The Armenians

B

The Peoples of Europe

General Editors James Campbell and Barry Cunliffe

This series is about the European tribes and peoples from their origins in prehistory to the present day. Drawing upon a wide range of archaeological and historical evidence, each volume presents a fresh and absorbing account of a group's culture, society and usually turbulent history.

Already published

The Etruscans
Graeme Barker and Thomas Rasmussen

The Lombards
Neil Christie

The Basques
Roger Collins

The English
Geoffrey Elton

The Gypsies
Angus Fraser

The Bretons
Patrick Galliou and Michael Jones

The Goths
Peter Heather

The Franks
Edward James

The Russians
Robin Milner-Gulland

The Mongols
David Morgan

The Armenians
A.E. Redgate

The Huns
E. A. Thompson

The Early Germans
Malcolm Todd

The Illyrians
John Wilkes

In preparation

The Sicilians
David Abulafia

The Irish
Francis John Byrne and Michael Herity

The Byzantines
Averil Cameron

The First English
Sonia Chadwick Hawkes

The Normans
Marjorie Chibnall

The Serbs
Sima Cirkovic

The Spanish
Roger Collins

The Romans
Timothy Cornell

The Celts
David Dumville

The Scots
Colin Kidd

The Ancient Greeks
Brian Sparkes

The Picts
Charles Thomas

The Armenians

A. E. Redgate

First published 1998

2 4 6 8 10 9 7 5 3 1

Blackwell Publishers Ltd
108 Cowley Road
Oxford OX4 1 JF
UK

Blackwell Publishers Inc.
350 Main Street
Malden, Massachusetts 02148
USA

British Library Cataloguing in Publication Data
A CIP catalogue record for this book is available from the British Library.

Library of Congress Cataloging-in-Publication Data
A. E. (Anne Elizabeth)
    The Armenians / A. E. Redgate.
      p.   cm. – (Peoples of Europe)
    Includes bibliographical references and index.
    ISBN 0-631-14372-6 (hb : alk. paper)
    1. Armenia–History.   I. Title.   II. Series.
DS 175.R43 1998
956.6'2–dc21   98-24617
                                             CIP

Typeset in 10 on 12pt Sabon
by Pure Tech India Ltd, Pondicherry
http://www.puretech.com
Printed in Great Britain by MPG Books Ltd, Bodmin, Cornwall

This book is printed on acid-free paper.

Contents

List of Plates

List of Figures

List of Maps

Preface

A generally accepted definition of the extent of Europe, whilst excluding much of historic Armenia, does include the present-day Republic of Armenia, the boundary between Asia and Europe being regarded as running along the Caucasus. Neither Armenia nor the Armenians however are routinely associated, by most people, with Europe and Europeans. European history has traditionally been narrowly conceived, concentrating particularly on western Europe, and an interest, in this context, in Armenia, is often expected to be explicable in terms of some personal connection, in a way which would not be expected of an interest in, say, France, Germany or Russia. I have no such connection, but as our world becomes more a global village and comparative history and world history more illuminating, a conviction that Armenian history is just as relevant to the history of the lands and peoples which have shared the heritage of Graeco-Roman civilization and of Judaeo-Christian religion as that of the Anglo-Saxons, though the latter is, for a west European, far easier of access, and vice versa. The book is intended for non-Armenian readers interested in the ancient and medieval histories of Europe, to 'demystify' the Armenians, and to illuminate their place in a European context. It is not to re-establish the emphasis on European influence and aspects which some modern scholars regard as having been overdone in the past, to the neglect of the Iranian and Syrian. Nevertheless, scholarly perception and accounts of Europe have also changed over time, so that those more familiar with the Armenians may also find a consideration of the Armenians as a people of Europe illuminating.

I should like to thank the editors for their invitation to contribute to this series, their patience and good advice; Professor J. A. Cannon, Professor R. I. Moore and Dr T. A. Sinclair for their comments on the text in draft; Mrs M. Brack, Miss J. Cummin, Mrs E. Cunningham, Miss J. Dalton, Mrs V. Douglass, Miss S. Dunkin, Mrs F. Griffiths, Mrs A. Macdonald, Mr R. Robson and Mrs I. Willis for secretarial assistance;

the Audio-Visual Centre of the University of Newcastle upon Tyne for reproducing some of the plates; the Inter-Library Loan Department of the Robinson Library, University of Newcastle upon Tyne; and Mrs A. Rooke, Senior Cartographer in the Department of Geography in the University of Newcastle upon Tyne who drew up the maps here from my hand-drawn versions.

Names and transliteration

Names of places and persons in Armenia and her history present themselves to the historian in a number of languages, ancient and modern.
Here familiarity and common usage, and ease of reference for the general
reader pursuing further reading in the history, especially ancient and
medieval, of Europe, the Near and Middle East, take priority over consistent application of academic convention.1

In the cases of Assyrian, Urartian, Persian, Arabic and Turkish the
usage of the 'standard' 'general' works, usually the *Cambridge Ancient
History, Cambridge History of Iran* or *Cambridge History of Islam* is
followed but generally without accents or diacritical marks except that,
for Turkish, ö, ü, and ğ and ş (rather than gh and sh) are used. Where
there are inconsistencies or differences between individual volumes
within the series, or between the works, then the more familiar and/or
the form more likely to be found elsewhere is preferred, for example
Azerbaijan, not Āzarbāījān or Āzarbāijān; Nimrud for the volcano in
Armenia in chapter 1, but Nemrut for the mountain in Commagene in
chapter 3 even though the name is the same. However, quotations from
secondary authorities are not changed. Where there is a major anomaly
and/or a different form is frequently found elsewhere, it is given in
parentheses on first occurrence – for example Khayasha (Hayasa), Seljuk
(Saljuq). There has been no attempt to standardize (between the different
languages) to represent the same sound always in the same way, except
that sh has been used instead of š, and in quotation of transcriptions of
cuneiform where ẖ and š have been changed to kh and sh.

Greek names and words, classical and Byzantine, are given in Anglici-
zations of Latinized forms, without accents, for example, Acilisene, not
Acilisena (Latin) or Akilisēnē (Greek). There are a few exceptions where
the name is not particularly well known in such a form and may be better
known in a 'correct' form, for example the names of Byzantine themes.
Where there are different versions of a place name then the form appro-

priate to the period in question is used e.g. Melid in the Assyrian period, Melitene in the classical and Byzantine, except where familiarity renders an anachronistic form more appropriate – thus Tiflis, not Tbilisi (its official name since 1935). Modern names are used for Urartian sites.

Since classical (Greek and Latin) sources pre-date Armenian ones, and take priority over them until, at the earliest, the third century AD, (no Armenian texts being written until the fifth), Armenian proper names are given in their classical rather than their Armenian forms in discussion of the antique period, for ease of reference in further reading in the context of ancient history. Thus, for example, Tigranes, Tiridates, not Tigran, Trdat, except where a particular context or the source makes the Armenian more appropriate. The periodization of ancient and medieval is debatable, but here *c.*640 is the dividing line: thereafter Armenian and medieval rather than classical forms are used.

Armenian forms are transcribed in accordance with the system advertised in R.W. Thomson's translations of the histories by Agathangelos, Moses of Khoren, and Ełishē, namely the Library of Congress system with two differences and one addition. The exceptions are twofold: some are well known in 'incorrect' and easier forms, thus Agathangelos not Agatʿangełos and Katholikos (Greek), not Katʿołikos (Armenian) or Catholicus (Latin), and where there is a well-known English equivalent it is preferred, thus for example Moses not Movsēs.

Ա	ա	A	a	Ն	ն	N	n
Բ	բ	B	b	Շ	շ	Sh	sh
Գ	գ	G	g	Ո	ո	O	o
Դ	դ	D	d	Չ	չ	Chᶜ	chᶜ
Ե	ե	E	e	Պ	պ	P	p
Զ	զ	Z	z	Ջ	ջ	J	j
Է	է	Ē	ē	Ռ	ռ	Ṙ	ṙ
Ը	ը	Ĕ	ĕ	Ս	ս	S	s
Թ	թ	Tᶜ	tᶜ	Վ	վ	V	v
Ժ	ժ	Zh	zh	Տ	տ	T	t
Ի	ի	I	i	Ր	ր	R	r
Լ	լ	L	l	Ց	ց	Tsᶜ	tsᶜ
Խ	խ	Kh	kh	Ւ	ւ	W	w
Ծ	ծ	Ts	ts	Փ	փ	Pᶜ	pᶜ
Կ	կ	K	k	Ք	ք	Kᶜ	kᶜ
Հ	հ	H	h	Օ	օ	Ō	ō
Ձ	ձ	Dz	dz	Ֆ	ֆ	F	f
Ղ	ղ	Ł	ł	Ու	ու	U	u
Ճ	ճ	Ch	ch				
Մ	մ	M	m				
Յ	յ	Y	y				

Notes, Citations and Bibliography

The notes are designed to identify quotations, original sources to which the text is closely related (though generally not in the case of well-known reconstruction of narrative), secondary authorities whose work lies behind particular points, some problems and differing interpretations.

Citations of primary sources are not given in full in every note. The translation quoted or paraphrased is in the case of classical texts that provided in the Loeb Classical Library series (where available), and for Armenian ones, unless otherwise stated, that provided in the translation which, for the convenience of the general reader, is also cited with page references. (Page references in the original Armenian editions, indicated in many of the translations, are not cited.) In other cases the translation used is indicated in the notes.

The Bibliography is restricted to works mentioned in the notes with a few more items which require acknowledgement and/or would be helpful to the general reader, in west European languages. Standard works of reference of obvious importance, and ease of access, like *The Cambridge Ancient History* (2nd edn) and *The Cambridge History of Iran* are *not* listed. For completeness, editions of the most used Armenian historical texts are listed, though they have not all been consulted nor are all editions listed. The translations of Armenian works which are listed are those which are most up to date and most cited in scholarly works in the west. Where such a translation is not in English, but an English version is accessible, this is also listed, and likewise recent translations into other western languages.

Where translations and even editions have, for ease of reference, been cited in the notes by their modern authors' names, the translations and editions of those texts are cited in full under Secondary rather than Primary Sources, with a cross reference appearing under Primary Sources. In cases where the same author's name is significantly differently transliterated in different publications the name has not been standardized but is given for each publication as it appears.

Note on Maps

The maps do not offer a series of snapshots in time. They are intended to help the reader unfamiliar with Armenian geography, to locate the more important places, territories and people (tribes and families) mentioned in each chapter, and to set them in a wider geographical context. Hence the maps include some places not mentioned in the text and the same map may include borders, polities and people of (sometimes quite widely) differing dates.

Although some historical continuities are thereby the more easily intelligible, nomenclature and representation require some clarification. Ancient and modern names for geographical features differ, as do their names in different modern languages; for example, Armenia's major river is the Turkish Aras, the Armenian Araks, but the classical Araxes, which name is commonly used in literature and/or maps regarding historical Armenia. Here the names used are, for ease of reference, those normally used in modern world atlases, but sometimes with the ancient form added in parentheses. Some territorial names, for example Egypt and Macedonia, have a varying significance, reflecting the territory's differing state and status at different times, as smaller or larger, less or more independent. The same name might sometimes refer to an empire, sometimes to a kingdom or territory 'proper', sometimes to a sub-unit of a larger, foreign kingdom or empire. Accordingly the placing and style of the lettering of the name may vary, reflecting historical change; for example Vaspurakan, appears as a 'province' in chapter 8, and a kingdom in chapters 1 and 9, whereas it did not constitute a political unit in the period covered by chapters 2–7 and hence is not mapped therein.

There are also some problems regarding the internal geography of ancient and medieval Armenia. Some districts originally shared a name with a family which owned it and lived there and they kept their names while their families moved, and their land-holdings changed over time, the relative size and status of an area is not necessarily the same, there is doubt about the boundaries of districts in Vaspurakan, and there are problems regarding the status and groupings of areas at particular times. Family surnames appear on the maps in the singular form. For clarity, only two sub-units are indicated – those of the region, or province, generally smaller than a kingdom or country, and the district, generally a smaller sub-unit. In general the maps follow the most recent specialized works, those by R. H. Hewsen, listed in the Bibliography, to which the reader is referred for authoritative judgements: here the intention is simply to aid in conjuring a mental picture of family and territorial adjacencies, sizes and distances. Where a geographical uncertainty is of particular historical importance however, it is referred to in the text.

The period after 1071 until the late twentieth century is discussed in chapter 11, but the small Armenian kingdoms which existed in the medieval period after 1071 are mapped in chapter 9.

Acknowledgements

The author and publishers offer grateful acknowledgements to the following for permission to reproduce copyright material:
Michael Baron (cover, plates 4, 10, 11); Deutsches Archäologisches Institut, Orient-Abteilung (plate 1); Bibliothèque Nationale de France (plate 2); Christian Collins (plates 3, 12); The British Museum (plate 5); François Walch (plates 6, 7, 8); Patrick Donabédian (plate 9); the Robinson Library, University of Newcastle upon Tyne (plate 14); plate 13 is reproduced by courtesy of the Director and University Librarian, the John Rylands University Library of Manchester.

The publishers apologise for any errors or omissions in the above list and would be grateful to be notified of any corrections that should be incorporated in the next edition or reprint of this book.

1

Origins

On 24 September 1896, at the age of eighty-seven, William Ewart Gladstone delivered his last great public speech. It was in his native city of Liverpool; it lasted for one hour twenty minutes; it was heard by more than 6,000 people and it was recalled in the House of Commons a quarter of a century later as 'one of the best speeches of his life'. His subject was the Armenian massacres. The vehemence of his attack on the Turks caused him to be accused of war-mongering – an ironic ending to his long career – and the leader of his own party, Lord Rosebery, to resign within two weeks, declaring that Gladstone's bellicosity was the *coup de grace*.

In a private conversation that same September Gladstone had remarked of 'the martyred people' to whom 'in his old age he felt the first obligation', that 'of all the nations of the world no history has been so blameless as the history of the Armenian people'. It had also been a remarkably long history and Gladstone was not the first western leader to have been concerned with Armenian issues. Almost exactly five centuries earlier, in September 1396, a crusade was decisively defeated outside Nicopolis, south of the Danube. This crusade had been promoted, as far as he was able, by the last of the kings of the Armenians, Leo V. He had hoped for the liberation of his kingdom – not Armenia proper, but the Armenian kingdom in Cilicia – which had fallen to the Egyptian Mamluks in 1375. Leo had gone to Paris in 1384, perhaps attracted by the current Anglo-French truce, visited Westminster in 1386, acted as mediator between the French and English kings Charles VI and Richard II and attended their peace conferences in 1392 and 1393. Leo died in 1393. His monument lies with those of French kings, in the cathedral at St Denis, near Paris, site of the royal abbey of France since the seventh century.

An earlier visitor to the west, Tiridates, brother of the Arsacid king of Parthia and the first Arsacid to rule Armenia, enjoys a very different kind of memorial. Tiridates visited Rome in AD 66, in the reign of the emperor Nero. The great states of Rome and Parthia had struggled to dominate Armenia, and had eventually reached a compromise. Armenia was to be ruled by Tiridates but he was to receive the crown from Nero. There is a case for saying that Tiridates' state visit is commemorated every year even now. For Tiridates was not only a king, but also a priest of the Persian religion of Zoroastrianism. He was a magus and brought other magi to Rome with him. It was about the same time that St Matthew's Gospel recorded a journey of wise men from the east to the infant Jesus in Bethlehem. Tiridates' journey seems to have contributed some elements to Iranian legend, and it may also lie behind the later Christian legend of the three Magi.[1] There may be a faint reminiscence of Tiridates' visit in the activities of hundreds of tiny children each year in Nativity plays.

The first surviving references to Armenia and Armenians were written a little over 500 years before the Nativity. The Achaemenid king of Persia, Darius I (522–486 BC), recorded in a trilingual illustrated inscription carved high on the cliff face at Behistun (Bisitun) how he had overcome opposition and secured his crown. Armenia appears in a list of twenty-three 'lands' or, more probably, 'peoples', who 'called themselves mine' at the beginning (that is, in 522 BC).[2] Two Armenians appear amongst the *dramatis personae*. One is the rebel Ara-kha whom Darius impaled for claiming to be king of Babylon, the other is Dâdarshish, a general of Darius himself. Armenians are referred to also in the writings of Darius's contemporary, Hecataeus of Miletus, who had travelled widely between 515 and 500 BC and knew the extent of Darius's empire. Hecataeus's two works have survived only as fragments in later texts. According to Stephanus of Byzantium (who wrote in the sixth century AD) he remarked in his *Description of the Earth* that the Armenians were situated south of the Chalybes (on the south-east coast of the Black Sea).

These four fragments of Armenian history, which span nearly twenty-five centuries, illustrate some of its major themes. The Armenians have had important links with a series of powerful neighbours to east and west. They have often been an object of rivalry between these neighbours. They have retained, in adversity, a sense of national identity. They have striven for national independence. Christianity has been a vital force in their culture. They have contributed to the history and culture of the peoples of Europe. But there are problems, for westerners, in apprehend-

---

[1] The historical prototype of the legendary Caspar, or Gadaspar in Armenian tradition, the Magi leader, was not Tiridates himself but Gundofarr king of Sakastan, with whose reign Tiridates' career overlapped. For this, and Tiridates' impact on Iranian legend see Herzfeld, 1935, pp. 63–6.

[2] Kent, 1953; Cameron, G. G., 1973.

ing the history of the Armenians. The Armenians seem far away, their language and the geography of their homelands unfamiliar. The evidence is patchy and their history can only be properly understood in the context of that of neighbouring peoples, sometimes even less familiar.

Plate 1   Ara-kha, the 'Armenian' Babylonian pretender, from Darius the Great's rock relief at Behistun.

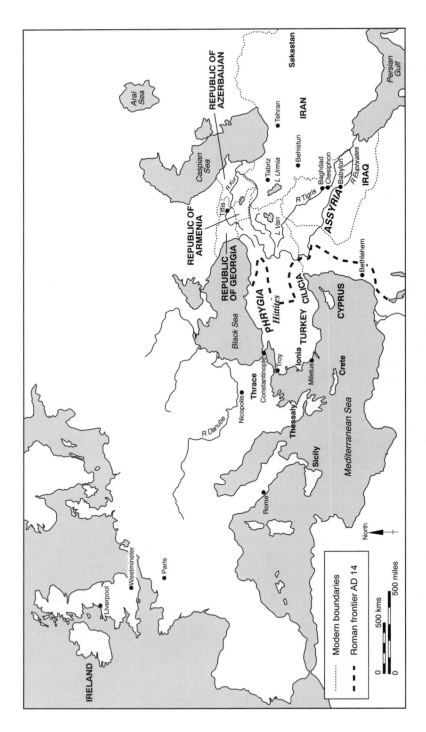

Map 1.1   Europe and west Asia

The story of the Armenians may be documented from about 1165 BC, when they came to eastern Turkey and subsequently spread over lands divided in the twentieth century between Turkey, the Soviet Union, Iran and Iraq. Although there are, as we shall see, different theories regarding the Armenians' origins, these origins were, probably, European. However, the most easily identifiable ancestors of the later Armenian nation are the Urartians. It would be wrong to regard the society and culture of Urartu, a powerful state between the ninth and early sixth centuries BC, situated where those Armenians referred to by Darius and Hecataeus lived, as an Armenian achievement. But it would be equally wrong to regard Urartu as external to Armenian history. Urartian culture was part of the Armenians' early experience, and late Urartian history was partly shaped by Armenians. Indeed, this early period, when Urartu was a world power, should be considered one of the highest points in Armenian history, rivalled only by the first century BC when the Armenian king Tigranes the Great forged a great, but short-lived, empire stretching down to Syria and the Holy Land. In the intervening centuries the Armenians had been subsumed into the Achaemenid Empire, regaining effective independence under a native dynasty only after the conquest of this empire by Alexander of Macedon. After the turn of the millennium Armenians were caught up in Roman–Parthian rivalry and became subject to the rule of relatives of the Parthian kings. With the Arsacids came an intensification of Iranian influence upon Armenian culture until Tiridates the Great, early in the fourth century, established Christianity as the state religion, trying, under Roman protection, to stave off the threat to the very existence of the Armenian kingdom posed by the Sasanians who had ousted the Arsacids in Parthia in the early third century.

The great glories of Armenian culture were its oral tradition, reaching back into the ancient past, its ecclesiastical building, which flourished in

Plate 2   Coin of Tigranes II 'the Great' of Armenia.

the late sixth and seventh, and the tenth and eleventh centuries AD, and its vernacular historical literature. Much of this literature was stimulated by religious persecution at the hands of the Sasanians and by the leadership of the church after the abolition of the Armenian monarchy in 428. Partition between the east Roman, or Byzantine, and Sasanian Persian empires was ended by Arab conquests in the seventh century, but independence and prosperity, interrupted by oppression in the eighth century, returned in the ninth, when kingship was revived. It was however a false dawn. The later tenth and the eleventh centuries resemble the sixth and seventh: first Byzantium gradually annexed Armenian territories, though this was not in itself necessarily a bad thing nor even universally unpopular, and then a new force burst upon the scene, to change the history of the world, the Seljuk (Saljuq) Turks. For some three centuries Armenians ruled in Cilicia, but thereafter their story is one of foreign domination and exile. They are perhaps best known to many westerners as victims of massacres in the early twentieth century and as claimants of territory in Turkey and the former Soviet Union.

Unfortunately the length and nature of the 'blameless' history of the Armenians, and the slender and ambiguous character of the earliest evidence, complicate the very first, most basic questions which arise: What was 'Armenia'? What are the 'Armenians'' origins? When did the 'Armenians' populate 'Armenia'? When and where was their first kingdom?

The Place

'Armenia' is not easily identifiable, partly because areas of Armenian settlement and culture have not coincided neatly with areas of Armenian rule, and partly because the extent of Armenian-controlled territory has varied considerably. Thus one estimate of what constitutes historical Armenia suggests an area of 239,320 square miles, another, considering historical and geographical Armenia, suggests about 154,440 square miles, whilst the territory actually under Armenian rule *c.*56 BC–AD 298 was much less, only about 108,108 square miles.[3]

It is this smallest territory which is treated in what seems to be a detailed medieval description of the ancient Armenian state, an account of fifteen 'provinces' comprising nearly two hundred *gawaṙs*, or districts. This is given by the Armenian *Geography* which was written probably shortly before AD 636 by the Armenian scholar Anania of Shirak. But the most recent explorer of Armenian historical geography has confirmed

---

[3] The approximate area of the fifteen 'provinces' listed in the Armenian *Geography*, according to the estimates of S. T. Eremyan (Hewsen, 1992, pp. 296–303). Hewsen's adjustments (1992, *passim*) yield some 3,861 less.

some earlier views that this account is not to be taken literally. It is not a valid picture of the geopolitical realities of ancient Armenia, either throughout the past, or even in any particular period, though it has been accepted as such by some scholars. Although the Armenian state had once (between *c*.56 BC and AD 298) controlled all the territory in question, not all the 'provinces' existed during that time and of the eleven that did, four were smaller than the document records. And when the text was written eight were long lost.[4]

These vicissitudes as to size may be explained in part by aspects of physical geography. For the natural internal state of geographical Armenia is not one of political unity. The population of historical Armenia may never have exceeded 5 or 6 million and most of its extent was not fit for settlement. The country is compartmentalized by its mountains, lava flows and, in antiquity, forests, and hence its pattern of settlement has been dispersed and its political communities self-contained. It was at their level, the level of the *gawařs*, that political society was most stable. When pre-Urartian Hittite and Assyrian sources allude to Armenia they refer most often to such 'lands' or 'countries' rather than to ethnic groups.

Separate communities might indeed be similar in many respects but some lack of uniformity is natural in terrain where there are mountains, and mountains dominate Armenia. Two arch-shaped, east–west aligned mountain ranges almost meet in Armenia, where heights reach nearly 9,000 feet near Erzurum and over 13,000 further east, though the ascent into the Armenian plateau from the west (beginning about twenty miles west of Malatya) is gradual. The more formidable mountains have over many centuries sheltered and engendered societies which differed from those below. It is clear for example from Assyrian sources that refugees, whether from poverty or politics, were attracted to the Sasun mountains in the seventh century BC.[5] And in the tenth century AD the Armenian writer Thomas Artsruni, a relative of King Gagik of Vaspurakan (the south-east and east parts of the Van region), described inhabitants of these same mountains, above Muş, as if they were objects of curiosity, though he admired their loyalty and courage.[6]

Another hindrance to internal unity is that communications in Armenia are not naturally easy. Rivers are only partially navigable because of winding gorges, rapids, currents and floods. Passes are closed and communications impeded where the mass of snow is not just an obstacle, but a positive danger, encouraging avalanches and hiding precipices. The geographer Strabo, who wrote early in the first century AD, had heard

---

[4] For these problems and for scholarly perceptions of the text, Hewsen, 1992, pp. 284–95 and Introduction, pp. 6–15, 32–5.

[5] See below, ch. 2 p. 38 and n. 45.

[6] Thomas Artsruni, *History of the House of the Artsrunis*, II, 7, trans. Thomson, 1985, pp. 187–8.

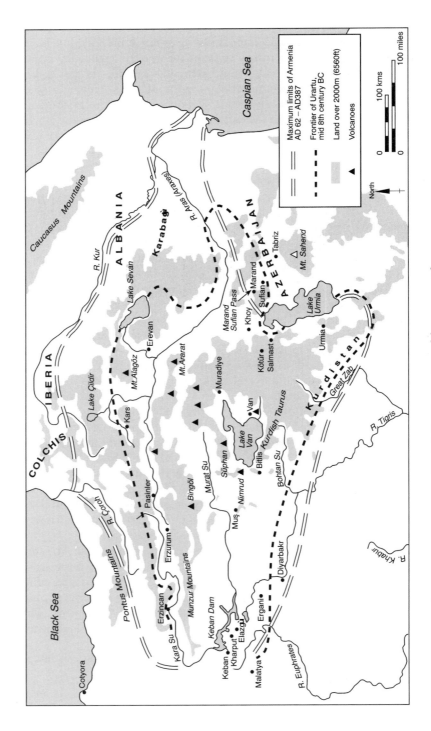

Map 1.2   Armenia and her geography

Plate 3   View from a mountain pass, north-western Armenia.

that on the most northerly passes whole caravans were sometimes swallowed up.[7] Another Greek, Xenophon, recorded *c*.400 BC how his army was severely troubled by snow when it marched through western Armenia. He records a depth of six feet, effects of snowblindness, the deaths of many animals and slaves and thirty soldiers, and the loss of toes through frostbite. The men had to be chivvied to keep going, so severely that when they reached Cotyora on the Black Sea, some of them indicted Xenophon for assault.[8] The eleventh-century Armenian historian Aristakēs of Lastivert records that in 1022 AD an army of the Byzantine emperor Basil II outside Khoy (Hoy) suffered badly from sudden rain, wind and snow: they fled the cold as an enemy and retreated to the Van region, abandoning their possessions.[9]

These particular difficulties were not however absolutely insurmountable. Strabo remarks that people carried staffs to signal with and help them breathe in the event of being buried. Elsewhere he mentions, like Thomas, the use of snow shoes and also the practice of sliding loads down from the summit on skins, though this seems to refer to the less snowy summer months.[10] Xenophon got his men through, unprepared though they had been. An Armenian headman passed on the tip of tying

[7] Strabo, *The Geography*, XI, xiv, 4.
[8] Xenophon, *Anabasis*, IV, iv, 8–12, v, 4–9, 12–21, V, viii, 1–26.
[9] Aristakēs of Lastivert, *History of the Armenians*, IV, trans. Canard and Berbérian, 1973, pp. 23–5.
[10] Strabo, XI, v, 6.

bags round the animals' feet so they could walk and not sink into the snow. In AD 1022 Basil II's infantry lost fingers and toes, and his tent-pegs were frozen to the ground, but the Byzantines were able to ride to Vaspurakan. Indeed in the winter of AD 627–8 the east Roman emperor Heraclius not only brought an army through Khoy to take the Persian capital Ctesiphon, near modern Baghdad, but brought it from the west via the much harsher, cold, cloudy, snowy Kars region. Such exploits were of course exceptional. Heraclius certainly surprised the Persians.

But since military campaigning should be ruled out in winter, winter conditions may be construed as one of the several advantages which nature has offered Armenians. Accounts of Arab campaigns and punitive expeditions against the Armenians reveal a norm of resting in winter quarters. Another benefit was the potential for prosperity. Armenia has produced a variety of crops (cereals, cotton, rice, silk, sugar cane, tobacco, water melons). Animal husbandry has been important. As Strabo observed, Armenia was 'exceptionally good "horse-pasturing" country'.[11] Assyrian inscriptions reveal that she had been a major supplier of horses, whether as booty or tribute, for Assyria, from the time of Tiglath-Pileser I (1114–1076 BC) to the late ninth century BC. Urartian inscriptions likewise record the taking of large numbers of horses by Urartian kings. Armenians' animal resources have included fish, birds, and wild animals, including leopards, tigers and wolves. Amongst their vegetable resources have been vines and trees (fruit trees, oaks, walnut, poplar, willow). There was once much more forest than nowadays. Extensive deforestation has occurred in Turkey, in antiquity and later, as land was cleared for pasture and timber cut for smelting and ship-building. In addition Armenians have had valuable mineral resources, for example, borax and arsenic to the north-west of Lake Van, gold and silver north of Erzurum, precious stones, gold, copper, and iron in the plain of Ayrarat, tin at Mount Sahend on the eastern frontier of Urartu, gold, silver and iron in the Taurus region.

The geography of Armenia was also advantageous for commerce. There is easy passage between present-day Armenia and Azerbaijan to Iran and to the Caspian sea via the lower Araxes valley. Armenian involvement in trade has varied but over the centuries trade routes passing through Armenia have connected the Black Sea with the Caspian, Anatolia and Russia with Iran and Mesopotamia.

Politically however, easy passage has sometimes had disadvantages. From their base south of Lake Urmia (now in Iran), the Scyths troubled Urartu as well as her rival Assyria. Azerbaijan is an arrow pointed at Armenia's heart. There are other weak points. The Tigris basin is vulnerable from the south and there is no clear boundary for Armenia on the

---

[11] Ibid. XI, xiii, 7, XI, xiv, 9.

west. The north is a little more secure as the Pontus mountains divide Armenia from the south-eastern Black Sea coast before sweeping round to the south of Lake Sevan and the lower Araxes. Beyond this north-eastern chain, of varied height but limited breadth except at Karabağ, where it will support forests, are the lands where the ancient peoples of Colchis (on the Black Sea) and of Iberia (modern Georgia) lived, and those of the Caucasian Albanians. Beyond them lie the Caucasus mountains and the Russian steppes.

The major regional unities and variations within geographical Armenia comprise the Euphrates, Tigris and Araxes basins, and the areas around Lakes Van and Urmia.

The Euphrates basin above Malatya is, at about 31,150 square miles, nearly three times the size of Republican (formerly Soviet) Armenia. Besides chains of mountains rising to nearly 9,000 feet near Erzurum, on the Euphrates' northern branch, the Kara Su, there are, in the east, volcanic cones. Most spectacular are those near Lake Van, Nimrud (Nemrut) to the west at 9,900 feet, whose crater measures $5\frac{1}{2}$ miles at its widest, and Süphan, on the northern shore, at over 14,000 feet. The larger part of the Elazığ plain, about 2,953 feet above sea level, used to be known as the 'Golden Plain', but most of it is now under water following the building of the Keban Dam. There are variations of climate. Malatya, 3,281 feet above sea level, has relatively mild winters with only a light snowfall. But at Erzurum, 6,168 feet above sea level, winter temperatures may be as low as $-17°$, the January mean temperature is about zero, snow falls for about three months, and lies for about four more. Some mountain passes are closed for six to eight months.

The Tigris basin is separated from the upper Euphrates basin by the Kurdish Taurus. This is not easily passable, except at Ergani about 75 miles east of Malatya and through the historic pass in the valley of the Bitlis river, near Nimrud, south-west of Lake Van. The climate and vegetation of south-east Turkey differ from those of the upper Euphrates. Diyarbakır, classical Amida, only 1,936 feet above sea level, has relatively warm winters with little snow. The higher mountains however, in Kurdistan in the south-east, are snow-bound in winter, and there are avalanches and floods. These and other aspects of physical geography lead the inhabitants to live in small communities in sites difficult of access but easily defended. The fierce and independent Kurds may be descended in part from the Carduchi described by Xenophon.[12] They are transhumant, and their economy partly pastoral.

The upper and middle Araxes (Turkish Aras) basin includes the plain of Erevan, historically one of the most fertile parts of Armenia. About 2,600

[12] Xenophon, *Anabasis*, IV, i–iii. But there are reasons for not identifying the Carduchi with the ancient Kurds. See Sinclair, 1989(b), p. 360.

Plate 4   The island of Alt‘amar, Lake Van, southern Armenia.

feet above sea level, this plain is overlooked by the (extinct) volcanic cones of Alagöz, at over 13,000 feet, to the north and of Ararat, at nearly 17,000 feet, to the south, and it is watered by streams from these mountains. The fifth-century AD Armenian writer Lazarus (Łazar) of P‘arp details its charms and resources and describes successful hunting, of onagers, goats, deer, boars and birds.[13] In the higher land, west of Erevan, conditions are more like those at Erzurum. Kars, capital of a small kingdom in the tenth century AD, 5,715 feet above sea level, can be even colder than Erzurum. The region is likewise particularly subject to earthquakes. High up north-east of Erevan, on a plateau surrounded by mountains, is Lake Sevan, historically about 547 square miles. It harbours fish, including trout.

The great lakes of Armenia are those of Van and Urmia. Lake Van, 5,451 feet above sea level, is, at about 1,440 square miles, almost exactly the size of the English county of Sussex. It is of salt water and harbours a unique species of fish. The Van plain, on the lake's eastern shore and limited to north and south by mountain chains, was the heart of Urartu. Access to the east is by a route to Khoy from Muradiye on the north-eastern corner of the lake, via the Kötür pass, and another route, leading to this one, from Van itself. To Van's east is Lake Urmia. This lake, some 4,000 feet above sea level is about 1,807 square miles in size. Its shallow alkaline waters have no fish, but according to Strabo they shared with the

---

[13] Lazarus of P ‘arp, *History of the Armenians*, I, 7, trans. Thomson, 1991, pp. 42–3.

waters of Van an ability to restore weathered garments.[14] The climate of this region, 19,900 square miles, is softer than elsewhere. Aristakēs of Lastivert saw the hand of God in the hardships which afflicted the Byzantine army in 1022, remarking that it was out of keeping with the area's normal conditions. Conditions can nevertheless be very severe. At Tabriz across the eastern plain the temperature can rise in summer to 40° and drop in winter to −20°. Access to the middle Araxes plain is possible via the Sufian-Marand Pass.

Origins

The ancestry of the modern and medieval Armenians of the Armenian plateau includes a number of different groups. The ancient population comprised speakers of Hurrian, Urartian and Indo-European Luwian who were joined later by speakers of Indo-European proto-Armenian. If we give priority to these last then we must begin Armenian history with their arrival in Armenia. But their arrival is difficult to describe.

There are two problems: geographical and chronological. The first is the easier. The conclusion that the 'Armenians' had come from the west to Armenia can be derived from the evidence, first, of language and, second, of the Greek writers Herodotus and Strabo. Armenian is an Indo-European language whereas Hurrian, Urartian and other proto-Caucasian languages are not. Proto-Armenian did not however belong to the same branch of Indo-European as Hittite and Luwian, the Indo-European languages which had become widespread in Anatolia by the beginning of the second millennium BC. Despite some scholarly disagreement, a scantiness of conclusive evidence, and the survival of only a few sentences from Phrygian, specialized study suggests that proto-Armenian most probably belonged to a Thraco-Phrygian sub-group which appeared in Asia in the twelfth century BC. And indeed, around 370 BC Eudoxus of Cnidus commented on the similarity of Phrygian and Armenian.[15]

Eudoxus was not the first to record an affiliation between Phrygians and Armenians. In the middle of the fifth century BC Herodotus had done the same. He observed that the Armenians who were in the Persian King Xerxes' army when he invaded Thrace in 480 BC were armed like the Phrygians, since they were, he said, Phrygian settlers.[16] Another tradition, recorded much later by Strabo, was that Armenia had been named after Armenus, a Thessalian and companion of Jason, whose followers had settled there. Strabo also remarked that the clothing of the Armenians

---

[14] Strabo, XI, xiii, 2, XI, xiv, 8.
[15] Diakonoff, 1984, pp. 109–10, 188–90 (n. 39, 40). Eudoxus is, like Hecataeus, quoted by Stephanus of Byzantium.
[16] Herodotus, *The Histories*, VII, 73.

and their style of horsemanship was said to be Thessalian.[17] Some modern scholars have cited, as archaeological evidence for a Thraco-Phrygian advance into Armenia, a relief found north of Irbil (ancient Arbela) in Iraq, which shows a figure wearing a cap of Phrygian type, and Thracian type tumuli discovered between Malatya, Kharput and Diyarbakır. These were reported respectively in publications of 1899 and 1901, but other scholars give the tumuli little credence since no archaeological confirmation for them can now be found.[18]

All of this evidence points to a western, Indo-European origin, but the matter of dating is more complex. Herodotus did not say when the Armenian settlers left their Phrygian kin, and, as he knew, Phrygian history stretched back many centuries. As Strabo noted, stories about them 'go back to earlier times than the Trojan War', that is to before the end of the thirteenth century BC. Herodotus himself observed that the Phrygians had once lived in Europe under a different name, and that they were believed by the Egyptians to be the most ancient of nations.[19]

We must nevertheless attempt to date the Armenian migration. The chronological question is important, for upon it depends the validity of treating Urartian history as a significant part of Armenian history rather than as merely a background to its beginning. Were the Armenians in the sixth century BC a relatively primitive people, rats who had deserted the sinking ship of the short-lived Phrygian Empire for firmer ground in the seventh century BC, or were they an advanced people, who had participated in the culture of the recently extinguished Urartian Empire?

The hypothesis of a seventh-century arrival is very attractive, for three reasons. It would seem most natural for Herodotus to have been thinking of the Phrygians nearest to himself in date. Second, the seventh century BC was indeed a period of change, in which the activity of the Cimmerians, Scyths and Medes resulted in the destruction of the empires of Phrygia, Assyria and Urartu. Third, it seems from Assyrian sources that in the early seventh century someone called Gurdi, who has been conjectured to be Gordias I of Phrygia, briefly took over from Assyria a town called Til-Garimmu.[20] Since Til-Garimmu is, perhaps, the Biblical Togarmah, Armenian Tᶜorgom, and since Armenian tradition records that the father of Hayk, the ancestor of the Armenians, was called Tᶜorgom, it is tempting to connect the proto-Armenians with Phrygian Til-Garimmu.[21]

---

[17] Strabo, XI, iv, 8, XI, xiv, 12.

[18] For the positive view, Adontz, 1946, p. 333; for the negative, Burney and Lang, 1971, p. 177.

[19] Strabo, XII, viii, 4; Herodotus, VII, 73, II, 2.

[20] Luckenbill, II, 1927, no. 290 (p. 138).

[21] For possible sites for Til-Garimmu, Garstang and Gurney, 1959, and Diakonoff, 1984, pp. 93, 179 (n. 292). For Togarmah – T ᶜorgom equation, Diakonoff, 1984, p. 179 (n. 297). For Armenian – Til-Garimmu connection, Toumanoff, 1963, pp. 53, 55; Adontz, 1946, pp. 125, 316–20.

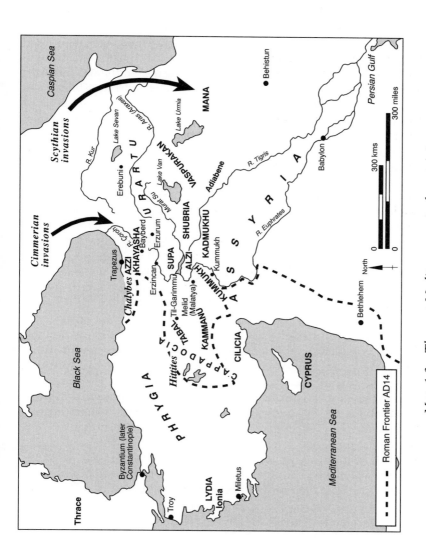

Map 1.3 The east Mediterranean and west Asia

Unfortunately, linguistic data seem not to support this connection. It has been argued that Old Armenian cannot be derived from Phrygian, that the two languages separated from a common base much earlier than the eighth or seventh centuries BC, and hence that the seventh-century 'Armenians' were *not* Phrygians. This specialized linguistic evidence is clearly crucial. It necessitates a trawl through pre-seventh century sources to discover some group settling in Armenia who might actually have been proto-Armenians. There is a good case, advanced by Diakonoff (D'iakonov), for identifying this group with the Urumeans, and, more certainly, with the Mushki, who settled *c*.1165 BC between the northern Taurus and the Sasun mountains. According to Assyrian sources, the Urumi, or Urumeans, came from the west and seized some Hurrian cities in about 1165 BC, and the Mushki occupied two Hurrian countries, the kingdom of Alzi and its neighbour Purulumzi, at the same time. Alzi was in the valley of the River Arsanias (Turkish Murat Su) extending as far as the mountains of Sasun. It is not clear who the Urumeans were, but the likelihood that the Mushki were a Thraco-Phrygian tribe is underlined by the fact that in later Assyrian sources the name Mushki designated Phrygians.[22]

The identification of the twelfth-century Mushki as proto-Armenians has the further attraction that it is reconcilable with Strabo's testimony. His 'ancient' story of Armenus is probably nonsense. But the association of Armenus with Jason at least suggests that Strabo's two fourth-century BC sources were thinking of a past much more remote than the period of Phrygia's decline. According to Greek tradition Jason went adventuring not long before the Trojan War. More important is Strabo's account of where the newcomers settled, some in Acilisene, others apparently in Syspiritis. Acilisene is the area of modern Erzincan in the upper Euphrates valley north-west of Alzi. Syspiritis should probably be identified with Shubria. Shubria is attested later than Alzi, and lay, probably, north-east of Diyarbakır in the Sasun mountains, just south-east of twelfth-century Alzi. Scholars are not unanimous concerning its exact location.

Teasing out the roots of the Armenian nation's family tree is a complex business. It is much easier to trace the progress of speakers of proto-Armenian, whom we might for convenience call 'Armenians', within the land where the state of Urartu was to flourish and which became known subsequently as Armenia. Our first narrative of 'Armenian' activity comes in the annals of the Assyrian king Tiglath-Pileser I, (1114–1076 BC) who recorded that in 1115 the Mushki captured the land of Kadmukhu (in the upper Tigris valley). He claims that a successful Assyrian counter-attack inflicted heavy casualties, took 6,000 captives and

---

[22] Diakonoff, 1984, pp. 109–12, 115–21, and for the relationship of Old Armenian and Phrygian, pp. 189–90 (n. 39, 47), 205 (n. 6).

imposed tribute on Alzi and Purulumzi. We know little about early
'Armenian' society. Tiglath-Pileser mentions 20,000 Mushki men-at-
arms and 4,000 Urumi and Kaska troops together.[23] Diakonoff calculates
that these newcomers were outnumbered three times or more by the local
population. This is assuming that the area of settlement later housed
about one quarter of the population of Urartu, assessed as between
1.5 and 3 million in the time of Sarduri II (*c.*763–*c.*734).[24] Modern
physical anthropology certainly suggests that the Thraco-Phrygians
were not dominant.[25] The 'Armenians' had five kings, but, according to
Diakonoff, the names used by the local dynasties continued to be Hurrian
and Luwian, suggesting that they either adopted local names or accepted
local rulers.[26]

By the ninth century BC the 'Armenians' had spread into the Tigris
valley. That they had settled down is implied by the Assyrian records that
Tukulti-Ninurta II (890–884) took cattle and sheep from them, burnt
their cities and cut down the harvest of their gardens, and that they paid
to his son Ashurnasirpal II (883–859) a tribute of bronze utensils and
wine as well as animals.[27] Some 'Armenians' may have settled at some
stage in the Malatya area (ancient Melid) and mixed there with the local
population, which was Luwian. Some Luwian names entered proto-
Armenian usage. Musheḷ, much used in both medieval and modern
times, was one such. As we have seen, there may also have been settlement of both Mushki and Urumeans in Shubria.

'Armenian' dissemination in the Urartian period was gradual. In the
early eighth century, Alzi, conquered in 856 by Shalmaneser III (858–
824) of Assyria, was incorporated into Urartu by the Urartian king
Menua. Some 'Armenians' may have been forcibly moved. The inscriptions of the Urartian kings record that they, like the Assyrians, frequently
resettled large numbers of people within their domains. Often this was a
matter of internal movement within expanding frontiers, but sometimes
captives were imported. Argishti I (*c.*785–*c.*763 BC) moved 6,600 warriors from Melid, and from Supa (north of Alzi), to Arin-berd (Urartian
Erebuni), the forerunner of modern Erevan. The campaign of Rusa II
(*c.*685–*c.*645) in 676, probably in alliance with the Cimmerians, against
Melid, the Phrygians and the Chalybes, resulted in forced transplantation
of some of the enemy population. The disturbed conditions caused by the
Cimmerian raids probably prompted some voluntary, if refugee, movement eastwards, at the very time when Urartu was distracted by the

[23] Grayson, II, 1976, LXXXVII, 12 (i 62) (pp. 6–7), 18 (ii 89) (p. 9).
[24] Diakonoff, 1984, pp. 123–4, 197 (n. 105).
[25] On these grounds it has been postulated that the Armenians were Anatolians, probably
Hurrians, related to the Urartians and that their speaking an Indo-European language
resulted from five centuries of Phrygian rule. (See Burney and Lang, 1971, pp. 177–9).
[26] Diakonoff, 1984, pp. 124, 197–8 (n. 106).
[27] Grayson, II, 1976, C 476 (r. 33) (p. 104), CI 547 (i 69) (p. 123).

appearance of the Scyths to her east. It is possible that these same conditions enabled some 'Armenians' to make conquests of their own within Urartu, thereby contributing to her decline.

After the fall of Urartu to the Medes in 590 BC the 'Armenians' simply infiltrated further, and mingled with the Urartians. The 'Armenians' presumably favoured Phrygian armour, but they had lost other aspects of Phrygian culture, for there are no Phrygian-style tumuli in Urartu. They had already mingled with the local populations of Alzi, Purulumzi, Melid, Shubria and elsewhere and so, presumably, imbibed some of their culture, as well as their proper names.

The First Kingdom

Til-Garimmu, Shubria and Melid have all been suggested as the home of the first 'Armenian' kingdom, as has a Scythian origin for its dynasty. There is no conclusive evidence against the possibility that it is with Gurdi's Til-Garimmu that the House of Togarmah, mentioned in those chapters of the Old Testament Book of Ezekiel which concern the war between Lydia and the Medes in 590–585 BC, should be connected.[28] Nevertheless, on linguistic grounds Til-Garimmu seems unlikely to have been 'Armenian'. A Scythian origin has been suggested on the grounds of 'Paroyr' and 'Skayordi', the names given by the eighth-century AD Armenian historian Moses of Khoren to the first Armenian king and his father. 'Paroyr' has been thought to be reminiscent of 'Bartatua' (Partatua), the name of the Scythian leader contemporary with Esarhaddon of Assyria (680–669), though there are linguistic difficulties attached to this.[29] 'Skayordi' perhaps means 'son of a "Saka"', Iranian for Scythian. But a different meaning for Skayordi, namely 'son of Hskay' (*hskay* being Armenian for giant), has also been postulated.

The grounds for locating the first Armenian kingdom in Shubria are stronger. This mountainous border zone maintained its independence for most of the period of Urartian history. The Armenian tradition that Hayk travelled north to the land of Ararad, from Babylon, might suggest a first entrenchment on the southern border of Urartu. Furthermore, proto-Armenian speakers had settled in Urme. There are differences of opinion concerning the separate identity and location of the countries of Arme, and Urme or Urmie, mentioned in Urartian inscriptions, but they may have been one and the same, and it may also be that Urme should be identified with, or within, Shubria rather than just to its north. It has been

---

[28] Ezekiel, 38–9.
[29] Moses of Khoren, *History of the Armenians*, I, 21, 22 trans. Thomson, 1978, pp. 108–10. The Armenian form cannot be traced back to the Old Iranian one. Diakonoff, 1984, pp. 177 (n. 271), 201 (n. 122).

argued that 'Hskay' conquered all or part of Shubria in about 714–712. These years are suggested because they were, as we shall see, a period in which Urartu had both internal and external problems to cope with, including disruption in the west caused by Assyrian activities. It is also likely that some more 'Armenians' came to Shubria after Esarhaddon had turned her into two Assyrian provinces in 673, and deported many of her inhabitants. For the depleted population seems to have been stocked up with transportees from lands west of the upper Euphrates. 'People, the plunder of my bow, of the upper and lower seas, therein I settled' Esarhaddon told his god Ashur.[30]

The Shubrian dynasty which Esarhaddon terminated seems from the names of its princes to have been Hurrian rather than 'Armenian', but it is not implausible that a new 'Armenian' dynasty should subsequently have risen to power. The report in Assyrian annals for 664 that it was the inhabitants of Kullimeri, centre of one of the new provinces, who slew great numbers of an invading force (from Urartu) led by one Andaria, suggests that Shubria was left to its own devices.[31] Finally there is in Moses of Khoren's *History* what seems to be an explicit connection between the father of the first Armenian king and Shubria. The brothers of Esarhaddon fled Assyria after assassinating their father Sennacherib (704–681).[32] According to the Bible they went to Ararat, that is, to Urartu. In Moses' account, however, one of them, Sanasar, was settled in Sasun, that is in Shubria, by 'our valiant ancestor Skayordi'. There is no reason to suppose that Moses meant a different Skayordi from the Skayordi whom he had designated a little before as the father of King Paroyr.

Yet despite the strengths of the Shubrian theory, the most convincing reconstruction is that which locates the first Armenian kingdom in Melid, whose capital was at Arslantepe (near Malatya). Diakonoff associates Ezekiel's sixth-century Togarmah with the dynasty of Mugallu, seventh-century king of Melid, rather than with Til-Garimmu.[33] This is plausible for three reasons. Til-Garimmu had belonged to Melid before Assyria subjugated both in 712 BC. Second, Til-Garimmu's subsequent bid for independence, under Gurdi, seems to have been crushed by the Assyrians in 695. Third, whereas Assyrian sources make no further references to Til-Garimmu, Melid is not only attested but appears to have recovered her independence and flourished. Enquiries of King Esarhaddon to his oracle show that Melid achieved independence under King Mugallu by, probably, 675.[34] The annals of Ashurbanipal (668–631? or 627?) show

[30] Luckenbill, II, 1927, 608 (p. 236).
[31] Ibid., 854 (p. 328).
[32] Moses, I, 23, trans. Thomson, 1978, p. 112.
[33] Diakonoff, 1984, pp. 96–9, 179 (n. 296).
[34] Starr, 1990, nos. 4–12, pp. 6–14, and LVII–LVIII (for comment).

that by 668 Mugallu had extended his control to Tabal[35] (north-west of Melid), another former kingdom, which had become an Assyrian province in 713. Mugallu's son, who controlled Tabal and perhaps Melid too, subsequently made an alliance against Assyria with the king of the Cimmerians. Diakonoff supports his argument that the original Armenian kingdom was Melid with the fact that Babylonian documents of the Achaemenid period refer to Urartu and Melid where they, apparently, mean the two Achaemenid satrapies in Armenia which Herodotus mentions.

As Diakonoff suggests, the dynasty of Mugallu was probably both a new dynasty, and descended from proto-Armenian settlers. There had been a hiatus in Melid at the end of the eighth century. The inscriptions of the Assyrian king Sargon II (721–705 BC) record that, after deposing the kings of Tabal and Melid in 713 and 712, he gave the city of Melid to Mutallu, king of Kummukh. When Kummukh became an Assyrian province, in 708, Mutallu fled, probably, since Sargon complained of Mutallu's trust in the Urartian king, to Urartu.[36] It is plausible that when Melid regained independence it was ruled by a new line. That Mugallu was 'Armenian' is suggested by the possibility, proposed by Diakonoff, that Ezekiel's ruler of Togarmah was the anonymous Armenian king to whom Xenophon referred in his *Cyropaedia* written in the 360s BC. This text concerns the life of Cyrus, king of Persia and founder of the Achaemenid Empire, who conquered the Medes in the middle of the sixth century. Xenophon relates that the Armenian king, having heard that the Medes were about to be attacked by the king of Lydia and others, refused to provide the Medes with either troops or the tribute which he owed.[37] Much of the *Cyropaedia* is fictional, its purpose to expound Xenophon's ideas about the model ruler rather than the historical Cyrus, yet it may also draw on Armenian oral tradition which Xenophon had encountered during his journey, with other Greek mercenaries, through Armenia which he described in his *Anabasis*. So his story may preserve some historical truth, albeit garbled. His suggestion that there had been a Median affiliation seems to be supported by Moses of Khoren. Moses, whose account is independent of Xenophon's, states that the first Armenian king was made king by the Medes in return for helping in the destruction of Assyria, an event which occurred in 612 BC.

By *c*.600 the geographical base of the 'Armenian' dynasty of Melid had indeed probably changed. For the strength of Melid had declined in the middle of the seventh century. The Assyrian king Ashurbanipal records that the god Ashur smote the son of Mugallu by fire and that his kin and

---

[35] Luckenbill, II, 1927, 781 (p. 297).
[36] Luckenbill, II, 1927, 45 (pp. 22–3) 64 (p. 32).
[37] Xenophon, *Cyropaedia*, II, iv, 12, (and II, i, 6 for numbers expected).

army then submitted to Assyria.[38] Pottery evidence suggests that the Urartians crossed the Euphrates and built a fort at Köşkerbaba Hüyük within 16 miles of Arslantepe. Tabal appears autonomous in a passage of Ezekiel referring to the 590s.[39] Furthermore, the area of Mugallu's kingdom of Melid and Tabal passed to the kingdom of Cappadocia. According to the *Cyropaedia* Cappadocia was not part of the Armenian kingdom, but had its own king, Aribaeus.[40]

Names and Identities

Names of peoples and countries signify internal senses of identity and external perceptions of them, but they do not reveal how these identities were attained. There is even a danger that such names might mislead the casual enquirer, prompting a feeling that the unities which they suggest constitute historical 'truths' and 'inevitabilities' instead of, as for example in the cases of Scotland and England, political and social constructs.[41] Hence we face the question of definition: who, in the context of a history of the 'Armenians', is to be considered 'Armenian', and on what grounds?

We might begin with a consideration of present-day Armenians, since 'the ancestors of those people who could today be considered Armenian' is an obvious answer to the question of who a history of the Armenians should be about. In 1979 there were nearly 3 million Armenians in Soviet Armenia, an area roughly the size of Belgium, and some 2 million elsewhere, including over 150,000 in France and over 500,000 in the USA and Canada,[42] where there have been substantial Armenian communities for many decades. To a great extent, even in the diaspora, these modern Armenians were both biologically and culturally Armenian. Historically their communities had maintained strong traditions of marrying within themselves, and nowadays many maintain a strong sense of Armenian identity. Paradoxically, in the USA this sense does not differentiate them dramatically from their fellow Americans; many other American

---

[38] Campbell Thompson and Mallowan, 1933, pp. 96–105.
[39] Ezekiel, 32:26, Diakonoff, 1984, p. 178 (n. 287).
[40] Xenophon, *Cyropaedia*, II, i, 5.
[41] There is a vast literature on the subjects of nationalism and ethnicity. See e.g. Anderson, 1983; Atkinson et al., 1996, for their relationship to historical and archaeological scholarship of the ancient and medieval periods in Europe and Russia, besides Scotland, esp. Banks, and Tierney.
[42] The Soviet, French and North American figures are taken from modern studies where they are attributed to the Soviet Census of 1979, and a compilation for 1976 in N. B. Schahgaldian, 'The Political Integration of an Immigrant Community into a Composite Society. The Armenians in Lebanon, 1920–1974', Ph.D Dissertation, Columbia Universtiy, 1979, p. 47. For difficulties in defining and estimating numbers of Armenians around the world, and for a table of estimated numbers with definition, date and source, see Takooshian, 1986–7.

communities, such as the Irish, Italian and Swedish, enjoy a similarly lively sense of identity, investigate their roots and retain an interest in their ancient homeland. Likewise in the medieval period there was some survival of Armenian culture and consciousness of being Armenian among immigrants into the Byzantine empire, both amongst the lower classes, for whom the evidence is greater, and in some Byzantine aristocratic families.

Deliberate choice is one of the many factors which are involved in ethnicity and the formation of nations. A recent study of Armenians in London suggests that the commitment and efforts of members of an ethnic group to delineate its boundaries and assert its identity are greatest when other lines of demarcation between it and 'outsiders', for example occupational, residential or economic, are becoming ever more blurred. This is very different from what is commonly implied, that ethnic consciousness serves actually to validate such non-ethnic group differences.[43] And not all Londoners who could claim to be Armenian do so. The most obvious threat to the continuity of the Armenian community is marriage outside it, which offers individuals alternative affiliations and alternative ancestors for their 'family history'. Evidence from the USA suggests that by the late 1970s the vast majority of Armenians there were marrying 'outsiders' and were being 'lost' to the Armenian community.[44] A particular case, from Britain, to which there must be many parallels, may serve as illustration both of the diminution of the Armenian community, and of the problems of definition: a woman now living in England whose surname before her marriage, to an Englishman, was Armenian, whose family tree, via her Irish mother and French grandmother, has as many and as deep roots in Ireland and in France as it does in the Caucasus, who is legally British, and regards herself as Irish. Should we regard her as Armenian? Which group of ancestors has the best claim to her interest should she choose to investigate her origins?

As in the modern, so too in the early medieval period, the ancestors of the Armenians included a number of different groups. It seems natural, in discussing the origins of the Armenian people, to give priority to those ancestors who seem culturally closest to their descendants, and hence it is upon the speakers of proto-Armenian that the spotlight has been trained thus far. But we should turn now to other ancestral groups, and to the issues of choice and articulation.

The first literary exposition, though not the first attestation, of Armenian national identity is that of Moses of Khoren, relatively late, in the

---

[43] Talai, 1989.

[44] Marriage records of Armenian churches in New England yield a figure of 81 per cent for mixed marriages in 1976 and show a ninefold increase over the period 1950–76 (Aharonian, 1983 and 1986–7).

eighth century AD. His work was a particular response to external pressures and internal problems. Yet if we agree, as some scholars suggest, that in the Middle Ages the telling of tales of migration and settlement was an expression of a present sense of community rather than a common history, that it was more usual for a group with a political identity to claim a common ethnic origin than vice versa,[45] then we can conclude that some sense of national identity existed among the 'Armenians' before the eighth century AD. Whether directly or indirectly, Moses drew upon oral tradition which referred back at least to the sixth century BC and perhaps much earlier. This tradition was probably itself continuous from these early times. Its plausibility contrasts markedly with the artificiality of explanations offered by Moses' near-contemporaries in Frankish Gaul, in the seventh and eighth centuries AD, for the origins of the Franks, such as that they were connected with the Trojans. Another Frankish story was that the grandfather of the comparatively recent, late fifth-century, King Clovis I was the child of a sea-monster. By his date the Armenians had been recounting for over 1,000 years their more credible stories of national origins and of deeds of national heroes.

When did 'Armenia' and 'Armenian' acquire the meanings with which we associate them? Moses of Khoren believed that 'Armenian' was derived from the name of an ancient ruler, Aram, actually the first attested king of Urartu. There are other names similar to 'Armenia' in Urartian history. The father of the late seventh-century king Rusa III (c.601 BC) was called Erimena. The names Urmeúkhini, and Urme also occur. These names have sometimes been interpreted as suggestions of an Armenian presence or even predominance but they are probably little more than coincidence. At Behistun (Bisitun) 'Armenian' had a geographical rather than an ethnic or political meaning. Two versions of the inscription read 'Armenia' and 'Armenian', but the Akkadian (Babylonian) has 'Urartu' and 'Urartian'. And the name of the Armenian Ara-kha's father, 'Khaldi-ti', incorporating as it does 'Khaldi', the name of the chief god of Urartu, suggests he was Urartian.

But 'Armenia' and 'Armenian' are in fact not of prime importance, for they were names bestowed not by 'Armenians' but by others. A series of borrowings lies behind this usage. The Greeks took 'Armenian' from the Persians. The Persians had taken it from the Aramaeans (who staffed, and whose language was used in, the Achaemenid chancellery). The Aramaeans had simply applied the name of the nearest proto-Armenian speaking group (who lived in the country of Arme), to all the peoples living where the state of Urartu had been.[46]

[45] S. Reynolds, 'National Identity, Nations and Nationalism', paper delivered at a conference held under the auspices of the Centre for Medieval Studies at the University of Leeds, 17 March 1990.

[46] Diakonoff, 1984, pp. 126–7, 199 (n. 115–17).

The important names, those which the Armenians came to use for themselves and their country, are *Hay* (pl. *Hayk^c*) and *Hayastan*. Their similarity to the name of the Khayasha (Hayasa) people, who are mentioned in Hittite records, have prompted a suggestion that this people played an important role in the formation of the Armenian nation. This is open to objections of coincidence and of the probable lack of geographical overlap. Khayasha had certainly been to the north of the areas of the earliest 'Armenian' settlement, though there are differences of opinion concerning its exact location. (It was either in the upper Euphrates valley between Erzincan and Erzurum or in the valley of the River Çoroh, with its centre near modern Bayberd.)

The most convincing explanation of the Armenians' name for themselves, *Hayk^c*, is that it derives linguistically from Urartian *Khatini*, meaning Hittite. Its use perhaps reflects the mingling of 'Armenians' and Urartians, by whom the 'Armenians' were outnumbered. 'Hittite' was used by both the Assyrians and the Urartians for the several Syro-Hittite states which succeeded the Hittite empire.[47] Both Til-Garimmu, which, as we have seen, was associated with the origin of the Armenians through the tradition that their ancestor Hayk was the son of T^corgom, and Melid were among these. 'Hittite' could have been used by the Urartians first for the proto-Armenians and later for themselves, as they merged. That the medieval Armenians were in a very significant sense of Urartian descent can be inferred from Moses of Khoren's account of Hayk and of the rulers who were his descendants. There are of course different interpretations, but one is that Hayk's family's history contains a streamlined and garbled but not inaccurate description of Urartian expansion over the Armenian plateau. This is the more remarkable, if correct, since the Armenian tradition seems otherwise to have forgotten Urartu. For although Moses' text does include information, such as his account of the inscriptions at Van, which has proved valuable in studying Urartu, this information is very mangled indeed.[48]

The formation of countries and nationalities not only involves choices and perceptions but also owes much to external stimulus and shared experience. Foreign invasion, exploitation and persecution can contribute, and subjection to a common, uniform, governmental system, and even culture, a process to which the Urartians contributed greatly, also plays a part. The history of the Armenians incorporates all these elements, just as it includes peoples who were not called Armenians in their own time. It is therefore with the first experiences of the speakers of proto-Armenian (the Mushki) in Armenia that this history begins.

---

[47] Ibid. pp. 126–7, 199–201 (n. 118–20).
[48] Hewsen, 1975; Moses, I, 10–16, trans. Thomson, 1978, pp. 85–101.

2

Early History: the 'Armenian' Environment c.1165–590 BC

The Armenian nation was forged out of disparate groups, a number of which are discernible and should be considered in their own right until about the mid-second century BC. The territory which was to be its homeland was far from empty when the Mushki ('Armenians') arrived in about 1165 BC. The Khayasha (Hayasa) -Azzi confederation had recently extended into the Euphrates valley, at least as far as modern Kemah, at the time of the great Shuppiluliuma, king of the Hittites (c. 1370–c. 1330), whose sister married the king of Khayasha. Hittite control of Khayasha and Azzi was shortlived, and the confederation itself seems to have fallen apart by the end of the thirteenth century BC. A different country, Dayaenu, appears in the annals of Assyria's Tiglath-Pileser I (1114–1076). Some scholars believe Dayaenu was in Khayasha, possibly the Çoroh valley, but this location depends on identifying Dayaenu with later, Urartian, Diauekhi. Another ancient kingdom which had reached into Armenia was Hurrian Mitanni in northern Mesopotamia. The Hurrians had spread through eastern Anatolia and northern Mesopotamia late in the third millennium, after about 2300 BC. Mitanni was in existence by the mid-sixteenth century BC. Her capital was Washshuganni on the River Khabur, but her territory probably extended northwards into Shubria and perhaps beyond. Little is known about the society and structure of Mitanni, but for some time she was a major power. In the fourteenth century she enjoyed marriage alliances with Egypt, and, like Khayasha, attracted fugitives from the Hittites. But she fell under Shuppiluliuma's domination and was finally destroyed by Shalmaneser I of Assyria in 1275.

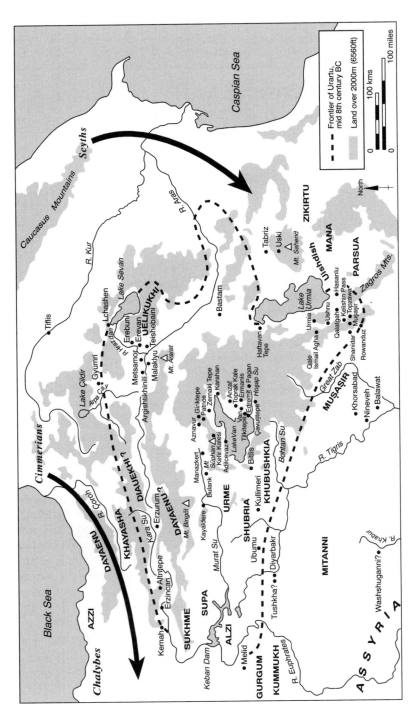

Map 2.1 Armenia

As for kingdoms entirely within Armenia, an inscription of Shalmaneser refers to eight lands and fifty-one cities in the land of 'Uruaṭri'.[1] He conquered them, apparently before he turned to Mitanni. Parts of Uruaṭri lay in the valley of the Upper Zab, and it may have extended to the west of Lake Van. The region was probably part of the 'Nairi' lands, whose forty kings the Assyrian Tukulti-Ninurta I (1244–1208) claimed to have conquered.[2] The names of twenty-three Nairi lands were recorded by Tiglath-Pileser I;[3] their southern point was Tumme, known to have been south-west of Lake Urmia, and their northern one Dayaenu.

The extent of Nairi is elusive. There is uncertainty about the exact location of Dayaenu, twenty-one countries in Tiglath-Pileser's list are otherwise unknown, and some scholars interpret his statement that he chased the kings to the Upper Sea as a reference to the Black Sea, whereas others prefer Lake Van. However, the information offered by the king's account of his victories of c.1112 BC regarding the structure and economy of Nairi is more helpful. Nairi was small-scale, and settled, ruled by a number of kings, perhaps in some league or confederation. Twenty-three kings are mentioned and then sixty, including those who had come to their aid. In another, shorter, version of events, the number of Nairi kings is thirty.[4] There were cult centres and cities for Tiglath-Pileser to conquer and destroy and herds of livestock to take. He imposed a tribute of 2,000 cattle and 1,200 horses. Nairi had much the same character in the ninth century. Ashurnasirpal II (883–859), who appointed governors over the Nairi lands, apparently took from the kings a tribute of chariots, horses, mules, silver, gold, bronze utensils, oxen, sheep and wine, and razed 250 of their fortified cities.[5] Shamshi-Adad V (823–811) recorded the names of twenty-eight persons 'kings of Nairi, all of them' upon whom he imposed a tribute of horses 'broken to the yoke'.[6]

The pre-history of the lands which were to become Armenia was diverse, and it reached back many millennia. We have a number of very important archaeological sites. There was early settlement at Van, at the mound of Tilkitepe, from some time before the late fourth millennium. The Araxes plain has been regarded by some scholars as the original home of what is sometimes termed the Kura-Araxes culture, which flourished in Armenia throughout the third millennium BC. This culture was uncovered first at Shengavit, near Erevan. A key site for the second millennium is that of Lchashen, on the shores of Lake Sevan. Here a

[1] Grayson, I, 1972, LXXVII 527 (p. 81).
[2] Ibid., LXXVIII 715 (p. 108), 721 (pp. 109–10), 773 (pp. 118–19), 795 (p. 123).
[3] Grayson, II, 1976, LXXXVII 30 (iv 43) (pp. 12–13).
[4] Ibid., LXXXVII 69 (25) (p. 21), 80 (6) (pp. 22–3).
[5] Ibid. CI 642 (r. 49) (p. 163), 589 (iii 118) (pp. 145–6), 551 (ii 12) (p. 127), 573 (ii 112) (p. 135).
[6] Luckenbill, I, 1926, 722 (pp. 257–8).

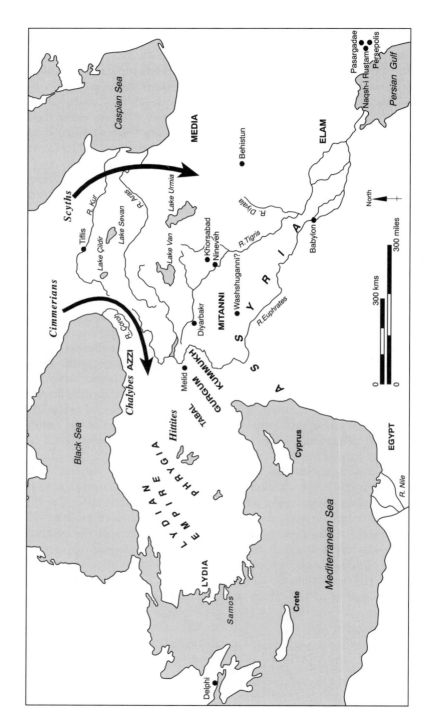

Map 2.2 The east Mediterranean and west Asia

wealthy barrow culture reached its highest point in the thirteenth century BC. The tombs of the chieftains contained gold work and wheeled vehicles as well as animals and slaves. The design of the vehicles suggests that this culture may have owed something to Mitanni.

More ancient still than these sites is that of Hasanlu, to the south of Lake Urmia. Here there was a settlement as early as the sixth millennium BC. Hasanlu was a major metal-working centre and prosperous in the very late second millennium. In the late ninth century BC it was part of the newly formed kingdom of Mana, which both Assyria and Urartu were to try to control, for strategic, commercial and economic reasons. Earliest of all is Shanidar, not far to the west, in present-day Iraqi Kurdistan. Shanidar lies close to the site of the city of Muṣaṣir (Urartian Ardini), which was important in Urartian history. Neanderthal men, whose species became extinct about 35,000–40,000 years ago, once lived in Shanidar cave. One, known now as Shanidar IV, was buried there with June flowers gathered from the mountainside.[7] His burial is the earliest known example of the offering of flowers at funerals.

The Rise and Fall of Urartu

Most of these territories were to come under the domination of the state known as Assyria and nowadays as Urartu, though the Urartians themselves called it Biainili.

The certain and continuous attestation of Urartu begins with the aggressive Assyrian Ashurnasirpal II, to whom the Mushki ('Armenians') had offered gifts in 883, and who had taken tribute from Nairi. Ashurnasirpal claimed in 879 BC that his dominion reached as far as Urartu.[8] Her first known king is Arame. He reigned, probably, from c.860 to the late 840s, and was attacked by Shalmaneser III (858–824) of Assyria three times. Arame's royal cities were Sugunia and Arzashkun, whose capture, in 859 and 855, Shalmaneser portrayed on the bronze gates of his palace at Balawat. Neither of these cities has been certainly located.[9] But under the next king, Sarduri I (c. 840–c.825), the capital was at Tushpa, modern Van, where it remained.

Exactly what had brought about the formation of Urartu is not clear, though various suggestions have been made, including a shift in trade routes and adaptation to increasing Assyrian aggression. This aggression may have stimulated its victims to co-operate under central leadership,

---

[7] Solecki, 1971, 1972; Leroi-Gourhan, 1975.
[8] Grayson, II, 1976, CI 651 (p. 166).
[9] Modern Adilcevaz is a strong candidate since not only have fragments of a large Urartian relief been found there, but its Armenian name, Artskhē, might be explained by that of Arzashkun (Sinclair, 1987, pp. 312, 275).

whilst simultaneously weakening some local dynasties. The expansion of Urartu, by contrast, can be reconstructed. We have dateable Urartian fortresses, details in the inscriptions of the Urartian kings, and information in Assyrian sources. But there are difficulties. Inscriptions offer statistics of booty and conquest, and claims that places were destroyed. They may contain both error and inflation, and they are certainly partial in their coverage. In some cases the gist may be more reliable than the details, but even that is not beyond suspicion. Furthermore, the concerns of the Urartians were not ours. Their inscriptions did not state the purposes of their wars and were more concerned with details of events than their dates and sequence. Precise chronology is sometimes a matter of scholarly disagreement. So too is Urartian political geography. Geographical disagreements are of major proportions and render it impossible to paint a neat and tidy picture. The moving of the capital to Van, for example, may be interpreted either as an early recovery against Assyria or as a retreat, depending on the view taken of the location of Arzashkun.

For nearly a century the leitmotif of Urartian history was expansion. King Ishpuini (c.825–c.810) with Menua, his son, co-ruler and successor, took over the lands between Van and Urmia and gained control of the kingdom of Muşaşir, to the south-west of Urmia in the Upper Zab valley. They also occupied at least some land west and north of Urmia and captured towns in Mana and Parsua to its south. Menua himself consolidated Urartian control to just beyond Hasanlu, which was burnt about 800 BC, and pushed northwards to the Araxes. He took tribute from Diauekhi. It was Menua who acquired the territories where 'Armenians' had settled. He may have built the fort of Altıntepe near Erzincan, he took tribute from Melid, conquered Supa (opposite Melid), wrested Sukhme (between the valleys of Erzincan and the Arsanias) and Alzi from Assyria, and conquered Urme and Kullimeri in Shubria.

Menua's successors continued his work. Under Argishti I (c.785–c.763 BC) the Urartians pushed further north. They reached the area of Gyumri (formerly Leninakan) as far as the country of the *Ish-qi-gu-lu-ú* (probably the Cimmerians), and crossed the Araxes. Sarduri II (c.763–c.734) campaigned, in the north, on the western shore of Lake Sevan, up to Lake Çildir, and against the Kulkhai (classical Colchis) in the Çoroh valley, and, in the south, in Urme. He also conquered the king of Melid and took from him nine forts on the western bank of the Euphrates. Rusa I (c.734–c.714 BC) extended control in the north-east towards Tiflis and the Kura river; he defeated twenty-three kings in the region of Lake Sevan, nineteen of whom came from areas to its east. There was subsequently further eastwards expansion, under Argishti II and Rusa II (c.685–c.645).

The new Urartian state certainly fended off Assyrian conquest but its very success naturally provoked Assyrian concern. Assyrian interests were endangered by Urartian success in the upper Euphrates valley,

Melid, Shubria, Mana and Parsua, by the campaigns of Argishti I and Sarduri in Babilu (perhaps the Diyala valley) and by the victory of Sarduri over the king of Kummukh, the neighbour of Melid, in 746. This victory gained for Urartu the support of the alliance of kingdoms in north Syria which had come together in the ninth century.

Urartu had, consequently, to cope with Assyrian ripostes, but there was no significant change in her fortune until about half way through Sarduri's reign, when Tiglath-Pileser III (744–727) began Assyrian reconquest in northern Syria with the defeat of Sarduri in Kummukh in 742. The upper Euphrates became the frontier of Urartu. Then in 735 Tiglath-Pileser invaded, as far as Van. There was however a brief Urartian recovery under Rusa I. Royal Assyrian letters from the reign of Sargon II (721–705)[10] reveal the manoeuvres which lay behind the events recorded in his inscriptions.[11] Rusa made various alliances: with Urzana of Muṣaṣir, probably between 726 and 722; with Phrygia, Tabal, and others, probably by 717; and with Ullusunu of Mana. Ullusunu had been established in Mana by Sargon in place of his brother, King Aza, whose assassination in 716 Rusa had instigated.

Sargon's response to Urartian success was even more energetic than Tiglath-Pileser's had been. He had already executed Bagdatti of Uishdish, one of the Mana rebels, when in 715 he seized the twenty-two border fortresses which Rusa had taken. In 714 he entered Mana, defeated Rusa at Mount Sahend, and invaded Urartu. His extensive ravaging culminated in the pillage of fabulous treasures, including statues of deities, from the palace and temple of Muṣaṣir whence about ten tons of silver and 220,460 lbs (3,600 talents) of bronze objects were removed.[12] Then Sargon attended to the west, and by 707 the kingdoms of Tabal, Melid, Gurgum and Kummukh had been turned into Assyrian provinces, and peace concluded with Phrygia. Rusa himself might have been able to survive 714 had Sargon's victory been the only disaster. But it seems not to have been. The Assyrian letters record that an Urartian king suffered a terrible defeat in the land of the Cimmerians, who subsequently invaded Urartu. This was probably Rusa. The precise chronological relationship of this defeat with the campaign of Sargon is unclear, but it seems to have been close.[13] According to Sargon, Rusa committed suicide after the news from Muṣaṣir.[14]

[10] Parpola, 1987; Pfeiffer, 1935; Waterman, 1930.

[11] Lie, 1929; Luckenbill, II, 1927.

[12] His expedition is described in detail in his Letter to Ashur, Luckenbill, II, 1927, 140–78 (pp. 73–99).

[13] For defeat, Parpola, 1987, nos. 30, 31; Pfeiffer, 1935, no. 11; Waterman, 1930, no. 197: for the chronology, Lanfranchi, 1983, esp. pp. 134–5, where a dating for the disaster shortly before Sargon's campaign but in 715 rather than 714, in the same year, is preferred. Kristensen, 1988, esp. pp. 80–93, argues that Rusa's disaster in the land of the Cimmerians and his defeat by Sargon's forces were one and the same event.

[14] Luckenbill, II, 1927, 22 (pp. 9–10), 59 (p. 30).

These blows were not, however, equally fatal for the state. A fragmentary letter suggests that the captured gods of Muṣaṣir may have been returned.[15] Argishti II extended the frontier eastwards. The Cimmerians went on to molest people further west. Rusa II had Cimmerian allies, both in his 676 campaign against Phrygia, Melid and the Chalybes and, at some point, against Shubria.[16] This was probably about 675, before Shubria was conquered by Assyria, but it might have been connected with Urartu's own, unsuccessful, invasion of Shubria in 664.

Yet despite these positive developments the seventh century was a period of irreversible decline. The Scyths, who, as the Cimmerians probably did, came from across the Caucasus, in the north, caused serious trouble. They were not invariably hostile. Scythian arrowheads in the stores at Karmir-Blur near Erevan could perhaps signify Urartian use of Scythian mercenaries, not simply of Scythian weapons. An inscription from Toprak Kale (Rusakhinili), a fortress and royal centre established near Van by Rusa II, suggests that a son of the Scythian king had visited.[17] But the Scyths attacked Urartu as well as Assyria from their base in Mana and the Zagros mountains to the south of Lake Urmia.

The precise role of the Scyths is difficult to establish, because one of our principal sources is the account entangled by Herodotus in his version of the history of the Medes, which is itself unreliable.[18] Herodotus' assertion that the Scyths dominated Asia Minor and Media, (meaning Mana, plus Media), for twenty-eight years is especially suspect. But according to Strabo, the Scyths terminated Cimmerian power at a battle in Cilicia, thought to have been in 636 BC.[19] It is likely that they had invaded and weakened Urartu *en route*. In his annals, written between 644 and 636, Ashurbanipal (668–631? or 627? BC) gloats that Sarduri, king of Urartu, sent him gifts in fear, and addressed him as lord, whereas Sarduri's predecessors had used terms of brotherhood in their messages to Assyria.[20] Pottery evidence suggests that sites which were abandoned or destroyed as Urartu expired, including Altıntepe, Armavir, Bastam, Karmir-Blur and Toprak Kale, had met their fate by 650 BC. Arrowheads betray the involvement of Scyths in the destruction.

Towards the close of the seventh century other predators appeared. Babylon, having contributed to the fall of Assyria in 612, advanced, according to the Babylonian chronicle, as far as 'the city of Urartu' in 609, and to the mountain of Bit-Khanunia in the 'district of Urartu'

[15] Parpola, 1987, no. 7.
[16] Melikishvili, 1960, no. 278 (pp. 341–2); Diakonoff, 1984, p. 90 and p. 175 (n. 257–60); Starr, 1990, no. 18 pp. 22–4.
[17] Melikishvili, 1960, no. 286 (p. 348).
[18] Brown, S. C., 1988.
[19] Strabo, *The Geography*, I, iii, 21.
[20] Luckenbill, II, 1927, 834 (pp. 320–1).

in 608.[21] The Medes, who had helped against Assyria and who were completely to absorb the Scyths by about 550, may have been involved in these assaults. They must certainly have dealt the final blow to whatever was left of Urartu when they moved west against Lydia in 590.

Government and Society in Urartu

1 War and building

The ability of Urartu to resist, rival and, perhaps, briefly outlast Assyria reveals a highly martial state. Her chief god, Khaldi, was god of war. It seems curious that Khaldi, god of subordinated Muṣaṣir, should precede Shivini, god of the capital, Tushpa. But some scholars suggest (partly because one inscription of Shalmaneser III refers to Muṣaṣir where we would expect Arzashkun), that Muṣaṣir may have been Arame's Arzashkun.[22] If so, Khaldi's priority is natural. Ishpuini and Menua took care to make Khaldi splendid gifts to ensure his favour. Their inscription at Meher Kapusu (Kapısı), near Van, sets out the sacrifices due, presumably on particular occasions, to the gods.[23] Khaldi's allowance, seventeen bulls and thirty-four sheep, is nearly three times that of the second god Teisheba, four times that of the sun god Shivini, and greater by about eight and seventeen times various others'.

The kings also took more practical steps to be sure of military success. Comparison of the Balawat illustrations with surviving weapons and armour, some pieces of which are themselves decorated with illustrations of military equipment, shows that the army was re-requipped in or by the time of Argishti I along Assyrian lines. There may have been a standing army by the time of Sarduri II (c.763–c.734), for he abolished what he called 'superfluous' service for the (armed) people – '92 chariots, 3,600 cavalrymen, 352,011 soldiers, riders or foot'.[24] This last number is taken to be the number of men hitherto liable for service. Horses were nurtured. There is a suggestion, based on finds of horse-bits, that a larger, more powerful breed of horses was introduced in Sarduri's reign. In 714 BC Sargon found that at the strong walled cities of Tarui and Tarmakisa (Tabriz) horses, reserved, and fattened each year, for the royal army, were stabled in the deep surrounding moats. He also recorded that in the district of Ushkaia

[21] Grayson, 1975, Texts nos 3, 4 (609, 608). Grayson translates 'district' of Urartu rather than 'city' in no. 3, but 'Urartu' has the determinative *uru* meaning city (p. 253).
[22] Pecoroella and Salvini, 1982.
[23] Melikishvili, 1960, no. 27 (pp. 143–9).
[24] Ibid., no. 155G (p. 298), Diakonoff; 1984, pp. 124, 197 (n. 105); Zimansky, 1985, pp. 55–7 and n. 77.

people had for years been catching native colts and raising them for the army.[25]

Even more important were the forts which were erected throughout the kingdom. Made up to about six feet, including foundations, of massive stone blocks, with mud bricks above, they were in naturally defensible sites, the larger ones having walls some nine to thirteen feet thick and perhaps up to sixty-six high, with buttresses (which seem to have been introduced by Menua), battlements, high, narrow towers and (decorative) false rectangular windows and, probably, projecting parapets. Our evidence for their appearance comes from excavation, from bronze and ivory remains of models, from illustrations on bronze belts and from Sargon, who recorded strong walled cities with deep surrounding moats and towers at the entrances to their gates, and fortress walls to a height of 240 cubits.

The chief function of these forts was to guard frontiers and access routes and provide bases for future expansion. Sargon complained that Ushkaia, perhaps modern Uski, on the west of Mount Sahend, 'bars the pass into the Zaranda district like a door'. Ishpuini's and Menua's forts at Anzaf, 12½ miles from Van, guarded the main Urmia-Van road. Rusa I's Kayalıdere commanded the approaches to the plains of Bulanık and Manazkert, and Rusa II's Bastam routes to the middle Araxes plain from the east. The connection between fortification and conquest is most clearly to be seen in the career of Menua, who excelled at both and used the one to further the other.

Sargon's account of his 714 campaign suggests that the number of Urartian forts was very large. One inscription claims the conquest of fifty-five walled cities together with eleven towering forts.[26] This was in just a part of Urartu. The forts varied in size and function however and their role might change. Some, like Argishti I's Arin-berd, founded in 782 'for the strength of Biainili and the suppression of the hostile countries',[27] were centres of production, cultivation and population. Arin-berd declined when Rusa II built Teishebaini, at Karmir-Blur, nearby, whose situation was safer from the Scyths. Sarduri II's Çavuştepe seems not to have been an agricultural centre, but was an administrative one, like Karmir-Blur and Bastam. Uaiais, perhaps modern Bitlis or Ushnu or Qale Ismail Agha or Qalatgah, according to Sargon the strongest of Rusa I's forts, appears in the Assyrian correspondence as a base where troops, spies, envoys and district governors with their retinues assembled.[28] Another important administrative centre, in the opinion of some scholars,

---

[25] Luckenbill, II, 1927, 159, 158 (pp. 85–6, 84–5).
[26] Ibid., 56 (pp. 27–9).
[27] Melikishvili, 1960, no. 138 (pp. 263–4).
[28] Uaiais also appears as Uesi, Uasi: Luckenbill, II, 1927, 167 (p.92); Waterman, 1930, nos 198, 380, 409, 444, 492, 515; Pfeiffer, 1935, nos 8, 9; Parpola, 1987, nos 29, 30.

Plate 5   Seventh-century BC *Urartian bronze models of a turret and part of a city, (British Museum WA 91250 and WA 91177), probably from the same model.*

despite its small size and the insignificance of its fortifications, was Haftavan Tepe, north-west of Lake Urmia, possibly the Ulkhu, 'the city of properties', whose walls and palace Sargon levelled in 714. Other forts served as refuges for the population, for whom flight was the major tactic in war. This may explain why the larger plains have no obvious central forts. Near Ulkhu there was the fort of Sardurikhurda.[29] Kefir Kalesi, possibly of late date, 7,874 feet high on Mount Süphan and with no

[29] Luckenbill, II, 1927, 161 (pp. 87–8).

buildings inside the fortress, probably had no permanent garrison, but was simply a mountain refuge, perhaps for users of the nearby summer pastures.

The Urartians established a road network to connect their sites, their road towards Elazığ from Lake Van, punctuated with way-stations, being the earliest known long-distance engineered road. They also provided irrigation works, canals and *qanāts* (underground channels) which have been admired through the ages. Describing his approach to Ulkhu, Sargon remarks, of the canal and irrigation channels dug by Rusa I, 'Like a god he made its people raise their glad songs.' The most famous canal is that of Menua, from the river Hoşap to Van, forty-five miles long and still used today. The medieval Moses of Khoren attributed it to Semiramis, legendary queen of Assyria.[30] His mistake may owe something to a memory of the laying out of a vineyard for *Ta-ri-ri-a-i*, daughter of Menua,[31] at a point beside Menua's canal. *Ta-ri-ri-a-i* was a near contemporary of the prototype for Semiramis, Sammuramat, mother of the Assyrian king Adad-nirari III (810–783 BC). Irrigation works were proclaimed with pride in the Urartian inscriptions. Until Argishti I had connected four canals to the river and laid out vineyards and orchards Armavir had, apparently, been a desert.[32] Rusa II made similar claims about Karmir-Blur, for which he constructed a canal from the river Ildaruni, modern Hrazdan.[33]

2   Economy

War and water together supported Urartu's economy. Irrigation works nourished vineyards, orchards, forests, fields of barley, grass and pasture. The early conquests had the result, and perhaps the object, of extending Urartian mineral resources. The building programme needed iron tools. At Metsamor, across the Araxes, there had been bronze and iron works for centuries. Beyond Diauekhi, Kulkhai was a rich metal-working area. Gold and iron came from there, and more iron from the Chalybes. Northern Syria may have attracted Urartu's attention because trade in iron passed through it. Mana likewise offered the opportunity of diverting trade from the east. Victory brought tribute and loot, detailed in the royal annals. Argishti I, in 785, imposed an annual tribute on Diauekhi of gold, 10,000 measures of copper, oxen, 100 cows, 500 sheep and 300 horses.[34] Sarduri II levied a tribute on Kummukh which included 40

[30] Moses, I, 16, trans. Thomson, 1978, pp. 99–100.
[31] Melikishvili, 1960, no. 111 (pp. 205–6).
[32] Ibid., no. 137 (pp. 262–3).
[33] Ibid., no. 281 (pp. 344–6).
[34] Ibid., no. 128 B1 (pp. 247–8).

measures of gold, 800 of silver and 2,000 copper shields and 1535 copper basins.[35] From Melid he took gold, silver and fifty war chariots.[36] From Mana, Argishti I took 170 horses, sixty-two camels, 2,411 oxen and over 6,000 sheep in 776.[37]

Glamorous though they are, precious metals appear on only four occasions in the inscriptions. The kings seem to have been more concerned with the regular acquisition of animate resources. Zimansky's tabulation of booty lists of Ishpuini, Menua, Argishti I and Sarduri II (i.e. *c.*825–*c.*734) shows that Argishti I claimed at least 10,427 horses, 447 camels, 131,871 oxen, and 557,516 sheep and goats, and Sarduri II at least 10,442 horses, 115 camels, 118,607 oxen and 442,949 sheep and goats. The profits of war also included thousands of people – captives such as the 52,675 Argishti took in 785, and the 29,284 which his campaigns against Melid and other places provided in 783. In all, his inscriptions claim at least 219,914, and Sarduri II's 102,196.[38] Not all survived: the annals repeat 'some I killed, but others I took alive.' It was probably more often males who perished, presumably to avoid the danger of subsequent rebellion and to intimidate others. Only twice do inscriptions indicate what happened to those who lived.[39] In 782, 6,600 warriors from Melid and Supa were settled at Arin-berd perhaps to garrison it. Captives were presumably set to work, in agriculture, in building, as some of Rusa II's captives were, or in some other useful occupation, as they certainly were in Assyria.

The connection between successful war and economic prosperity is apparent too in the importance of hunting. Hunting had both an economic and a martial function. As Xenophon explains in the *Cyropaedia* it 'seems to be the best preparation for war itself', for similar qualities and techniques were required in both.[40] It was clearly a familiar occupation. Hunting scenes with bulls, lions, leopards, goats and fantastic animals are to be found on Urartian bronze belts and on seals. And, finally, it was forts and warriors who protected the economy, from enemy deportations and pillage, and from destruction. Some destruction, such as that of vines and trees, takes a long time to rectify.

The inner workings of the economy, however, are difficult to gauge.[41] The medium of exchange, if any, or unit of account, is unknown. The evidence for such things as land tenure, taxation, transfer of goods, the redistribution of agricultural surplus and the role of slaves is both

---

[35] Ibid., no. 155 E 36–57 (p. 303).
[36] Ibid., no. 158 (pp. 306–8).
[37] Ibid., no. 127 V (pp. 225–9).
[38] Zimansky, 1985, table 8 and pp. 57–9. Readings of numbers have varied. Zimansky has checked his against photographs of the texts.
[39] Zimansky, 1985, pp. 57–8; Melikishvili, 1960, nos 138 (pp. 263–4), 278 (pp. 341–2).
[40] Xenophon, *Cyropaedia*, I, ii, 10.
[41] Zimansky, 1985, pp. 2–3, 6, 33, 45–7, 57–8.

difficult to interpret and very slight, for most administrative records were written on perishable materials.

The level of Urartu's international trade is also difficult to assess. Direct evidence of commerce has been found elsewhere in the Near East, but not in Urartu. It might be that trade is implied where there appears to have been movement of goods. Textile fragments found at Toprak Kale (Rusakhinili) have been identified as Chinese silk dating from the middle of the eighth century. Some eighth-century Urartian seals may have been of foreign manufacture. One Urartian bell has been found on the Greek island of Samos. Then there are the controversial bronze cauldrons whose ornamental handles, riveted to the basins, comprise a human head and body with bird wings and tail, and which have been found in Phrygia, Greece and Italy. Current opinion supports a north Syrian origin rather than an Urartian one, for several reasons.[42] Despite claims to the contrary, no human-headed handles have been found in Urartu, and their artistry is Syrian. Inscriptions demonstrate that north Syria was a centre of production, Kummukh paid a tribute of vessels to Sarduri II, and there were vessels from Tabal at Muşaşir. On the other hand, lead isotope analysis suggests that cauldrons at Delphi, in Greece, might be Urartian after all.[43]

But the movement of goods, and especially of luxury goods, may be the result, not of trade, but of war, diplomacy and the movement of people, which movement is well attested. For example, Sarduri II complained of 'fugitive slaves' in Melid,[44] and fugitives from both Assyria and Urartu were attracted to Shubria. Esarhaddon (680–669) complained about them – governors, scribes, superintendents and constables as well as robbers and other criminals. When he conquered Shubria he returned Urartian fugitives to Rusa II.[45]

In general foreign trade was not a necessity, though tin, probably from Afghanistan, was needed to produce bronze. Urartu was fairly self-sufficient – with, for example, her own bronze and iron industries – and prosperous. Her system of settlement remains obscure, but a multiplicity of towns is suggested by both literary and archaeological evidence.[46] Statements in inscriptions are probably exaggerated. Shalmaneser III (858–824 BC) claimed to have destroyed fifty Urartian cities, and his successor to have captured eleven strong and 200 small ones. Tiglath-Pileser III, recording his march through Urartu, listed twenty-six places as

---

[42] Muscarella, 1970; Van Loon, 1977.

[43] Muhly, in Curtis (ed.), 1988, p. 338.

[44] Melikishvili, 1960, no. 158 (pp. 306–8).

[45] Luckenbill, II, 1927, 606 (p. 235), 612 (p. 237), 607 (p. 236). For references in Assyrian correspondence, Lanfranchi and Parpola, 1990, nos. 52, 53, 54; Waterman, 1930, nos 252, 251, 1176.

[46] Zimansky, 1985, ch. 3, Settlement and Defensive Networks, pp. 32–47, includes detailed comment on sites mentioned by Sargon, pp. 62–5 for 'palace'/'fortresses' and 'cities' in Urartian inscriptions.

cities and strongholds of Urartu.[47] The reality was less impressive, a variety of walled cities (for example Karmir-Blur), citadel-towns (for example Çavuştepe) and villages. In the south, Sargon II differentiated 'strong' or fortified cities, sixty in five provinces, some with walls, moats, citadels, stores and houses, from 360 'cities', all but two anonymous, which must have been villages. Further north, after a campaign of 785, which started in Diauekhi and involved three nearby countries, Argishti I claimed that he destroyed 105 forts and burnt 453 towns.[48] Most of these must also have been villages.

The archaeological evidence for genuinely urban life is strong. In the Van region there were, besides Van, at least thirteen towns. They include Edremit, the city of Alniunu whence came the stone for Sarduri I's citadel at Van, and Karahan, perhaps the *Ar-ṣu-ni-ù-i-ni* mentioned at Meher Kapusu, whose foundation is recorded in inscriptions found near Karahan in 1977.[49] The town at Upper Anzaf Kale was probably about five acres in size. Van, once blessed with Menua's canal, could have supported 50,000 people, though very little is known about the settlement beneath the citadel rock. Armavir covered 400–500 hectares and its population was about 30,000. It had a palace, store rooms, temples, gardens, vineyards, walls, towers, and a citadel.

3   Administration

Urban building programmes, irrigation works and fortifications were all, like the raising, provisioning and equipping of troops, the work of a strong and centralized administrative system. This system both stimulated and used towns. Consider Karmir-Blur, where the town outside the ten-acre citadel covered at least seventy-five acres. It has been inferred from the regularity of its layout and its different types of housing that it was built in advance, for inhabitants who were to be transferred from elsewhere. The unfinished Zernaki Tepe has often been regarded as another example, but its early Urartian attribution has been challenged.[50] Even Urartian art likewise implies strong central control. Some specialists have remarked on a lack of regional variation and of chronological development. The apparent exceptions are mass-produced bronze belts,

[47] Luckenbill, I, 1926, 588 (pp. 210–11), 717 (p. 255), 785 (pp. 281–2).
[48] Melikishvili, 1960, no. 128 B1 (pp. 234–6).
[49] Sinclair, 1987, pp. 183, 219–20, 283.
[50] There is a Urartian fortress-town at Zernaki Tepe as well as this unfinished town. The latter could have held perhaps 15,000 people over about 0.4 of a square mile; its intersecting streets forming square blocks are typical of Roman towns; its hill site is unusual for an Urartian town; and it is probably first or second century AD. Sinclair, 1987, pp. 281–2, 16, 87. See also Burney, 1957, Burney and Lawson, 1960 and Zimansky, 1985, pp. 65–6. Zimansky believes (1985, p. 76) that the Urartian reputation for building and planning cities is an unwarranted twentieth-century creation.

which suggest both, and votive bronze plaques, unknown until 1970, whose style has been termed 'barbaric'.

An efficient administrative system is suggested also by the tribute of sheep, cattle, foodstuffs and precious metals, which was levied throughout Urartu, from tributary states like Diauekhi and from the local population. At major sites there were wine cellars, huge granaries and storehouses, to keep dues in kind. The construction of storehouses is attested in inscriptions. Sarduri II, for example, built eight, to take in total at least 90,020 *ka-pi*, a unit of dry measure, probably for grain. It is frustrating that there are two possibilities for the quantity represented by the *ka-pi*, – about a half gallon or about twelve. Archaeologists have unearthed less evidence for such storehouses than for those meant to store liquids.[51] Long lines of earthenware jars of three feet high or more, often labelled, have been found. Altıntepe had two storerooms, one some 52 by 33 feet with jars in rows of ten by six. Some of the jars in the wine cellars at Arin-berd could hold more than 200 gallons. In the citadel at Karmir-Blur about 9,000 gallons could be contained in eight wine stores, and about 750 tons of grain in others.

Besides the archaeological evidence, the administration has left some official government statistics. Like the Assyrians, the Urartian kings had inscriptions made, written in an adapted form of Assyrian cuneiform, which record information about their building works, victories and tributes, including the number of animals and persons captured. Ishpuini and Menua led 106 war chariots, and at least (some numbers are missing) 9,174 horsemen and 2,704 infantry against *Me-ish-ta*, probably Hasanlu. On another occasion they led sixty-six chariots, 1,460 cavalry and 15,760 foot.[52] The annals of Argishti I repetitively enumerate the yearly tally of horses, oxen, sheep, and sometimes camels, youths, women and warriors acquired through campaigning.

The royal inscriptions were set up in a variety of places, on rock faces, in fortresses, temples, and on steles. Menua, Argishti I and Sarduri II were the most prolific authors, as they were the most successful, and the last two have left lengthy annals at Van. The earliest inscriptions, three short ones of Sarduri I, were in Assyrian, which suggests that Assyrian personnel were used, but the later ones are in Urartian. The inscription of Ishpuini and Menua at Kelishin was bilingual.[53] This might suggest that for a short period a bilingual text was the norm. But the fact that the inscription of Rusa I at nearby Topzawa[54] was also bilingual suggests other reasons. Both inscriptions concerned Urartu's relationship with

[51] Zimansky, 1985, table 15 and pp. 73–5.
[52] Melikishvili, 1960, nos 24 (pp. 138–42), 21 (pp. 135–6); Zimansky, 1985, table 6 reads 1460 instead of Melikishvili's 460.
[53] Melikishvili, 1960, no. 19 (pp. 125–31).
[54] Ibid., no. 264 (pp. 323–7).

Muṣaṣir, which, being near the Assyrian frontier, was a natural Assyrian target, and perhaps had a mixed population. It may simply be that the two kings felt that two texts were necessary here, to reach all interested parties. The inscriptions use regular formulae, for example in summarizing the year's booty, recording the killing of captives, and associating the royal deeds with the god Khaldi. Some of the formulae are analogous to those used by the Assyrians, but others are related to Hittite annals, suggesting that the Urartians may have used the expertise of some intermediary Hurrian centre whose identity is now lost.[55]

There were several categories of administrative personnel. Behind the masons who carved the inscriptions were scribes, who composed them and counted up booty, like the clerks depicted on Assyrian reliefs, on one of which the clerk is accompanied by a war-artist. Scribes, presumably, kept the records of the contents of stores. One record from Karmir-Blur lists 224 calf-, 172 sheep- and eighteen goat-skins and fifty-two wool skeins.[56] From Toprak Kale comes a text which seems to be a personnel roster, enumerating 5,507 people divided into six major categories, some of them subdivided. It seems to refer to more than just palace personnel, but what it is exactly is unknown, as is the precise significance of most of the headings. This Toprak Kale text suggests there were different grades of accountants. Royal letters found here and at Bastam refer to four other kinds of officials, but the evidence is too scanty for us to be sure of their role.[57] Ambassadors appear on an Assyrian relief celebrating Ashurbanipal's victory over Elam in 663 or 653 BC, and farm rent collectors, spies and messengers, besides emissaries, appear in Assyrian correspondence.[58] Messages were authenticated, and property marked, with seals. Amongst the booty Tiglath-Pileser III took from Sarduri II was the 'seal-cylinder, (hung) about his neck',[59] visible in the depiction of Sarduri in flight on Tiglath-Pileser's palace reliefs. Urartian seals, of different types (cylinder seals to be rolled on clay, and stamp seals), and seal impressions have been discovered at Bastam, Karmir-Blur and Toprak Kale. The kings had multiple seals, to be used on their behalf by subordinates.

Both archaeological evidence and the administrative documents reveal, at least from the time of Rusa II, a degree of decentralization. Rusa's foundations of Bastam, Karmir-Blur and Toprak Kale were all major administrative centres, whose reach was deep.[60] Their documents deal with a variety of business, including land disputes, a marriage, an abduction and reports of spies.

---

[55] Diakonoff, 1984, pp. 39, 144–45 (n. 130).
[56] Piotrovsky, 1969b, p. 156. For administrative records, Zimansky, 1985, pp. 79–83.
[57] Zimansky, 1985, pp. 82–9 for the roster, letters and personnel known from administrative records.
[58] Parpola, 1987, no. 10; Pfeiffer, 1935, nos 6, 95.
[59] Luckenbill, I, 1926, 769 (pp. 272–4).
[60] Zimansky, 1985, pp. 80–4.

The efficiency of its administration is not the only conclusion which can be drawn regarding the structure and government of the Urartian state. Adontz concluded that there were a few Urartian-dominated independent kingdoms, such as Mana, 118 conquered territories, and about fifteen provinces in Urartu proper (the regions of Tushpa and Arzashkun).[61] The provinces, and those lands whose kings were deposed, were ruled by governors, but there are very few references to their appointment. Argishti I and Rusa I recorded their replacement of kings with governors in, respectively, four countries near Diauekhi, and Uelikukhi on Lake Sevan.[62] New governors might sometimes have been former kings. The Topzawa inscription records that Rusa established Urzana, king of Muṣaṣir, as ruler there.[63] A number of conquered kings, including the kings of Diauekhi and the twenty-three around Lake Sevan[64] are said to have been made *bu-ra*, slave, a term which Adontz took to mean vassal.[65] They seem to have remained in place in return for tribute, and may have had councils. The Urartian king had a commander-in-chief and he in turn a deputy. The governors had vice-governors, officers and armed men, whom they accompanied into battle.[66]

4   Society

Little can be said about the structure of society. There were slaves. There were the kings' transported captives. Whether these people remained the personal property of the kings has been debated by Soviet scholars. There were free (armed) men liable for military service. There are hints that the troops normally received a share of captured animals and people. The existence of private property has been inferred from references in inscriptions to the vineyard of *Ta-ri-ri-a-i*, the orchard of *Gi-lu-ra-a-ni-e*, and the garden of *Ish-pi-li-ni*.[67] Burials confirm the economic and social differentiation which is suggested by the different types of housing at Karmir-Blur. In this town were blocks of houses, each with a courtyard and two to three rooms without storerooms, presumably for those maintained by the

---

[61] Adontz, 1946, pp. 208–13.

[62] Melikishvili, 1960, nos 128 B1 (pp. 247–8), 265 (p. 328)

[63] Ibid., no. 264 (pp. 323–7). Kristensen, 1988, pp. 24–35 connects this with Sargon's description of a royal coronation at Muṣaṣir, often taken to refer to Urartian coronations. An Assyrian letter refers to 'Abaluqunu' 'the governor' of Muṣaṣir: Lanfranchi and Parpola, 1990, no. 84; Waterman, 1930, no. 381.

[64] Melikishvili, 1960, no. 266 (pp. 328–30).

[65] Adontz, 1946, p. 220.

[66] Sargon refers to counsellors amongst Rusa's personnel, Luckenbill, II, 1927, 154 (pp. 81–2). The hierarchy appear in e.g. Parpola, 1987, nos. 29, 30, 31; Pfeiffer, 1935, 4, 11, 3, 8. For extensive discussion, Zimansky, 1985, pp. 89–94.

[67] Zimansky, 1985, pp. 2, 57, 70; Melikishvili, 1960, nos 111 (pp. 205–6), 277 (pp. 339–40) for the three individuals.

authorities, and larger houses with more rooms. There was certainly a wide range of occupations, besides those already mentioned. The people deported by Esarhaddon of Assyria from Shubria included charioteers, cavalry, governors, chiefs, bowmen, workmen, sappers, shieldbearers, 'killers', farmers, shepherds and gardeners.[68] The Urartian court apparently included eunuchs. A category of 3,784 eunuchs appears in the Toprak Kale roster, and a much smaller subgroup is designated 'eunuchs of the palace'. There may have been family or clan settlements. Sargon refers to Arbu, the city of Rusa's father's house, and Riar, the city of Sarduri, and to seven cities of their neighbourhood where dwelt the brothers of Rusa. These were probably sites of royal domains and the text suggests they were garrisoned rather than fortified. Its reference to 260 of Rusa's royal kin implies that the effective kin group was an extended one.

Rusa I's *rabute*, mentioned in the Assyrian correspondence, have been variously translated, as officers, magnates and nobles. Adontz postulated that they were great lords, either possessors of part of their ancient patrimony, or recipients of lands as fiefs, and were the same as the *ashariduti* whom Sargon captured when he defeated Rusa. The captured *pit-khalli* Adontz suggested were 'knights'.[69]

Although it is not possible to establish with any certainty the exact relationship between king and aristocracy it is most likely that his position in society was exalted. Urartu was not immune from the influence of Assyria, where monarchs underlined in words and pictures their close association with the gods. Likewise, in Urartu the king represented the supreme god. Inscriptions proclaim that it was Khaldi to whom the kings owed their position, power and success, and that they acted in his name. Their close association is suggested also by the choice of the walls of the temple at Aznavur (near Patnos) for the inscription of Menua's annals and by the presence, recorded by Sargon, of statues of Argishti, Rusa, and Sarduri son of Ishpuini (possibly an error for Ishpuini son of Sarduri), in Khaldi's temple at Muṣaṣir in 714. Argishti's had the diadem of a god and a hand raised in blessing.

One of the Urartian royal titles offers a further hint of exaltation. 'King of kings' may, as sometimes suggested, have meant something like 'ruler of a confederacy', 'first among equals'. But until the thirteenth century, when the Assyrian Tukulti-Ninurta I (1244–1208 BC) used it, 'king of kings' was used only of gods, and it may be that kings took this title precisely to suggest their association with the gods. Much later it was used by the Medes, copying, probably, Urartian rather than the less frequent Assyrian usage, and then by the Persian Achaemenids, who, in

---

[68] Luckenbill, II, 1927, 606 (p. 235).

[69] Officers: Waterman, 1930, no. 197; magnates: Parpola, 1987, no. 31; nobles: Pfeiffer, 1935, no. 11; Sargon's enumeration of Rusa's personnel: Luckenbill, II, 1927, 154 (pp. 81–2); equivalents: Adontz, 1946, pp. 218–19.

the opinion of some scholars, claimed to be divine. Another Urartian title however is perhaps less bombastic than it first appears. 'King of the universe' or 'king of all', used less often in the inscriptions than are other titles, is thought to have originated in Mitannian Mesopotamia. It may signify merely a claim to control of northern Mesopotamia.

The bearers of these titles were anxious to impress upon both gods and men that they were powerful and glorious monarchs, who did good to their people. They did this predominantly in the inscriptions, of which they had a monopoly and in which they were selective. The account of the defeat of Sarduri II by Tiglath-Pileser III for example could only be read in victorious Assyria.[70] Another forum was ceremony. According to Sargon royal Urartian coronations were at Muṣaṣir.[71] Countless cattle and sheep were slaughtered before the image of Khaldi, gold, silver and treasure from the king's palace presented to him, and a banquet provided for the whole city. The king was then crowned before Khaldi and given his sceptre, and hailed by the people.

Repression and respect kept the dynasty of Sarduri I on the throne. For nearly two centuries son succeeded father (assuming that the Muṣaṣir statue of Sarduri was really one of Ishpuini) in remarkable continuity. Joint rule may possibly have been used as a device to ensure smooth succession, but it was only used by Ishpuini, and, briefly, Menua. The one, slight, piece of evidence for joint rule by Rusa II and Sarduri III, in the mid-seventh century, is disputed. After Sarduri III the dates, order of succession and relationships of the kings are extremely unclear. The scanty evidence consists of names and patronymics in a few inscriptions on items found at Karmir-Blur. But there is nothing to suggest that the dynasty itself was losing its hold, though what it held was clearly crumbling.

The dynasty was not however so remarkable that it had never known rebellion. The statement, under the statue of Rusa I, that with his two horses and one charioteer he had attained the kingdom, probably alluded to an outbreak and suppression of revolt following Sarduri II's defeat by Assyria. Assyrian letters reveal another, later, rebellion identifying two groups of rebels. Their target was probably Rusa, though some scholars have thought it was Argishti II.[72] The rebellion involved some governors

[70] Luckenbill, I, 1926, 769 (pp. 272–4), 785 (pp. 281–2), 813 (p. 292) at Nimrud.

[71] A differing interpretation of the passage in question, namely that it refers to the coronation of Urzana of Muṣaṣir as a vassal of Rusa, at Rusa's behest, following his defeat by Sargon in 714, has been suggested (Kristensen, 1988, pp. 24–35).

[72] For the letters: Waterman, 1930, nos 146, 197, 144; Pfeiffer, 1935, no. 4; Lanfranchi and Parpola, 1990, nos 92, 91. Lanfranchi, 1983, reconstructs the course of events suggesting that after Rusa had fled the scene of his defeat by the Cimmerians and was believed dead, his son Melartua was made King by the army and was subsequently killed by the rebels. Kristensen, 1988, pp. 72–9, sees the entire revolt as stemming from Melartua's election, and his murder as instigated by Rusa. For the election, Lanfranchi and Parpola, 1990, no. 90, Waterman, no. 646; for the killing, Lanfranchi and Parpola, 1990, no. 93.

in Uasi, perhaps prompted by the Cimmerian victory over Urartu, in which several governors including the governor of Uasi had perished. Also involved was Narage, a commander (probably) at Van, with twenty eunuchs. The leaders were captured and 100 men at Van executed. There is also a slight hint of internal insecurity in the building of the fortresses of Çavuştepe and Kef Kalesi. Çavuştepe was near Van, but not on a major invasion route. Kef Kalesi, built by Rusa II (*c*.685–*c*.645), was not necessary for the protection of the nearby town (Adilcevaz).

Religion

Much can be deduced about the aspirations, the problems and the lifestyle of the Urartian kings, but their religious ideas are more elusive. A possible source of evidence is the treatment of the dead, for particular treatments may seem to offer suggestions about beliefs. Thus, interment may derive from a supposition that the dead live in the tomb, and cremation from one that souls must metamorphosize or be set free for the next life. Funeral customs may derive from fear that the dead will be troublesome if not satisfied or disabled; hence the deposit of grave-goods, the making of offerings, the destruction of property which might tie the deceased to this world and the provision of magical protection, for the dead, and for the living against them.[73] But tradition, fashion and economics also come into play. In Late Roman Gaul for example, the rich came to prefer interment not because the Christian church did, but because the kudos of an expensive sarcophagus was more lasting than that of the conspicuous consumption of expensive fuel.[74] In early Frankish Gaul the church did not interpret the burial of grave-goods as indicative of pagan rather than Christian belief.[75] For Urartians cremation and then burial in urns was normal. It was not customary at Malaklyu. The Urartian cemetery (*c*.650 BC) in the rock crevices there received one inhumation, the deceased being quite likely the local wife of an Urartian and their two children.[76] Did their beliefs differ? We cannot tell.

Cremation seems to have been reserved for the lowly-placed. The elite preferred rock-cut complexes of tomb chambers of which there were several at Van, though only the tomb of Argishti I is identifiable. There are similar tombs elsewhere, for example in a cliff at Kayalıdere, and near Patnos and Adilcevaz. The dead were provided with grave-goods. At Altıntepe three masonry tombs sealed with huge blocks of stone, datable to the reign of Argishti II, were designed as houses. Two had three rooms.

---

[73] Rush, 1941.
[74] Nock, 1932.
[75] Bullough, 1983.
[76] Barnett, 1963.

Two of the dead rested in plain stone sarcophagi, the others perhaps in wooden coffins. The deposits included rich clothes, jewellery, weapons, bronze belts, horse-trappings and bits, a war chariot, cauldrons, chairs and tables. Some of them had been deliberately damaged before they were left. In cremations, bodies were burned wearing clothes and ornaments. Items such as weapons, bracelets and metal ornamental equipment were added to the ashes for burial. The Malaklyu urns had holes, made before filling, perhaps for the souls of the dead to escape.

There was almost certainly a cult of the dead. Offerings were probably placed in the niches within rock tombs, before the tombs were sealed, or outside, or both. The Altıntepe tombs had such niches. Outside and adjacent to them was an open air temple comprising four steles and a round stone altar facing them.

The Urartians had also to propitiate their gods. According to the Meher Kapusu inscription, Urartu had seventy-nine divinities, of varying importance. They included gods of particular towns and gods of the earth and water. A cult of a fish god or gods is suggested by small statuettes, of bearded figures wearing fish skins and heads, found near an altar in a cellar at Karmir-Blur, and by seal scenes featuring fish and a fish-dressed god. The sacred tree appears in the wall paintings in the hall at Altıntepe, where it is tended by genii. The (later) consultation, by pagan Armenian priests, of the sound and movement of the plane (or poplar) tree for oracles, attested by Moses of Khoren,[77] may have been a continuation of Urartian practice. Most of the gods were male, but sixteen Meher Kapusu deities were goddesses. Bagbartu, the wife of Khaldi, was venerated at Muşaşir, where she lost to Sargon her jewels and begemmed gold seal ring used for validating her decrees. The scene of a goddess worshipped by a woman is depicted on a gold medallion from Van and on a box lid from Toprak Kale.

The gods were worshipped in house shrines, before stone slabs or niches carved in rock, and in regular, square, temples. At a 'temple' established by Ishpuini and Menua near Pagan, a rock cut stair leads to a platform. It was furnished with six steles. In the rock itself is carved a 15 foot-high panel, with a commemorative inscription prescribing sacrifices to Khaldi and the goddess Uarubani. Niches generally resemble temple doorways, and their inscriptions, like that at Meher Kapusu, refer to 'gates', whilst 'gates' of gods in some other Urartian inscriptions, for example at Patnos, seem to refer to temple buildings. The temple building at Altıntepe was set back in a courtyard which had a drain and columned porticoes all around. There were altars before and behind the building in which the god's statue had been.

Offerings to the divinities were prodigious. Animal sacrifice was prescribed in the Meher Kapusu inscription. A room at Karmir-Blur has

---

[77] Moses, I, 20, trans. Thomson, 1978, pp. 107–8.

yielded bones of 4,000 headless and legless lambs and calves, apparently sacrificial remains accumulated over a period of no more than thirty-five years. In addition, human sacrifice may have occurred. The suggestion has been prompted by a seal scene showing a beheaded man, and female skeletons at the palace at Giriktepe. Human bones, without skulls, have been identified, together with animal bones, at Toprak Kale, as the remains of sacrifices, though this human identification has been questioned. Another offering was weapons. Indeed, Khaldi's temple was sometimes designated 'house of weapons'. Altıntepe has yielded spears, mace- and arrowheads, helmets and shields. Shields were hung, as the Khorsabad relief depicting the temple of Muṣaṣir shows. Royal votive shields, richly decorated and designed to be seen from just one position, quivers and helmets inscribed to Khaldi have survived. Gods were also honoured with cities and forts. Tushpa itself (*Ṭu-ush-pa-a*) was named after the goddess Tushpuea (*Ṭu-ush-pu-e-a*). Rusa I built forts named 'the city of Khaldi' and 'the city of Teisheba' on Lake Sevan and Rusa II's Teishebaini (Karmir-Blur) was named for Teisheba.

Temples might, consequently, grow very wealthy on the proceeds of piety. The fabulous booty Sargon took from Khaldi's temple at Muṣaṣir included six gold and 25,212 bronze shields, ninety-six silver and 1,514 bronze spears, thirty-three silver chariots, nine gold embroidered vestments, a bejewelled ivory and silver bed, four cauldrons and a number of statues including Khaldi's own. There is some evidence that temples could loan or sell cattle to community members.[78]

Gifts to gods must have been meant, in part at least, as a *quid pro quo* for past or future help in this life. There are other examples of the Urartians appealing to supernatural forces. Some inscriptions incorporate curses upon anyone who should tamper with the royal works and inscriptions. A magical purpose may lie behind the triplication of the text in most of Ishpuini's inscriptions and some half dozen of Menua's. (The majority were very short and recorded royal building.) Bells, belts and seals had a protective function. Urartu has been termed the 'homeland' of horse- and harness-bells, which survive from the reign of Menua and afterwards, some inscribed with a king's name. It has been suggested that the Assyrians put bells on the harnesses of their horses to protect them against demons, and it is likely that the Urartians shared the ancient belief in the efficacy of ringing bells against evil.[79] The repertoire of belt decoration included bulls and lions, the animals of Teisheba and Khaldi, goats, also associated with a god, scenes of gods and sacred trees and scenes of hunting, possibly meant as representation of the afterlife, as in later, Sasanian and Islamic, art. Belts

---

[78] Diakonoff, 1985, pp. 80, 169 (n. 176).
[79] Porada, 1967. Bells also have more tangible practical use, drawing human and animal attention to the presence of the wearer.

themselves may have had magical significance, for enclosure within a circle was an ancient method of fending off evil. Seal scenes resembled those on belts, thereby ensuring magical protection for anything the seals safeguarded. Worn round the neck the seal could function as an amulet. Decorated medallions, pectorals and pins did likewise. Wall paintings too had a role. The Altıntepe paintings depicted lions and bulls, as did Arin-berd's, genii tending sacred trees, whose fruit seems to be pomegranates, and a frieze of stylized pomegranates. The pomegranate, a fertility symbol, was used in modern times in the eastern Mediterranean against the evil eye, and this use may be very ancient.

Debts and Legacies

In their deployment of magic symbols the Urartians were no different from the Assyrians, whose colossal gateway figures, like some figures on their reliefs, had magical protective purposes. The culture of Urartu bore many similarities to that of Assyria and in fact owed much to it. Royal titles and inscriptions, military dress and equipment, the bud garland motif on a horse-blinker of King Menua, the iconography of cylinder seals, the fish gods, the bulls, lions, genii costumes, colours and techniques of the wall paintings at Altıntepe and Arin-berd all betray this. A seal design and an ivory figure from Toprak Kale suggest that the Urartian kings and courtiers dressed like Assyrian ones. The soldiers of Malaklyu wore bracelets with lion head terminals derived from those of Assyrian royal attendants. There were of course other influences too. Syrian influence is strong in Urartian ivories. Local cultures and languages (Hurrian, Luwian and proto-Armenian) survived.

But Urartian culture also had original elements, and even, perhaps, some contributions to make to Assyria. Originality and independence may be seen in the animal processions on shields, the development and invention of animal motifs and composite creatures, the iconography of stamp seals and stamp cylinders, the skill of metal-workers and the building of fortresses. Urartian example may have inspired Tiglath-Pileser III in some reorganization of his large provinces, ruled by hereditary governors, into smaller ones, ruled by government appointees.[80] The *qanāt* system used in Assyria from the reign of Sennacherib (704–681 BC) may have derived from what Sargon II saw at Ulkhu.

Yet although the magnificence and achievement of Urartu were great, her legacy was slight. There are traces in Achaemenid Persian culture. Urartian rock tombs were emulated at Persepolis, and at Naqsh-i Rustam, where there are four. There is resemblance between a tower there and one

---

[80] The view of some scholars that Tiglath-Pileser III brought about administrative 'reforms' seems to be unsubstantiated. (Kuhrt, 1995, 2. p. 506).

at Karmir-Blur, and it may be that Achaemenid temple towers go back to Urartian prototypes. So too might the columned halls of the Achaemenid palace at Pasargadae, built by Cyrus (559–530 BC), though there were also prototypes at Hasanlu IV and at Median sites of the eighth to seventh centuries BC. Columned halls were built at most Urartian palaces, for example at Armavir, Bastam, Çavuştepe and Kef Kalesi. The most impressive, at Altıntepe, 130 feet by 75 feet with eighteen columns, in six rows of three, seems to be Achaemenid work.[81] The sight of the annals of Argishti I on the cliff face at Van may have inspired the inscription of Darius at Behistun. The winged figure shown near Darius there wears a crown, thought to derive from those of some Urartian gods. There are a few other artistic similarities. Some Urartian elements were passed on through the Medes: the title 'King of Kings'; some prototypes for the form of Achaemenid inscriptions, for example, their subdivision into paragraphs; perhaps, the use of stamp cylinders; perhaps, the few artistic elements. But as the regime had collapsed, so had the empire, into its constituent parts, and the glory of Urartu passed into oblivion.

[81] Summers, 1993.

3

Foreign Rule: Medes, Persians and Greeks, 590–190 BC

Armenia after the Fall of Urartu

By 590 BC, when the Medes dealt the final blow to Urartu, the Armenians were probably spread through parts of Urartu and in possession of a kingdom therein. Its ruling dynasty had probably come to power a century earlier, in Melid, and benefited, directly or indirectly, from the activities of the Medes. If the Medes established a short-lived empire, then this new Armenian kingdom should be considered as part of a new, structured, polity. But the suggestion that they did so rests on the testimony of Herodotus, and his reliability with regard to Median history is now considered weak.[1] On these and other grounds, including the evidence of Assyrian and Babylonian records and archeology, the existence of a real Median empire with a unified structure has been questioned.[2] It seems that a new beginning came only with the Persian Achaemenids, following the conquest of the Medes by Cyrus in the sixth century, and an idea of empire only with Darius.

The nature and paucity of the evidence means that much of the society and conditions in sixth-century Armenia are beyond our ken. The extent of Armenian domination and the nature of the relationship between Urartians and Armenians are two areas of uncertainty. Xenophon's *Cyropaedia* records that in the first half of the sixth century there was hostility between the Armenians and their neighbours, the poor and warlike 'Chaldaei', who lived in the mountains. This, he says, was resolved with the help of Cyrus. The defeated mountain people were to be allowed down to farm uncultivated land, and the Armenians to pasture their herds

---

[1] Brown, S.C., 1988.
[2] Sancisi-Weerdenburg, 1988.

in the hills. Both agreed upon the right of intermarriage and upon a defensive alliance, whilst Cyrus himself installed a garrison in the heights to ensure peace was kept.[3] Some scholars have taken 'Chaldaei' to mean 'worshippers of Khaldi' that is, Urartians. But there is a different view, though likewise not beyond questions, that these 'Chaldaei' were actually the north-western Khalitu (*ḫa-li-ṭu*) or Chalybes, against whom the Urartian Rusa II had campaigned a century before.[4] The name 'Urartian' actually became 'Alarodian' in Greek and according to Strabo it was the ancient Chalybes who were later called 'Chaldaei'.[5]

The testimony of Herodotus regarding the Armenian–Urartian balance of power, though initially beguiling, is no more conclusive. Herodotus provides a list, perhaps derived from Hecataeus, of the twenty satrapies into which Darius divided the Achaemenid Empire. In its thirteenth satrapy were Pactyica, the 'Armenians' and their neighbours 'as far as' the Black Sea. In its eighteenth satrapy were the Alarodians, the Matieni and Saspires, their tribute being 200 talents, half the sum which was due from the thirteenth.[6] Herodotus' evidence seems therefore to imply that by 522 BC the Armenians had come to dominate western Armenia whereas the Urartians were concentrated in the east and were inferior to them in influence and wealth. Unfortunately the accuracy of Herodotus' list is questionable and such conclusions may be quite wrong. Variation in Herodotus' wording implies that not all the information within his list was from the same source, and hence that it is not all equally reliable. Herzfeld has argued that in reality Darius had not two but only one satrapy in the region of former Urartu. This was effectively a combination of most of Herodotus' satrapies 'thirteen' and 'eighteen' with his 'nineteen', (comprising the Moschi, Tibareni, Macrones, Mossynoeci and Mares, assessed at 300 talents), excluding the thirteenth's Pactyes, actually a tribe far to the east in the Kabul region of Afghanistan, and the eighteenth's Matieni, whom Herzfeld believed belonged to the Median satrapy.[7] If Herzfeld is correct then Armenians and Urartians (Alarodians) might be considered roughly equal to each other and to the other six groups within the satrapy.

Whatever the balance of power between Urartians and Armenians in the sixth century BC there was some, limited, continuity between conditions in Urartu and those in Armenia. If the Old Testament Book of Ezekiel's remarks about Togarmah really do refer to the first Armenian kingdom, then its allusion to its trading, in the 590s, in the fairs of Tyre

---

[3] Xenophon, *Cyropaedia*, III, ii, 1–III, ii, 24.

[4] Though *Chalybes* seems to have been used by the Greeks for any group in the Pontus trading in iron ore. Diakonoff, 1984, pp. 65, 117, 162, (n. 103, 104), 172 (n. 225) and p. 90. Strabo, *The Geography*, XII, iii, 19.

[5] Strabo, XII, iii, 19.

[6] Herodotus, *The Histories*, III, 89–94.

[7] Herzfeld, 1968, pp. 296–7, 313–14, 301–2.

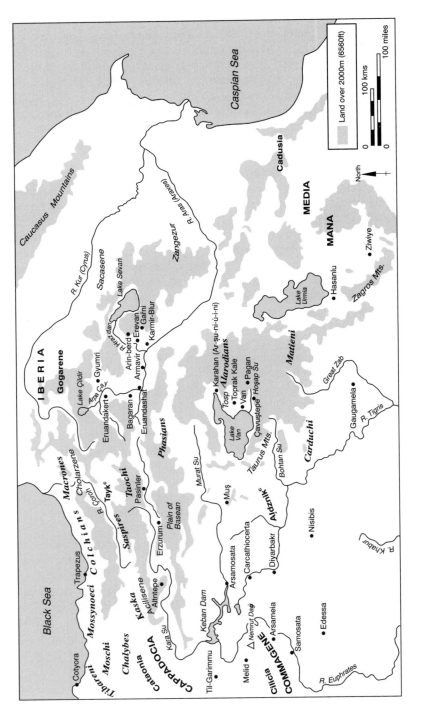

Map 3.1 Armenia

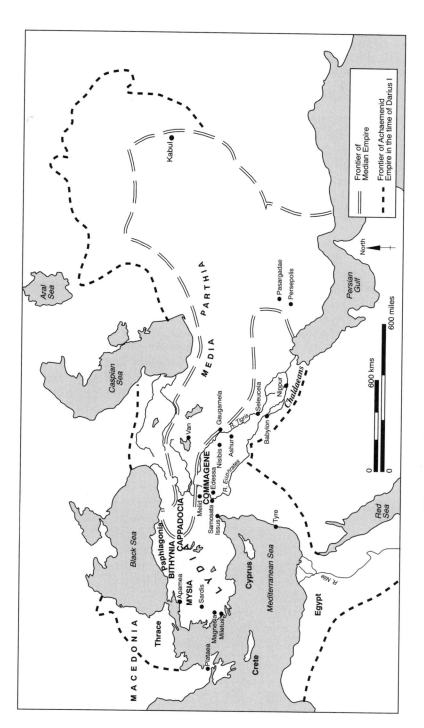

Map 3.2   The east Mediterranean and West Asia

with horses and horsemen and mules,[8] suggest that horse breeding, trade, prosperity and communications had not been seriously disrupted. There is archaeological evidence for reoccupation, or continued use, in the Achaemenid period at Van, Altıntepe, Arin-berd and Armavir. An Urartian castle at Pagan was occupied from the late seventh century into the first half of the sixth. Other Urartian sites however show evidence of disuse. Karmir-Blur and Toprak Kale had been burnt. A humble settlement did return to Çavuştepe soon after its firing by the Scyths, but it was extinguished after a few years. At Hasanlu part of the site may have been reused in the sixth and fifth centuries. There were perhaps survivals in religion and mythology. Pagan Armenians venerated trees, and later tales of their god Vahagn overcoming dragons seem related to earlier myths about Teisheba.

There is a significant amount of evidence for continuity among the upper classes. The attire of the Urartian ambassadors on the Assyrian king Ashurbanipal's celebratory relief of the mid-seventh century resembles that of the Armenians depicted on the relief of the Achaemenid king Xerxes at his palace at Persepolis, one of the Achaemenid capitals. A number of Armenian place and family names preserve or recall an earlier substratum. Erebuni survives in Erevan, Tushpa in Tosp. Mandakuni and Slkuni, surnames of two medieval aristocratic Armenian families, may preserve the names of the tribes of Manda and Sala, mentioned in Hittite records. (Sala was somewhere in Armenia, but Manda is not precisely identifiable.) *Ar-ṣu-ni-ú-i-ni* (Artsuniuini) looks like an Urartian form of 'Artsruni', the family name of the kings of Vaspurakan in the tenth century AD, though their origin may not be Urartian. Toumanoff concluded that the origins of a number of other early medieval Armenian aristocratic families did indeed go back to Urartian times.[9] Of twenty-nine dynasties which held some fifty princely states in, roughly, the first to fifth centuries AD, five had Urartian origins (in four cases, royal ones). Five other houses were, he suggested, dynasties of territorialized remnants of even more ancient groups, Hurrians, Mannaeans, the Pala, Sala and Kaska or Kashka peoples. The Pala and Sala are mentioned in Hittite sources. The Pala had lived in Paphlagonia but may have extended as far as the River Çoroh before 1500 BC. The Kaska had come to the Upper Euphrates Valley with the Urumeans in the twelfth century BC.

One thing which was not preserved was political autonomy. The victories of Darius meant that Armenia was incorporated into the Achaemenid Empire and was not to be independent again until this empire itself

---

[8] Ezekiel, 27:14.
[9] Toumanoff, 1963, pp. 154–227, the Orduni, Apahuni, Bzhnuni, Manawazean, Řshtuni, Khorkořuni, Mandakuni, Paluni, Slkuni, K ᶜajberuni families (pp. 218, 199, 216, 218, 213, 208–9, 212, 215, 206).

fell to Alexander of Macedon in 331 BC. After that it was the royal dynasty of the Orontids who ruled Armenia, until the beginning of the second century BC when their realm was broken up and a new line of kings was recognized by Rome in 188 BC.

Armenia in the Achaemenid Empire

Unfortunately, the keynote of the period 522–188 BC is, for Armenia, a lack of evidence. The inhabitants wrote almost nothing that has been discovered (though there are some confused memories in the *History* of Moses of Khoren) and there is almost no archaeological evidence from the Achaemenid period. The Greek and Iranian literary sources suggest that Armenia was now on the fringe of world events instead of being a major power, and her society seems to have regressed. Her history is scarcely discernible and depends as much on its context as on direct testimony.

The incorporation of Armenia into the huge Achaemenid Empire did not, probably, involve much meddling by Achaemenid kings in Armenian affairs. Rather than aspiring to cultural unification and uniformity, they preferred to maintain their own culture, untainted by influence from subject peoples, and to leave unchanged these subject peoples' law and government and their political and economic structures. Achaemenid intervention was limited, its priorities to stimulate the economy, collect taxes and maintain control, the latter through royal scribes, officials called 'the king's eyes' and 'the king's ears', and the royal roads.

The history of Armenia's place in the administrative structure of the empire is not entirely clear. Xenophon's *Cyropaedia* records that by the time of the death of Cyrus Armenia was grouped with Media and Cadusia, in one satrapy.[10] We have no information as to whether any Armenian kingdom still existed. The satrapy was given to Cyrus' younger son. Under Darius however, Armenia was separate from Media and Cadusia, and comprised, probably, as we have seen, a single satrapy. Sculpture on the tombs of Xerxes (485–465) and Artaxerxes suggest that this satrapy was later divided into two, which may explain why Herodotus mistakenly thought that Darius had had two satrapies. Likewise Xenophon's *Anabasis*, describing his own adventures in 401 BC, refers to two Persian officials in Armenia, one the Persian king's son-in-law Orontes, the other Tiribazus,[11] sometimes taken to be the satraps of these two satrapies, the 'eighteenth', eastern, and the 'thirteenth', western, satrapies respectively. Yet Xenophon identifies Tiribazus as the subordinate of Orontes, which means that if there had once been a division of the satrapy into two, it had been discontinued by 401. Another pair, an Orontes and a Mithraustes,

[10] *Cyropaedia*, VIII, vii, 11.
[11] *Anabasis*, II, iv 8, 9, III, iv 13, v 17, IV, iv 4.

are mentioned by Arrian, writing in the second century AD, as commanders of the Armenians in the battle of Gaugamela in 331 BC,[12] where
Alexander defeated the last Achaemenid king, Darius III (337–330 BC).
They too have sometimes been assumed to represent two satrapies but
may instead have been superior and subordinate. If, as is possible,
Mithraustes was the Vahē whom Moses of Khoren says rebelled and
was killed by Alexander,[13] they were also kinsmen.

Whatever the administrative theory, the Achaemenid hold over Armenia was reasonably strong, though it did decline, like the empire itself,
after the defeat of the Persians by the Greeks at Plataea in Boeotia in 479.
Like their Assyrian and Urartian predecessors the Achaemenids exacted
tribute. Herodotus gives details in his satrapy list and King Xerxes'
apadana reliefs at Persepolis show Armenians with other peoples of the
empire presenting tributes in kind. Strabo records that the satrap sent
20,000 foals per year to the king, and Xenophon reveals that in 401 the
Armenians were rearing horses as tribute.[14] There were seventeen such
colts in the village where he was quartered. Texts from Persepolis suggest
that the Achaemenids also exacted, also in kind, taxes for the financing of
the satrapies in their various activities. There are traces of the existence of
Achaemenid chancelleries in Armenia. The chancelleries used Aramaic,
and in a stratum of words in Armenian whose derivation is Aramaic there
are terms connected with state scribal offices. The use of Aramaic continued through the period and appears in the second century BC in the
inscriptions of the Armenian king Artaxias.

Military repression and recruitment were other aspects of Achaemenid
rule. Xenophon's *Oeconomicus* refers to the requirement that governors
supply maintenance for a number of horsemen, archers, slingers and light
infantry so that they should be strong enough to control their subjects. It
also refers to the maintenance of garrisons in the citadels.[15] Both Arin-
berd and Van have been suggested as satrapal capitals, though the only
evidence for a Persian presence at Van is that Darius had a niche cut for
an inscription on the cliff, to which Xerxes added a text. It is certainly
likely that the Persian troops used at least some of the Urartian forts.
Achaemenid satraps and kings also used native troops. The multinational
army which Xerxes took to Thrace in 480 included contingents from all
the groups within the Armenian satrapy. A Babylonian document attests
a military colony of men of 'Urartu' (Urashtu) and 'Melid' (perhaps the
equivalent of the Greek Alarodians and Armenians) at Nippur on the
Euphrates in the time of Darius II (423–404).[16] Forty thousand Armenian

---

[12] Arrian, *The Anabasis of Alexander*, III, viii, 5–6.
[13] Moses, I, 31, trans. Thomson, 1978, p. 124.
[14] Strabo, XI, xiv, 9; Xenophon, *Anabasis* IV, v, 24, 34.
[15] *Oeconomicus*, IV, 5, 6.
[16] Cardascia, 1951, p. 7.

foot soldiers and 7,000 Armenian cavalry supported Darius III against Alexander.

But Achaemenid control was not total. Xenophon described three groups in the mountains bordering Armenia as 'not subjects of the king'. They were the Carduchi in the south, and the Taochi and Chaldaeans in the north. By Chaldaeans Xenophon may mean Chalybes. Some Taochi and Chalybes did however serve the Persians as mercenaries. The Mossynoeci, who according to Herodotus were part of the satrapy, Xenophon found to be lords of an outlying group of Chalybes, self-governing with chiefs and a king, and an official representative at the Greek city of Trapezus.[17]

Another threat to royal control was the ambition and power of satraps. The dynasty founded by the satrap of Armenia under Artaxerxes III (404–358), Orontes, was to rule Armenia for 300 years. Orontes had been affronted to be placed under the command of his erstwhile subordinate, Tiribazus, satrap of Lydia after 395, when Artaxerxes made war against Cyprus in the 380s. His machinations against Tiribazus led ultimately to his own degradation, though he did subsequently become satrap of Mysia in western Asia Minor. Orontes then took part in the satraps' revolt of 362, but deserted his confederates. The evidence that he stayed in the west and rebelled again in the 350s is not conclusive, and it is most likely that he regained Armenia as a reward for his loyalty and spent the rest of his career there. Royal control was reinforced when the future Darius III became satrap of Armenia, but the Orontid dynasty nevertheless maintained its position. The Orontes at Gaugamela was most probably the son of Artaxerxes III's Orontes.

Society

The society of the satrapy of Armenia during the Achaemenid period was clearly not homogeneous. From Herzfeld's analysis of Herodotus' satrapy list we may infer that its people, the ancestors of the Armenians of Late Antiquity, comprised eight different groups, including Herodotus' 'Armenians' though neither the origins nor, as we shall see, the locations of all of them are certain. It seems likely that five were Georgian or proto-Georgian groups, speaking a form of Georgian: the Moschi, much discussed, who have been connected with the Georgian Meskhi; the Macrones and Mossynoeci, both thought to have come to Pontus after the mid eighth-century BC Urartian conquest of Diauekhi, the Tibareni, perhaps the Kashka tribe of Tibia mentioned in the fourteenth century BC, and the

---

[17] *Anabasis*, V, v, 17; mercenaries: ibid. IV, iv, 18; Carduchi: ibid. III, v, 15–16, IV, i–iii; Taochi, Chalybes: *ibid.* IV, vii, 1–18; Mossynoeci: *ibid.* V, iv, v 1.

Saspires.[18] In King Xerxes' army, the Moschi, Tibareni, Macrones and Mossynoeci were, according to Herodotus, equipped alike, as were the Saspires and Alarodians.[19] However, this account does not tally exactly with what is depicted on the reliefs at Persepolis. Xenophon alerts us to a further group, the Phasians.[20] The Chaldaean mercenaries whom he records as being among Orontes' troops were however probably not 'Armenian' in any sense. The Chaldaeans were a people of Babylonia, grouped with the Assyrians in Xerxes' army.[21]

For the location in Armenia of these different peoples we depend upon Herodotus and Xenophon. But even supposing that their testimony is accurate, it is not always very clear, and the question is complicated by the fact that Xenophon's route through Armenia still provokes disagreement. But it seems that by 400 BC the group Xenophon called Armenians were dominant in the south-west of the plateau, between the Euphrates, the Centrites (Bohtan) and the mountains north of the Araxes in the plain of Basean.[22]

Besides the Georgian, Armenian and Urartian elements in Armenia there was probably an Iranian-speaking element too, whose penetration may have begun in the seventh century BC. It perhaps infiltrated from Media and from Mana, where Old Iranian was present, although not strong in the late eighth century. Furthermore, both the Scyths and the Cimmerians were, probably, Iranian speakers, and some of them may have settled in Armenia. There is archaeological evidence for Scythian settlement in Shakashēn (Sacasene) in Azerbaijan, in the seventh century BC, and in Mana, where a splendid princely burial, probably Scythian, was deposited at the end of the century at Ziwiye, about 62 miles south of Hasanlu. The Urartian king Rusa II may have allowed some Cimmerian settlement. There were also Medes in Achaemenid Armenia. The names Mardi and Mardastan, south of Erzurum and near Van respectively, found in the seventh century AD Armenian *Geography*, have been thought to signify areas of Median settlement, and Moses of Khoren refers to such settlement in the Araxes valley in the time of Cyrus.[23]

In the *Anabasis* of Xenophon the Armenians and four other peoples connected with the Achaemenid satrapy of Armenia appear. The Armenians' political organization was rudimentary, and their social organization was that of the clan. The villages where Cheirisophus and Xenophon were quartered each had a chief (comarch). Xenophon's chief accompan-

[18] For the origins of all these groups, Diakonoff, 1984, pp. 66–7, 103, 116–18, 162 n. 108 (Moschi); 67; 103, 117, 163 (n. 115), 183 (n. 11) (Tibareni); 102, 183 n. 6 (Saspires).
[19] *The Histories*, VII, 78, 79.
[20] *Anabasis*, IV, vi, 6.
[21] Ibid., iii, 4; Herodotus, *The Histories*, VII, 63.
[22] Hewsen, 1983a. For Xenophon's route, Manfredi, 1986, esp. pp. 4–5 for map showing varying reconstructions.
[23] Moses, I, 30, trans. Thomson, 1978, pp. 119–21.

ied him to visit Cheirisophus and whenever, in other villages, he caught sight of a kinsman, he would 'take the man to his side'. Some at least of the villages were walled, and the villagers' goats, sheep, cattle and fowl were reared in their underground houses.[24] Of course, Xenophon did not see everything. Other groups or places may have retained elements of the more advanced society which they had known under Urartu. The 'king' of Armenia who appears in the *Cyropaedia* may represent a higher rank of aristocracy than do the village chiefs. This higher class may have continued into the fifth century and later, besides the successors of the Urartian sub-kings who were the ancestors or predecessors of Armenian princes of the Arsacid period.

In the northern borderlands were the Taochi, successors of the people of Diauekhi. They apparently lived in strongholds, had others which were just refuges and preferred death to falling into Greek hands. In what had been the south-west and north-west frontier regions of Urartu Xenophon encountered Carduchi, Chalybes and Mossynoeci.[25] The Carduchi opposed the passage of the Greeks for seven days, a feat which suggests that they had some political unity and organization. They fought with huge bows and slings. Both the Chalybes and Mossynoeci had strongholds and towns (πόλισμα). The name 'Mossynoeci' means 'living in towers' and their king dwelt in a wooden tower in their chief citadel in their city Metropolis, control of this citadel being the qualification to rule. His people showed the Greeks their fat tattooed children, and struck Xenophon as less civilized than any people he had encountered, habitually doing in public what others did in private.

Economy

Lack of homogeneity and of sophistication did not inhibit prosperity. If corrected as Herzfeld suggested, Herodotus' satrapy list implies that the Armenian satrapy paid Darius tribute of something under 600 talents. By comparison, Assyria and Babylon together paid 1,000 talents plus 500 boy eunuchs, Egypt 700, and Cilicia 500 plus 360 white horses. Armenia's wealth derived ultimately from agriculture. Aristagoras of Miletus described the Armenians as 'rich in flocks'.[26] Since they were used in tribute the rearing of horses must have been a major element in the economy. The palace and villages around it, near to where the Greek army camped 'had all possible good things in the way of supplies'. Xenophon mentions animals, grain, fine wine, dried grapes, all sorts of

[24] *Anabasis*, IV, v, 9–11, 24; 30–2; 9, 25.
[25] Cf. above n. 17.
[26] Quoted by Herodotus, *The Histories*, V, 49.

beans, ointment and fragrant oil made out of 'pork fat, sesame, bitter almonds, or turpentine', and elsewhere, at table, lamb, kid, pork, veal, poultry and both wheat and barley bread. In a stronghold of the Taochi he found large numbers of asses, cattle and sheep. Further south the Carduchi had many fine houses, abundant supplies, especially of wine, and great numbers of bronze vessels.[27]

There is less evidence for commerce though there is some. Herodotus mentions exports, mostly wine, from Armenia to Babylon.[28] This trade was conducted by Assyrians. The Achaemenid royal roads, punctuated with way stations, passed through southern Armenia. There are terms connected with trade and handicrafts in the Aramaic stratum of Armenian. Armenia's neighbours to the south-west were Aramaic-speaking, and these terms may have entered the Armenian language in the Achaemenid period, though some at least may be due to the large numbers of people whom Tigranes the Great transported to Armenia in the first century BC. The discovery of sixth-century Athenian coinage in Zangezur, of fifth-century coins from Miletus at Arin-berd, and of fifth-century Cretan coins may demonstrate trade between Armenia and Asia Minor. Xenophon records that a group of Chalybes subject to the Mossynoeci lived mostly by working in iron, which suggests some trade.[29]

The evidence for urban life is even more scanty. Xenophon says that the Chalybes and Mossynoeci had towns and he records a large city at Gymnias, in Scythian territory.[30] This may have been Gyumri, though another suggestion is Pasinler. Nothing suggests that the Armenians themselves were intimately involved in trade or towns, for the Armenian settlements Xenophon saw were villages. Nevertheless it is likely that beginnings of urban life were being stimulated by the attractions and requirements of the two satrapal palaces to which the *Anabasis* refers.[31] The *Oeconomicus* records the concern of the king that his countries should be densely populated and cultivated. Persian palaces had large parks, or 'paradises', artistically laid out with trees and 'all the good and beautiful things that the soil produces' and were provided with wild animals to hunt.[32] In Armenia, according to Xenophon, one palace was associated with a large village, most of whose houses had turrets, the other had many villages around it, and all had plentiful provisions. Altıntepe, where there was an Achaemenid hall, walls, a large settlement on a nearby hill and possibly in-between, may have been one of these

---

[27] *Anabasis*, IV, iv, 7–13, v, 31; vii, 14; ii, 22, i, 8.
[28] Herodotus, I, 194.
[29] *Anabasis* V, v, 1.
[30] *Anabasis*: Chalybes IV, vii, 17; Mossynoeci, V, iv, 31 (using *polisma* – buildings of a city, town – and *polis* – city – respectively); Gymnias, IV, vii, 18–19.
[31] IV, iv, 2, 7.
[32] Xenophon, *Oeconomicus*, IV, 8, 13–14 and *Anabasis*, I, ii, 7 for animals at a palace of Cyrus in Phrygia.

sites.[33] That the Persians influenced Armenian society is obvious from the fact that Persian was spoken in villages Xenophon visited.[34]

Religion

It is likely that the Persians also influenced Armenian religion. The Achaemenids followed, probably, an early form of Zoroastrianism. This involved belief in a supreme creator God, Ahura Mazda, opposed by an uncreated evil spirit, each helped by subordinate spirits, and veneration of ancestral spirits. The role of righteous men was to promote truth, and to respect the created elements, especially fire, to which end there were various regulations and rites. Doctrine was transmitted orally. The Armenians certainly did not follow the Achaemenid lead absolutely, for they sacrificed horses to the sun god,[35] whereas the Achaemenid kings seem to have accepted Zoroaster's disapproval of animal sacrifice. Yet there has been much diversity and development within Zoroastrianism, and it may, as Russell has argued,[36] have acquired a hold in Armenia during this period. The evidence is varied. A fire temple was provided at Arin-berd. There are a few Armenian religious terms which may derive from Old Iranian, probably Old Persian, and a seal scene of, possibly, religious significance. Artaxerxes II promoted the cult of the ancient Iranian goddess Anahita who, as Strabo records, came to be exceptionally honoured in Armenia. The Zoroastrian calendar was, probably, introduced throughout the empire, though there is disagreement about the date. The establishment of Zoroastrianism in Armenia would not however have been by compulsion. The Achaemenids did not try to eradicate the gods of the peoples they conquered. Instead they sought their support.

Armenia and Greek Rule

There is little sign of any direct Greek impact on Armenia under the Achaemenids, despite the Greek colonies on the Black Sea coast, and a Greek element in Achaemenid society and culture. There were Greek physicians at the royal court and some Greek influence in art and architecture is detectable, for example, in cameos, and at Pasargadae, and, to a lesser extent, at Persepolis. Darius III knew Greek well enough to speak privately with the leader of his Greek mercenaries. Greek influence in the

---

[33] Summers, 1993.
[34] *Anabasis*, IV, v, 10, 34.
[35] Xenophon, *Anabasis*, IV, v, 35.
[36] Russell, 1987, pp. 14, 47; ch. 2 (pp. 39–71) includes the Median, Achaemenid and Orontid periods.

east generally was to be intensified after Alexander of Macedon conquered the Achaemenid Empire at Gaugamela in 331.

The most important consequence for Armenia of this conquest was a greater degree of independence. Justin, a writer of the third century AD, states that neither Alexander nor his successors conquered Armenia.[37] It was the Orontid dynasty who now really ruled there, in unbroken descent from father to son until the early second century BC. Our evidence for the continuity of the dynasty is the inscriptions on steles on Nemrut (Nimrud) Dağ. There Antiochus I of Commagene (69–34 BC) commemorated his ancestors and proclaimed his direct descent from Darius the Great via the wife of the satrap Orontes. It was the son of Orontes who was first to take the title of king, and the most likely time for him to have taken it is the aftermath of 331.

Alexander's general policy was to continue the Achaemenid administrative system and to appoint Iranian satraps, but to provide them with troops and generals drawn from his own followers. For Armenia he appointed Mithrenes, the Persian-speaking commander of Sardis who had surrendered to him. Mithrenes was probably the son of King Orontes, by now dead or deposed, the son whose own name survives in the Nemrut Dağ inscription only as '...anes'. Alexander also, according to Strabo, sent soldiers and a Greek general, Menon, to the gold mines in Syspiritis (modern İspir). It is unclear from the text whether the natives guided Menon, or killed him.[38]

Armenia under the Orontids

Alexander's empire was short-lived. After his death, in 323 BC, Armenia was briefly drawn into the rivalries and wars of his successors, the Diadochi. A certain Neoptolemus, satrap of Armenia, was defeated by another satrap, Eumenes. In 301 BC Armenia passed to Seleucus, former satrap of Babylon, who in 304 had taken the title of king and had then consolidated his position as ruler of the east.

The dynasty of Seleucus was to control Armenia under her Orontid kings only fitfully, and mostly only nominally. The deeds of the Orontids may be traced in classical sources. One king, Orontes, helped Ariarathes II of Cappadocia to regain Cappadocia from the Macedonian strategus Amyntas, in about 270 or 260 BC. Either Orontes or King Samus provided refuge for Ziaelas, future king of Bithynia, in about 260 BC. King Arsames sheltered the Seleucid rebel Antiochus Hierax from his brother

---

[37] Justin, *Epitome*, XXXVIII, vii, 2.
[38] The text's 'led up' has been emended by some but apparently only on the grounds that it 'seems wrong'. Strabo, *Geography*, XI, xiv, 9 note 3 Loeb edition. The gold mines are at Pharangion, north-east of Bayberd.

Seleucus II. In about 212 BC the Seleucid Antiochus III attempted to collect tribute which the father of King Xerxes had failed to pay. Antiochus besieged Xerxes in Arsamosata, and persuaded him to pay part of the tribute, in money, horses and mules, and to marry his sister. Around 200 BC Antiochus was, perhaps, involved in the removal of the last Orontid king, Orontes IV. Strabo says Antiochus turned the country over to two of his generals, Artaxias and Zariadris.[39] But Seleucid suzerainty was nearly over. Antiochus provoked Rome by invading Greece. He was defeated at the battle of Magnesia in 190 BC, whereupon his two generals 'joined the Romans' and were recognized as independent, with the title of king, at the Peace of Apamea in 189/8.

The geographical extent of Orontid Armenia is identifiable, from Strabo's account of how Artaxias and Zariadris enlarged it. It included[40] all western, southern and central Armenia, from the borders of Taykᶜ, Cholarzene and Gogarene, to the Araxes and the Taurus mountains and the Muş plain. The Orontids may have held Melid. They also held ancient Kummukh, later Commagene, kingdom of their descendant Antiochus I. But they did not control the Matieni, nor the Chalybes and the Mossynoeci who consolidated their independence, round Erzurum and further west. They lost Acilisene to the Cataonians, and Taykᶜ to the Iberians.

It was under the Orontids that Greek civilization spread in Armenia, as it did elsewhere in the Seleucid empire. Seven Greek inscriptions of the early second century or later, found at Armavir, have suggested to some scholars the presence of a Greek colony, perhaps with its own temple and priesthood, and also the use of Greek by the last Orontid king and his associates, since, according to Moses of Khoren, the Orontids used Armavir as a capital. Samus, Arsames and Xerxes issued coins. There was a partial revival of urban life, a very Greek element, perhaps stimulated by the passage of international trade through Armenia and encouraged by the various Seleucid foundations, for example at Nisibis, Edessa and Seleuceia on the Tigris. Samosata (modern Samsat), on the site of an old town, perhaps the capital of Kummukh, may have been founded by King Samus. It was probably his son Arsames who founded Arsameia (Eski Kâhta), also in Commagene, and Arsamosata (modern Haraba and mostly under the waters of the Keban Dam lake) where there had been a small, probably Urartian settlement on the citadel site between the tenth and seventh centuries BC. The site, probably, was chosen for security, and lived by agriculture rather than trade. The old town of Carcathiocerta, modern Eğil, was to be the capital of the Orontid kingdom of Sophene in the next century, so it too must have been an Orontid base. In the northeast Garni was occupied and fortified in the third century. The reoccupied

---

[39] Strabo, XI, xiv, 15.
[40] Hewsen, 1984.

Urartian Armavir was not, contrary to Moses' assertion, deserted when the last Orontid king, perhaps around 220 BC, constructed a new fortified town at Eruandashat on the Araxes plain.[41] This was founded partly because of a shortage of water caused by a shift in the course of the Araxes.

The newly introduced Hellenistic influence did not replace the long-standing Iranian influence. This appears for example in the name of Bagaran, the new town which was to be this king's religious centre, where his brother was high priest. The name is from Iranian *bag*, god. In his construction of a walled hunting park, gardens, vineyards and a royal residence at another town, Eruandakert, this same king combined Hellenistic and Iranian interests. His successors were to introduce Armenia to the interests of Rome.

[41] Moses, II, 39, 40, trans. Thomson, 1978, pp. 181–2.

4

Autonomy and Empires: Artaxias I to Tiridates I, 189 BC–AD 63

The accessions of Artaxias (189–160 BC) and Zariadris in 189 BC were a milestone in Armenian history in at least four respects. First, Armenia had encountered Rome and begun her entanglement in the hostility of the great powers of east and west. Second, the territorial integrity of Orontid Armenia was destroyed, possibly as a price for Armenia's independent status. It may have been at this time that Commagene, and also Lesser Armenia (in north-west Armenia), perhaps part of the Orontid kingdom, and now with its own potentates, emerged as separate entities. Melid passed at some point to Cappadocia. Artaxias and Zariadris themselves divided Armenia between them. Zariadris took Sophene (ancient Supa), and perhaps the region around Arca, about twenty-two miles west of Melitene, and Artaxias the rest.

A third milestone depends on the view taken of the origins of these two kings. Their accession may represent an attempt, only initially successful, by the Seleucid king, Antiochus III, to crush the independence of Armenia, using two outsiders as his tools, as Strabo suggests.[1] Another possibility is that Artaxias' removal of king Orontes IV was an Armenian and aristocratic revolt against Iranian, central, power, which was forced to retreat to Sophene. Zariadris seems to have been an Orontid,[2] and in Moses of Khoren's account Artaxias appears as a native dynast.[3] It has even been suggested, on the flimsy grounds of his family's use of the name Tigranes, that Artaxias was connected with the family of the Armenian prince Tigranes who appeared in Xenophon's *Cyropaedia*.[4] On the other

[1] Strabo, *The Geography*, XI, xiv, 15.
[2] Toumanoff, 1963, pp. 290–4.
[3] Moses, II, 37, 43–6, trans. Thomson, 1978, pp. 179–80, 184–7; Toumanoff, 1963, p. 285.
[4] Xenophon, *Cyropaedia*, III, i, 7.

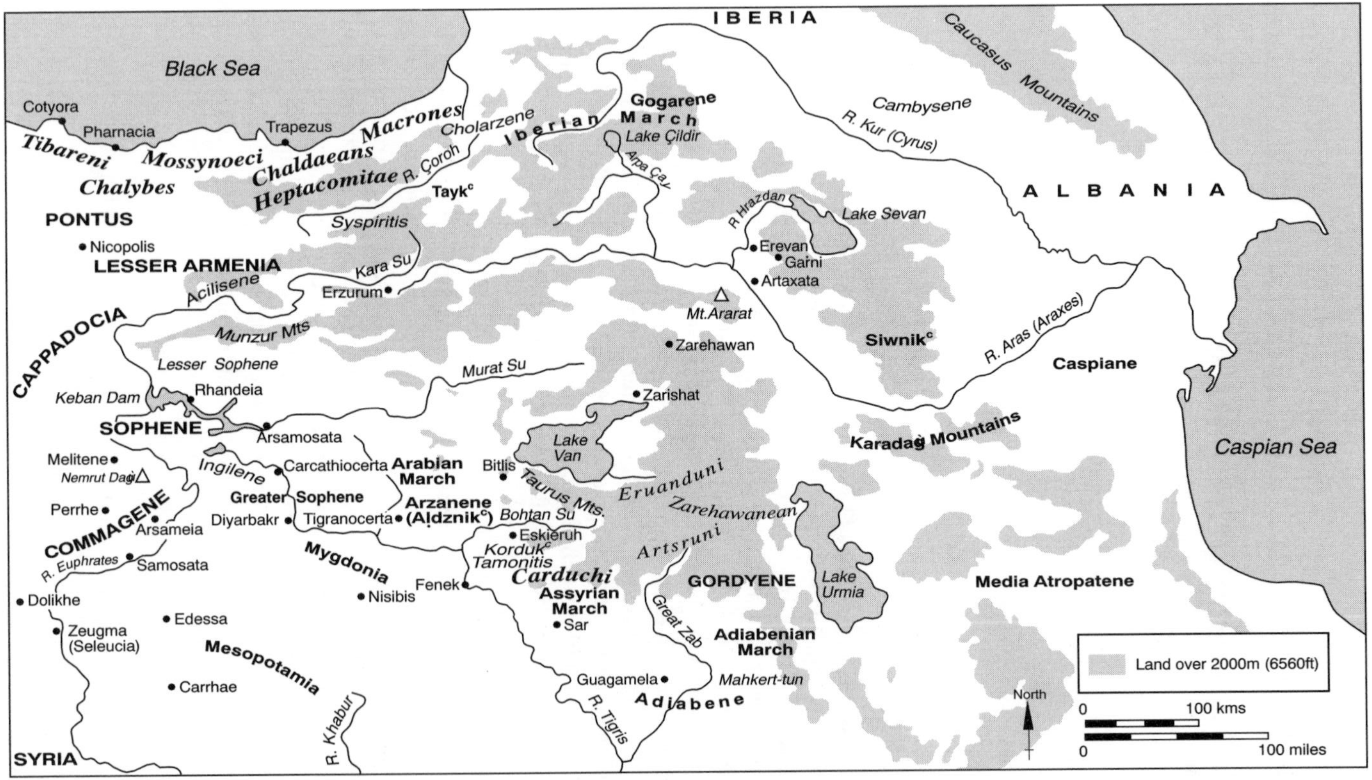

Map 4.1 Armenia

hand if Artaxias' claim in his inscriptions to be an Orontid[5] was true, and Zariadris of Sophene was related, perhaps brother or nephew to him, then their accessions represent only the replacement of one branch of the ruling family by another. Armenian autonomy was gained by their clever exploitation, first of Seleucid aspiration and then of Seleucid weakness, and, no doubt, with the support of at least some of the aristocracy of Armenia. This last emerges from Moses' account, though his mendacity in giving starring roles in Armenian history to members of the Bagratuni (Bagratid) family, his patrons, where his sources make no reference to them, prevents us from taking the details, like the contribution of Smbat Bagratuni, seriously.

Fourth, the new kings began a programme of expansion which was to reach its zenith a century later. Their acquisitions are summarized by Strabo. It was probably Zariadris who acquired Acilisene and 'the country around the Antitaurus', possibly the district of Muzur or west of the Euphrates. It was probably Artaxias who took lands from the Medes, including modern Karadağ and the stretch from Lake Sevan to the Araxes, later known as Siwnik^c, and acquired Tayk^c, Kıaŕjk^c (classical Cholarzene) and Gugark^c (classical Gogarene) from the Iberians and Tamonitis from the Syrians. It is unclear which of the two kings took the region of modern Erzurum and land further west from the Chalybes and Mossynoeci. Some of the acquisitions may have come from Lesser Armenia, which had expanded up to the territories of Pharnacia and Trapezus. According to Strabo it was as a result of these Artaxiad acquisitions that 'they all speak the same language'.[6]

The details behind these successes are, for the most part, elusive. Classical sources allow only a partial reconstruction of Artaxias' manoeuvrings but they do show that he and the other Armenian potentates had confrontations with Pontus, Seleucid Syria and Cappadocia. Artaxias was, according to the Greek writer Polybius (*c*.200–*c*.118 BC), included in the treaty which followed the victory of a group of Anatolian kings over Pharnaces of Pontus in 181 BC. This forced Pharnaces to abandon all his recent gains in the west, except Sinope, and fined Mithridates of Lesser Armenia, possibly Pharnaces' ally, 300 talents for attacking Cappadocia.[7] As for Syria, in 166 or 165 BC Artaxias had to recognize Seleucid sovereignty after Antiochus IV invaded Armenia and captured him, but this recognition was short-lived. Artaxias subsequently allied with Timarchus, satrap of Media under (the Seleucid) king Demetrius, who having obtained Roman recognition as an independent king proceeded to armed rebellion. It may have been in reward for this alliance that Artaxias gained his Median lands. (Timarchus himself proved unsuc-

---

[5] With a father called Zariadris, Périkhanian, 1971 b.
[6] Strabo, XI, xiv, 5; Hewsen, 1985.
[7] Polybius, *The Histories*, XXV, 2.

cessful in his rebellion.) Another episode involved Ptolemaeus, governor of Commagene and grandson of the Orontid king Arsames. In 163 or 162 BC, Ptolemaeus, emulating Timarchus, seized independence from Syria. He also tried to take Melid from Ariarathes V (163–130 BC) of Cappadocia. Ariarathes had already blocked an attempt by Artaxias to annexe part of Sophene after its king (presumably Zariadris) had died, by refusing to countenance Artaxias' suggestion that the two of them assassinate the heir, Mithrobuzanes, and divide the kingdom between them. Now Ariarathes baulked Ptolemaeus. It is possible that this recalcitrance reflects something of Roman policy towards Armenia. Ariarathes was not only an ally of Rome but had been educated there. Such an education was unusual at this time for a king, though it was common later.

That Artaxias was an ambitious monarch of international stature can be inferred from the reputation he left behind him. In Armenian oral tradition he was remembered as a great king and warrior. Moses of Khoren drew on 'songs about Artashēs' (Armenian for Artaxias) 'and his sons'. He recorded, amongst other things, that Artaxias defeated Alan invaders and wished 'to subject the whole west',[8] in two accounts which combine truth with tradition of dubious historicity, confusion, and literary borrowings. The Greek writers Plutarch (c.AD 45–c.123) and Strabo record a suspect story that Artaxias sheltered Hannibal of Carthage after the battle of Apamea.[9] But Artaxias' programme lapsed after his death, as his kingdom was pressed by Pontus and Parthia, the latter ruled by the dynasty of the Arsacids. Mithridates VI of Pontus advanced through Lesser Armenia, part of which he was ceded, in about 120 BC, by one of its kings, Antipater, and built seventy-five forts there. Parthia took Media from the Seleucids in about 148 and Mithridates II campaigned against Armenia in about 110 gaining both the submission of King Artavasdes, and a hostage, the future king Tigranes the Great (c.95–55 BC).

Empire

The provocation which Tigranes the Great subsequently offered Rome, as a powerful and glorious hindrance to Roman expansion, was one of the causes of classical historians writing detailed accounts of the wars, the shifting alliances, and the boundary changes in which Armenians were involved in the first century BC. There are of course some uncertainties but the gist of the narrative is clear.

---

[8] Moses, I, 30, II, 48, 49, 50, trans. Thomson, 1978, pp. 120–1, 189, 190, 192 for songs; Moses, II, 50, trans. Thomson, pp. 191–2 for Alans; Moses, II, 12, trans. Thomson, p. 148 for western ambition.

[9] Plutarch, *Lives: Lucullus*, XXXI, 3; Strabo, XI, xiv, 6.

Tigranes acceded, perhaps in succession to a Tigranes I, in about 95 BC. That he acceded with Parthian help has prompted some scholars to believe he was a tributary 'vassal',[10] but another suggestion is that, having agreed with Parthia that the Euphrates should be their frontier, Rome insisted on the accession of Tigranes in the hope that the existence of an independent kingdom situated between Parthia and Pontus would hinder any subsequent alliance between them. Rome was apprehensive, and with good reason, of Pontus, and it was this apprehension which was to cause the destruction of the empire which Tigranes was to build. There was a foretaste quite soon. Tigranes, married to Cleopatra, daughter of Mithridates VI, twice helped his father-in-law in his attempts to control Cappadocia, in about 95 and 91 BC. Twice Rome checked Pontus, by restoring the Cappadocian nominee, Ariobarzanes, to his throne.

Tigranes was much more successful on his own account. He took Sophene. He recovered seventy valleys, probably in Media Atropatene, which had been the price paid to Parthia for his accession. He subjugated Atropatene, Adiabene, and Gordyene, whose people, according to Strabo,[11] were the ancient Carduchi. He raided Media, subordinated Commagene and Osrhoene (Mesopotamia), and took over Syria as far as Egypt. This last was, according to one source,[12] by invitation of the Syrians, exhausted by the wars between the last of the Seleucids, and impressed by Tigranes' strength and his alliances with Parthia and Pontus. The widowed queen, Cleopatra Selene, however was still holding out in Ptolemais, under siege, in 70 BC. She fled to Commagene only to be imprisoned and slain by Tigranes in Seleuceia. Tigranes also conquered Phoenicia and Cilicia. By 70 BC he was perceived in Judaea as a potential threat. Its queen, Alexandra, won him over with treaties and gifts. The extent of Tigranes' empire may also be gauged from the composition of the army he brought to defend his new capital, Tigranocerta, against a (successful) Roman siege in 69 BC. This comprised men of Armenia, Gordyene, Media, Adiabene, Albania, Iberia and Arabs, plus some from around the River Araxes who were apparently not his subjects. The subjugation of Albania is unrecorded, but it seems to have resulted in the brief acquisition of Cambysene, north of the Kura river, between Albania and Iberia.

Tigranes' empire was dismembered by Rome in the 60s BC. Tigranes had tried to avoid involvement in the (third) war between Rome and Pontus which began in 73 BC. He nevertheless refused the demand of an offensive Roman envoy, Appius Clodius, that he surrender his father-in-law, who had fled to him in 71, and his refusal dragged him in. Yet the Roman general Lucullus had no authority to wage war on Tigranes, a fact

[10] Chaumont, 1985–8, p. 23.
[11] Strabo, XVI, i, 24.
[12] Justin, *Epitome*, XL, i.

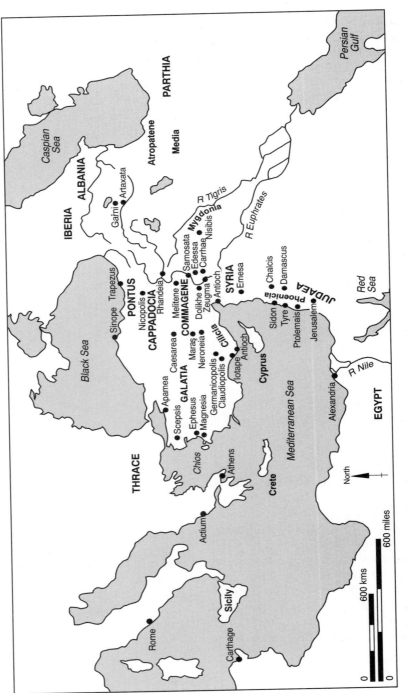

Map 4.2   The east Mediterranean and West Asia

which may explain why Tigranes was ill-prepared for the siege of his capital. Tigranes and Mithridates nearly recovered their positions. Lucullus was beaten off from Artaxata in 68 BC and by 66 BC most of his conquests had been regained. But Syria was lost, having reverted to Antiochus III, son of Cleopatra Selene, after its governor had left to help Tigranes. The deciding factor was the rebellion of Tigranes' son, also named Tigranes, and his alliance with Pompey, appointed to replace Lucullus. The king made peace and agreed to pay an indemnity.

Pompey then rearranged the political geography of the east. The exact details of the changes and their chronology are not always clear. Some were changed after Pompey and the young Tigranes fell out and after Parthian intervention. But the upshot was that by 59 BC Syria and Phoenicia had passed to Rome, Sophene to Cappadocia, and Adiabene to Parthia. Lesser Armenia went, probably, to Brogitarus, son-in-law of Deiotarus king of Galatia,[13] and Caspiane to the Albanians. Commagene had regained independence and acquired Seleuceia and parts of Mesopotamia across the Euphrates from Samosata. Antiochus I (69–34 BC) issued coins showing him wearing the Armenian tiara with five points, a star and eagles. This may have been as propaganda, its purpose to proclaim Antiochus a fully legitimate local successor of Tigranes.[14] As friend and ally of Rome Antiochus received a gift of a *toga praetexta* in 59 BC and he may well have been made a Roman citizen.

Royal Government

Antiochus' implied esteem of Tigranes was probably not due solely to his military successes. The evidence indicates that Artaxiad Armenia had enjoyed efficient government, with the support, or at least the acquiescence, of the aristocracy. There may be some truth, in principle, in the innovations ascribed by Moses of Khoren to figures who are identifiable as Artaxiads. In Moses' account, Artaxias gave high rank, insignia, offices and estates to members of six families, one related to his Alan queen, and set his sons over his household, religion, and the four divisions into which he divided his army. One of these sons, Artawazd (classical Artavasdes) manipulated Artaxias into destroying one of the elevated families, engineered the departure of another, and aroused the jealousy of his brothers. Then, as king, he forbade them to live in Ayrarat, the royal residence, establishing them in two provinces to the north and north-east of Lake Van. Another Artawazd did the same with his brothers and sisters, assigning them the income and rents of the 'royal portion' in

---

[13] Adcock, 1937.
[14] Sullivan, R. D., 1973.

the villages. And 'Tiran', successor to the first Artawazd settled his kin likewise in the same places, but promoted his brother-in-law, married to the last of Artawazd's wives.[15] Behind Moses' suspect details probably lies a reality of rearrangements and efficiency, of reward and punishment for aristocracy, and of concern and suspicion regarding relatives, who were simultaneously potential props and potential rivals.

This hypothesis accords perfectly with what we know from other sources. Artaxias I certainly paid attention to internal stability. He set up inscribed boundary stones, several of which survive, to mark the territories of villages and, presumably, to obviate disputes, which might be especially bitter in times of food shortages. This measure was recorded by Moses.[16] Tigranes the Great exploited and controlled his relatives and his aristocracy with a combination of continuity, change and supervision. Various conquered potentates, like those of the Medes, Adiabene and Gordyene, kept their royal titles. So did Tigranes' kinsman Antiochus of Commagene. The Orontids of Sophene of course did not, but the family was permitted to survive. The commander Mithrobuzanes, whom Lucullus defeated prior to besieging Tigranocerta, may have been the son or brother of its last king, and perhaps an ancestor of the tenth-century Artsruni kings. For the Artsrunis had favoured the name Mithrobuzanes and were of Orontid descent. Toumanoff has demonstrated the Orontid origin of twelve dynasties including the Artsrunis, some of major importance.[17] In Sophene, the Orontids survived as the dynasty of Ingilene, known as the house of Angḷ (Angḷ being Eğil, the site of the former royal capital Carcathiocerta), and the dynasties of the principalities of Greater and Lesser Sophene, like the princes of Arzanene and the princes of Adiabene, the latter possibly closely related to the Artsrunis, were all Orontid.

It is possible that the ancestors of the Orontid dynasties were allowed significant responsibility by Tigranes. The later location of the Artsrunis, Eruandunis and Zarehawaneans in the south-east has been attributed to royal transfer, and the transfer of the Artsrunis has been attributed to Tigranes himself.[18] The motive behind such transfers is just as likely to have been to strengthen the frontiers as to weaken rebellious tendencies in Sophene. The Bagratunis, who attained royal status in the ninth century, were another family of Orontid origin, though their family had, probably, branched off before 200 BC. They too, Toumanoff suggests, were persuaded, perhaps by Tigranes, to exchange their original territory, in central Armenia, for Syspiritis on the Georgian border.[19] The Bagadates who

[15] Moses, II, 47, 51–3; II, 51–3, 61; II, 22, 62, trans. Thomson, 1978, pp. 187–8, 194–6; 193–6, 203; 159, 204–5. The Artawazd who comes first in Moses' account is historically later than the one who comes second.
[16] Périkhanian, 1971a, and 1971b; Moses, II, 56, trans. Thomson, 1978, pp. 198–9.
[17] Toumanoff, 1963, pp. 297–305.
[18] Ibid. pp. 199–200, 310.
[19] Ibid. pp. 306, 320–4.

supervised Syria and Cilicia, between 83 and 69 BC, for Tigranes, may have belonged to this family, though this is not universally accepted.

It is possible that great power was placed in a small number of hands. That the Greek historian Appian (*c.*AD 90–*c.*165) terms Bagadates στρἄτηγόϛ,[20] may suggest the continuation of the Seleucid office which bore this title. The four marches, or vitaxates, whose rulers are called *bdeashkh* or *bdēshkh* in Armenian sources, are clearly attested only for the later Arsacid period. But they may have been Artaxiad creations, despite their title's being a Parthian (Middle Iranian) loanword. According to Toumanoff, the Assyrian march comprised the former kingdom of Sophene and may have been held by Mithrobuzanes; the Arabian one, held by the princes of Arzanene, comprised the lands taken from Gordyene and Mygdonia (the area around Nisibis) and included Tigranocerta; the Median or Adiabenian march, held perhaps by the princes of Adiabene, comprised lands from Adiabene and Atropatene; and the Iberian march comprised Taykᶜ, Cholarzene and Gogarene, lands taken from the Iberians. Toumanoff also argued that the very institution of the march implied a 'feudal kind of dependence' upon the *bdēshkh* by the princes within it.[21]

This account of the marches has however recently been challenged. Hewsen[22] suggests that the marches of Assyria and Adiabene both bordered Adiabene's northern frontier, and were formed later than the others; that these two at least were Arsacid creations, and that they were commanded not by Orontids and Artsrunis but by, respectively, the princes of Kordukᶜ, whom Toumanoff suggested were descended from the royal line of Gordyene, in whose old territory Kordukᶜ lay, and by the princes of Mahkert-tun, of Medo-Carduchian origin. The latter appear to be the only princes known for certain to have reigned within the area of the vitaxate and so cannot be held to have lorded it over other princes. By much diminishing the Arabian march Hewsen similarly lowers the status of the prince of Arzanene, making him not a super-dynast, but a lord of his own principality plus a number of smaller, princeless, lands. His role was to guard the Bitlis Pass.

Hewsen's geographical scrutiny of the vitaxates is entirely convincing, but the evidence concerning the dates of their formation is so slight that questions remain. Much depends on the credence and interpretation given to the remark of Plutarch that there were four kings who were always with Tigranes, like attendants,[23] whom Toumanoff took to be his marcher lords.

[20] Appian, *Roman History*, XI, (*The Syrian Wars*), viii, 48, (has Magadates for Bagadates).

[21] Toumanoff, 1963, pp. 154–92 for *vitaxae*, (pp. 166–79 Assyrian march; 179–82 Arabian; 163–6 Median; 183–92 Iberian), pp. 123–4, 154, for feudal dependence.

[22] Hewsen, 1988–9, and 1990–1.

[23] Plutarch, *Lives: Lucullus*, XXI, 5.

Plutarch's often cited remarks certainly suggest that Tigranes kept the aristocracy under his eye. Many kings, apparently, waited on him. These were presumably men of lesser power than the kings, of, say, Gordyene. Appian says Tigranes had conquered many of the neighbouring tribes who had kings (he calls them dynasts) of their own,[24] and Pliny the Elder (AD 23/24–79) records that, by the middle of the first century AD, Greater Armenia was divided into 120 prefectships (*praefecturas*), 'with native names, called in Greek' generalships (*strategias*), 'some of which were formerly actual separate kingdoms'.[25]

Tigranes' 'kings', who supported him in his military undertakings, are often referred to as his 'vassals'. But the exact terms of their relationship are not sufficiently known to warrant such an appellation. What is clear is that Anatolian dynasts preferred to work through ties of marriage and blood.[26] If the Artaxiads were really Orontids, then most of their powerful subordinates were their kinsmen. Tigranes set his brother over Nisibis, which he had taken from Parthia and which contained his treasures and most of his other possessions. He made a marriage alliance with the dynasty of Media Atropatene. But non-kinsmen were not excluded from power. Mancaeus, who defended Tigranocerta for Tigranes, may have been an ancestor of the Mamikonean family, dynasts of Tayk^c perhaps as early as the Achaemenid period, and possibly of Georgian origin.

Little is known of the structure of Artaxiad society, but various groups are perceptible. The forces Tigranes deployed against Lucullus included men from around the River Araxes who were 'not subject to kings' but were persuaded by 'favour' and by 'gifts',[27] a reference which suggests to some scholars that they comprised 'vassals' acting out of duty and mercenaries coming for pay. A subsequent army was recruited from the whole population, perhaps the same group as the Armenian citizens who bore arms, who were to choose Tigranes' grandson Artaxias II to be king. Another group comprised transportees, both native subjects and foreign captives. Tigranes compelled the principal inhabitants of the country, under penalty of confiscation of their goods, to move to Tigranocerta, where he also installed Greeks from Cilicia and people from Adiabene, Assyria, Gordyene and Cappadocia.

Tigranes exacted obedience and expected respect. Because he had conquered neighbouring kings, he assumed the title King of Kings and was vexed if it was not recognized. When Lucullus addressed him only as king, he responded by refusing to address Lucullus as 'autocrator'. Tigranes did not, however, always use his title. On some of his coins,

---

[24] Appian, XI, viii, 48.
[25] Pliny the Elder, *Natural History*, VI, x, 27.
[26] Sullivan, R. D., 1970.
[27] Plutarch, *Lives: Lucullus*, XXVI, 4.

for example those struck at Antioch, he restricted himself to 'king'. It has been suggested that the grander title was used only on coins struck in Armenia. It is not improbable that the Artaxiads had followed the Achaemenid tradition of close association with the gods. Artavasdes II (55–34 BC) and Tigranes III (c.20–c.8 BC) bore a divine epithet on their coins. Russell[28] interprets figures of eagles from Artaxata, and eagles and stars on coins, as representations of the royal 'glory' and 'fortune' which in Iranian society were thought to protect the legitimate king, and, by extension, his realm, even after death.

The attitude of Tigranes' subjects towards him is less clear than is his to them. Plutarch believed that success went to his head, that his four attendant kings behaved towards him like slaves, that he was pompous and haughty, ruled as a tyrant, was so unused to free speech that he executed the messenger who reported Lucullus' advance towards Tigranocerta, and treacherous. He told his father-in-law Mithridates how Mithridates' own envoy, Metrodorus, had advised against helping him, and after Mithridates engineered Metrodorus' death, salved his conscience by giving Metrodorus a splendid burial.[29] Such a character could hardly have been popular. Yet we should not take Plutarch's account at face value. Denigration of the enemy, and a traditional distaste for oriental protocols, may lie behind it. And Tigranes' contemporaries were not blameless. Mithridates, apparently, poisoned both his own son and a man who surpassed him in driving race horses. The responsibility for Tigranes' war with Rome rests with Appius Clodius, a man known from other sources to have been shameless and abominably behaved.

There were certainly three categories of malcontents. The loyalty of the many foreigners in Armenia was doubtful. Greeks, variously reported as mercenaries and transportees from Cilicia, let Lucullus into Tigranocerta. Second, some of the conquered were restive. Appius Clodius had made secret agreements with 'many of the enslaved cities'[30] and won over many of the princes (dynasts), including the king of Gordyene, whom Tigranes subsequently put to death for his treachery. When Lucullus advanced through Sophene, the inhabitants seem to have received his army gladly. They, the Gordyeni, and the kings of the Arabs joined his cause after the fall of Tigranocerta. Third, if, as is likely, the reign of Tigranes was crucial in the subordination of the separate kingdoms within Armenia to which Pliny alludes, there must have been resentment. Tigranes the Younger certainly profited from discontent, before and during his rebellion. Cassius Dio (c.164–after 229) records that 'some of the foremost men' went with him to Parthia because King Tigranes 'was not ruling to suit them'.[31]

[28] Russell, 1987, pp. 80, 82–4.
[29] Plutarch, *Lives: Lucullus*, XXI, 3–6, XXV, 1, XXII, 1–4.
[30] Ibid. XXI, 2.
[31] Cassius Dio, *Roman History*, XXXVI, 51, 1.

The prince was further stirred up against his father by some Armenians who deserted the king on his way to meet Pompey. Two of his brothers were equally disloyal. One died in battle against their father, the other was executed for taking the royal diadem after the king was thrown on the hunting field.

Decline

The century that followed the destruction of Tigranes' empire was one of great change for Armenian lands, that is Commagene, whose kings were of Orontid descent, Lesser Armenia and Sophene and Greater Armenia. Commagene enjoyed a reasonable stability. But Lesser Armenia was passed by Rome to potentates of Cappadocia (38 BC), Pontus (36 or 35 BC), and Media Atropatene (31 BC), to the son of Cotys, king of Thrace (AD 38), and to the son of Herod, king of Chalcis in AD 54. Sophene was given in that same year to Sohaemus of Emesa. We do not know how long he kept it. For the Artaxiad dynasty these were decades of decline into extinction. A detailed narrative of Armenian experiences would comprise a series of accessions, depositions, restorations and other changes, in which it is difficult to see a pattern, except one of rivalry between Rome and Parthia.

For a brief while however Artaxiad decline was staved off. Young Tigranes was out of the picture, kept in detention in Rome by a friend of Pompey, until 'rescued', by a relative of Appius Clodius, for an unknown fate. Tigranes' brother, King Artavasdes II, gave good advice to Crassus, governor of Syria, namely to march via Armenia, when he decided to invade Parthia. Whilst Crassus disregarded this and marched instead to his own defeat at Carrhae, Artavasdes came to terms with Orodes of Parthia, marrying off his sister to Pacorus, son of Orodes. Artavasdes even contemplated expansion. In 51 BC he thought of attacking Cappadocia, and he betrothed a daughter to the son of Deiotarus of Galatia, ruler of Lesser Armenia since 52 BC.

The balance of power and alliances were altered by the victory of Julius Caesar in civil war with Pompey, in 48 BC, and Rome's defeat of Pacorus in 38 BC. Deiotarus' Lesser Armenia passed to Cappadocia. Antiochus of Commagene had not, unlike Deiotarus, sent sufficient support to Pompey to antagonize Caesar. But being the father-in-law of Orodes he was besieged in Samosata, though eventually he bought off the Romans, under Mark Antony, with 300 talents. Artavasdes shifted his support to Antony and to Monaeses, a Parthian dissident, against the new and murderous king of Parthia, Phraates IV (37 BC–AD 2). But then, rightly or wrongly, Antony attributed the failure of his own invasion of Media Atropatene to Artavasdes' desertion, and gave Artavasdes, with members of his family, as a present to Cleopatra of Egypt, where he was killed in 31

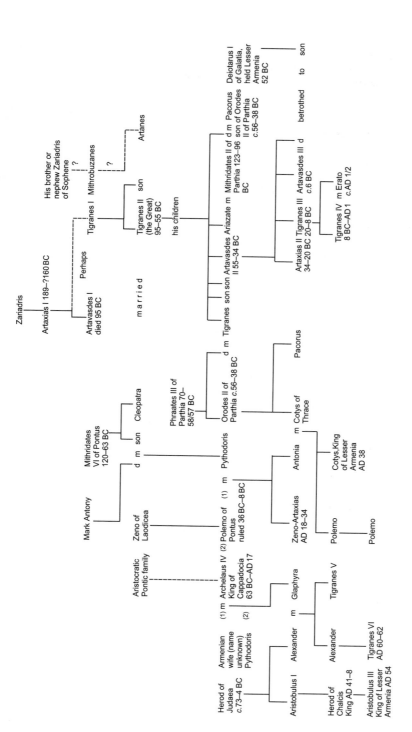

Figure 4.1   Partial genealogical table: the Artaxiads and their connections

BC. Artavasdes had refused obeisance to Cleopatra, but he did not for very long have the consolation of being remembered as a hero. He appears in Moses of Khoren's text as a slothful glutton who lost Mesopotamia to the Romans.[32] His son Artaxias II (34–20 BC) regained the Armenian kingdom from Parthia, whither he had fled. He then killed all the Romans left there by Antony.

Artaxiad rule was to last only a little longer, and the monarchs were increasingly dependent upon Roman support. Around 20 BC the Armenians requested Rome to replace Artaxias with his brother, Tigranes III, whom Rome had not returned from Egypt after the deaths of Antony and Cleopatra, and they murdered Artaxias. Around 8 BC Tigranes' son, Tigranes IV, succeeded him, but without Rome's approval. Artavasdes III was imposed in his place by the emperor Augustus (27 BC–AD 14), but lasted only a few years. Tigranes IV then successfully petitioned Rome for the kingship. From 2 BC to AD 1 he reigned with his sister and wife, Erato. She was the last Artaxiad monarch because some time after Tigranes' death in battle with barbarians she reigned briefly on her own, until she was expelled.

Thereafter Armenia was prey to several foreigners' interventions. Rome was dominant until AD 34. She imposed two Medians (Ariobarzanes II and his son Artavasdes IV), Tigranes V, and Vonones, once a Roman hostage and subsequently king of Parthia until ousted by the Parthians. Vonones ruled from AD 11 until 16, when Parthian threats and a lack of Armenian support led to his removal. At this point Archelaus of Cappadocia may have attempted the restoration of his grandson Tigranes V. Such an attempt could explain why Archelaus was tried for treason before the Roman Senate. He died (before the verdict) in the same year, AD 17, that Rome annexed Commagene, at the request of her men of substance. Armenia then enjoyed sixteen years of stability under the next Roman nominee, Zeno (18–34), who was son of the king of Pontus, stepson of Archelaus of Cappadocia, and, probably, a Roman citizen.

When instability returned, both Parthia and Iberia were involved. First Artabanus III of Parthia (AD 12–*c.*38) installed his eldest son, Arsaces. But then Pharasmanes of Iberia, in alliance with Rome, installed his own brother, Mithridates, in AD 35. The attendants of Arsaces had been bribed to kill him, and this introduced the element of bloodfeud into relations with Parthia. War followed. Mithridates managed to keep his throne but he had a chequered career. He was imprisoned by the Roman emperor Gaius (Caligula) (37–41 AD), and his restoration, by the emperor Claudius (41–54) in AD 41, was despite the resistance of Cotys, king of Lesser Armenia, and of some of the nobility, including a certain Demonax, perhaps a ruler of one of Pliny's prefectures. His cruelty subsequently provoked rebellion, and he was murdered by Radamistus of Iberia (simul-

---

[32] Moses, II, 22–3, trans. Thomson, 1978, pp. 159–60.

taneously his nephew, son-in-law and brother-in-law), in about AD 52. Radamistus himself was subsequently driven out. There were changes too in Commagene. Gaius had restored Antiochus IV in AD 38, and augmented the kingdom with holdings in Cilicia, but subsequently deposed Antiochus, leaving him to be restored again, with further Cilician holdings, by Claudius in AD 48.

The fifties and sixties saw the failure of Rome to prevent the Arsacid king Vologases I of Parthia securing Armenia for his brother Tiridates. Yet at first Roman resistance was successful. The Roman general, Corbulo, dispatched against Tiridates, secured the surrender of Artaxata and Tigranocerta, and the emperor Nero (AD 54–68) established as king Tigranes VI (nephew of Tigranes V), reduced, apparently, by long residence in Rome to slave-like docility.[33] Nero entrusted the rulers of Lesser Armenia and of Commagene, Tigranes' kinsmen, and possibly also those of Iberia and Pontus,[34] with the protection of Tigranes' kingdom. But Tigranes' invasion of Adiabene provoked Parthia. After some fighting, in which Rome made much use of Commagenian territory and of native dynastic forces, it was finally agreed, at the peace of Rhandeia in AD 63, that Tiridates should be king, but be crowned by Nero. Some border changes seem to have been made at the same time. Hewsen suggests that the reversion of Caspiane to Media Atropatene was one of the provisions of the treaty. Gogarene had been retained and Cholarzene regained by Iberia after the expulsion of Radamistus.

What explanations are there for the twists and turns of the years between 38 BC and AD 63? The classical sources imply that, in Greater Armenia, Armenians had tended to switch support from one ruler to another. Though this may be interpreted as indicating aristocratic resentment of strong government, it could equally well indicate a search for strength. Peace and stability may be more propitious than war and disruption for an aristocracy's pursuit of its 'own interests'. The supporters of different candidates for the throne are often labelled as pro-Roman, and pro-Parthian. But it is not necessarily the case that their divisions were actually *caused* by differing attitudes towards the two great powers. Tacitus did indeed remark that Armenia was untrustworthy regarding Rome at the time of Vonones. But he attributed it to resentment of Antony's dreadful behaviour to Artavasdes.[35] The Roman coronation of Zeno, who took the name Artaxias, was perfectly acceptable. It took place at Artaxata in the presence of consenting nobles and a great concourse of people, won over by Zeno's preference for Armenian dress and institutions.

---

[33] Tacitus, *Annals*, XIV, xxvi.
[34] This is according to a traditional emendation of Tacitus (AD 56/7–after 113/114), *Annals*, XIV, xxvi, questioned in Barrett, 1979.
[35] Tacitus, *Annals*, II, iii.

It would be agreeable to be able to explain Armenian attitudes in terms of responses to Roman and Parthian policies towards Armenia, which in turn were aspects of Roman and Parthian policies towards each other. But these subjects have provoked differences of opinion. Roman frontier studies have become a growth industry. It is possible that Rome and Parthia were content for the Euphrates to be their frontier, as they were in their agreements of 66 BC and 20 BC. Some scholars believe in a Roman strategy of linear defence, and that the creation of the eastern frontier provinces was neither piecemeal, nor the result of creeping advance. But another suggestion, advanced forcefully by Isaac,[36] is that concern for borders and frontiers is modern rather than ancient, that Roman frontiers congealed or arose by default rather than planning, that expansion was opportunistic, more the result of desires for glory and plunder than of the search for sensible frontier lines, or of defensive considerations, or of concerns to protect the people in the provinces. Indeed, he argues that Roman geographical knowledge was so pitiful that a 'sensible' policy is impossible to credit. This might explain why the Romans never solved their Armenian problems; supply lines that were too long, troops that were too few, and Parthian tactics and power that were too effective. Some scholars see Rome as almost entirely predatory. According to their views, Rome's generals were eager for triumphs, her soldiers for loot, and her business class of merchants and financiers for profit. Appius Clodius seems deliberately to have provoked war with Tigranes II, in order to further his family's interests in the east. Crassus' treacherous invasion of Parthian Mesopotamia in a time of peace was due not to policy but to rapacity, together with the expectation of an easy but prestigious victory.

Rome's requirements of her client kingdoms have also been variously assessed. Their role as buffer states for her protection has been asserted, denied and refined. The job of their kings may alternatively have been, primarily, the management of new acquisitions. In some cases the kings had considerable freedom of action. They have been termed 'vassals', but Braund,[37] the most recent scholar to study them, emphasizes that the Romans had no juridical concept of a client state. Client kings mostly did not, he argues, pay tribute, though they might pay indemnities, and they had to pay troops and to provide resources and supplies when Rome requested military assistance. Their royal troops could form the backbone of imperial defences.

Roman policy towards Armenia probably developed on an *ad hoc* basis, but certain principles seem to emerge at different times. One constant was Rome's use of native Anatolian dynasts and exploitation of their interrelationships. Every Roman nominee could claim internal sup-

---

[36] Isaac, 1990.
[37] Braund, D. C., 1988; 1984, pp. 63–6, 91–3.

port upon the grounds of legitimacy, and external support on the grounds of kinship. A second constant was apprehension of Pontus, and a third, a foreboding that Parthian control of Armenia would facilitate a Parthian invasion of Pontus or of Roman territory. Fourth was a preference, inaugurated by Augustus, for avoiding direct confrontation with Parthia. Hence Roman concern for Cappadocia and Media. Cappadocia could check both Pontus and Armenia. Media Atropatene could press both Armenia and Parthia. Rome could exert control over Armenia from either of them, if not directly. Exactly why things never settled down in Armenia as easily as they did in Commagene is harder to explain, for in several respects the two kingdoms were comparable. In Commagene too Parthia had maintained an interest, and dynastic rivalry, to which indeed Roman–Parthian rivalry may have contributed, was not unknown.

Culture and Religion

Iranian and Hellenistic influences combined in the culture of Commagene as they did in that of Armenia. Their combination in Armenia appears even in Artaxias I's inscriptions. These reveal a continued use of Aramaic, suggest a middle Iranian pronunciation of some words, and use epithets for the king which accord with Iranian ideas. On the other hand, in one inscription, his name appears in its Greek form, Artaxerxes,[38] and the erection of boundary markers was a Hellenistic practice, common in the Greek city states in western Asia Minor.

Iranian influence is detectible in names and in the culture of Armenian high society. 'Artaxata' and 'Tigranes' are Iranian. 'Ariazate', the name of the daughter of Tigranes II who married Mithridates II of Parthia, means 'daughter of an Iranian', though if Tigranes meant this to indicate where his loyalties lay, he was probably referring to his ancestors, not his contemporaries. More significant is the setting, in historical texts, of hunt and banquet for certain key episodes in the careers of some of the royal dynasty. For in Iranian culture the hunt featured in epic and literature as a context in which an individual's true character and destiny could reveal itself. The banquet played the same role. Moses of Khoren records that two sons of Artaxias ambushed and killed a brother in the hunt, and that one, King Artawazd, died hunting, having fallen into a great pit, in fulfilment of a curse put upon him by Artaxias.[39] Appian records the episode in which Tigranes II's son presumptuously took the royal diadem on the hunting field.[40] According to Moses it was at a banquet that Artawazd engineered the decisive breach between Artaxias and the prince

---

[38] Périkhanian, 1971 b.
[39] Moses, II, 55, 61, trans. Thomson, 1978, pp. 198, 203–4.
[40] Appian, *Roman History*, XII (*The Mithridatic Wars*), xv, 104.

of the Muratsean.[41] Just as the Parthians, according to Tacitus, despised Vonones for his rare appearance in the chase and his disdain of banquets, so the Armenians liked Zeno for liking them.[42]

The exact truth of these accounts is not important. It is how they were remembered that suggests Iranian influence. Yet some allowance must be made for the chronological distance between the writers and the Artaxiads, even in the cases of Tacitus and Appian. They were all writing after Armenia had passed to Arsacid rule, under which Iranian influence in Armenia intensified, and this intensification may have added Iranian elements to Armenian story-telling. It is unfortunate that the contemporary account of Tigranes the Great by Metrodorus of Scepsis, apparently renowned for his hatred of Rome,[43] does not survive.

The religion of the Armenians was, probably, Zoroastrianism, as Russell argues.[44] The repertory of symbols on Artaxiad coins includes the cypress tree, sacred to Zoroastrians, and the Greek god Heracles, whom he believes represents Vahagn, the Zoroastrian deity of strength and victory. The Hellenistic figure of Tyche, and an enthroned male figure with sceptre, may signify Anahita and Ahura Mazda, but this identification is conjectural. The terracotta bas-reliefs of a ruler in Parthian dress, found at Artaxata, may represent the Iranian god Mithras. Russell's interpretation of Moses of Khoren's report that Artaxias moved the ancestral idols from Bagaran to Artaxata as an indication of the Zoroastrian cult of the *fravashi*s, (spirits of one's ancestors) is more doubtful.[45] For Moses was adapting a passage from another work about the much later conversion of Armenia to Christianity.[46] Greek sources confirm that Armenian Zoroastrianism was strong. Strabo records that Anahita was particularly revered by the Armenians, and had temples in different places, especially in Acilisene, where male and female slaves were dedicated to her service and where ritual prostitution was practised by the daughters of the most illustrious families with men of their own rank.[47] The references of Pliny the Elder to Acilisene as the Anaetic region, and of Cassius Dio to the 'land of Anaitis' suggests the existence of temple estates.[48]

We lack any helpful descriptions of burial rites which might indicate whether or not the Zoroastrian prohibition of the pollution of the earth

---

[41] Moses, II, 51, trans. Thomson, 1978, pp. 193–4.

[42] Tacitus, *Annals*, II, ii and lvi.

[43] Plutarch, *Lives: Lucullus*, XXII; Pliny the Elder, *Natural History*, XXXIV, xvi, 34. For Metrodorus' account, Jacoby, 1929, no. 184.

[44] Russell, 1987, pp. 73–111.

[45] Moses, II, 49, trans. Thomson, 1978, p. 190 and his n. 11. Russell, 1987, pp. 80 and 102 (n. 40) and 323–59.

[46] Thomson, 1978, p. 190 n. 11.

[47] Strabo, XI, xiv, 16.

[48] Pliny the Elder, *Natural History*, V, xx, 83; Cassius Dio, *Roman History*, XXXVI, 48, 1.

was observed. At Garni there were graves which were dug in the ground and then covered with slabs. In Sophene, the kings were buried in tombs at Carcathiocerta. The family of Antiochus I of Commagene favoured tumuli. His own, 150 feet high, topped his highest mountain, Nemrut Dağ, visible from almost everywhere in Commagene, which, he thought, was in closest proximity to the heavenly throne of Zeus. The location was presumably meant to emphasize Antiochus' own status as god. The colossal statues, 25–29 feet high on a 20 foot-high platform, were meant as embellishments for a throne room of all the gods, who included his father. Here posterity was to worship twice monthly in celebration of his own birth and accession.

The fire altar at the centre of this shrine is an Iranian feature. But both Commagene and Armenia were also part of the Hellenistic milieu. The heads of Antiochus' statues may be the work of Greek artists. In his sculptured gods Hellenistic and Iranian deities are fused, for example Apollo and Mithras in his Sun god. Two of Antiochus' inscriptions show an interest in the cult of Greek Artemis, to whose temple at Ephesus he made a gift.[49] Antiochus IV was honoured in Chios, to which he made gifts, and where he was an eponymous magistrate and, probably, the patron of a gymnasion, and also in Athens on a monument erected by his grandson Philopappus.[50] There was a rhetorician from Athens at Tigranes II's court (who committed suicide after falling into disfavour), though it is not impossible that it was his wife Cleopatra rather than Tigranes who encouraged Greek culture. Plutarch says that Euripides' *Bacchae* was being read at the wedding reception of Artavasdes II's sister when the head of Crassus was brought in, appropriately enough at a moment when the text required a head.[51] Artavasdes himself was an author of tragedies, orations and histories. It would of course be wrong to assume that Iranian and Hellenistic culture were antithetical. Crassus' enemy, the bridegroom's father, Orodes of Parthia, was well acquainted with Greek language and literature. Roman influence contributed to Armenian military organization. In the seventies BC, Mithridates VI of Pontus had reorganized his forces along Roman lines and he subsequently did the same for an army of Tigranes II under his command.

Economic Resources

Hellenistic influence is most apparent in the promotion of urban life. Cities in Armenian lands (Lesser Armenia, Sophene, Greater Armenia and Commagene), were few, and had a foreign flavour. In Lesser Armenia the

[49] Sullivan, R. D., 1970, p. 170.
[50] Ibid. pp. 186, 210–11.
[51] Plutarch, *Lives: Crassus*, XXXIII, 1–4.

city of Nicopolis was founded by Pompey. In Sophene, Carcathiocerta was too small to rank as a city, and was not a centre of trade and industry. In Armenia itself there were four new, Artaxiad, foundations. Zarehawan and Zarishat probably date from the reign of Artaxias. Both names preserve that of Zariadris, Artaxias' father. Artaxata, 'joy of Artaxias', was of Hellenistic type. Strabo and Plutarch believed it had been built by Hannibal and so Plutarch called it the Armenian Carthage. Razed by Corbulo, it was rebuilt early in Tiridates I's reign by permission of the emperor Nero who provided Italian workmen. Excavations have revealed a coherent plan, maintained each time it was rebuilt. Artaxata had an acropolis, theatre, bath houses and a number of fine buildings embellished with columns. Fragments of frescoes have prompted comparison with frescoes from Roman Pompeii (near Naples). Various objects, for example, amphorae and figurines, of Hellenistic style have also been found. Artaxata may have obtained from Tigranes II the right to mint its own bronze coins, like cities in Syria and Asia Minor. Garni too has yielded material of Hellenistic and Roman type. Such finds reflect the presence of the many foreigners in Armenia. They included Roman soldiers, like those left by Antony, the prefect and centurion who commanded the garrison at Garni for King Mithridates, and the thousand legionaries, three cohorts of infantry and two *alae* of cavalry whom Corbulo left to protect Tigranes VI.

The exact site of Tigranes II's foundation of Tigranocerta has to be deduced, from indications in the fifth-century Armenian *Epic Histories*, in the classical sources and on the ground. These indications are not entirely consistent and scholars have considered six possible sites. Most recently Sinclair has argued convincingly that Tigranocerta was modern Arzn.[52] Arzn has not been excavated, but it seems to have had a grid-plan. Tigranocerta may not however have been absolutely new. Appian says Tigranes had 'assumed the diadem' there.[53] It became full of wealth and votive offerings, many foreigners, mostly Cilicians, private persons and princes (dynasts) competing with the king in its adornment. It had a theatre, whose formal dedication had been planned to include many dramatic artists from all quarters. There were more traditionally Iranian touches too, such as the large parks and hunting grounds and lakes in the suburbs, the stables in the base of the high walls, the strong fort nearby and the unfortified palace.

In Commagene there were the ancient towns of Samosata and Arsameia and Caesarea Germaniceia (Maraş), restored probably in AD 38. Of the origins of Doliche, which minted coins from the time of the emperor Marcus Aurelius (161–80), nothing is known. Perrhe, probably the Anti-

---

[52] Sinclair, 1989b, pp. 295–9, 361–4 and Sinclair, 1994–5.
[53] Appian, XII, x, 67.

och upon Taurus mentioned by the geographer Ptolemy (who wrote between AD 127 and 148),[54] was given city status by Antiochus IV. Antiochus IV himself founded six cities: in his newly acquired Cilician lands he built Neroneia, Claudiopolis and Germanicopolis, named in honour of, respectively, Nero, Claudius and probably Gaius (Caligula), Antioch in Lamotis, and Iotape and Philadelphia. But it is improbable that Antiochus ruled his kingdom through the cities. Commagene probably had a centralized system whereby the king had direct authority over villages and cities. Some of his cities may have been military colonies, populated by his mercenaries. Urban life was peripheral rather than central to the royal and aristocratic Armenian lifestyle.

Artaxiad Armenia was prosperous, and her kings were concerned to encourage, guard and exploit this prosperity, though, like the cities, manufacture and trade seem to have been in foreign, rather than Armenian, hands. Tigranes II's transportees included nomadic Arabs, to be used, according to Plutarch,[55] in trade and commerce. It is to Tigranes that the fifth-century Armenian *Epic Histories* ascribe responsibility for the presence of 100,000 Jewish families in the cities of Armenia in the early 360s AD,[56] but the transportation of their ancestors was probably the work of Artavasdes, who in 40 BC took many prisoners from Judaea. The Aramaic derivation of some Armenian words relating to trade and handicrafts is an additional piece of evidence suggesting that non-Armenians made a major contribution to the economy.

Most of the cities were involved in trade. The rise of Zarehawan and Zarishat has been attributed to flourishing east–west trade. Sinclair suggests that Zarishat and Tigranocerta were founded, in part, to encourage a new trade route.[57] Arsamosata and Carcathiocerta, though probably not trading centres, were both on important routes, the former on the ancient Royal road of the Persians. Artaxata, sited in a fertile and well-watered spot, occupied 450–500 hectares, of which 100 comprised the fortified citadel and central districts, on nine hills. Its population could have reached 100,000. It had forges, armouries and a flourishing pottery industry. There is evidence of copper, gold and silver work, spinning and weaving. Towards the end of the period production of enamel work and glass began. Such items had earlier been imported from Mesopotamia, Syria and Sidon. Artaxata was at a junction of trade routes. Goods from India and Babylonia went, via the Medes and Armenians, to the tribes of the Siraci and the Aorsi on the Caspian coast. Goods also passed westwards and to the Black Sea coast. The presence in Artaxata of coins of

---

[54] Suggested by Jones, 1971, p. 264.
[55] Plutarch, *Lives: Lucullus*, XXI, 4.
[56] *Epic Histories*, IV, lv, trans. Garsoïan, 1989, p. 176 and her Commentary p. 305 (n. 20).
[57] Sinclair, 1987, p. 87.

Tigranes II, struck outside Armenia, and other finds show that Armenian money circulated widely in his empire.

Economic strength was concentrated in the cities and in the south, the areas where Hellenistic culture was most influential. Tigranes II's conquests had given him access to great wealth. Nisibis was, like Tigranocerta, a repository of treasure. It was from Sophene that the money Tigranes promised Pompey came. He gave 6,000 talents of silver to Pompey, and 50, 1,000 and 10,000 drachmae to each soldier, centurion and tribune. Commagene was the richest of the Roman client kingdoms. Its wealth was remarked upon by Tacitus and the Jewish historian Josephus[58] (AD 37–after 95), with regard to Antiochus IV, and it is evident in the building works of Antiochus I, and of his father Mithridates Callinicus (*c.*96–*c.*69 BC). Mithridates built his Hierothesion at Arsameia with colossal statues and a processional way featuring a 21 foot-wide stairway. Antiochus not only erected his monument atop Nemrut Dağ, but also improved the fortifications of Arsameia, provided it with supplies and weapons, and with statues and reliefs of gods. Here too his birthday was to be celebrated monthly, with music and with offerings of food and wine. His kingdom was not only naturally fertile, but on a major east–west trade route. Samosata and Zeugma were the major crossing points of the Euphrates.

Lesser Armenia too was fertile and on a major trade route. It had towns, according to Pliny, at Caesarea, Ezaz and Nicopolis.[59] Society in its mountain regions, however, was less wealthy and sophisticated. The soldiers of Lucullus complained when they were asked to go into the desert of the Tibareni and Chaldaeans to fight Mithridates of Pontus. Strabo reported that the Tibareni, Chaldaeans, Macrones (by his time called Sanni), and the Mossynoeci were utterly savage, some living in trees or turrets, subsisting on wild animals and nuts, and jumping down from scaffolds to attack wayfarers. The worst of them, the Heptacomitae, set 'crazing honey' extracted from tree-twigs, on the roads to tempt Pompey's troops. Six hundred drank it, lost their senses, and were cut down.[60] Tigranes' different subjects offered him different talents. He had Mardian mounted archers and Iberian lancers upon whom he relied, apparently, 'beyond any other mercenaries'. He used people of Gordyene as masterbuilders and constructors of siege engines, for which activities they had an exceptional reputation.[61]

Conquest increased resources and resources facilitated further victories and lent resilience in the face of major defeats, though the classical authors may have exaggerated the latters' severity. Even after the empire

[58] Tacitus, *Histories*, II, lxxxi; Josephus, *The Jewish War*, V, 461.
[59] *Natural History*, VI, x, 26.
[60] Strabo, XII, iii, 18.
[61] Plutarch, *Lives: Lucullus*, XXXI, 5; Strabo, XVI, i, 24.

was dismembered, the Artaxiad kings were not immediately impoverished. Artavasdes II took 6,000 horsemen with him to visit Crassus, and promised to provide and maintain a further 10,000 mail-clad horsemen and 30,000 foot. He also asserted that should Crassus march through Armenia his troops would be in the midst of plenty. For Antony Artavasdes provided 6,000 horse and 7,000 foot. Although Lucullus had plundered Tigranocerta and, according to Strabo, pulled it down and sent home the people who had been compelled to settle there,[62] it did, nevertheless, recover. For we know that it subsequently surrendered to Corbulo, and was besieged by the Parthians in 61. It was only in the last years of the Artaxiads and in the first century AD that economic decline of their kingdom was marked. The coinage of Tigranes IV was limited to copper. Corbulo devastated the districts hostile to Rome and razed Artaxata.

The Treaty of Rhandeia allowed Armenia a recovery, and a new direction. Artaxata was soon rebuilt, with Roman help, and Armenia moved back into an Iranian orbit.

[62] Strabo, XI, xiv, 15.

5

Arsacid Rule: Tiridates I to Tiridates IV, AD 66–AD 298/9

Roman–Parthian conflict in and over Armenia had been resolved with the agreement that Tiridates, brother of Vologases of Parthia, be crowned king of Armenia by the Roman emperor, Nero. So Tiridates went to Rome, attended by his wife, his sons, the sons of his brothers the kings of Parthia and of Media Atropatene and the sons of Monobazus of Adiabene, servants, 3,000 Parthian horsemen and numerous Romans. His journey, overland, took nine months, costing the public treasury 800,000 sestertii daily. At a gladiatorial exhibition at Puteoli, Tiridates distinguished himself as a good shot, and he ingratiated himself in Rome.

Tiridates' coronation marked him as a client king. The form of address which he used to Nero may derive from ceremonies where the king of Parthia received the allegiance of sub-kings. His assertion that Nero was his 'fortune'[1] must have been a flattering equation of the Roman emperor with the royal 'fortune' which in Iranian society was associated with legitimate kings. And although the grandeur which Rome accorded Tiridates was exceptional, in other respects he was being treated just like other clients. By this date it was normal for kings to apply for recognition before accession, instead of afterwards, and for the emperors to be in charge of the associated ceremonies.

On the other hand, it could be held that Nero had *de facto* ceded Armenia to Parthia. At least some contemporary observers felt this. According to one source,[2] when Terentius Maximus, an Asiatic pretending to be Nero, claimed asylum in Parthia in AD 79, it was as recompense for the restitution of Armenia. The Arsacid monarchs of Parthia, and the

---

[1] Cassius Dio, *Roman History*, LXIII, 5, 3.
[2] John of Antioch, fragment 104, cited in editorial note to Cassius Dio, *Roman History*, LXVI 19. 3b.

Sasanians who replaced them in 224, seem to have regarded Armenia as the proper domain of their very closest kin.

The beginning of the reign of Tiridates I is well reported, but the next two and a half centuries of Arsacid rule in Armenia are not. Our sources comprise snippets of information provided by classical writers, Roman coins and inscriptions, third-century Sasanian inscriptions and the tangle of Armenian historical tradition. The history of the kings can be pieced together only partially, and there are disagreements concerning the dates and identities of some of them. What is most clear is that both Rome and Parthia were jealous of their rights, and conscious of Armenia's strategic importance, and that Armenia was affected by Rome's generally expansionist policy. Wars between the two empires, usually begun by Rome, involved Armenia, and Armenia sometimes provided the cause, nominal or otherwise. Nevertheless, for over 150 years, conditions were generally peaceful. There was more turbulence after 224. The Armenian Arsacids wanted vengeance on the Sasanians, and Sasanian ambition to restore the empire of the Achaemenids led to wars with Rome.

Reconstructions

The accession of Tiridates I brought relief from external aggression to his own kingdom, Greater Armenia, but it imperilled those of Lesser Armenia and Commagene. To allow their independence, now that Greater Armenia was under Parthian control, may have seemed to Rome to mean leaving the Euphrates frontier vulnerable. The emperor Vespasian (AD 69–79) annexed them both, probably in AD 71 and 72. The circumstances surrounding the removal of Aristobulus from Lesser Armenia are unknown, but he appears in AD 72 as king of Chalcis, helping in the annexation of Commagene. Her king, Antiochus IV, had been accused by the governor of Syria, Paetus, of contemplating revolt and being in league with Parthia. But this seems to have been just a pretext. Like Sohaemus of Emesa and Sophene, Antiochus had supported Vespasian in his campaign for the imperial throne and in the suppression of the Jewish revolt (AD 66–74), when auxiliaries from Commagene had assisted Vespasian's son Titus in the siege of Jerusalem (AD 70). And despite their flight, to Cilicia and Parthia respectively, Antiochus and his two sons were allowed to live in Rome with every mark of honour. Antiochus' grandson Philopappus was even elected to the senate, with praetorian rank, and became consul in AD 109. Vespasian most probably wanted Commagene for her wealth as well as for her strategic position.

Greater Armenia was by contrast unmolested for nearly fifty years. The exception was an invasion of Alans, a fierce and militarily accomplished nomad people, in 72, in which Tiridates I narrowly escaped capture, and,

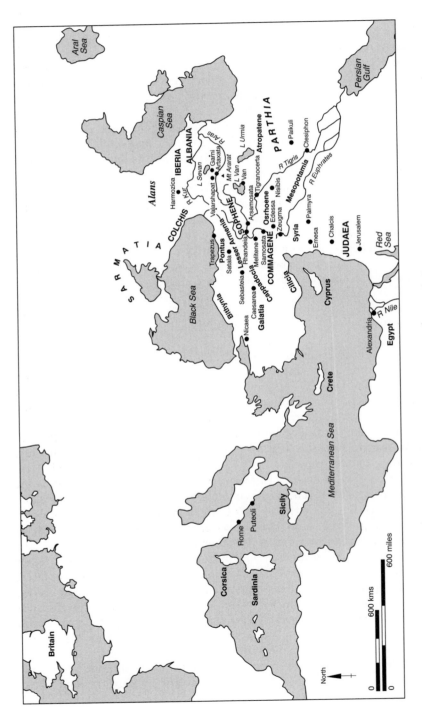

Map 5.1 Europe and west Asia

like his brother Pacorus in Media, lost people and booty. At the end of the century Armenia was ruled by King Sanatruk. According to his near contemporary Arrian (*c.*85 – sometime after AD 145), Roman governor of Cappadocia in the 130s, Sanatruk was good at war, a strict guardian of justice, and, being 'modest' 'in his way of life', equal to the best Greeks and Romans.[3]

Tranquillity was interrupted by the Roman emperor Trajan's (98–117) policy of expansion. Trajan found in Armenia an excuse to launch war against Parthia. By AD 110 the Armenian throne had passed to Axidares, son of the king of Parthia, Pacorus. Axidares' replacement, by his brother Parthamasiris, as a consequence of a coup d'état in Parthia, breached the agreement of Rhandeia. The excuse Parthia gave was that Axidares had been unsatisfactory to Rome as well as Parthia. Trajan nevertheless insisted on war. He invaded Sophene in 114, captured Arsamosata, visited Melitene and Lesser Armenia, cemented good relations with the kings of Sarmatia (north of the Black Sea), Iberia, and Colchis and of the Heniochi (south-west of Colchis), invested a king for Albania and received gifts, including a horse that had been trained to do obeisance,[4] from satraps and kings who came to greet him. Finally he met, but refused to crown, Parthamasiris. Parthamasiris was killed by the leader of his Roman escort as he left the camp, probably at Trajan's order, and those kings who initially refused obedience to Trajan were subdued, without battle. These stirring events had an impact on Armenian historical tradition. Confusion between Axidares and Artaxias I explains Moses of Khoren's making Artaxias a contemporary of Trajan, and some elements in his account of their relationship.[5]

Trajan incorporated Greater Armenia into a huge province with Cappadocia and Lesser Armenia. He also acquired Gordyene, from its king Manisarus, and Adiabene, on his way to the capture of Ctesiphon in Iran. But the new arrangements did not last. In 116 there was rebellion in the conquered territories. In Armenia it was led by Vologases, son of Sanatruk, and Rome was defeated by Armenian and Parthian forces. Soon after, Vologases was recognized by the emperor Hadrian (AD 117–138) as king. It may have been then that Armenia regained Sophene.

The calm that followed was only disturbed in 136, this time by another Alan invasion, in which Albania, Media and Cappadocia also suffered. The complicity of Armenia's old enemy Iberia in the invasion caused Rome to receive a complaint from Vologases. Scholars disagree over whether this was Vologases of Armenia or Vologases II of Parthia or indeed whether the two were one and the same. The Alans were

---

[3] Arrian, *Parthica*, fragment 77.
[4] Cassius Dio, *Roman History*, LXVIII, 18, 2.
[5] In one of his two accounts, Moses, II, 54, 55; trans. Thomson 1978, pp. 197–8 and his p. 197 n. 2.

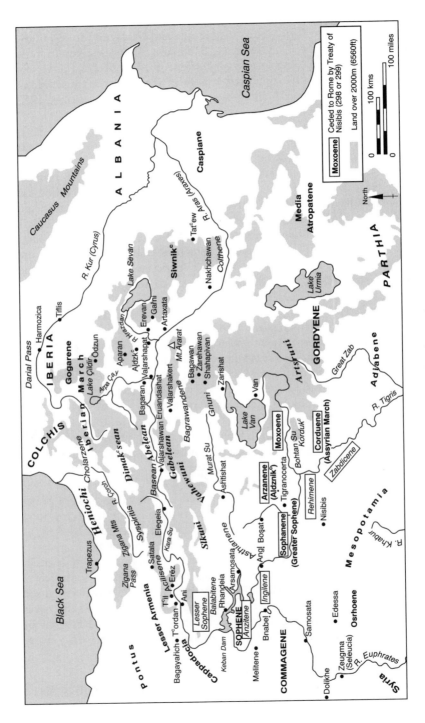

Map 5.2 Armenia

persuaded to depart by gifts from Vologases and by their own dread of Arrian. Like Trajan's activities, these events contributed elements to the stories subsequently recorded about Artaxias I. In Moses of Khoren's muddle, the Alans, in alliance with Iberia, attacked Armenia but Artaxias subsequently married the Alan king's daughter, helped her brother to gain the Alan throne, and elevated some of her relatives.[6]

The next major war was in the 160s. Between AD 140 and 144 the emperor Antoninus (AD 138–61) had invested an Armenian king. This may have been either the Pacorus attested for the 160s or Sohaemus of Emesa, a descendant of the Achaemenids and Arsacids, and a Roman senator and consul. Pacorus may instead have been installed by the Parthians when, after Antoninus' death, they invaded Armenia and Syria. But Parthia's victories were short-lived. Priscus, previously governor of Roman Britain, took Artaxata in 163. Valarshapat, now renamed Caenepolis, 'New City', was garrisoned, and Pacorus exiled to Rome. Sohaemus was king (again?) by 164. He had one further crisis to surmount. In the 170s a 'satrap', Tiridates, deposed him, killed Rome's client the king of the Heniochi, and responded to the concern of the governor of Cappadocia with threats. This behaviour naturally provoked a Roman response. Tiridates was exiled to Britain, Valarshapat captured, and declared to be the capital, in 172, and Sohaemus was restored. We may infer from Moses of Khoren that Sohaemus was succeeded by Vologases II, an Arsacid, in 180.[7] This Vologases may have been the Vologases who became King of Kings in Parthia in 191, in which case he was succeeded in Armenia in 191 by his son Khosrov.

We know only a little of Armenian politics in the three decades that followed the reign of Sohaemus. There was aggression against Iberia. The Armenian king became involved in a rebellion against Amazaspus II (AD 185–9), and his son, who was Amazaspus' nephew, subsequently overthrew and replaced Amazaspus as Rev I (189–216). Armenian policy towards Rome was more conciliatory. In 191 the king stayed neutral in the struggle for the imperial throne between Niger and the ultimately victorious Septimius Severus (AD 193–211). In 197, the king, whose name is again unrecorded, diplomatically deflected a threat of Septimius to invade Armenia, sending him money and gifts and hostages.

This tranquillity was interrupted in the second decade of the next century. In 214 the king, perhaps the same one as in 197, was persuaded by the emperor Caracalla (AD 211–17) to visit Rome. Caracalla then held him prisoner, and rebellion ensued. The king's son Tiridates won a victory in 215. Caracalla also began a war with Parthia, finding an excuse in the Parthian refusal of a marriage alliance and attacking Adiabene. But

---

[6] Moses, II, 50–52, 58, trans. Thomson, 1978, pp. 191–5, 200.
[7] Ibid., 64, trans. Thomson, 1978, pp. 208–10.

Caracalla was assassinated in 217 and Tiridates profited from the Roman–Parthian treaty of 218. Tiridates (II) accepted his crown from the emperor Macrinus (AD 217–18), his mother was freed, and Rome restored booty taken from Armenians. There was also some sort of promise that the annual Roman subsidies, discontinued in the time of Tiridates' father, would be resumed and his father's lands, perhaps private royal estates, in Cappadocia returned.

A much longer period of war was inaugurated in 224 with the deposition of Artabanus IV, last Arsacid king of Parthia, by Ardashir, the first of the Sasanians of Persia. Tiridates, confused in Armenian tradition with his son Khosrov,[8] was nephew to the victim, and obliged to exact vengeance. In 227/8 he organized resistance, with the Medes and the sons of Artabanus, and this seems to have checked Ardashir for a while. In 232 he helped Rome respond to Sasanian aggression in Syria and Cappadocia. One wing of Rome's army was to travel through Armenia to attack Media. It had some success, but difficulties elsewhere caused an overall retreat, leaving large numbers to perish in the Armenian winter.

Despite these efforts however, by 253 Armenia was lost. Sasanian aggression in Mesopotamia, beginning in 238, had indeed produced another Roman response, in 242. But the death in battle of the emperor Gordian (AD 238–44), defeated by Shapur I (242–72), had proved disastrous. Rome seems to have abandoned Tiridates, perhaps by making a kind of non-intervention pact. Shapur proceeded to conquer Armenia in 252–3, claiming some Roman provocation, the nature of which is unknown, and he made his own son, Hormizd-Ardashir, Great King there. Tiridates' sons accepted this, but Tiridates himself fled to the Roman empire. He had little prospect of help, since Persia continued to be successful in her wars. Shapur even captured the emperor Valerian (AD 253–60) in 260, though, thanks to the prince of Palmyra, he was checked soon after, and lost his conquests in Mesopotamia, Syria, Cilicia and Cappadocia. He nevertheless conquered Iberia and Albania, and he added Siwnik᷂c to his empire, though Siwnik᷂c retained a status different from that of the rest of Armenia. After Shapur was succeeded by Hormizd, in 272, Armenia passed, at some time before 293, to Hormizd's brother, Narses.

The events and personalities of the last quarter of the third century have provoked a range of opinion and sharp disagreements. The most convincing reconstruction is as follows.[9] In 279/80 Narses ceded western Armenia to the Roman emperor Probus (276–82), who then enthroned Khosrov (279/80–87), presumably the son of Tiridates II. Khosrov was murdered, and replaced, in 287 by his own brother, Tiridates III (287–

---

[8] Toumanoff, 1969, clarifies the third-century Arsacids.
[9] Ibid.

98). Khosrov's son, the future Tiridates IV (298/9–330), fled to Caesarea in Cappadocia and pursued a career in the Roman army. Tiridates III meanwhile acquired the rest of Armenia after Narses made himself King of Kings (of the Persian Empire) in 293. Narses was subsequently defeated by Caesar (deputy emperor) Galerius in 298. The emperor Diocletian (284–305) then concluded the Treaty of Nisibis (298 or 299) with Persia. This treaty established Tiridates IV as king.

The Treaty of Nisibis both restored and extended Rome's influence in her eastern frontier regions. This was done mostly at Sasanian expense, but partly at the expense of Armenia. Nisibis was to be the sole place of commercial exchange. This provision was economically more advantageous to Rome than it was to Persia and may also have been intended to curb Persian espionage. The travelling and multi-lingualism of merchants fitted them for spying, and it seems from a Roman edict of 408/9 that they had something of a reputation for it. Iberia reverted to alliance with Rome, whence her kings were to receive their insignia. The Armenian frontier was extended eastwards up to an otherwise unknown Zintha in Media.

This gain may have been some compensation for the substantial losses which Armenia suffered. Unfortunately for us, the treaty survives only in a summary by the sixth-century Byzantine writer Peter the Patrician. Its territorial arrangements have been much debated, often with reference to the later Roman–Persian treaty of 363 which in some respects reversed them. It seems that in 298/299 Rome took nine southern regions (running, roughly, between the Kara Su and the Great Zab – see map 5.2): Ingilene and Sophene (both formerly parts of the former kingdom of Sophene) and Arzanene (the Arabian march), Corduene (the Assyrian march), and Zabdicene, all listed by Peter, plus Moxoene and Rehimene[10] (both lost to Persia in 363), Sophanene and Anzitene (like Sophanene attested in an imperial rescript as belonging to Rome in 536). These regions comprised at least 17,374 square miles,[11] about one-sixth of the kingdom. Peter's statement that the Tigris was to be the Roman–Persian frontier, obviously irreconcilable with these dispositions,[12] may either refer to regions further south, or reflect the *de facto* situation after 299.

---

[10] Rehimene is not mentioned by Peter, but appears in the 363 treaty. Its location is uncertain. Hewsen, 1988–9, suggests the district of Nisibis, Sinclair (private communication) the area immediately south of Amida and west of the Tigris. See also Hewsen, 1992, map I for a different location and p. 344 for discussion of possibilities. Adontz viewed Rehimene as part of Zabdicene, (Adontz–Garsoïan, 1970, p. 36), Dilleman, 1962, p. 210 as part of Corduene, Toumanoff, 1963, pp. 166, 182, part of Zabdicene or Arzanene.

[11] Hewsen, 1985–6, suggests some 17, 942 square miles. For figures and map, Hewsen, 1992, Appendix IV (Eremyan's estimates of districts' sizes) and commentary, and map I (where there seems to be a mistake in the scale).

[12] One solution is that the eastern Tigris, the Bohtan Su was meant. Another is that the clause applied to the area south of the ceded territories. Blockley, 1984, p. 23. Résumé and suggestions regarding 298 and 363 borders, Sinclair, 1989b, pp. 365–7 and refs.

To what extent the ceded principalities were actually supposed to be answerable to the Armenian king as well as to the Roman emperor is not clear.[13] They did keep in touch. The princes of Ingilene, Arzanene, Corduene, Sophene, Moxoene and Zabdicene attended a council of Tiridates IV and the consecration, as bishop, of his evangelizer, Gregory the Illuminator, in Caesarea in Cappadocia in 314.

Government and Society: Continuity or Change?

Just as the succession of kings between Tiridates I and Tiridates IV is difficult to discern, so too are their internal policies and achievements. What is clear is that they seldom had a free hand. Rome supplemented diplomatic encirclement, created by alliances with various client kings, with direct supervision. Sometimes there was actually a military presence though we have only snippets of information about this. In AD 64–5 (between the Treaty of Rhandeia and Tiridates I's coronation) the legion *III Gallica* is recorded as engaged in building, probably a fort, near Kharput. *VI Ferrata* probably wintered in Armenia around the same time. After Trajan's annexation *IV Scythica*, probably the garrison of Zeugma in Commagene, is recorded as involved in unspecified building work at Artaxata in 116. Caenepolis was garrisoned in 163, though the men were on the verge of mutiny in 172. By 175 there were detachments in Caenepolis from *XII Fulminata* and *XV Apollinaris*. The latter was still there in 185.

The Roman presence was probably minimal but there were always troops stationed just inside the Roman frontier and within striking distance of, and therefore able to interfere in, Armenia. *XII Fulminata* came to Melitene in the early seventies, and remained there until at least the end of the fourth century. *XVI Flavia Firma* was in annexed Lesser Armenia, at Satala, only about 25 miles north-east of Erzincan, in the kingdom, by 76. Its later replacement, *XV Apollinaris*, remained there until the early fifth century. Satala and Melitene not only commanded the two main routes into and out of Armenia but could if necessary maintain vexillations (detachments, probably of about 1,000 men in this case) up to 620 miles east of the Euphrates. The frontier was punctuated with auxiliary forts about a day's march apart. A major road linked them to the Black Sea and to Syria. In the north, Trapezus, headquarters of the Pontic fleet, controlled access to Armenia via the Zigana Pass, and a series of coastal forts stretching nearly 200 miles east helped maintain the Roman allegiance of local tribes. When Vespasian assisted the king of Iberia to guard the Darial Pass, by building a wall at Harmozica, he may

---

[13] Sinclair, 1989(b), p. 368 for résumé.

have left troops there. In the south, the Roman annexations, in 195, 198 or 199 and 212/213, of part of Osrhoene, Mesopotamia, and then the rest of Osrhoene, gave Rome command of the southern approaches.

It cannot have been only when relations were hostile that the Roman army interacted with Armenians. The civilian population of the empire normally had to support preparations for war, for example, providing supplies, and paying for their transport. In peace-time the army was normally involved in keeping order, including tax collecting. It could, as in Judaea, couple intensive interference with brutality.

The Arsacid kings had to work with this Roman background. Their degree of internal control, their methods and the changes they brought about are more easily identifiable in general than in particular terms. We need not believe that they made any fundamental changes to the structure of society, despite the explicit assertion to the contrary made by Moses of Khoren. In a detailed account Moses claimed that the first Arsacid king, whom he calls by the Armenian form of 'Vologases', instituted principalities, and established their dynasts, giving, to most of them, particular offices, and that he set up protocol, secretaries and judges at court, and judges in the towns.[14] But this account cannot be accepted at face value. For one thing, Moses had confused the Arsacids with the Artaxiads, and treats the Artaxiads as successors of 'Vologases'. Adontz indeed saw the Arsacid period as one of change, believing that other innovations which Moses ascribed to Artaxiad figures should actually be credited to the Arsacids. But in Toumanoff's view, Armenian socio-political structure was essentially the same under the Arsacids as it had been under the Artaxiads.[15] Toumanoff has demonstrated both the ancient origin of a number of the fifty princely houses (belonging to twenty-nine dynasties, including the Arsacids), which existed in the Arsacid period, and some anachronisms in Moses' account. Of Moses' 'Arsacid appointees' the Bagratunis and Artsrunis for example were Orontids, and the Dziwna-kan, Hawenunis and Spandunis, although of Arsacid origin, are not otherwise attested for the Arsacid period.[16] Most of the dynasties of this period were probably descended from the earlier potentates of the region, including those of the districts which had once been the separate kingdoms within Greater Armenia to which Pliny had alluded.

The evidence which best illuminates the relationship between crown and princes between 66 and 299 is contained in the fifth-century Armenian accounts of the conversion of Tiridates IV to Christianity, and of other events of the fourth century.[17] Modern evaluation is heavily indebted to

[14] Moses, II, 3, 7, 8, trans. Thomson, 1978, pp. 132, 136–45.
[15] Adontz – Garsoïan, 1970, pp. 331–43, 368–71; Toumanoff, 1963, pp. 108–11.
[16] Toumanoff, 1963, pp. 154–227 for houses (including *vitaxae* pp. 154–92) in the Arsacid period.
[17] Agathangelos, *History of the Armenians*, text and trans. Thomson, 1976; *Epic Histories*, trans. Garsoïan, 1989.

the work and interpretations of Adontz and Toumanoff, which must therefore be briefly summarized, even though, as we shall see in chapter 10, the utility of the labels 'feudalism' and 'feudal system' is now very questionable. Adontz argued that Arsacid Armenia resembled France, 'in the period of the flowering of feudal institutions', meaning the twelfth and thirteenth centuries AD.[18] Toumanoff however saw the Armenian aristocracy as representing a symbiosis of full feudalism and full dynasticism, meaning by dynasticism a system in which dynasts ruled fully sovereign states, and thereby adding to Adontz's 'feudalism' a greater emphasis on the antiquity of Armenia's aristocratic families and on their original rights.[19] The 'feudal' aspect arose, Toumanoff argued, from the attempt of the crown, whether Artaxiad or Arsacid, to involve the dynasts in serving the monarchy, and so to imply that their (ancient) dynastic sovereignty had actually been delegated by the crown. This attempt is reflected in Moses' assertion that the majority of the princely houses were 'raised' by kings, whereas in fact most of them are demonstrably of (ancient) dynastic origin. This involvement of dynasts, presumably meant to buttress the monarchy, could however equally well serve to weaken it, and to limit the opportunity to create a strong but dependent, and hence dependable, elite. Since, according to Toumanoff, every 'dynastic', independent principality was simultaneously a 'feudal', delegated dukedom, the two kinds of power reinforced, and became confused with, each other.[20]

Such distinctions are largely theoretical, and in practice were often neither perceived nor maintained: they are not reflected in the usage of Armenian authors. For example, although Toumanoff distinguishes particular Armenian terms as 'dynastic' and 'feudal', regarding *ishkhan* and *nakharar* for instance as 'prince' and 'duke', Armenian authors, as he emphasizes, tended to use them indiscriminately.[21] What it comes down to is that the kings had to cope as best they could with a nobility which was hereditary, largely ancient, and entrenched, though open to some degree of manipulation. This openness would inevitably have been greater in the times of Artaxiad expansion. Successful war can keep a nobility occupied and respectful, and newly conquered lands can be used to reward the loyal and so, indirectly, weaken dissidents. Lack of expansion can diminish aristocratic obligation and contribute to noble independence. This is what the Arsacids of Parthia found.

The ranks of aristocratic society comprised the *vitaxae* (the marcher lords), then the princes or dukes, the *sepuhk*^c (aristocrats who were not

---

[18] Adontz–Garsoïan, 1970, pp. 343–61, citing Luchaire, 1892, for France.
[19] Toumanoff, 1963, pp. 34–144, esp. for dynasticism, pp. 112–14, their combination, pp. 34–40, 112, 115–19.
[20] Ibid., pp. 115, 79–80, 110–11, 115–16.
[21] Ibid., pp. 114, 115, 116–17.

heads of houses), and then the *azat*s (literally 'the free'). *Azat*s were not dynasts, but they served in the cavalry, paid dues to the princes and may, Toumanoff suggests, have evolved from the heads of small clans or from dynastic warbands of much earlier times.[22] Toumanoff believes there may have been some subinfeudation – that is, the granting, by a person enfeoffed by the crown, of part of his fief or a territory to another person.[23] Below the nobility were the rest of the population, including peasants who were personally free though attached to the soil and who owed military and labour service and dues to their superiors.

In their turn the princes had to provide the crown with cavalry. The Armenian *Military List*, composed sometime between the reign of Khosrov (Chosroes) I of Persia (531–79) and 750, using official records and historical texts, purports to record the contingents of eighty-six families, though some of the names are simply formed on toponyms. The *List* states that the total owed was 84,000, and that this, combined with those who served the royal court, gave the crown 120,000 cavalry. The average size of the contingents in the *List* is about 1,000. The individual numbers range from fifty to 19,400.[24]

The princes also owed castle-guard and monetary contributions, and advice, though the *Epic Histories* record that the royal council included non-nobles and peasants as well.[25] They may have sworn an oath of fealty. It has been suggested that an oath sworn by the *sparapet* (commander-in-chief) to king Pap (*c*.368–74), who had doubted his loyalty, 'I shall live and die for thee like my ancestors for thy ancestors', was a renewal of one first sworn at his investiture.[26] Grants were of course recorded. A Greek inscription recording a grant was found at Aparan in 1908, and Moses of Khoren refers to Tiridates IV making a grant with perpetual jurisdiction by written edict.[27]

The authority of the Arsacid kings was buttressed by traditional, Iranian, concepts regarding kingship. One was the concept of the protective royal 'fortune' and 'glory', to which Tiridates I alluded in Rome, and which is clearly attested for the fourth century. The protection it afforded was perhaps weakened by the belief that it would not attend an illegitimate or evil king. Several anecdotes in the *Epic Histories* reveal the belief that the person of the king was inviolable, at least by his inferiors. This might be related to the view of the Parthians and Sasanians that their kings were divine, if indeed such a belief really did exist. Some scholars

[22] Ibid., pp. 124–7, 35–8.
[23] Ibid., p. 126.
[24] Ibid., pp. 135–6, 229–41, the *List* appears in table V, pp. 239–41.
[25] *Epic Histories*, III, xxi, IV, li, trans. Garsoïan, 1989, pp. 97–8, 168 and, for comment, her p. 572.
[26] *Epic Histories*, V, iv, trans. Garsoïan, 1989, pp. 190–1; Widengren, 1956, p. 92.
[27] Moses, II, 84, trans. Thomson, 1978, pp. 235–6. See below n. 30 for Aparan.

regard the evidence that it did as representing convention, rhetoric and confusion rather than actuality.[28]

The power of the kings over the aristocracy was nevertheless limited by the tendency of offices to become hereditary. By the fourth century the privilege of crowning the king was regarded as belonging to the Bagratuni family, the office of *sparapet* to the Mamikoneans, and that of *hazarapet*, entailing supervision of the peasantry, belonged to the house of Anzitene, though in the middle of the century the king gave it to the Gnunis.

Furthermore, the lack of evidence for royal interference in the principalities may imply that they were autonomous. But royal judicial rights did include rights to punish, to confiscate territory and to oversee succession. Succession was agnatic (though it could pass through women), patrilineal, and, basically, one of primogeniture. Princely property essentially belonged to the family as a whole, the 'prince' acting as administrator. The system is reflected in a tale in the *Epic Histories* about the punishment of a treacherous *vitaxa*. The king brought about the deaths of the *vitaxa* and of his brothers and sons, married off the *vitaxa*'s daughter, and made her husband *vitaxa* and successor of the house, because there was no-one else left in the family. But later a son, who had secretly survived, returned and took possession.[29]

This background to royal government, a background of Roman supervision, socio-political continuity and aristocratic power, is relatively easy to establish. The details of particular royal deeds are more elusive. The Aparan inscription seems to record the gift of the district (Nig) as an hereditary estate, by Tiridates I to a son of the former king Radamistus.[30] Some legislative activity might conceivably lie behind Arrian's reference to Sanatruk as guardian of justice. It has been suggested that the Amatunis, recorded by Moses as immigrants who were endowed by Artaxias I, were the refugee royal family of Adiabene, deposed after they fled from Trajan, and, presumably, welcomed by Vologases I.[31] The picture Moses paints of the first Arsacid king, 'Vologases',[32] may incorporate some genuine historical material whether about Tiridates I, Vologases I or even Vologases II. For it was Vologases II who established a permanent branch of the Arsacids on the Armenian throne. A few new families emerged under Arsacid rule. The Kamsarakans and the princes of Asthianene were of Arsacid origin. The Rop'seans were related either to the

---

[28] Widengren, 1959; Frye, 1972.

[29] *Epic Histories*, III, ix, trans. Garsoïan, 1989, pp. 76–7.

[30] Chaumont, 1976, pp. 185–8 challenges its interpretation as a grant by Tiridates II to a Gnt'uni prince, advanced by Trever and followed by Toumanoff (1963, pp. 204–5) and Hewsen, 1992, pp. 293, 311.

[31] Neusner, 1966; Moses, II, 57, trans. Thomson, 1978, pp. 199–200.

[32] Moses, II, 3–8, trans. Thomson, 1978, pp. 132–45.

Arsacids or to the dynasty of Emesa. The Aṙaweḷeans and Dimakⁱseans, both perhaps of royal Alan origin, the Bagratunis of Colthene and the dynasty of Moxoene seem to have risen to eminence under the Arsacids.[33]

Some details of enlargement of Armenian territory in the Arsacid period are discernible.[34] Gogarene and Cholarzene were regained from Iberia sometime before AD 148, for the geographer Ptolemy, who seems to have written between AD 127 and 148, regarded them both as Armenian lands. It was perhaps in the late 180s that Cholarzene was incorporated into the Iberian march (by Vologases II) when its duke joined in the rebellion against Amazaspus II. The kingdom of Gordyene was, probably, given to Sohaemus by the Romans. The extent of this former kingdom is disputed, but Hewsen suggests that it was larger than the later Kordukⁱ and that Sohaemus divided it, taking eastern Gordyene as royal land for the cadets of his royal house, and leaving the western portion to the Gordyenean royal line subsequently the princes of Kordukⁱ.[35] It may have been then that the Assyrian march was created.[36] Caspiane reverted from Media to Armenia, to be incorporated in the royal domain and administered directly by the crown. This occurred under either Vologases I or Vologases II, for Moses records that 'Vologases' established military governors in this area.[37]

It is difficult to gauge the extent and seriousness of internal disunity or opposition to the kings. Such indications as there are mainly connected with possession of the crown and quarrels within the royal family. If, as one doubtful piece of evidence suggests,[38] the late first-century king Sanatruk took part in the rebellion against Trajan in 116 which preceded Armenia's resumption of independence, then he may have been deposed, since the rebellion postdates his reign. The 'Roman' Sohaemus was deposed at least once. It may have been internal tensions which caused him, apparently, to prefer to site his tomb at Garni rather than Ani (Kemah) where Sanatruk had built a tomb, and which was to become the Arsacid necropolis. Sohaemus' preference is suggested by the Graeco-Roman Ionic building which was built at Garni in the second half of the first century AD. There is no direct evidence for its normal interpretation as a temple of Mithras, and Wilkinson has shown that it is more likely to

[33] Toumanoff, 1963, pp. 206, 172, 213, 199, 204, 203–4, 181–2.
[34] From studies of Armenian historical geography by Toumanoff, (1963, pp. 435–99, The Armeno-Georgian marchlands, chronology, pp. 498–9) and by Hewsen, (1973, 1988–9, 1990–1).
[35] Hewsen, 1988–9, summarized in Hewsen, 1992, pp. 170–1.
[36] Hewsen, 1988–9, pp. 276–95.
[37] Hewsen, 1973, suggests Vologases II; Hewsen, 1985, p. 72 (taking a different view of the ambiguous evidence of Ptolemy) the Roman annexation, 114–17, before Roman recognition of Vologases I. Hewsen, 1992, pp. 253–8 suggests Vologases I (presumably a misprint for II) (180–91) or 298 (the Treaty of Nisibis) (p. 255).
[38] The account given by the sixth-century John Malalas, considered by Chaumont, 1976, p. 141.

have been a tomb, built in about AD 175, for a Romanized ruler. The most likely candidate would seem to be Sohaemus.[39]

(Royal) family disagreements are increasingly noticeable in the third century. When Caracalla, in 214, lured the Armenian king into captivity it was by promising to make peace between the king and his sons. Why any mediation was necessary is unknown. Tiridates II was deserted by his sons after the Sasanians had conquered Armenia. Many of the aristocracy will have followed, and perhaps even anticipated, their example, encouraged by the new regime. Moses of Khoren's account of King 'Artashir'[40] (Armenian for Ardashir) probably applies to Shapur I. It suggests that after quashing resistance, Shapur became conciliatory, recalling princes who had fled, restoring to the Arsacids their hereditary domains, and generally, as Moses said, 'organized Armenia in a splendid fashion and re-established its former order'. Support for the Sasanians must have been nurtured at the courts of the Sasanian kings of Armenia, Hormizd and Narses. The murder of the Armenian king Khosrov in 287 seems to have been the work of a pro-Sasanian party to which Khosrov's own brother belonged.

Royal Resources

As supporters of the crown, the aristocracy were not, then, wholly reliable. But kings could also look to their own household, territory (about two-sevenths of the kingdom) and income. There is some evidence to suggest that the royal household, wardrobe, fortresses, and treasures therein were supervised by a eunuch grand chamberlain. The royal fortresses were not confined to the royal domain, Ayrarat. There were strongholds, like Angl and Bnabel (both in ancient Sophene), within princely territory. Their treasures came from various sources. There might be gifts and subsidies from Rome, as Tiridates I and Tiridates II found. There was booty. Agathangelos (Agatᶜangelos) records that 'Khosrov' took a fifth of the enormous booty collected after victory over the Persians, and made gifts to the (pagan) priests and soldiers.[41] It may be that one-fifth was the normal royal share. There were taxes. Taxes might be paid in kind, as later ecclesiastical sources suggest. The tax which, in the fifth century, after the abolition of their kingship (in 428), the Armenians paid to Persia was perhaps the same tax they had once paid their own kings.

A fifth source of royal income must have been the cities and the trade which passed through them. A memory of royal sponsorship of urban

---

[39] Wilkinson, 1982.
[40] Moses, II, 76, 77, trans. Thomson, 1978, pp. 223–5.
[41] Agathangelos, 22, text and trans. Thomson, 1976, pp. 40, 41.

growth is embodied in Moses of Khoren's report that the first Arsacid king ordered Van to be restored, numerous other cities built, and urban residents respected by peasants.[42] Tiridates I restored Artaxata as Neroneia. It may have been Tiridates who was responsible for the repairs of the first and second century to the fortifications of Gaṙni. Sanatruk, according to the *Epic Histories*, founded the city of Mtsurn,[43] whose exact location is unknown. Nakhchawan was known to Ptolemy and may date from the Arsacid period. Caenepolis, the later Ējmiatsin, was probably founded by Vologases I, for its original name was Vaḷarshapat ('founded by Vaḷarsh', i.e. Vologases). In 364 when Persians sacked it, there were, apparently, 19,000 families there.[44] Vaḷarshawan, in Basean, and Vaḷarshakert, in Bagrewand, have also been ascribed to Vologases I. Gaṙni was embellished not only with Sohaemus' tomb but also with a palace, with a columned hall, similar to Parthian palaces, and Roman baths. The mosaic pavement in their vestibule, which shows Greek mythological figures and has Greek inscriptions, is normally ascribed to the second half of the third century, but both it and the palace may belong, as Wilkinson suggests, to the first half of the fourth.[45] Tigranocerta, although mentioned only in geographical texts, must have retained an urban character: in 364 the Persians, according to the *Epic Histories*, deported 40,000 families from it.[46]

These cities must have benefited from the economic development of Armenia's neighbours. In the Roman Empire, Trajan tried to improve communications and develop urban centres. Melitene received the title of Metropolis and the status of city. After the annexation of Commagene, Samosata expanded, perhaps beyond the walls. The Severan emperors did not found new towns, but they did try to establish market-centres to promote trade. In Iran, urban life was encouraged more by the Sasanians than by their Arsacid predecessors who had concentrated rather on controlling the old towns, in most of which Hellenistic-style organization and some autonomy survived. Shapur I used deportees to found new cities and reinvigorate old ones, making his prisoners build, decorate and work. Many of his captives were skilled textile workers. The fruits of their labours both gratified their new masters and provided items of trade. By the sixth century such persons as merchants, tradesmen and artisans were reckoned to comprise a fourth 'estate' in society, beside the traditional three. Armenian prosperity may admittedly have been dis-

---

[42] Moses, II, 8, trans. Thomson, 1978, p. 144.
[43] *Epic Histories*, IV, xiv, trans. Garsoïan, 1989, p. 140 and for comment her pp. 479–80.
[44] Ibid., lv, trans. Garsoïan, 1989, p. 175 and for comment her pp. 304 (n. 15) and 498–9.
[45] R. D. Wilkinson, 'Armenia in Hellenistic and Roman Times' (MA Diss., Cambridge Univ. 1972) p. 200 (baths), p. 204 (residence), pp. 193–4 (fortress repairs) cited by Hewsen, 1985–6.
[46] *Epic Histories*, IV, xxiv, trans. Garsoïan, 1989, p. 157.

rupted in the third century by Sasanian aggression and by the so-called 'third century crisis' in the Roman Empire, if indeed there was one.

Armenian profits derived from transit trade in oriental luxury goods and some export of raw materials. In his *Natural History*, Pliny refers to laserwort, a medicinal plant; emery whetstones; a mineral, probably malachite (basic copper carbonate), which after being dried, pounded, sieved and dyed was used by painters; another mineral (azurite) named after Armenia, whose price had recently dropped dramatically due to the discovery of alternative material in Spain and which produced a dark blue pigment; and alum, used amongst other things for dye, medicine, deodorant and earwash.[47]

Artaxata was a major commercial centre. In one of its buildings about 2,000 clay seals, from packs or jars of merchandise, have been found, dating from the first and second centuries. Trade routes linked Artaxata to the Black Sea coast, Colchis, Media Atropatene, Nisibis in Syria, Satala in Lesser Armenia, and Tigranocerta and other places in Greater Armenia. Six itineraries have been reconstructed and Ptolemy's version of Armenian geography seems to have been based, in part, on at least one road map of Armenia, or a list of towns with distances between them.[48] A reference in one of Juvenal's satires, written in the first half of the second century, has often been quoted to suggest that the wealth of Artaxata was so great as to make it a place of luxurious and loose living. In fact, Juvenal's particular and limited use of the east in his work means that his remarks cannot be treated as accurate observations.[49]

It is unfortunate for us that the Armenian kings did not mint their own coins. If they were forbidden to it must have been by Parthia: Rome allowed client kings to mint. Armenia consequently depended on her neighbours for currency. Coin hoards suggest that, before the advent of the Sasanians, the circulation of coins from the east was limited, but that thereafter it was Sasanian silver coinage which was used for trade. In the absence of native coins, little can be said about native art. The few pieces of sculpture which have been found are not particularly accomplished. If Wilkinson's datings are correct, the strongly Graeco-Roman tomb at Garni is the only artistic monument of pre-Christian Arsacid Armenia to survive.

Culture: Contacts and Comparisons

The tomb at Garni, the economic life and the political history of Armenia testify to some involvement of Armenians in Roman culture and society.

---

[47] Pliny the Elder, *Natural History*, XIX, xv, 40–4; XXXVI, x, 54, xlvii, 164; XXXIII, xxvii, 89; XXXV, xxviii, 47; XXXV, lii, 184–186.
[48] Hewsen, 1982a.
[49] Juvenal, *The Satires* II, 164–170; Braund, S. H., 1989.

But in other respects this involvement was slight. There is no Armenian parallel to the participation in Roman life of the elite of neighbouring Commagene and Pontus-Bithynia. The first Roman senators of oriental origin included descendants of Commagene's king Antiochus I. Rome's equestrian officers were recruited from Pontus-Bithynia as well as from other eastern provinces. But analysis for the period from Augustus to Valerian (AD 253–60) has detected none of Armenian origin.[50]

Armenian involvement in Iranian society and culture on the other hand was extensive. The lifestyle of the Armenian kings and aristocracy was similar to that in Iran. Their similarity does not however necessarily imply that one derived from the other. We must remember that some elements are probably very ancient and are shared with other societies which themselves were not influenced by Iran. A strong oral tradition is one. Moses of Khoren drew on it extensively. There was, clearly, what Russell terms an 'Artaxiad epic'.[51] Epic tradition was transmitted by professional minstrels, who, in the Iranian as in the Germanic worlds, sang not merely to entertain but also to eulogize their patrons. They were members of the royal court, and went to war so that they could encourage and record heroic deeds.

Aristocratic fosterage of aristocratic children is another institution shared, probably, with Iran but also found elsewhere, for example in early Germanic and Irish society. Fosterage of children by inferiors occurred in some Caucasian groups up to the nineteenth century. Fosterage created a special bond between foster-father and foster-son, probably not just of affection but of reciprocal obligations, especially help in time of need. Behind the practice of fosterage must lie anticipation of such need. And fosterage could be used like marriage, to cement friendly relations. It could also safeguard a family's survival. Because property belonged to the family, and because of bloodfeud, well attested in the *Epic Histories*, the only sure way to eliminate an enemy, take over his property and enjoy it in safety, was to exterminate his family. This would be the more difficult if children resided apart from their parents, with foster-parents eager to protect them. The cliché of infants being rescued by their foster-parents, applied to Tiridates IV, appears several times in Armenian tradition.

Armenian elite society shared with the Iranian an essentially non-urban character.[52] In the fourth century AD, the nobility normally lived in forts, while the kings were normally peripatetic. There might be a 'principal camp' but this was not in a city. The 'principal camp' of Arsaces (Armenian Arshak) II (350?–67/8), at Shahapivan, was adjacent to a walled hunting preserve and horse-racing course and furnished with tents or pavilions.[53]

---

[50] Dejiver, 1989.
[51] Russell, 1986–7.
[52] This is demonstrated by Garsoïan, 1987.
[53] Garsoïan, 1988–9. The exact location of Shahapivan is unknown.

There was a palace at Vaḷarshapat, in which Tiridates IV resided, and another at Gaṙni, but there is no evidence for one at Artaxata. Even in death the monarchs shunned cities. Ani was only a fortified stronghold in 364, and Aḷdzkᶜ, whither the royal necropolis then moved, was a village. Very few sites are termed 'city' by early Armenian authors. Of these only Artaxata is attested as the site of one of the seven major pagan shrines. Urban life remained largely the concern of foreigners, mostly Jews. The *Epic Histories* report the numbers of Armenian and Jewish households in Artaxata, Eruandashat, Zarehawan, Zarishat, Van and Nakhchawan in 364.[54] The exact figures, totalling 97,000 and 82,000 may be unreliable, but they suggest a contemporary perception that, except at Artaxata, urban Armenian households were outnumbered by urban Jewish ones, though in varying proportions. At Artaxata the proportions were 4:1, at Nakhchawan 1:8, at Zarishat 5:7. Excepting Artaxata, the proportions were about 1:2 overall, including Artaxata about 11:13.

Culturally, Iran had much more direct influence upon Armenia than had Rome. When Tiridates I and Parthamasiris visited Nero and Trajan, they had Parthians with them, and other Arsacid kings must also have had Parthian attendants. Parthian forces often worked in Armenia, as for example in 162 when Vologases attacked the Romans at Elegeia. They will have depended on Armenians for sustenance since, according to Dio (c.164–after 229), the Parthians did not lay in supplies of food or pay.[55] The Sasanian kings who ruled Armenia must have spent some time there. Narses was there in 293 when he was invited to become King of Kings. At the fourth-century Armenian court the princes had thrones and cushions arranged according to their rank. Rank was closely related to the numbers of cavalry owed, both, presumably, reflecting the realities of power. Royal favour might also affect rank. The *Gahnamak*, (*Throne List* or *Rank List*) composed later, probably in the Arab period, using Armenian historical works, purports to record the order of seventy families in the early fifth century.[56] It asserts that this order was brought from Persia, at the request of the katholikos (katᶜolikos) (head of the Armenian Christian church) Sahak. The same system operated at the Sasanian court.

The extensive contact between Armenians and Iranians and their shared interests have left their mark on the Armenian language. *Aspakani*, meaning hunter, for example, is of Iranian derivation, conceivably from some Iranian term meaning 'leading horses and hounds'.[57] Many words in the Armenian vocabulary for social and political organization and law are related to Iranian ones of the Parthian or near-Parthian

---

[54] *Epic Histories*, IV, lv, trans. Garsoïan, 1989, pp. 175–6, and for comment her pp. 304–5.
[55] Cassius Dio, *Roman History*, XL 15.6.
[56] Toumanoff, 1963, pp. 229–30.
[57] Considine, 1979.

period, as loan words or derivations. Besides *ishkhan* and *nakharar*, there are a number of words related to Armenian terms in the inscription which Narses set up, sometime between 293 and 296, to justify his accession in Persia. There is a strong historiographical tradition, stimulated by the Iranian connections and especially by the vocabulary of Armenian aristocratic society, that this society was essentially the same as that of Parthian Iran. But, as Toumanoff pointed out, to borrow a word does not necessarily imply the borrowing or sharing of the institution it is used for.[58] Furthermore, things may change, while their names remain the same. Some names for Armenian (Christian) ecclesiastical vestments, used in the Armenian Bible and in later medieval texts, for example, are Zoroastrian religious terms. *Patarag*, the word for the rite of offering, which came to be used for the Christian divine liturgy, may be a loan from Parthian (Middle Iranian).[59]

Fortunately, the implications of these objections are, for Armenian society, largely academic, since it is normally, though not always, the Armenian evidence which is used to supplement the paucity of the Parthian evidence rather than vice versa. For example, although the office of Armenian *hazarapet* is attested also for Sasanian but not for Parthian Iran, yet it has been suggested that it was common to all three societies.[60] In Iran it involved military command, in Armenia, according to the evidence, it did not. *Sparapet* is another title of Parthian origin, but there is insufficient evidence to establish the degree to which the Armenian office resembled its Iranian equivalent.

The pioneer in identifying Iranian words in Classical Armenian was Hübschmann. His collection of 686 words, made in 1895, has been added to and the number of words known to be borrowed from Iranian is now considered to be between 800 and 900.[61] Iran influenced everyday as well as specialized vocabulary, supplying, for example, terms for 'answer', 'time', 'death', 'urine' and 'black'. Some royal and aristocratic names, for example Tiridates, Khosrov, Vologases, Vahan and Vasak are Iranian. Iranian influence is apparent in words for 'temple' and in place names incorporating *bag* (god), and Zoroastrian influence in other place and personal names.

Religion: Continuity and Challenge

The linguistic evidence is a useful supplement to the literary evidence for Armenian Zoroastrianism, that is material contained in the account of

[58] Toumanoff, 1963, p. 114 (n. 184).
[59] Russell, 1987, pp. 496 and 512 (n. 81).
[60] Chaumont, 1973, criticized by Gignoux, 1976.
[61] Considine, 1979.

Tiridates IV's conversion by Gregory the Illuminator, to Christianity. This account, written up in approximately 460 by an Armenian known as Agathangelos is our major source for pre-Christian religion in Armenia. There is little archaeological evidence, though remains of temples and sacrifices dating from the second century BC to the third century AD have been found at Shirakawan.

Most of Armenia's gods were Iranian, but some were equated by Armenian authors with Greek ones. Agathangelos' reference to the 'seven altars of the temples' most probably means that there were seven major sites of worship,[62] which sites are identified later in his text. Aramazd, that is Ahura Mazda (Zeus), had a temple at Ani. Anahit (Anahita-Artemis) was, as in the Artaxiad period, exceptionally honoured, with major shrines at Erēz in Acilisene, Artaxata and Ashtishat. Tiridates IV reportedly regarded her as 'the glory of our race and our savior',[63] who gave Armenia life, fertility and protection and was honoured by all kings, and especially the (Roman) emperor. Also worshipped at Ashtishat was Vahagn (Greek Heracles, Iranian Verethragna), god of strength and victory. The descriptions of the temples and Tiridates' prayer for the blessings of the gods reveal that Vahagn had replaced Mihr (Mithras-Hephaistus), to whom he was in many respects similar, as a member of the major triad.

The other major gods were Astḷik (Syriac Astarte), equated with Aphrodite and worshipped at Ashtishat, and Tir (Apollo), Mihr, Barshamin and Nanē. Tir, the 'interpreter of dreams', had 'a temple of learned instruction' at Artaxata,[64] and Mihr a temple at Bagayaṙich. The Syrian Barshamin, originally, like Aramazd, a supreme creator god, was worshipped at Tᶜordan, and the goddess Nanē (Athena) at Tᶜil. Her origin was Semitic, and although she was not a *yazata* (being worthy of worship), she was widely worshipped in Iranian lands. Vanatur, a god of hospitality, was of indigenous origin. He was worshipped with Amanor, the bringer of the new fruits, in a harvest festival at Bagawan. There was also some sun worship. There was a 'Sun-gate' at Vaḷarshapat. Zoroastrians were supposed to recite hymns to the sun three times a day. There may have been some reverence too for the moon. The fifth-century Armenian writer Eznik refers to belief that the moon caused epilepsy.[65] Armenia certainly shared in the Zoroastrian veneration of ancestral spirits. Agathangelos refers to *uru* worship. *Uru* apparently means 'soul' in early writers, though later it came to mean 'evil spirit' and 'ghost'.[66] He also

---

[62] Agathangelos, 22, text and trans. Thomson, 1976, pp. 40, 41, and for comment his p. xl.

[63] Ibid., 53, text and trans. Thomson, 1976, pp. 64, 65.

[64] Ibid., 778, text and trans. Thomson, 1976, pp. 316, 317.

[65] Eznik, paragraph 258 (text p. 488, translation p. 630). See also Ananikian, 1925, pp. 47–8 for beliefs about the moon.

[66] Russell, 1987, pp. 334–36; Agathangelos, 16, text and trans. Thomson, 1976, pp. 30, 31 where *uruapasht* is translated 'idolatrous', a translation criticized by Russell, 1987, p. 354 n. 82.

records that King 'Khosrov', in thanks for victory, offered the royal ancestors various gold and silver objects, silks, and animals – oxen, rams, horses and mules, all of them white.[67]

The temples and their attendants were, as this suggests, wealthy. Anahit's image at Erēz was of gold. Vahagn's temple was full of gold and silver and had received many offerings from the greatest kings. 'Khosrov' had given splendid gifts to the priests at Vaḷarshapat out of his Persian booty. Besides treasure, temple property, comprising nearly 5 per cent of the kingdom, included estates. At T͑ordan the temple of Barshamin owned the whole village with its properties and territories, and at Ani the town and its fortress belonged to Aramazd.

Though there were many similarities between Armenian and Iranian Zoroastrianism there were, nevertheless, also some differences. The Persian Ahriman, the uncreated evil invader opposed to the good Creator Ahura Mazda, is noticeable by his absence. There may have been magi in the royal and major religious centres, but there were not in the rest of the kingdom, which was left to native priests and idolatrous beliefs. Third, there is little evidence that the cult of fire had had much impact. It receives almost no attention in Agathangelos' account of Gregory's discourses and deeds. There is a reference, in a prayer, to ancestral 'ash-worship',[68] meaning, presumably, the care of the ashes of the holy fires, the fires being allowed to smoulder under the ashes until needed for services. But otherwise, Armenian religion is characterized by Gregory as the vain and foul worship of useless idols made by the hands of men. It is nevertheless likely that Armenian society, like so many others, did have some kind of cult of fire, manifested in certain seasonal festivals. The ancient Iranian fire festival, celebrated by Zoroastrians in April, survives in Armenia in the celebrations surrounding the Feast of the Presentation of the Lord to the Temple, celebrated on the evening of 13 February and on the next day. A fourth difference between Armenian and Iranian Zoroastrianism is that although it is easy to identify polygamy, consanguineous marriage and concubinage in Armenia, it is much harder to discover the elaborate system of proxy and substitute marriage which obtained in Iran. That system was part of Zoroastrian family law and ensured that a man could, legally, have a son, even if he could not manage it biologically.

Words for 'sarcophagus' and 'grave' or 'tomb' suggest Iranian influence on burial customs, and graves at Gaṙni suggest a change in custom in the first century which may reflect the Zoroastrian prohibition of the pollution of the earth. Graves lined as well as covered with stone slabs came to

---

[67] Agathangelos, 22, text and trans. Thomson, 1976, pp. 40, 41.
[68] Ibid., 89, text and trans. Thomson, 1976, pp. 100, 101, (where it is translated 'fire-worship') and for comment, his p. 464.

be preferred to unlined ones. Other methods were burial in a jar, or stone sarcophagus. Rock-cut tomb chambers were still used. At Boşat is a Parthian rock relief which may date from the end of the second century or beginning of the third, above the entrance to a tomb chamber. It shows a horseman, possibly Mithras or an Armenian king. It has been suggested that the relief has been altered, but that the original, probably only slightly earlier, perhaps depicted a sacrifice which would have been performed there for the person whose tomb it was.[69]

It is difficult to say more, with certainty, about pre-Christian Armenian religion since the evidence is so limited. Modern Armenian practice, contemporary and medieval folklore, and etymology allow a number of additions.[70] Russell has given us an exhaustive account of what can be deduced. Folklore about *vishaps*, (serpents or dragons), owed something to Iranian influence. The same name is used of ancient megaliths, often near water, some carved with representations of water, and some shaped like fish. Armenians seem to have sacrificed to them. There may have been some veneration of dogs. In Zoroastrian belief the dog is an intermediary between living and dead, with the power to protect souls from evil, and its presence at funeral rites is necessary. Fifth-century writers allude to belief in the *aralēz*, a dog which can cure battle wounds by licking. There may also have been some veneration of cats, despite the fact that the cat is regarded by Zoroastrians as a noxious creature. The early eighth-century Paulician heretics, who may have included unconverted Armenian Zoroastrians, were accused of cat worship.

We have other glimpses of belief. The legend that the chains of Artawazd, cursed by his father and imprisoned alive by spirits, were strengthened by the sound of blacksmiths' hammering, preventing his escape and his destruction of the country, suggests that blacksmiths once had some role of religious significance. According to another tradition, a site which later became a monastery was originally sacred to Anahit and was called Rock of the Smiths. There was a belief that children could be swapped for a demon changeling. Artawazd was said to be such a changeling. The evil eye was feared. Moses of Khoren records a tradition concerning the last Orontid king, that his glance split stones brought each daybreak by his attendants.[71]

Notwithstanding the absence of Ahriman from Armenia, the influence of Iran on Armenian beliefs and attitudes concerning the powers of evil was strong. Particular plants may have been used against evil spirits; garlic, the mandrake and rue, whose name in Armenian is a loan from Middle Iranian, and which was scattered at Zoroastrian shrines. Some of

[69] Nogaret, 1983; Sinclair, 1989b, p. 281.
[70] Russell, 1987, for what follows (and all aspects of Armenian Zoroastrianism).
[71] Moses, II, 42, trans. Thomson, 1978, pp. 183–4.

the terminology of sorcery is related to Iranian words, and many aspects of Zoroastrian demonology are attested, in various periods. The *al*, the personification of a disease which strikes a woman in childbirth, is of Iranian origin. The *aysk^c*, wind demons, could appear as men or serpents, could marry each other, and had a king. The *k^cajk^c*, who according to legend imprisoned Artawazd, were, according to the sixth-century Armenian David the Invincible, earthly and corporeal and good, and according to the fourteenth-century Gregory of Tat^cew were thought to rule in the rocks. Folklore suggests that they lived like the nobility, and Russell thinks they may originally have represented the royal ancestral spirits who were revered by Artaxias I, the father of Artawazd in the legend.[72] Other demons however do not appear to have particular links with Iran.

Armenian Zoroastrianism, which dated back, probably, to the Achaemenid era, was well-established in the Arsacid period. But it was threatened in the third century, by two forces, the Sasanian reformers, and the Christians. As to the first, Kartir, the moving force in Sasanian Zoroastrianism, whose aim was to purify practice and belief and extinguish idolatry, claimed in an inscription to have worked throughout Shapur's empire. The Armenian evidence supports him. Moses of Khoren asserts that Artashir, probably meaning Shapur, destroyed the ancestral statues at Artaxata and ordered fire to be kept perpetually burning at Bagawan.[73] And there is archaeological confirmation for a promotion of the fire cult. A fire altar under the cathedral of Ējmiatsin (Vaḷarshapat) probably predates the official Christian conversion of Armenia. (Its alternative date is 451.) The particular influence of Ardashir I and Narses, who both promoted Anahit, may lie behind the disappearance of prostitution at her temple in Erēz. Russell suggests that the promotion of Vahagn in Armenia was an expression of opposition to Kartir.[74]

Christianity provided the second threat to Zoroastrianism. Precisely when it reached Arsacid Armenia is unknown, but by the accession of Tiridates IV in 298 or 299 Christians had been nearby for nearly two centuries. Pliny the Younger (AD 61–c.112), as legate in Pontus and Bithynia, had corresponded with Trajan about measures to be taken against them. By the middle of the second century Christianity had spread to Nisibis. There were Christians in the legion *XII Fulminata* in the 170s. The wife of the governor of Cappadocia at the turn of the century was a Christian. By 201 there was a church in Osrhoene, at Edessa. There were Christians in Lesser Armenia when the emperor Decius inaugurated persecution in 249. The fourth-century historian Eusebius of Caesarea refers to Bishop Dionysius of Alexandria (248–65) writing about apos-

---

[72] Russell, 1987, ch. 14, 'Evil Spirits and Creatures' (pp. 437–80), pp. 451–4 and p. 77 for K^cajk^c and Artaxias.
[73] Moses, II, 77, trans. Thomson, 1978, p. 225.
[74] Russell, 1982.

tates to Meruzhan, bishop of the Armenians. Meruzhan may have been bishop of Sebasteia (modern Sivas). There were Christians in Melitene by the late third century. Diocletian's persecution of 303 was partly provoked by a revolt there, itself apparently instigated by Christians.

It is probable then that Christianity had infiltrated Tiridates' kingdom before his accession, though there is no evidence that it had gained many elite adherents. Some town dwellers may have been Christian, for Christianity was often spread through Jewish communities. The Armenian word for a Christian altar may derive from Hebrew. Christianity had very likely arrived from Syria, to which early Armenian Christianity was to owe a great deal. The fifth-century author of the *Epic Histories* stresses, in some parts of his work, that the first evangelizer and head of the church in Armenia was Thaddaeus (Jude),[75] an apostle, and the traditional founder of the church of Edessa in the first century. The legend presumably reflects some early evangelization from Edessa. Syriac, the dialect of Aramaic in Edessa and Osrhoene, furnished the later stratum of the words in Armenian which are of Semitic derivation, and which is of ecclesiastical-literary nature. The *Epic Histories* emphasize that the first church of Armenia was at Ashtishat, in the south,[76] rather than in the northern city of Vaḷarshapat, which Tiridates IV and Gregory the Illuminator made into the mother church. The Syrian bishop Daniel, supervisor of Ashtishat, has been, tentatively, identified as the Armenian Acrites who, with the then head of the Armenian church, Aristakēs, attended the Council of Nicaea in 325.[77] Even Agathangelos' account of Gregory's work, which makes the Armenian church dependent on Cappadocia, betrays Armenian Christianity's Syrian origins. The baptismal rite it describes is related to Syrian rather than to Greek practice, and some Syrian Christology is detectible.[78]

Syrian Christianity was however to be a casualty of fourth-century politics. As they sought Roman protection from Sasanian ambition Tiridates IV and his successors were to prefer Greek to Syrian Christianity, which was driven underground.

---

[75] *Epic Histories*, III, i, xii, xiv, IV, iii, iv, trans. Garsoïan, 1989, pp. 67, 82, 89, 110, 112 and for comment her pp. 411–12.

[76] Ibid., III, iii, xiv, xix, IV, iv, trans. Garsoïan, 1989, pp. 68, 87, 93, 113 and for comment her pp. 257–8 (n. 11), 449–50.

[77] Garsoïan, 1988, pp. 257–8 (n. 35).

[78] Winkler, 1978, 1980, 1982.

6

The Establishment of Christianity and the End of the Monarchy, c.300–c.428

The establishment of Christianity is a landmark in Armenian history not merely for its importance in the fourth century but because to modern eyes Armenia's church and Armenians' Christian faith seem to have been the major contributors to the shaping and preservation of Armenians' identity as a people. As for many of the peoples of Europe, so for Armenians Christianity was both the harbinger of new institutions and new relationships, between themselves and with a wider world, and a vehicle of continuity, preserving, if in adapted forms, much of the ancient inheritance whose formation has been considered in preceding chapters.

Its immediate context, of course, was one of Roman rule, or protectorate. After Diocletian had established Tiridates IV as king, most Armenians were under Roman sway and they remained so for many years. Places where Armenians had settled and ruled in ancient times, Melitene (ancient Melid), Commagene and Lesser Armenia, had been incorporated into Roman provincial organization. Swings of political fortune, alliances with Rome, and pressure from the Sasanians had encouraged some Armenians to leave the Arsacid kingdom for lands further west, and this western Armenian presence continued. Tiridates IV had presumably used the Cappadocian estates of Tiridates II during his exile. Both his cousin Gregory and Gregory's great-great-grandson, the future patriarch Nersēs were educated in Caesarea. Cucusus, a small town between Caesarea and Germaniceia seems to have been something of an Armenian centre.[1] It was from Cucusus that the fêted Armenian rhetor Proaeresius (276–367/368), departed to study first in Antioch and then in Athens where he became professor of rhetoric. Armenian names appear in an

[1] Dédéyan, 1986.

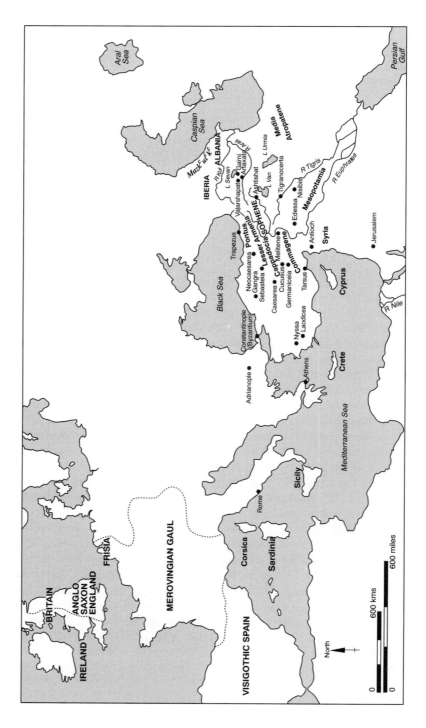

Map 6.1 Europe and west Asia

account of a saint of Cucusus who was martyred in 362. And John Chrysostom, patriarch of Constantinople 398–404, got to know Armenian Christians after he was exiled to Cucusus in 404. A panegyric to Gregory the Illuminator is ascribed to him, possibly correctly.

Diocletian reformed the provincial organization of the Roman empire and he guarded his territories with forts and garrisons. Lesser Armenia became one of seven provinces in the diocese of Pontica. It included Cucusus and its capital was at Melitene where *XII Fulminata* was still stationed. The Armenian regions which Diocletian had acquired at Nisibis were not, however, incorporated into the provinces. The evidence for the fourth century suggests that these principalities were allowed much self-government under their native rulers, now fictionalized into Roman appointees, but whether this accorded with Diocletian's original intentions is not clear. It may have been Diocletian who built the large fort at Hizan, south of Lake Van, which may have been garrisoned with cavalry. Hizan guarded the route from Lake Van to the Tigris, that is, into Rome's newly gained Arzanene, the old Arabian march.

Within the kingdom, Tiridates IV depended on Roman support, to the extent that his territory could even be perceived as a province.[2] The fifth-century 'Verona List' of Roman provinces, which used fourth-century sources, inaccurately but suggestively includes Greater Armenia. Agathangelos, the historian of Tiridates' conversion, quotes Tiridates, in an edict, referring to his kingdom as the *dastakert*, or property, of the Caesars.[3] Assuming the quotation to be accurate, such a statement must have been meant to warn dissidents and Sasanians that Tiridates had protectors. His own Romanization is detectible in his residence in towns and in building work at Garni, which he made one of his bases. The inscription referring to the construction of a fort and some building for the queen should probably be attributed to him, rather than to Tiridates I as many scholars have thought. The Roman-type tower, of second- to fourth-century date, that archaeologists have detected may be his work. So too may the Roman baths, with their mosaic depicting fabulous creatures and divinities, including Oceanus and Thalassa, and the palace with a columned hall.[4]

Tiridates' Roman orientation was strengthened by the fact that trouble with Persia was practically guaranteed. There was an obligation on him to prosecute bloodfeud against the Sasanians, reflected in Agathangelos' statement that throughout his reign Tiridates fought the Persian Empire, 'seeking vengeance in battle'.[5] It was likely that Persia would seek to regain her lost territory in Media. It was still Sasanian policy to abolish

[2] Hewsen, 1985–6.
[3] Agathangelos, 127, text and trans. Thomson, 1976, pp. 138, 139 where he translates as 'province', and his pp. 467–8 (note) and xlvi. Garsoïan, 1989, p. 520 and refs. for the term.
[4] Wilkinson, 1972, cited by Hewsen, 1985–6. See above, ch. 5, n. 45.
[5] Agathangelos, 132, text and trans. Thomson, 1976, pp. 142, 143, 144, 145.

the Armenian kingship, and Sasanian intrigue in Armenia must have continued. The claim in a Roman edict of 311 of six victories over the Armenians may reflect direct Roman intervention in Armenia on Tiridates' behalf.[6]

It would be surprising if, in these circumstances, the king could be proved to have done anything that ran counter to Roman policy. This includes his becoming a Christian. Unfortunately the fact that Tiridates' religious policy adhered closely to that of Rome is obscured in what became the received tradition of the conversion of Armenia, whose author Agathangelos claimed to be Tiridates' contemporary but actually wrote long after the conversion, in about 460.[7] According to Agathangelos, Tiridates had Gregory the Illuminator, who was in his service, tortured to persuade him to give up Christianity. Gregory's refusal and Tiridates' realization that Gregory was the son of his own father's murderer, led to Gregory's imprisonment in a dungeon, in a snake-infested pit. Tiridates then, apparently, proceeded to a general persecution of Christians. Some refugee nuns from Rome (one of whom, Hṙip꜀simē, Tiridates tried to rape), and their abbess Gayianē, came to a painful end. Divine punishment followed: Tiridates behaved like a wild boar, torments fell on his household and demon-possession afflicted the people of Vaḷarshapat. Happily the king's sister had an instructive vision, after which Gregory was released (after thirteen or fourteen years in the pit), the martyrs buried and the afflicted cured and converted. Subsequently, Agathangelos relates, the pagan shrines were overthrown, and Gregory was consecrated bishop at Caesarea.

This conversion is traditionally dated 301, before Diocletian began persecuting Christians in 303, well before the conversion of the Roman emperor Constantine (306–37), in 312. But 301 is wrong. The chronology is admittedly difficult to establish, but the scholarly consensus is to prefer c.314.[8] Tiridates, far from being a trail-blazer, trod imperial paths. First he followed Diocletian's lead against Christians. Agathangelos' details of Tiridates' persecution are more legendary than historical, but the probability is that it encountered significant resistance. The Christian Armenians against whom the emperor Maximinus Daia (305–14) brought troops, in 311/12, may even have been Tiridates' subjects, rather than Christians in Lesser Armenia or in the ceded principalities.

Tiridates' attitude to Christianity changed only when Rome's did. In 311 Galerius (emperor 293–311) issued a deathbed edict of toleration, in 312 Constantine became a convert, and both Constantine and his rival Licinius tried to gain Christian support. Tiridates' new policy was to convert his kingdom and to promote the cult of martyrs who were Roman, rather than

[6] Hewsen, 1985–6.
[7] Thomson, 1976, Introduction and esp. pp. lxxxix–xcvii for dating.
[8] Ananian, 1961, states the case.

Armenian, in order to impress the emperor. Behind Agathangelos' fiction that Tiridates visited the newly Christian Constantine in Rome[9] probably lies a reaffirmation of the Armenian–Roman alliance. The king's Greek-educated cousin Gregory was not therefore the prime mover in the conversion, but a convenient tool, the more attractive since a religious alliance with him might heal the rift in the royal family.

And there were other temptations. Uniting the family might weaken the pro-Persian 'faction' to which Gregory's father had belonged. Conversion might lessen aristocratic receptiveness to Sasanian influence, for the Sasanians had persecuted Christians briefly, in the late third century, and might be expected to do so again – and indeed they did, when provoked by Constantine. In 324 Constantine represented himself to Shapur I as the protector of Christians in Persia. When he prepared to invade, as their liberator, in 337, at least some of them fervently hoped for Roman victory. The result, in Persia, was mistrust and martyrdoms. More practically, if the new church, replacing the existing establishment, were to spread its own power and personnel throughout Armenia, it might prove an instrument for royal power, more dependent and dependable, and also more authoritative, than the aristocracy.

The alliance of Church and Crown certainly proved, at first, mutually beneficial. Tiridates himself gave the Church temple properties, and four fields in every estate and seven in every town.[10] The Church was also to profit from unsuccessful aristocratic recalcitrance. In the 330s after the warring Manawazeans and Ordunis had spurned the mediation of Albianos, bishop of Manazkert, who was acting at the request of the king, Khosrov III (330–8/9), and of the patriarch, and subsequently been annihilated by the *sparapet*, their estates passed, respectively to Albianos and to the bishop of Basean.

The chronology and separate identity of the fourth-century kings after Tiridates has been a matter of debate, but what is clear is that the royal-patriarchal family partnership was reinforced by a number of marriage alliances and it is evidenced in the diplomatic activities of the clerics. Gregory's grandson, Patriarch Yusik I (*c.*341–7?), and Yusik's twin sons, all married royal princesses. Vrt^canēs, patriarch in the 330s, visited the Roman imperial court, to secure assent to the royal succession. Patriarch Nersēs (353–73) did likewise, to arrange fiscal privileges and a marriage alliance for Arsaces II (350?–67/8). Vrt^canēs's son Grigoris was martyred when he tried to convert the Mazk^ut^k^c, a group whose identity is disputed but who may have been Alans, and who were ruled by a relative of the Armenian king. They had perceived his preaching as 'a plot of the Armenian king' to halt their plundering raids.[11]

---

[9] Agathangelos, 872–80, text and trans. Thomson, 1976, pp. 406–15.
[10] Ibid., 837, text and trans. Thomson, 1976, pp. 372, 373.
[11] *Epic Histories*, III, vi, trans. Garsoïan, 1989, pp. 72–3.

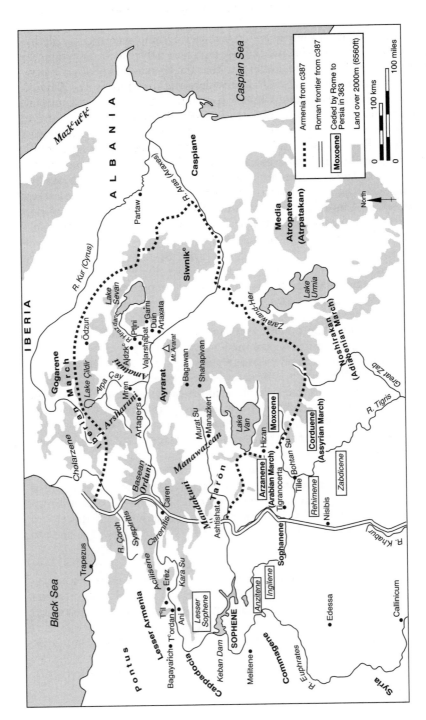

Map 6.2 Armenia

One view of Tiridates' conversion is that it was motivated primarily by concern to secure his throne, that in pursuit of this he abased himself obsequiously before Rome, and hence that the spectacle is scarcely edifying.[12] An alternative is that Tiridates deserves his epithet 'the Great', because in the long run the Church contributed to the maintenance of Armenian national identity and tradition.[13] Proponents of each have regarded the strong opposition which Tiridates encountered as an indication that political considerations were of prime importance. One could however, equally logically, suggest that Tiridates' determination to impose Christianity despite resistance implies religious zeal as much as political calculation. The relationship between higher and baser motives is complex and must always be questioned where political leaders are concerned, as it has been, of course, in that of the emperor Constantine himself. Ultimately it is not susceptible of proof.

Conversion and its Consequences: Early Medieval Armenian Christianity

1 Problems and tensions

Political considerations aside, how appealing is Christianity likely to have seemed to Tiridates and his subjects?

Belief in a god who is one and yet three, Father, Son and Holy Ghost, one of whose dimensions, the Son, is both God and man, incarnated and resurrected, and who forbids worship of graven images, must have seemed strange to those who frequented the Armenian temples. The difficulty of accepting it must have been compounded by fear of the consequences if Christianity was in fact not true. Punishment in this world must have seemed a possibility, and likewise for eternity, for there is evidence that Zoroastrians believed apostasy (from Zoroastrianism) would be punished by hell fire. In this respect conversion must have been more difficult for Armenians than for Romans, whose paganism lacked such a concept.

Besides the intellectual problems, there were differences and difficulties of lifestyle to be faced. One involved marriage. Zoroastrianism not only permitted polygamy but it promoted consanguineous marriages between the closest of relatives as acts of particular virtue with a sacramental value. Offspring of such marriages were regarded especially highly, and it is even possible that, under Parthian law, an heir born of a consanguineous marriage had the strongest claims in inheritance. Zoroastrian marriage functioned to preserve the purity of classes and the integrity

---

[12] Hewsen, 1985–6.
[13] See below, esp. ch. 10 for its contribution.

of family property. Christianity, however, preached continence and monogamy, discouraged widowed persons from remarrying, and abhorred incest. Christian marriage threatened disruption to a convert's existing social relations and to his future prospects. This difficulty was not easily overcome. Patriarch Nersēs taught against consanguineous marriage and betrayal of spouses,[14] but old habits died hard. An allusion in the *Epic Histories* to the wives (plural) of a *vitaxa*, and their record that King Arsaces II was simultaneously the husband of both an Armenian and a Greek, (previously the fiancée of the deceased emperor Constans), and that after the Greek wife's death Arsaces considered marrying a Persian princess,[15] reveal that polygamy continued. The Council of Shahapivan condemned consanguineous marriage in 444. At the Council of Partaw in 768 it was thought necessary to emphasize that a third marriage is detestable adultery and an inexpiable crime.

Other Christian–Zoroastrian differences involved the treatment of the dead, and mourning customs. The Church in the Roman Empire had come to prefer inhumation to cremation. Zoroastrianism prohibited the pollution of the earth. This difficulty however could be sidestepped, since the church did not regard burial as crucial, and since burial could be accomplished without pollution. But Christian ecclesiastics would not have approved decarnation, the exposure of bodies in a 'tower of silence' to decompose before burial, probably first institutionalized by the third-century Sasanian reformer Kartir.

The Christian Church also discouraged traditional mourning customs, whose origins lay in the cult of the dead, and whose original purpose was to inform the spirits that they were being honoured, in order to make them tractable, prevent their being discontented and dissuade them from any hostile activity. These customs included, for example, wailing, and the pulling of hair and the use of red garments, both substitutes for blood sacrifice. Armenian traditions were similar enough to Graeco-Roman ones to justify and inspire in Armenian prelates the kind of ecclesiastical disapproval which was expounded, in the Graeco-Roman world, by such luminaries as Bishops Basil of Caesarea (*c.*330–79) a near neighbour, his brother Gregory of Nyssa (*c.*330–*c.*395) and John Chrysostom. Like them, the Caesarea-educated Patriarch Nersēs condemned excessive weeping, loud wailing and unbridled mourning. This last included the rending of garments and tearing of hair, the slashing of arms and laceration of faces, monstrous dances, and the playing of trumpets. The view of the authorities was that Christians should regard death as the summons of Christ to the place prepared for the soul, and should look forward to resurrection. Their funerals should have, like Nersēs' own, in 373, psalms

---

[14] *Epic Histories*, IV, iv, trans. Garsoïan, 1989, p. 114, and her Commentary, p. 273 (n. 25).
[15] Ibid., V, xvi, IV, xv, xx, trans. Garsoïan, 1989, pp. 201, 145, 151–2.

and hymns (which were signs of the joyful concept of death), incense, lamps, and candles and quiet tears. But the old ways were persistent. They returned, to be condemned again, at Shahapivan and in the late 480s by the Albanians, whose church was dependent on that of Armenia.

The Armenian minstrel tradition also came under ecclesiastical censure, for several reasons. The Albanian decrees testify to minstrels' involvement in inappropriate mourning.[16] Dances were associated with Dionysius, god of wine, and could lead to lust. The fifth-century John Mandakuni, Patriarch 478–90, refers to minstrel-mad drunkards who gave themselves up to debauchery.[17] And the very content of oral tradition was both suspect and dangerous: suspect because it preserved tales of pagan gods, and of ancestors, who, as non-Christians, were doomed to hell, dangerous because the fear and affection which gods and ancestors inspired were hindrances to conversion.

Such differences between the interests of traditional culture and those of Christianity must have contributed just as much as did its political implications to the fierce opposition which it had to meet. Moses of Khoren records that Tiridates had 'enemies', against his Christian policy, whom Moses regarded simplistically but perhaps not totally inaccurately, as 'following the will of their wives and concubines'. The king consequently abandoned his throne for the life of a hermit, and was poisoned when he refused to return. Gregory's son and successor, Aristakēs, had already been slain in Sophene, by an aristocrat whom he had reprimanded.[18] The next patriarch, Vrtᶜanēs, was actually besieged by 'up to two thousand' men belonging to families of pagan priests, emboldened by the queen, Tiridates' daughter-in-law, who had been rebuked for adultery and dissolute ways.[19]

In such circumstances it is not surprising that many Armenians were for over a generation relatively untouched by Christianity. Agathangelos' tale of Gregory's extensive missionary work has to be discounted, since it is modelled on two other accounts: one about the work of Mesrop (Mashtotsᶜ), inventor of the Armenian alphabet, written by his pupil Koriwn in about 443, the other about Patriarch Nersēs by the author of the *Epic Histories*. Some thirty years' endeavour had had only a limited impact, according to the *Epic Histories* when in 347 Patriarch Yusik I was murdered for his constant admonition of persistent transgressors. Christianity had been accepted 'under duress' 'as some human folly', only those people with some Greek or Syriac learning had any understanding of it, and the majority, aristocrats as well as peasants, still believed in their songs, legends and epics, and performed the old rites.[20]

[16] Moses Daskhurantsᶜi *History of the Albanians*, I, 26, trans. Dowsett, 1961b, p. 52.
[17] Boyce, 1957.
[18] Moses, II, 92, 91, trans. Thomson, 1978, pp. 251, 249.
[19] *Epic Histories*, III, iii, trans. Garsoïan, 1989, pp. 68–9.
[20] Ibid., xii, xiii, trans. Garsoïan, 1989, pp. 82–85.

It was Nersēs who tackled these difficulties, gave the church some systematic organization, and extended its contact with the people. His council at Ashtishat, *c.*354, set down canonical regulations. It was ordered that almshouses and hospitals were to be established throughout Armenia. Overseers were set over them, and hostelries and resthouses were built. Nersēs' model in these charitable activities may have been Eustathius of Sebasteia.[21] He also set up Greek and Syriac schools, built dwellings for consecrated virgins, increased the number of churches and ministers, and appointed more bishops. Even then however, bishoprics were few; only seven are identifiable at the end of the fourth century, compared to nineteen by the mid-fifth century and twenty-eight by the mid-sixth.[22] Nersēs' work is recorded as having been successful, and certainly the new faith proved sufficiently well established to survive the setbacks that were to follow his death.

2   Compensation and continuity

Just as it was to do in other societies, the success of Christianity in Armenia was to involve compromises and accommodations with traditional attitudes and behaviour which compensated for the tensions between them. The church offered opportunities, for example, for continuity in religious imagery, in personnel, in festivals, in saints' cults and in protection against evil. There are numerous examples of continuity of religious imagery and symbols. Serpents, though they had demonic connotations and had been unpleasant company for Gregory in his pit-prison, were also regarded by the people as protectors of houses, and have traditionally been associated with wisdom. They appear in ecclesiastical architecture and are still to be found ornamenting the cross on the staff of the *vardapet* (teacher, doctor of divinity). The light and fire imagery in Gregory's vision of the church which was to be built at Ējmiatsin, as recounted in the fifth century by Agathangelos, derive from Iranian religious tradition as well as from Biblical images.[23] The banquet, common on Greek funeral steles, and the hunt could still characterize the afterlife. In a passage on Paradise, Agathangelos combines two common Christian images for it, the feast with the bridegroom, and Abraham's bosom for the repose of the faithful, into another, that of Abraham's banquet.[24] Hunting scenes, symbolizing victory over evil, and hence salvation, became part of the repertoire of Christian sculptural images. The reliefs of the royal necropolis built at Aḷdzkᶜ in the 360s

[21] Rather than Basil of Caesarea, Garsoïan, 1983.
[22] Adontz–Garsoïan, 1970, pp. 269, 254–60.
[23] Hultgård, 1982.
[24] Thomson, 1976, p. lxxxv regarding Agathangelos, 149.

include one of a hunt scene. At the church of Ptḷni, (probably sixth-century, though possibly early seventh-century) Manuēl, Lord of the Amatunis, is sculpted in a hunting scene below images of Christ, angels and apostles. And for the funeral crowns with which pagans had honoured the dead the Church Fathers provided Christian substitutes, even if they were only images, like the crown of martydom. Gregory, or perhaps our fifth-century source using him as mouthpiece, offered his audience a share of the crown of the martyred nuns, and he promised that at the Resurrection the just and the sinners would have crowns of flowers and thorns.[25]

Armenian worshippers lost their visually splendid temples, full of treasures and statues, but they were given Christian replacements. Impressive churches offered sculptured reliefs, wall paintings and holy objects. An attack on opponents of images, written by Vrtᶜanēs Kᶜertᶜoḷ, *locum tenens* of the headship of the church 604–7, attests with approval representations of the Virgin and Child, of Gospel scenes, of the martyrdom of Gregory, Gayianē and Ḥripᶜsimē, of prophets, apostles and saints, and of the Cross, and Gospels painted in gold and silver on purple parchment and bound in ivory.[26] An example of a cult image may be the enthroned Virgin and Child, now in a niche in the church at Ōdzun, which was carved in the late sixth or very early seventh century.

A number of measures neatly combined allowing continuity, but in a new context, with weakening the old order and removing opportunity for non-conformity. There is some evidence to suggest that members of the pagan priestly class were retrained as Christian clerics. Pagan properties, for example the goddess Anahit's property, personnel and land at Artaxata, were transferred by Tiridates and Gregory to the new, Christian church.[27] Pagan sites were made into Christian ones. Thus at chapels in Ashtishat, Gregory installed relics of John the Baptist and of St Atᶜanaginēs, martyred in Sebasteia under Diocletian.[28] Tᶜordan and Tᶜil were the burial sites for Gregory's line of patriarchs: his own remains, and those of Vrtᶜanēs and Yusik, went to Tᶜordan, where the memory of Vrtᶜanēs was commemorated annually, and those of Aristakēs and Nersēs to Tᶜil.[29] Some pagan festivals were ousted by Christian ones. Feasts of John the Baptist and St Atᶜanaginēs were established, in about 356–9, to replace the festivals of Amanor and Vanatur on New Year's Day at Bagawan, and a feast of Vahagn. The Annunciation replaced, between

[25] Agathangelos, 719, text and trans. Thomson, 1976, pp. 260, 261; Thomson, 1970, p. 29 and pp. 160–62 trans. of *The Teaching of St Gregory* paras 648–51. See also below n. 47.

[26] Der Nersessian, 1944–5, 1946.

[27] Agathangelos, 781, 840; 778–81, text and trans. Thomson, 1976, pp. 320, 321, 374, 375 (and his notes, pp. 484, 494); 316–21.

[28] Ibid., 809–15, text and trans. Thomson, 1976, pp. 346–53.

[29] Garsoïan, 1989, pp. 496, 495.

Plate 6   Upper half of sculpted enthroned Virgin and Child, (sixth or seventh century) set in the interior of the north wall of a seventh-century church at Ōdzun, but possibly originally a cult object.

468 and 471, a feast of Anahit, and the Transfiguration was established, probably by Patriarch Sahak (387?–439), to replace one of Aphrodite.

There was a large element of continuity too in saints' cults, folklore and custom and ritual. Passages in the *History of Tarōn* by Ps. John Mamikonean, written purportedly in the seventh century but actually in the tenth, suggest that some of the qualities of Vahagn had been transferred to John the Baptist. The name of a flower used in popular rites on Ascension Day, hawrot-mawrot, preserves names of two divinities, Haurvatāt and Aměrětāt guardians of the waters and plants, so its use may be connected with Zoroastrian practice. Elements of the cult of fire survive in Candlemas celebrations.[30] And animal sacrifice continued. One tradition, in the so-called Canons of Sahak, probably compiled early in the seventh century, says that Gregory allowed this in order to conciliate former pagan priests who feared poverty, promising them an increased share in the proceeds. It was perhaps to distinguish the Christian rite from Zoroastrian practice that young animals were used rather than mature ones. Where sacrifice was in memory of the dead it was effectively a Christian substitute for sacrifice to them.

Nor did Christianity leave people helpless against old demons and rejected gods. The early church condemned sorcery, which it associated with paganism, but it had its own rites and miracles. These in their turn prompted pagan accusations that the church itself practiced magic and it is possible, as some scholars believe, that there was actually no significant difference between Christian and pagan 'magic' other than whether it enjoyed ecclesiastical approval. John Chrysostom's approval was limited to praising the will of God and to making the sign of the Cross, but this sign could, apparently, be far more efficacious than any pagan spell or amulet. According to Agathangelos, by making it, Gregory brought down Anahit's temple at Artaxata and a wind blowing from a wooden Cross which he held destroyed the temples at Ashtishat.[31] (These attacks will have been between 312 and 330/331.)[32] Elsewhere in the early Christian world the Cross came to be used as a protective device against demons, for example on bookcovers and at entrances to buildings, which were thought particularly to need protection. By the late fourth century this had become a well-established practice in nearby Syria. On floors, since they would be trodden on, crosses were unsuitable (and indeed forbidden in the Roman Empire by an edict of 427); there other decorative motifs, including the ancient apotropaic symbol of the knot, were used. Angels

[30] Russell, 1987, pp. 199–201, 202–3, 217 (for Vahagn and John the Baptist); 375 (for flower); 497–503 (for fire cult).

[31] Agathangelos, 779, 813, text and trans. Thomson, 1976, pp. 318, 319; 350, 351.

[32] If Agathangelos' descriptions are accepted, then these attacks anticipated similar events in the Roman Empire by some fifty years. But his reconstruction may be anachronistic, coloured by a (fifth-century) perception of such attacks as natural.

were another source of protection. The Church taught that the souls of the faithful were carried to heaven by angels who guarded them from dangers on the way. That some people hoped for more than this is suggested by the concern of the mid-fourth-century Council of Laodicea that angels were sometimes the object of exaggerated veneration resembling magic.

Protective motifs of these kinds occur at entry points in Armenian churches. On each side of the central window of the sixth- or seventh-century church at Ōdzun for example is an angel holding a snake, and the snakes' bodies intertwine to form a knot above it. A similar serpent knot tops the centre of the window of the south portal at the seventh-century church of Mren. Christ, two angels and six apostles guard a window in the Ptḷni church. Protection was not, of course, the only purpose of such ecclesiastical art. The serpents, for example, may have been meant as reference to Gregory in the pit. There are often several images together: the combinations affect their meaning, and it is probable that artistic representations were, even singly, meant to function at more than one level.

3   Compromise and adjustment

The Church's ability to offer its converts some religious continuity and effective protection against rejected gods and evil spirits enhanced the acceptibility of Christianity but it went hand in hand with compromise and adjustment. Some compromises may sometimes seem, to us, extreme, and, like other people, the Armenians may be charged with the adulteration of Christianity. As an example let us consider Christian continuation of the ancient use of charms, perhaps in Christianized or new forms. That some fourth-century clerics made amulets and that some Christians wore them is suggested by the fact that the Laodicean synod forbade both. A homily on charms, attributed to the fifth-century Armenian patriarch John Mandakuni, but probably written by the sixth- to seventh-century scholar John Mayragometsʿi, suggests that Armenians shared this predeliction for amulets.[33] Yet whether such accommodations between Christianity and society as some Christians approving of amulets should be interpreted as signs that Christianity had had only a superficial impact in society is a matter for debate. It touches upon anthropology, Christian polemic, historical change and modern outlooks. Fourth-century clerical amulet-makers might themselves be scandalized by 1990s Church of England vicars doubting the Resurrection. None can tell which God prefers.

In fact, opinion and practice within church and society was no more uniform in antiquity than it is now. At one extreme lie the twin sons of

---

[33] Feydit, 1986, and Mahé, J.-P., 1988–9.

Yusik I who became deacons, albeit, apparently, against their own wishes. They enjoyed themselves with harlots, singing girls, minstrels and buffoons at the bishop's residence at Ashtishat. Our fifth-century source disapproved, recording that God struck them down.[34] The clerics at the fourth Council of Duin in 645 also took a rigorous stance against relaxed attitudes. They condemned the way 'some nobility' and 'plebeian cavalry' desecrated monasteries by lodging there with their minstrels and dancing girls.

The Armenian church adapted to secular society in a number of ways. One was the accumulation and exhibition of wealth. A perception of simple susceptibility to secular mores is illustrated in accounts of King Arsaces II's (350?–67/8) patronage of Khad, Nersēs' deputy whilst Nersēs was in exile from 359 to 368. Arsaces gave Khad gold, silver, royal ornaments of silk woven with gold and many royal horses, in the hope of softening his opposition to royal policy.[35] Moses of Khoren informs us that Khad was mocked by people he reproached until he gave up his glamorous clothes and horses for a hair shirt and a donkey.[36] Zawēn, the patriarch of the late 370s, maintained an ostentatious attire, with braided and spangled garments, sables, ermine, wolf skins, and fox pelts.[37] Since in primitive societies priests may wear animal skins to acquire the sanctity or qualities of their original occupants, Zawēn's costume may have been a continuation of a pagan practice. A particular, and worthy, purpose of ostentation was to maintain episcopal dignity. John of Ōdzun, patriarch from 717/8 to 728/9, routinely appeared in fine clothes, his long white beard glistening with gold dust fixed with sweet-smelling ointment. His justification was that, in default of miracles, splendid garments were necessary 'to impress the simple and immature minds of men with the fear of God'. His underclothes by contrast were of goat's hair.[38]

As Khad's sad case suggests, the property of the church was to include many horses, which, besides being associated with aristocratic lifestyle, were of course of practical use. The Albanian council of the 480s stipulated that for the soul of every royal and noble man should be given a saddled, harnessed horse and whatever else he could afford. In commemoration of the dead it required an offering from all laymen annually, specifying a horse and an ox if the dead man had owned any. Other ecclesiastical revenues mentioned include payments to priests of fruits of the earth, and by priests, to bishops, of money on ordination and of annual gifts.[39]

---

[34] *Epic Histories*, III, xv, xix, trans. Garsoïan, 1989, pp. 91, 93–4.
[35] Ibid., IV, xii, trans. Garsoïan, 1989, pp. 134–6.
[36] Moses, III, 31, trans. Thomson, 1978, pp. 288–9.
[37] *Epic Histories*, VI, ii, trans. Garsoïan, 1989, p. 234.
[38] John Katholikos, *History of the Armenians*, XXII, 10–31, trans. Maksoudian, 1987, pp. 110–11.
[39] Moses Daskhurants‘i, I, 26, trans. Dowsett, 1961b, p. 51.

Prospects and realities of wealth can of course lead to cupidity and to resentment and censure. Such sentiments may lie behind stories of the late fourth-century bishop John: that he forcibly ordained an unbaptized catechumen and evildoer, in order to take his horse as a reward, and that he played the buffoon whenever he was with the king, crawling and braying, 'I am a camel' 'put the sins of the king on me', so that the kings put sealed deeds, for villages and estates, on his back in exchange for their sins.[40] Yet consideration of the wider context, the early history of the Church in general, suggests that even in this caricature there may have been worthy purpose. It was only in times of persecution that the mere profession of Christianity was demanding and so signified sincere commitment to it. In other times, the Church made further demands on its members to test them. Some of these demands were hard. Consequently mechanisms for dealing with post-baptismal sins evolved, to save from despair and damnation those members who were incapable of monotonous virtue. Thus the early church developed confession and penance, and beliefs in the efficacy of intercession and of donations for the salvation of the soul. Gifts to God could be perceived as compensation for offences against Him. In Armenia a concept that a gift which is made to atone for sin somehow incorporates that sin is implicit in the tale of John's braying and is also found in one of the canons attributed to St Sahak.

The early church not only came to terms with ostentation and sin, it also adapted its definitions of good practice and virtue. In Armenia this involved an evolution of an alliance between patriarch and aristocracy. One of its manifestations is that spiritual office came to be viewed, as secular aristocratic office was, as hereditary. A Byzantine council of 692 criticized the Armenian restriction of ordination to descendants of families of priests. There were at least three episcopal families in Armenia in the fourth century. Khad was succeeded by his son-in-law. John the buffoon was the son of Patriarch Pᶜaṙēn, who may himself have belonged to the dynasty of Aḷbianos of Manazkert, although another suggestion, because he was buried at Ashtishat, is that he belonged to Gregory's. Gregory's family may also have spawned the scholar-missionary Mesrop (Mashtotsᶜ) for he may have been the son of Vrik, the illegitimate son of Pap, son of Patriarch Yusik, and hence a second cousin of Patriarch Sahak.[41] More important than these family connections is that ecclesiastical norms were transgressed in order that the patriarchate should remain in the Illuminator's family. Gregory's grandson Grigoris was made bishop at fifteen. Grigoris's twin nephews Pap and Atᶜanaginēs, were, with the assent of the bishops, forcibly ordained as deacons, as

---

[40] *Epic Histories*, VI, viii, x, trans. Garsoïan, 1989, pp. 236–7, 237–8.
[41] Garsoïan, 1989, pp. 428, 431, 399, 427.

preparation for rule, though they subsequently opted for a military career. Atᶜanaginēs's son Nersēs was also forcibly ordained, and made patriarch at the urging of the council, though strictly speaking, as a military man, he was ineligible.

Strength of family feeling is perhaps one explanation for the failure of the Gregorid leaders of the Armenian church to espouse virginity, as the influence of Syria on early Armenian Christianity could theoretically have led them to do.[42] In the early Syriac-speaking church veneration of celibacy was such that, even in the third century, baptism was conditional upon renunciation of sexual activity, though it had ceased to be so by the 330s. The more relaxed attitude of the Gregorids is perhaps also explicable by the legacy of Zoroastrianism which condemned sexual continence, and by the influence of the Greek church. The canons of the Council of Gangra, c.340, were prefaced with a letter to the bishops of the province of Armenia where the ideas it denounced were strong. The council had anathametized condemnation of marriage and refusal of the Eucharist celebrated by married priests. Admittedly Gregory's son Aristakēs preceded his brother as patriarch because he was celibate, Grigoris did not marry, and his brother, Yusik, limited conjugal relations to the first night, despite the disapproval of his in-laws. But our fifth-century clerical source chose to represent Yusik's subsequent continence as the consequence of an unhappy vision of his twin sons, rather than of a belief that marriage would pollute. And Yusik's own father, Vrtᶜanēs, had long been attempting procreation before begetting his own twins.

As the church accommodated wealth and aristocratic family feeling so too it compromised with the warrior ethic of Armenian elite society. The passage of Nersēs from military to ecclesiastical leadership was far from the only instance of this adjustment. Military prowess and Christian profession were closely connected, in various ways. One was Christian use of force. Gregory had taken troops to pagan sites. The 'demons' who opposed him at Erēz and Artaxata in the shape of an army carrying shields, and of cavalry and infantry, may have been temple military contingents.[43] The pagans, up to 2,000, who besieged Vrtᶜanēs at Ashtishat, were defeated, apparently by being miraculously and invisibly tied up, but probably by armed men.[44] Another accommodation was the willingness of Christians to fight. Christians had offered armed resistance to persecution in 311/312. The patriarch Zawēn even, for some reason unknown, decreed in the 370s that all priests were to wear military dress, and his two successors followed his regulations. The canons of the 645

[42] Ibid., pp. 53–4.
[43] Agathangelos, 786, 778–9, text and trans. Thomson, 1976, pp. 324, 325; 316, 317 and his p. 484 (note) for criticism of Chaumont's theory that the 'demons' were humans. Hewsen, 1985–6, accepts the military interpretation.
[44] *Epic Histories*, III, iii, trans. Garsoïan, 1989, pp. 68–9.

Council of Duin envisage clerics abandoning their spiritual duty in order to become soldiers. Those who did not return within three years were to be rejected from the privilege of the church, which was to be given to their relatives. Not until the eighth and ninth centuries do clerics seem to have ceased to perform military service.

By the late fifth century, and possibly earlier, fighting itself had acquired a religious aura. This development is best understood in the context of the early church's refinement of its ideas about martyrdom.[45] One stimulus to this refinement was the cessation of persecution, which, previously, had generated martyrs. Another was philosophy. Contemplation, self-purification and suffering, as Christ had done, were recommended as means to union with God.[46] In philosophical terms, a harsh life was actually preferable to martyrdom by blood. As a consequence it acquired a high status. According to Jerome (*c*.348–420) 'the service of a devout soul is also a martyrdom and a daily martyrdom'. Its crown was of lilies, while that of traditional martyrdom was of roses and violets.[47] Doing penance was, later, to be regarded by the Irish as a third type of martyrdom.[48]

Armenian came to use two words for martyr, *vkay* and *nahatak*, seemingly to signify passive and active witness respectively.[49] *Nahatak* and words associated with *nahatak* have meanings of hero, bravery and the like. They are used in Armenian translations for Greek words meaning champion and combatant, terminology which is itself much used, in both Greek and Syriac, to describe martyrs and ascetics.[50] Agathangelos almost always prefers *vkay* in his account of Hřipᶜsimē and her fellow martyrs, but he does also use *nahatak* of them sometimes. And, he says, they prayed for 'the cup of *nahatak*dom', rendered martyrdom in the authorative translation by Thomson, so that 'we may receive the crown as reward'.[51]

The use of *nahatak* for laymen fighting against anti-Christian enemies (as in the sixth-century Eḷishē's account of the mid-fifth-century Armenian rebellion against Persia),[52] implicitly gave military and political

---

[45]   Malone, 1950, demonstrates that 'the ascetic and then the monk came to fill the place that had been left vacant by the martyr' (p. vii). Cf. also Brock, 1973, who views the ascetic as 'in many ways the successor of the martyr' emphasizing that 'much of the terminology', e.g. athlete, 'previously applied to martyrs' was 'used in connection with ascetics' (p. 2). For the athletic image, see Malone, 1950, pp. 64–90.

[46]   Petterson, 1984.

[47]   Rush, 1941, pp. 145–8 for the crown of martyrdom; pp. 148–9 for the crown of sanctity; p. 147 for Jerome's identification of the crowns of martyrdom and of virginity as crowns of roses and violets respectively; and p. 148 for Jerome's view of sanctity as a daily and second kind of martyrdom (*Letters*, no. 108, col. 905), and of the two different crowns, one of roses and violets, the other of lilies.

[48]   Stancliffe, 1982, esp. pp. 33–46.

[49]   Frendo, 1985, p. 7 n. 14.

[50]   Thomson, 1976, p. 488, note to Agathangelos, 799, and 1982b, pp. 17–18 and p. 58, n. 2.

[51]   Agathangelos, 210, 148, text and trans. Thomson, 1976, pp. 216, 217, 156, 157.

[52]   Thomson, 1982b, pp. 17–18, 58, n. 2.

actions and heroes therein an aura of sanctity. More explicit is the fifth-century *Epic Histories*' account of Patriarch Vrtᶜanēs's reaction to the defeat of the Persian invasion of about 338. The Persians would have restored Zoroastrianism, so he referred to the dead as 'our pious martyrs' and told the grieving king and army that 'the memory of their valour' should be preserved 'as martyrs of Christ'.[53] A third indication that violence against enemies of the church was regarded as intrinsically pious may lie in the oral tradition concerning Mushel Mamikonean which is preserved in the same text. Mushel was commander-in-chief in the 360s. He destroyed Zoroastrian temples which had been erected after another Persian invasion and roasted their adherents, and he had Persian sympathizers flayed and stuffed in vengeance for his father.[54] Other elements in the text, for example, Mushel's betrayal at a royal banquet, where he was seized by twelve men primed by the king, and his house-hold's expectation of his resurrection, have prompted a suggestion that Mushel was actually perceived as being Christ-like.[55]

We should not, of course, expect early Armenian Christian heroes to have opted out of war. It is true that some luminaries of the early church had reservations about military service, but these are more likely related to a consciousness of particular non-Christian practices and beliefs within the Roman army than to a belief that Christians should be pacifist. By the fourth century, many Christians had pursued military careers. Neverthe-less, the Armenian attitudes had an element of originality. The tenth-century Byzantine Church was to reject the suggestion of the emperor Nicephorus II (963–9) that those who fell in Byzantium's wars should be ranked as martyrs. It cited Basil of Caesarea, Mushel's contemporary, as its authority. According to Basil, war was sinful, and killing in war necessitated penance, abstention from the Eucharist for three years, though it seems that the Byzantine Church in practice tended to disregard his recommendation.[56]

The drawing together of patriarchate and aristocracy, and of their interests, can be seen not only in hereditary succession and pious warfare but also in the anti-urban policy of Nersēs, and in the failure of the church to establish itself in cities.[57] The only fourth-century urban project was the foundation, by King Arsaces II, of Arshakawan (not precisely located in our sources, but in Ayrarat, south of the River Araxes). It grew to more than 20,000 households. Arsaces built a royal palace there. His intention was, probably, to make Arshakawan a centre of royal authority, and perhaps of trade, along the lines of towns sponsored by the Sasan-

---

[53] *Epic Histories*, III, xi, trans. Garsoïan, 1989, pp. 80–1.
[54] Ibid., V, i, trans. Garsoïan, 1989, pp. 186–7.
[55] Bedrosian, 1983, p. 22.
[56] McLin, 1981.
[57] Garsoïan, 1987.

ians. He had encouraged settlement there by offering newcomers immunity from any bloodfeud or legal process currently pending. Hence Arshakawan was stigmatized as a refuge for outlaws, debtors, renegades and evildoers of all kinds. Nersēs' vicar Khad refused to set up an altar in its church. Nersēs himself cursed both Arshakawan and Arsaces when he refused to demolish it. And it was soon destroyed – by plague, in fulfilment of the curse, according to the *Epic Histories*,[58] but by aristocratic attack and slaughter, according to Moses of Khoren.[59] Nersēs' anti-urban preferences can also be seen in his charitable activities. His foundations spread over villages, hamlets and deserts, but none, in contrast to his Greek models, were near cities. His council and headquarters were at a village, Ashtishat.

Nersēs' successors and colleagues likewise eschewed towns. In life the patriarchs were often at the royal court and in death at their villages of Tᶜil and Tᶜordan. Of the churches we know about, neither the large churches, built between the fourth and seventh centuries, nor the many smaller ones were near towns. The meeting place of the 444 church Council, Shahapivan, was a royal camp site. Whereas in the Roman Empire bishops were bishops of towns, Armenian bishops were representatives of aristocratic families and their domains. The normal episcopal signature at councils took the form of 'X, bishop of the [family name]'. The creation of separate bishoprics for the more powerful families may have begun, as Adontz suggested,[60] during the peaceful regency of Manuēl Mamikonean, *c.*379–*c.*384.

Crown, Church and Aristocracy

Although one of Tiridates IV's purposes in introducing Christianity was to strengthen the crown, what eventually occurred was that the alliance of church and aristocracy grew stronger, whilst the partnership of patriarch and king broke down. The climax was the murder of Nersēs by King Pap (*c.*368–*c.*374), poisoned at a banquet because of his perpetual reproof. Pap was murdered in his turn, by Roman hands, true, but with the complicity of the commander-in-chief, perhaps in vengeance for Nersēs.

How had this come about? Royal policy, both foreign and domestic, had after all been relatively successful until the late 330s. Peace between Rome and Persia had lasted, and the Iberian alliance which the Roman emperor Diocletian had restored had been further cemented by the marriage of Tiridates' daughter Salome, to Rev, son of the first Christian king

---

[58] Garsoïan, 1989, pp. 52–3, and 134–9, translating *Epic Histories*, IV, xii–xiii.
[59] Moses, III, 27, trans. Thomson, 1978, pp. 282–3.
[60] Adontz–Garsoïan, 1970, p. 286.

of Iberia, Mirian III, and co-king there from 345 to 361. Once Narses of Persia's son Shapur II, born in 309 after Narses' death, reached adulthood, however, instability had recurred. Tiridates had been murdered in 330/1, to be succeeded, probably, by his son Khosrov III (330–8/9). War between Rome and Persia had revived *c.*336. In Armenia there was pagan and aristocratic revolt, and an invasion, in which Shapur II was involved, of the Mazkᶜutᶜkᶜ. Their (Arsacid) king, Sanēsan, held Armenia in subjection for a year. It may have been in connection with these events that Rome nominated Hannibalianus, nephew of the emperor Constantine, as king of Armenia in 335/6. There was also a Persian invasion. Yet despite these traumas, Khosrov III survived. Hannibalianus died in 337, rebels were annihilated, enemies defeated, and the greatest magnates ordered to remain with the king, under his eye. For the *sparapet* who dealt with the Mazkᶜutᶜkᶜ remained loyal and there was support from Rome. Rome sent an army to assist against the prince of Arzanene, one of the Roman principalities, who was waging war against Khosrov with Persian support and princes of Rome's other principalities also joined in on Khosrov's side.

Rome yet again saved the kingship after Khosrov was, nevertheless, subsequently driven out of his kingdom (as is suggested in a work of the future Roman emperor Julian (361–3)). In 338 the emperor Constantius II (337–61) came to Arzanene, defeated the Persians, pardoned the Armenian rebels and, probably in consultation with the patriarch, restored the Armenian king. This king was, probably, Tiran (338–50?). Constantius also strengthened the border. The fort at Tille, at the confluence of the Tigris and Bohtan Su, on the border of rebellious Arzanene and Corduene, was probably one of his constructions.

It was the Arian heresy which from the late 330s had undermined Tiridates IV's plans and the established order. Arianism was espoused by all the Roman emperors, except the pagan Julian, after the death of Constantine in 337 until 380.[61] The Armenian kings followed their lead. But the Armenian patriarchs did not. This explains their mutual estrangement. The patriarch Yusik I was beaten to death and his nominated successor strangled for their rebuke of Tiran. The kings could not afford to conciliate their patriarchs if this would have offended their imperial protectors, for they needed Roman assistance in their defence against and pursuit of vengeance upon the Sasanians. Tiran seems subsequently to have been reported to Shapur II for intending, with imperial help, to oust the Sasanians. As a result he was arrested and blinded.

The reign of Tiran's son Arsaces II saw some royal successes but ended disastrously. Arsaces' installation had followed the Roman–Persian truce inaugurated by Shapur II's third failure, in 350, to take Nisibis. Roman

---

[61] Garsoïan, 1967b.

sources represent Arsaces as a loyal Roman ally, but he may, for a while, have aligned himself with Persia. For not only do the *Epic Histories* record that Arsaces ravaged Roman territory for six years, and participated in a Persian campaign near Nisibis, but the embassy on which in 358 Arsaces sent the patriarch Nersēs to the Roman Empire is probably the same one recorded by the contemporary Roman soldier and historian Ammianus Marcellinus (*c.*330–*c.*395) as a Persian embassy from Shapur.[62] Whatever Shapur wanted, Arsaces won the return of royal hostages (his nephews Gnēl and Tiritᶜ), taxation exemptions and a marriage alliance.

Arsaces also managed to exercise strong internal control. Gnēl had ambitions to reign himself, and had considerable aristocratic support, but Arsaces had him executed in 359. He retained alliance with the family of Siwnikᶜ by wedding Gnēl's widow, Pᶜaṙandzem. (It is unclear whether these nuptials came before, or after, Arsaces' marriage to his Roman bride, Olympias, whose murder Pᶜaṙandzem arranged *c.*361.) He appeased the Mamikoneans, his foster-family, who had broken away under Tiran, restoring the office of *sparapet* to them. He kept the nobility at court. According to the *Epic Histories* he renewed the kingdom, 'every magnate on his throne, every official in his station'.[63] He also seized from the aristocracy many domains, including the great fortress of Artagers, for the royal treasury. The resentment which his foundation of Arshakawan aroused demonstrates that his urban policy was, temporarily, a success.

But in 359 problems arose. Shapur II invaded Roman Mesopotamia and Patriarch Nersēs was exiled, probably for his opposition to Arianism. Arsaces himself did reasonably well in the new Roman–Persian war, despite the defections of Vahan Mamikonean and Meruzhan Artsruni (head of the house of Roman Sophene) and the capture of Tigranocerta. The Persians pillaged the royal tombs at Ani, except for Sanatruk's, but the royal bones were recovered by the *sparapet* so that their attendant 'glory' would not pass away.[64] The prince of Corduene, who had been a hostage in Syria, remained loyal. Unfortunately the emperor Julian's campaign of 363, which Arsaces supported, was a failure with disastrous repercussions for Armenia. The peace which Julian's successor, Jovian, made with Persia, reversing some provisions of the 298/9 Treaty of Nisibis, was described by Ammianus as 'shameful'. Jovian ceded (see map 6.2) the Armenian territories of Arzanene, Moxoene, Zabdicene, Rehimene[65] and Corduene[66] with fifteen castles, which probably

---

[62] Garsoïan, 1969.
[63] *Epic Histories*, IV, ii, trans. Garsoïan, 1989, p. 108.
[64] Ibid., xxiv, trans. Garsoïan, 1989, p. 158 and her p. 294 (n. 12).
[65] Cf. above, ch. 5 pp. 95 and n. 10.
[66] Cf. above, ch. 5 p. 101 and n. 35.

included Tille. Worse, Rome undertook not to give Armenia any military assistance against Persia.

The results were dire. Persia invaded. Sasanian policy was to engineer the transfer of Armenian noble allegiance, either to Persia or to Rome, and to abolish the Armenian kingship. A number of nobles deserted, mostly to Persia, and, since no-one was willing to fight for him, Arsaces surrendered. Ammianus records that he was subsequently blinded and executed, the Armenian sources that he committed suicide. Others suffered too. The great cities were destroyed. Their inhabitants were deported. Some aristocrats fled. Captives were killed. Vahan Mamikonean and Meruzhan Artsruni, to whom Shapur entrusted his gains, began to restore Zoroastrianism and establish the cult of fire.

But yet again Rome intervened, installing another king, Pap (c.368–c.374), son of Arsaces and Pᶜaṙandzem, who had been a hostage at the imperial court and educated at Neocaesarea (now Niksar) in Pontus. Pap's tasks were to suppress Zoroastrianism, to exact vengeance from those who had supported the Persians, and to beat off Persian offensives, in alliance with imperial forces which were, under the emperor Valens (364–78), to campaign in Armenia for nearly eight years. In about 370 the *sparapet* Mushel regained a great deal of territory which had been lost to Persia: Gordyene, Arzanene, domains in Media Atropatene, Norshirakan, Caspiane, Gogarene (disputed with Iberia), and the lands up to the Kura river, (disputed with Albania). Mushel also conquered three Roman territories, Sophanene, Anzitene and Ingilene. These last may have caused, or may signify, tension between king and emperor over territory, reflected also in the strange statement of the *Epic Histories* that Pap claimed Caesarea, Edessa and other cities from Rome.[67]

Whatever the reason, their alliance broke down. When Pap was murdered it was by a Roman official, in obedience to imperial order. Pap's Arianism[68] ought to have protected him, but it had led to internal difficulties. The opposition of the orthodox Nersēs, who had returned from exile at Pap's accession, had been a serious problem, for the church had become a powerful institution. Church property, comprising former temple lands, royal grants and confiscated principalities comprised about one-seventh of the kingdom, whilst the crown's comprised about twice that. The Patriarch himself apparently held fifteen 'districts', perhaps estates rather than entire 'districts',[69] some quite large and many in

[67] *Epic Histories*, V, xxxii, trans. Garsoïan, 1989, p. 213 and for comment, her pp. 324 (n. 3), 455–6, 497.

[68] The *Epic Histories* depict Pap as a sodomist possessed by demons visible as snakes. The accusation of sodomy was often levelled against early medieval heretics, Garsoïan, 1967b. Devotion to demons could signify paganism/Zoroastrianism.

[69] *Epic Histories*, IV, xiv, trans. Garsoïan, 1989, p. 139 and for comment, her p. 283 (n. 3).

Ayrarat, the royal domain. Ecclesiastical influence had been extended by Nersēs' charitable foundations and organizational work. And the fact that Nersēs' disapproval of Arsaces' Arshakawan had contributed to its destruction boded ill for any future royal projects. Pap had responded to Nersēs' unwelcome power by dismantling the charitable foundations, forbidding the payment of dues to the church and confiscating five-sevenths of the lands which Tiridates IV had given for the support of the church.[70] Though our sources place it afterwards, Pap's assault may have preceded and so partly caused the final crisis in his relationship with Nersēs and the latter's murder. This caused a breach with the Church of Caesarea, on which the Armenian Church had hitherto been dependent. To replace his opponent, Pap had looked, like his predecessors, to the dynasty of Aḷbianos of Manazkert. The figures are shadowy, and there are different views about their careers, but it seems that the murdered Yusik had been followed by Pᶜarēn (348–52?) and then Shahak (Isaac), probably the Isacoces who represented Greater Armenia at the Council of Antioch in 363. Pap appointed Yusik II. Then came Yusik's brothers, Zawēn, another Shahak and Aspurakēs.

Armenian Christianity was not, however, imperilled by these 'alternative' patriarchs. Only Zawēn failed to win respect. Epipᶜan and Gind, disciples of the Syrian bishop Daniel of Ashtishat, continued their careers as hermits and as overseers of eremetical communities. These resembled communities which were being formed at this time in Syria.[71] Such monks and holy men must have helped in the destruction of pre-Christian religion among the rural population in Armenia, as they did not only in Syria but elsewhere in the Roman east. Their impact must have contributed to the strength of the Syrian influence in religious terminology.

The End of Royal Power

Pap's murder of Nersēs led, paradoxically, to a weakening of his Roman alliance. The imperial general in Armenia colluded with Armenian dissidents and made allegations against him. They included a suggestion that the king's subjects so hated him that they were likely to support the Persians. So Pap was summoned to Tarsus, and then he fled back to Armenia. His own murder was organized by the very general who had brought him to power, an orthodox friend of Basil of Caesarea whom Pap had alienated by his appointment of Yusik II, in collusion with the *sparapet*, Musheḷ Mamikonean.

---

[70] Ibid., V, xxxi, trans. Garsoïan, 1989, pp. 211–13. For the suggestion as to timing, Dédéyan (ed.), 1982, p. 152.
[71] Vööbus, 1960, pp. 53–8; Garsoïan, 1989, p. 273 (n. 19).

These events opened the way to bloodfeud and to annexation. At first, however, they were thwarted by Armenian distaste for Persian religion and by the *rapprochement* of emperor and *sparapet* against Persian expansionism. Valens nominated Pap's nephew Varazdat (*c.*374–8), perhaps the son of Pap's younger brother Tiridates, as king. In 377 Roman envoys, visiting Shapur II, accepted some small territories in Armenia which Shapur offered, but Rome refused to ratify their transfer and Persia recovered them. It is not clear what lies behind this episode, but it may be that Rome was refusing to cooperate in a renewal of Persia's policy of 363, of encouraging Armenian defection to Rome or Persia. Valens and Mushel agreed that *azat*s and army should receive an imperial stipend. But their decision that new cities should be built, proved, as could have been predicted, a mistake. It was one of the reasons whereby Varazdat was persuaded by his foster-father to suspect the loyalty of Mushel and to consent to his murder in vengeance for Pap. In response, Mushel's kinsman Manuēl brought about the fall of Varazdat, *c.*378. Varazdat fled to the Roman Empire and, according to one tradition, was exiled in Britain. Manuēl became *sparapet*, and acted as regent for Pap's widow and Pap's two sons, Arshak (Arsaces) III (378–90?), who was also Manuēl's own son-in-law, and Valarshak, who died soon after. Armenian allegiance and tribute were transferred to Persia but subsequently Manuēl drove the Persian 'governor' out.

The autonomy Armenia enjoyed during Manuēl's regency had been facilitated partly by Rome's preoccupation with the Goths, who had defeated and killed Valens at Adrianople in 378, and partly by the death of Shapur II in 379. But this proved brief. After Manuēl died, *c.*384, Persia, asked by some of the aristocracy to nominate a king, installed Khosrov IV (384–9?), possibly the son of Varazdat. Whereupon Rome, unwilling or unable to defend the interests of Arsaces III, agreed with Persia to divide Armenia. This occurred, probably, in 387.[72] Rome took Sophene, Anzitene, Ingilene and Sophanene and Persia took Arzanene, Gordyene, Norshirakan, the domains in Atropatene, Zarawand-Her, and the territory between Lake Urmia and the Caspian Sea, including Caspiane (see map 6.2). Albania and Iberia recovered their losses of *c.*370. Cholarzene had already passed to Rome after the collapse, in favour of Persia, of the division of Iberia which had been made in 370. The two Armenian kings retained only Armenia's central districts. Arsaces' kingdom, nearly a sixth the size of Khosrov's, was the more westerly, bordering Lesser Armenia (which was now augmented and divided into two provinces).

This was the beginning of the abolition of the Armenian kingship. After five years Khosrov was denounced by his aristocracy for intrigue with

---

[72] 384, 387 and 389 have been suggested, and the precise boundary lines were probably settled later (Blockley, 1987).

Rome, and deported. His brother Vṙamshapuh (393–414) succeeded only after an interregnum. After Arsaces III died, his kingdom was made a Roman province (390). Within it the Arsacids retained Carenitis, the Bagratunis Syspiritis, the Gregorids Acilisene (which the Mamikoneans inherited in 438). After Vṙamshapuh's death in 414 the surviving kingdom, just under half the size that the third-century kingdom had been, was ruled again, briefly, by Khosrov IV, then by Shapur, son of the Persian king, and lastly by Vṙamshapuh's own son, Artaxias IV (422–8). Details of the Roman–Persian boundary were finally settled after Persia, again at the request of the nobility, removed Artaxias in 428. The abolition of the kingship was thereby complete.

The final realization of the long-standing Sasanian dream was diplomatic, but pressure of arms had prepared the way. The destruction of the cities must have greatly impoverished Armenia's crown. Admittedly the destruction was not total. Artaxata regained vitality for, according to an imperial edict of 408/9, it was then one of three points of commercial exchange between Rome and Persia, the other two being Nisibis and Callinicum (on the Euphrates). Vaḷarshapat survived as a religious centre. Perhaps its shops and glass-making, which Agathangelos mentions in connection with the refugee nuns,[73] did too. Tigranocerta survived. Epipᶜan built a martyrium there, and the city is mentioned in sixth-century sources under Syriac and Greek forms, namely Arzon and Chlomaron, of its local name (Arzn and Kᶜḷimar in Armenian).[74] But other cities decayed and were not refurbished. By the late fifth century Zarehawan was in ruins. The Crown's financial and political standing might have been improved if it had been successful in war. Captives could have repopulated cities, booty swelled the treasury and new lands sweetened the aristocracy. Unfortunately royal impoverishment was exacerbated by the loss of territories, only briefly reversed by Musheḷ Mamikonean.

Improvement in the exploitation of its resources could likewise have prolonged the life of the Arsacid monarchy, but no such improvement seems to have occurred. There is very little evidence for the existence and development of a bureaucracy such as the Sasanians had. Though officials at Arsaces II's court are referred to, in the *Epic Histories*, they seem to have been nobles.[75]

The downfall of the Arsacids may also be blamed on bloodfeud. That bloodfeud had survived the advent of Christianity is perfectly clear, both from Agathangelos, who includes struggles for revenge in his definition of the subject-matter of his history, and who records major events, for example the murder of 'Khosrov' and the imprisonment of Gregory, in

---

[73] Agathangelos, 150, text and trans. Thomson, 1976, pp. 160, 161.
[74] Sinclair, 1994–5 esp. pp. 194–5, 211, 214 and 1989b pp. 295–9, 361–4.
[75] *Epic Histories*, IV, ii, trans. Garsoïan, 1989, p. 108 and for comment her pp. 527–8; and 1976, cols 187 and 230 (n. 74).

terms of the exaction of vengeance,[76] and from the *Epic Histories*. The murder of Pap began a spiral of instability. In addition, honour dictated that the kings continue the bloodfeud with the Sasanians which had begun in 224. Yet to pursue it was to provoke retaliation, suffering and intrigue.

The church could have strengthened the monarchy. It had been intended that it would, but Tiridates IV's policy had backfired. Ecclesiastical opposition to imperial Arianism led to ecclesiastical alliance with the aristocracy rather than with the crown. Only in the fifth century was the church to realize its role of stiffening Armenian resistance to Persian encroachment.

[76] Agathangelos, 12, 25, 121, text and trans. Thomson, 1976, pp. 22, 23; 44, 45; 132, 133 where 'son of a guilty man' renders the literal 'son of one meriting vengeance' (*vrēzh* signifying vengeance) (See his p. 466, n.).

7

Culture and Repression: Partitioned Armenia c.428–c.640

Christian Teaching c.400–450

The story of the last years of Arsacid kingship in Armenia, c.384–428, was one of weakness, decline and foreign domination, culminating in abolition. But there was one glimmer of light in the gloom. The partnership between king and patriarch was renewed, evangelization was extended, and the church was equipped for the role which Tiridates IV had envisaged and which it was to play, albeit without a royal partner, over the next centuries. This achievement was the work of Sahak, Patriarch Nersēs' son, himself appointed patriarch, probably in 387, by Khosrov IV, and of Mesrop, possibly Sahak's second cousin, an ascetic and scholar.

Under Sahak's patronage and with royal backing, Mesrop formulated an Armenian alphabet, probably in 400. The details and dating of this invention have prompted much discussion, especially with regard to the testimony of Mesrop's biographer and pupil, Koriwn, that for two years letters of Syrian origin, learnt from a Syrian bishop, Daniel, and then perfected, were used, but that after these letters had proved deficient, Mesrop fashioned a new alphabet, in Edessa, and perfected it in consultation with a Greek scribe, in Samosata. Modern studies indicate that a twenty-sign code did indeed undergo two stages of development, under the influence of Greek, and that Mesrop's changes were to improve legibility and to represent sounds particular to Armenian.[1] He introduced only one new letter, *ք* (kᶜ), a form of the Greek monogram for Christ, placing it last, so that the alphabet begins with *ա* (a) representing God, and ends with Christ.

---

[1] Mouraviev, 1980a, 1980b.

The motivation behind Mesrop's creations was concern for his people's salvation rather than for its worldly prospects, but their timing may nevertheless have been related to the contemporary political situation. In the late fourth century Persia was probably tolerant of Armenian contacts with Christians in Mesopotamia, but suspicious of any sign of Roman influence or sympathy. Mesrop's rejection of the 'Syriac' letters may have been facilitated by the accession to the Persian throne of Yazdgard I (399–421), who in his early years was sympathetic to the Christian West.

Once the alphabet was settled, Armenian scholars embarked on a programme of translating and teaching. Their first translation of the Bible betrays the influence of Syria but its revision, after 431, shows that of the Greek church. Instruction was provided, at court and in the provinces. Students of Mesrop left Armenia to study Syriac and Greek and to translate patristic works. Many of these translations have been identified, by analysis of style and language, and they suggest that a large number of translators with a common training was involved. Mesrop's circle also produced original works. His pupil Eznik composed a treatise on God, dealing with the origins of evil and with free will, known as the *Refutation of the Sects*. Koriwn wrote a biography of Mesrop in about 443. The *Teaching* of St Gregory, a long exposition of the faith incorporated in the *History* of Agathangelos, is, probably, a representation of Mesrop's preaching, by one of his group. It betrays the influence of works of John Chrysostom (patriarch of Constantinople 398–404), of Basil of Caesarea (c.330–79) and of Cyril of Jerusalem (313–86).[2] The influence of Jerusalem is also apparent in the Lectionary used in the Armenian church until the eleventh century. Based upon one used in fifth-century Jerusalem, it was probably adopted in Armenia, under the aegis of Sahak, between 417 and 439.

This dynamic educational programme was not restricted to Persian Armenia. Sahak and Mesrop obtained permission from Constantinople (capital of the Roman Empire since the time of Constantine I), to include Roman Armenia, where schools were set up. Mesrop's missionary work also took him to Siwnikᶜ, and to the kingdoms of Iberia and Albania, for both of which he invented alphabets. There has been debate about whether a vernacular Albanian literature ever came about, but it seems that it did not and that it was Armenian language and culture which predominated in Albania.

It was probably in this period too that the development of the role of the *vardapet*, peculiar to the Armenian church, began. As a rank in the church *vardapet*, originally meaning 'teacher', is first attested at the 444 Council of Shahapivan. By then *vardapet*s had authority both to

[2] Thomson, 1970, pp. 31–7.

excommunicate and to readmit excommunicates, as bishops had. By the seventh century *vardapet*s could authorize marriages and depose and reinstate *chorepiscopi*, and they were teaching in monasteries. They could not demand payment, but were entitled to respect and, if necessary, support, from their disciples. *Vardapet*s seem to have resembled the *herbad*s, priest-teachers of Zoroastrianism.[3]

Persecution and Resistance, 428–484

One of the stimuli to these developments in Christian teaching must have been ecclesiastical fears concerning Persian policy. For the Persian monarchy's increasing dependence on the Zoroastrian religious establishment for support led to an increase in pressure on Armenian Christians to convert to Zoroastrianism. The methods used were persuasion, repression, bribery and force. Two crises resulted, in 450–1 and in 482.

The initial hope of the shah that friendly contact, facilitated by direct Persian rule, would encourage noble apostasy, may have been partially realized. Repression came only after Patriarch Sahak refused to consent to the deposition of Artaxias IV in 428. For a while it was relatively limited. Vahram V (of Persia) replaced Sahak, first with Surmak, and then with a Syrian, Brkishoy. Both displeased the Armenian princes; and Sahak, whose restoration some of them requested, recovered spiritual authority in 432. But his temporalities went to another Syrian, Samuel (432–7) and a power struggle ensued. Samuel looked for excuses to expel bishops and to seize their domains, as well as those of dead bishops whom he did not allow Sahak to replace. These ecclesiastical–political tensions may partially explain why Koriwn, in his biography of Sahak's partner, Mesrop, parades biblical references to legitimize Mesrop, as a new Moses, as a follower of the apostle Paul in his educational work, and as an example to be emulated. Koriwn's purpose was, presumably, to defend Sahak's party.[4]

The crisis of 450–1 began when in *c*.449 Yazdgard II (438–57) not only increased Armenian taxation, but also levied it on the Church. He then ordered conversion to Zoroastrianism. When they refused, the magnates and senior members of the lesser nobility in Armenia, Iberia and Albania were summoned to his court. They feigned apostasy and returned home with Zoroastrian teachers. There the sad and scornful reaction of their compatriots caused the princes to swear an oath, form a covenant and, taking advantage of Persia's military engagement in the east, to rebel, led by Vardan Mamikonean. Vasak of Siwnik[c], the Persian-appointed

---

[3] Thomson, 1962.
[4] Mahé, 1992.

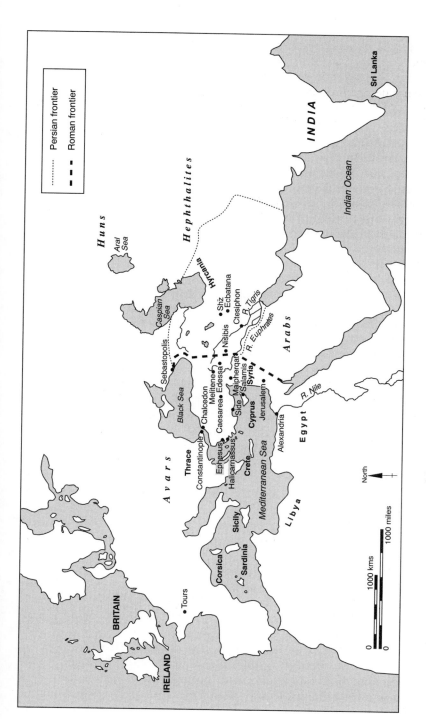

Map 7.1 Europe, west and south Asia

governor, or *marzpan* (*c*.442–51), joined them, but, partly because his sons were hostages at the Persian capital, Ctesiphon (near modern Baghdad), subsequently deserted, obtaining from Persia a promise of religious toleration. Nor was he the only Armenian on Persia's side. Within none of the aristocratic houses was there total consistency in members' sympathies.

Armenian Christians' circumstances were the more difficult because the Roman Empire did not offer the same prospect of help as she had in the past. For Armenia was never, during the fifth century, of major concern to Rome. Rome after all had serious problems in the west, where her provinces were lost one by one. And Roman–Persian relations were generally peaceful, Persia being preoccupied with the defence of her northern frontiers against invasion from central Asia. For this defence Persia seems to have been entitled to some Roman subsidy, regularly to have asked for substantially more, and to have seized opportunities presented by Rome's western problems to extract it by force. Leo I (454–74) paid up in 464. Zeno (474–5, 476–91) likewise contributed to Persian wars against the Kidarite Huns and the Hephthalites.

Rome did not, of course, completely abandon her north-eastern interests. Annexed Armenian principalities were required to furnish her with military aid. And the frontier was still protected. The early fifth-century *Notitia Dignitatum*, a list of the offices of the imperial administration, though its trustworthiness has been questioned, suggests that the Black Sea coast was still garrisoned, and that the legions *XV Apollinaris* and *XIV Fulminata* were still at Satala and Melitene. Satala indeed played an important role in the wars of 421–2 and 441–2 in which Persia invaded Syria, Cappadocia and Roman Armenia. Defences were improved. By the 430s the emperor Theodosius II (408–50) had built the fortified city of Theodosiopolis, modern Erzurum, in Carenitis. It was erected on an earlier site, probably the site of the centre held in Carenitis by the late fourth-century Arsacids.

But despite this continuing propinquity the Armenian rebels received no help from Rome. They did however manage an alliance with some Huns and they did achieve something. There was an heroic battle against Persia at Avarayr in 451 in which many, including Vardan, died. Freedom of religion was granted, the taxes were remitted and Vasak of Siwnik' was deprived of his principality. Less happy results were that the patriarch Joseph and some clerics were executed and some nobles were imprisoned and then required to do military service.

Apostasy continued to be the price Persia exacted for positions of power, and hence there was another crisis in the 480s. It began in 482 when the king of Iberia executed the apostate *vitaxa* of Gogarene. This *vitaxa* had martyred his Christian wife, Vardan's daughter Shushanik, in 475, and acquired from Persia both a royal spouse and control of Alba-

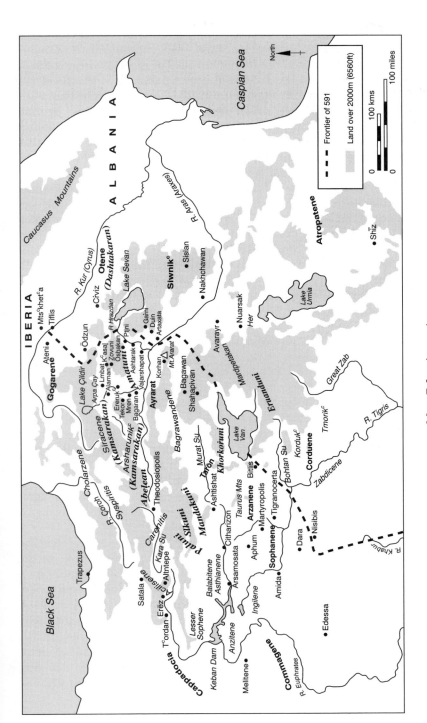

Map 7.2 Armenia

nia. Some Armenians, persuading Shushanik's cousin, Vahan Mamikonean, to lead them, joined this Iberian revolt. The rebels swore an oath on
the Gospel, appointed the Bagratuni prince Sahak II as *marzpan*, and
were reinforced briefly by some Hun mercenaries sent from Iberia and
also, judging by the 'Greek' origin of one of the elite casualties,[5] by some
Romans. They had some military success, but the Iberian king was put to
flight, Sahak and others were killed and, like Vardan before him, Vahan
had to suffer desertion and opposition from other Armenian princes.

   The situation was saved in 484 by the death of the Persian king, Peroz
(459–84), at the hands of the Hephthalites. Following negotiations
between Vahan and a Persian envoy who had come to Nuarsak (a village
in Her), the Armenians were granted freedom of religion, and right of access
to the king. Merit rather than apostasy was to be the basis for promotion.
The triumphant conclusion was that Vahan was appointed *marzpan*, in
485. The new political context enabled the Iberian king, Vakht^cang I, to ally
with Rome. It was probably in connection with his marriage to Helena, a
relative of Zeno, that the territory of Cholarzene was returned to Iberia.

Leadership *c.*400–*c.*500: Mamikoneans, Patriarchs and Historians

The two fifth-century crises reveal not only that the Mamikoneans and
the patriarchs worked in concert, but also that each had assumed, in their
leadership of Christian society, some aspects of the abolished Arsacid
kingship. The Mamikoneans had indeed also aquired much of the Gregorid inheritance, for Patriarch Sahak, who died in 439, had no heir but
his daughter, married to Hamazasp Mamikonean. Gregorid estates
(in Acilisene, which was now in the Roman Empire, part of Tarōn around
Ashtishat, and Bagrewand) made the Mamikoneans the greatest of
the Armenian landowners. They seem also to have assumed some
Gregorid obduracy and prestige, the martyrs Vardan and Shushanik
being Sahak's grandson and great-granddaughter.

   As for the patriarchs, their power rested in part on ecclesiastical
wealth, deriving from former temple estates, gifts given to atone for sin,
dues, and exemption from taxation. The patriarchal assumption of
aspects of a kingly role can be seen in the career of Sahak even before
the abolition of the kingship. When King Vramshapuh refused to invest
Hamazasp as *sparapet* without Sasanian permission, it was Sahak who
obtained it from Vahram IV (388–99). It was Sahak who arranged that
the survivors of the Kamsarakans and Amatunis who had offended
the Persian king be granted their lives and restored to their domains,
that Khosrov IV be restored, in 414, that Artaxias IV accede in 422 and

---

[5] Lazarus of P^carp, *History of the Armenians*, III, 83, trans. Thomson, 1991, p. 212.

that the order of precedence at court be confirmed, (probably by Vahram V (420–38)). The reality of patriarchal leadership is underlined in the fifth-century *Epic Histories'* account of reactions to the death of the fourth-century patriarch Nersēs, wherein the *sparapet* attributed victories over the enemies of Armenia to Nersēs' prayers and 'those of his clan' and predicted that there would be no more.[6]

Whereas the Mamikoneans provided military might, the patriarchs and their circle offered exhortation, both orally and in writing. When, in around 460, 'Agathangelos', who purported to be the secretary of Tiridates IV and hence an eyewitness, recounted the conversion of Armenia by Gregory the Illuminator some 150 years earlier, it was not really to record the distant past but rather to justify the recent past, to legitimate the present and to insure the future.[7] Mesrop's recent missionary work was given authority as a fulfilment of a Gregorian blueprint by the simple expedient of modelling the account of Gregory's work on Mesrop's. The contemporary cathedral of Ējmiatsin was sanctioned by a vision of Gregory, in which, some scholars believe, an actual building, either complete or still under construction, is described.[8] And Gregory's apparent direction of King Tiridates and of the nobility had the function of precedent and model for the current role of the church,[9] which quite clearly included political leadership. Patriarch Giwt (461–78) was deposed by Persia for canvassing for Roman help and attacking apostates. John Mandakuni, patriarch 478–90, kept in close touch with the rebel Vahan Mamikonean and his army and would bless them before and after battle.

Agathangelos may have hoped that the loyalty of Gregory the Illuminator's fratricidal father to the Sasanian king and the representation, actually a fiction, that Tiridates' conversion had been independent of that of the Roman emperor Constantine would make Armenian Christianity less suspect to any Persians who learnt of the conversion as he portrayed it. He may also have hoped that the Armenians would be encouraged by the *Teaching* of Gregory, which he included, to remain steadfast under pressure. For one of its lessons is that men must make their choice between Heaven and Hell when they hear the message, and that there is no second chance after death.[10] To reinforce this theme the explanation offered regarding Gregory's vision of the 'future' refers to a time when many 'impious ones' 'will abandon the holy covenant', perhaps a reference to those who deserted Vardan.[11] The impious will of

[6] *Epic Histories*, V, xxx, trans. Garsoïan, 1989, pp. 210–11.
[7] Thomson, 1976, pp. lxxv–xciii, esp. lxxxix–xciii.
[8] Agathangelos, *History of the Armenians*, 731–56, text and trans. Thomson, 1976, pp. 272–97; Thomson's pp. lv–lvii; Hultgård, 1982.
[9] Thomson, 1976, p. xciii.
[10] Thomson, 1970, p. 27, and pp. 125–6, *The Teaching of St Gregory*, para. 535.
[11] Agathangelos, 754, text and trans. Thomson, 1976, pp. 292, 293, and his pp. lvi–lvii.

course be 'handed over to unquenchable fire'. Agathangelos makes it clear that Zoroastrianism is no protection. Tiridates' punishment for martyring the nuns is charged, as Garsoïan has shown, with Iranian imagery. Tiridates becomes a boar, the animal identified with the god Vahagn, instead of an ox or bull like his biblical model Nebuchadnezzar, and wallows, in a parody of his 'divine' protector, helpless before the Christian God.[12]

The account of Armenian history between about 330 and 387 provided by the *Epic Histories*, whose author, an anonymous cleric, wove together in the 470s oral traditions about the patriarchs, the kings from Khosrov III to Arsaces II, and the Mamikoneans, is less sophisticated. Princes who may, perhaps, have been within their rights when they failed to follow Arsacid policies, are simply regarded as traitors to their legitimate lord.[13] Patriarch Sahak's sentiments about Artaxias IV, that however sinful he might be he was nevertheless a Christian king and so should be served, are anticipated in an address of Patriarch Nersēs to the council of the realm. The Mamikoneans figure as the protectors of the realm, for when they lead the army it is victorious. Willingness to die for the cause is lauded and death for the cause is equated with martyrdom. 'Die bravely for your God-serving realm, since that is in itself a death for God, for His church and His covenant, and for the true-lords of this realm', is simultaneously Manuēl Mamikonean's deathbed injunction to his son and successor in *c.*384, and our 470s compiler's injunction to his contemporaries,[14] albeit the Arsacid mantle now rested on others.

The momentous events of the fifth century likewise provided opportunities for exhortation. The history by Lazarus of Pᶜarp, which takes up where the *Epic Histories* end and continues to 485, was commissioned by the *marzpan* Vahan Mamikonean. Vahan wanted the virtues of clerics and good deeds of brave men to be written down so that others would emulate them.[15] The fact that the Mamikonean rebel leaders had actually apostasized before rebelling could of course have turned out to be embarrassing. But Lazarus conveniently portrays the mid-century pseudo-apostate Vardan embracing a self-imposed penance of exile, and being entreated by his fellow pseudo-apostates, in the realization that without Mamikonean leadership 'no Armenian affairs or undertakings were brought to completion' to abandon it. Mamikonean authority is enhanced by Vardan's statements that salvation is the most important thing in the world, and that his family was always more concerned for a friend's well-being than its own. Vahan, likewise an insincere apostate, is portrayed as waiting anxiously for a favourable moment to declare his true faith and so avoid

---

[12] Garsoïan, 1982.
[13] Garsoïan, 1989, pp. 6–16 (date and authorship); 22–35 (sources); 48–9 (attitude).
[14] *Epic Histories*, V, xliv, trans. Garsoïan, 1989, pp. 228–9.
[15] Lazarus, I, 4, trans. Thomson, 1991, pp. 37–9, and for discussion his pp. 1–8.

Hell. Both heroes, apparently, were initially reluctant to help their colleagues, remembering that their ancestors had suffered deceit and treachery, and they were admired and honoured by Persian nobles and monarchs. Lazarus particularly emphasizes the worthiness of the Mamikoneans as leaders by Vahan's defiance when urged by a Persian adversary to submit. He had won his victories, he said, with inferior numbers and without any foreign aid, and had only lost the recent encounter because of dissent and treachery on his own side.[16]

Lazarus also made it indubitably clear that Vahan's cause was that of God. On one occasion victory was announced in Duin, whither the capital was transferred in the second half of the century and, likewise (by Patriarch Giwt) the seat of the patriarch, with the proclamation that the power of the Cross had conquered and would always prevail. Finding the bridge at Artaxata destroyed and the river swollen, Vahan gained passage for his troops by making the sign of the Cross on himself. And his appointment as *marzpan* was celebrated in church. The patriarch chose as one of the readings the biblical passage where David had Solomon anointed king.[17]

Like the author of the *Epic Histories*, Lazarus emphasized a relationship between martial resistance and martyrdom. Vardan urged his associates to hurry to the banquet of Christ. Wives of prisoners and the widows of the martyrs 'were living martyrs'. The face of Vahan's brother Vasak was illuminated before he died, in token of his imminent translation to the army of angels. And in 451 the protagonists were, apparently, not simply willing to suffer martyrdom, but actively seeking it. They found the Persians unprepared at Avarayr, but held off because they wanted martyrdom more than victory.[18]

Social Change: Aristocracy, Heresy, Intellectual Life *c.428–c.570*

The extension of Christianity, the abolition of the kingship and the more pronounced leadership of the Mamikoneans were not the only changes Armenian society underwent in the fifth century. Another was that the central administration was reduced. The grand chamberlainship had disappeared with the kingship. The total strength of the noble cavalry after 428, about 30,000, was much less than under the monarchy. And

---

[16] For Vardan, Lazarus, II, 30, 46, trans. Thomson, 1982b, pp. 270–3, 300, and 1991, pp. 97–9, 130–1; for Vahan, Lazarus, III, 63, 65, 66, 75, trans. Thomson, 1991, pp. 164, 171–3, 194–5.

[17] Lazarus, III, 69, 94, 99–100, trans. Thomson, 1991, pp. 181, 232–3, 240–5.

[18] For Vardan, Lazarus, II, 38, trans. Thomson, 1982b, pp. 285–6 and 1991, p. 114; for the women, Lazarus, III, 61, trans. Thomson, 1982b, p.326, 1991, p. 161; for Vasak, Lazarus, III, 77, trans. Thomson, 1991, p. 201; for Avarayr, Lazarus, II, 38, trans. Thomson 1982b, p. 284, 1991, p. 112.

indeed the aristocracy as a whole was also reduced. Naturally the involvement of the lost principalities in Armenian affairs decreased, though Arzanene, Ingilene, Sophene, Asthianene, and Acilisene were asked for help against Persia, and Arzanene and Corduene may have tried to help. The sixth-century writer Ełishē blamed Vasak of Siwnikᶜ for holding back Arzanene and for urging the garrisons of Tmorikᶜ and Kordikᶜ, adjacent to Corduene, not to support the rebels.[19]

The historical record would suggest that a number of Armenian dynasties declined or even disappeared after the failure of the rebellion of 450–1.[20] They include the dynasties of Arzanene, of Corduene and of Zabdicene, the Orontid Eruandunis, the Ṙopᶜseans, the Slkunis, and the Ĕntsayatsᶜis, the Kᶜoḷeans, and the Sruandzits (who are all three attested solely in 450). The Mandakunis are not attested after 500, nor the Palunis after 505/506. In sum, Toumanoff concludes that seven houses belonging to six dynasties did disappear between 400 and 500, leaving thirty-five houses and twenty-two dynasties.

By contrast, the position of some other families improved. The Mamikoneans acquired some of the 'extinct' families' lands. The Artsrunis took over Mardpetakan (between Lakes Van and Urmia), hitherto under the grand chamberlain. The Khorkhoṙunis' increasing importance was probably due to their assumption of a margravial role after the loss of Arzanene. The princes of Siwnikᶜ, in the east, did likewise. Some new dynasties appeared, albeit short-lived and of minor importance: including besides the Ĕntsayatsᶜis, the Kᶜoḷeans, the Sruandzits, the Abeḷeans and the Dziwnakans, and the Dashtakarans and the Spandunis, the first two mentioned last in 555, the latter two in the seventh century. Toumanoff argues that the 'new' houses represent cadet branches of older dynasties. Another development was the practice of forming apanages for the *sepuh*s, making them, Toumanoff says, tenurially dependent on the family head, instead of independent, as co-possessors of family estates.[21]

As for the church, it had other problems besides Persian persecution. Though Arianism had been vanquished there were a number of other heresies to face. Disapproval of early Syrian doctrine may, as Winkler suggests, be reflected in the 'official' attribution of Armenia's conversion to Gregory, thereby denying the Syrian contribution.[22] The first Christians of Edessa had included members of Gnostic circles, followers of Mani, and Marcionites. The Marcionites, who preached a radical asceticism, were refuted by Eznik in his treatise on God, as were the pagans,

---

[19] Ełishē, *History of Vardan and the Armenian War*, IV, trans. Thomson, 1982b, pp. 145, 146.

[20] Toumanoff, 1963, pp. 154–227 for dynasties' histories (including *vitaxae* pp. 154–92); pp. 227, 229 for statistics; pp. 135–241 for cavalry strengths.

[21] Ibid., p. 248; pp. 219–28 (for houses existing only in post-Arsacid period); p. 252 (cadets); p. 124 (apanages).

[22] Winkler, 1980.

Greek philosophers and Mazdaeans (Zoroastrians). Eznik's reason for including them may have been that he believed there were Marcionites in Armenia. There were probably some Manichees too, though there is no evidence that they were numerous.

Another group of heretics were the Messalians. The Messalians had been condemned around 390 by the Council of Side, and their beliefs have to be gleaned from orthodox writings. Messalians seem to have rejected manual labour, asceticism, marriage, the sacraments and the ecclesiastical hierarchy, and to have embraced a dualist theology along the lines of Manichaeism, and a defective Christology.[23] The Armenian church condemned Messalians at the Council of Shahapivan in 444, though by an unfortunate coincidence the name used for them also means simply 'filthiness', and some scholars have argued that some other group of deviants were meant by it.[24] They may be the same heretics whom Lazarus of P^carp described, in a letter to Vahan Mamikonean, as ignorant, lazy and inconstant, but 'not named for any teacher'.[25] There were also the Borborites, who came to the attention of the patriarch Atticus of Constantinople (405–25). According to Epiphanius of Salamis, a contemporary of Basil of Caesarea, the Borborites had Gnostic origins.

Doctrinal disagreement with outsiders began after the first Council of Ephesus of 431. This had addressed the nature of Christ, and affirmed the status of the Virgin as *Theotokos*, mother of God. The Armenian Church had not been represented at this council but it soon became aware of its concerns. In 433 or 434 Bishop Acacius of Melitene expressed to the patriarch, Sahak, his fears that there were followers of Theodore of Mopsuestia in Armenia. Theodore, who had died in 428, had come under suspicion since, and partly as a result of, the Ephesus Council. Theodore's writings had earlier been promoted in Edessa, where Mesrop and some of his disciples had worked and where Brkishoy and Samuel (the Syrian replacements of Sahak) had, possibly, studied, and they were certainly known in Armenia. The surviving version of Sahak's reply to Acacius rather evasively denies the presence of false doctrine. Sahak proceeded to seek clarification from Constantinople and when his delegates returned, with the *Tome* of Patriarch Proclus and the canons of Ephesus, the Council of Ashtishat was held (in 435/436) and the decisions of Ephesus accepted.[26] Theodore himself escaped condemnation, but some Armenian clerics, dissatisfied, joined in the continuing campaign against him.

The 451 Council of Chalcedon, whose Armenian representatives were from 'lost' territories (from Theodosiopolis, and from Sophene, Anzitene, Ingilene, Sophanene, and Balabitene whose metropolitan superior was

[23] Meyendorff, 1970.
[24] Garsoïan, 1967a, pp. 207–10.
[25] Lazarus, *Letter*, trans. Thomson, 1991, pp. 254–6; Garsoïan, 1967a, pp. 156–209.
[26] Winkler, 1985.

the bishop of Amida), and which defined the orthodox dyophysite doctrine of the nature of Christ, was to prove more troublesome. For its Christological doctrine provoked schism with the eastern Monophysites who all stressed His single nature, and ultimately, though not immediately, with Armenia. In 451 Armenian attention was of course focussed on rebellion against Persia, and in 482 the emperor Zeno, attempting to heal the breach with the Monophysites, issued his *Henoticon*, which Armenia accepted at the 506 Council of Duin. But Constantinople subsequently repudiated the *Henoticon*, Papal opposition having provoked an east–west schism, which ended only in 519. Armenia in turn subsequently rejected both Chalcedon and so-called Nestorianism, which the Persian church had adopted in the early sixth century, at another council or councils at Duin, in 555 or (if indeed there were two councils) in 552–3 and 555. Relations with the Syrian church, this council's chief concern, soured. Followers of Julian of Halicarnassus, who were a minority in Syria, found support in Armenia.

It is possible that the later sixth-century church had yet another heresy to face, that of the Paulicians, whose name means 'followers of Paul'. For their early history may belong to this period though the evidence is slight. The fifth-century John Mandakuni's *Call to Repentance* and the Oath of Union of the 555 Duin Council allude to Paulicians, but there are doubts about the authenticity of both these references.[27] The Katholikos John of Ōdzun's (717–28) *Against the Paulicians* records that the Paulicians hid somewhere on the border, after the death of Katholikos Nersēs. (The first known use by the head of the church of the title Katholikos is in Nersēs II's synodal letter of 555. But it was probably in use earlier, for it appears in Armenian historical writing of the second half of the fifth century, sometimes used, anachronistically, for fourth-century patriarchs.) John may have meant Nersēs II (548–57), but he could equally well have meant Nersēs III (641–66). Then, John says, they were joined by iconoclasts who had been rebuked by the Albanian Katholikos.[28] Other texts attest a group which cited Old Testament prohibitions against idolatry to support its opposition to images and paintings. This group seems to have formed, and been noticed by the Armenian authorities, in the period c.590–610. It was perhaps reacting against the current ecclesiastical involvement in Roman-Persian rivalry, Roman and Persian Armenia each having, in the 590s, their own Katholikos.[29] The Albanians took action against these iconoclasts in about 633. By the 670s the schismatics had become heretics and were rejecting baptism.

[27] Garsoïan, 1967a, pp. 87 and n.24, 90 n. 28e, 131; and for the oath, ibid. pp. 88–9, 90 n. 28, and Lemerle, 1973, p. 54.
[28] *Against the Paulicians* in Aucher, 1834. Discussed in Garsoïan, 1967a and Russell, 1987, pp. 515–28.
[29] Der Nersessian, 1944–5, 1946; Alexander, 1955.

Heretics were dealt with by preaching, punishment and ecclesiastical legislation. To convert the Borborites Mesrop tried punishments, imprisonments and tortures. When they remained obdurate, they were scourged, branded and expelled. The 444 Council decreed branding and hamstringing for Messalians and for priests who failed to report them. Former dissidents could be admitted to penance. Studies of the earliest rites of penance, generally conceived in the early church as a second baptism, suggest that they may have been originally composed for accepting apostates and heretics back into the fold.[30]

Despite the various political and ecclesiastical problems Armenian intellectual life continued to thrive. The late fifth century onwards produced further translations into Armenian of Greek writers, including Aristotle and Plato, and the medical writers Hippocrates and Galen. Lazarus of P[c]arp studied in the Roman Empire, before being appointed, by the *marzpan* Vahan, as abbot of a monastery in Valarshapat. (When his efficiency, financial probity and orthodoxy were impugned, he took refuge in Amida, whence he cleared himself, and was then recalled.) An organized form of communal monasticism seems to been a new development in Armenia in the fifth century. Armenia appears also to have resumed, in the sixth century, some missionary enterprise, probably with political overtones, in response to the onslaught of the Huns upon the Roman Empire. About 535, according to a Syriac source of 569, a bishop with seven priests went from Albania to minister to Roman captives, and in seven years made many Hun converts and translated some books into the Hun language. This success was followed up a little later by another initiative on the part of another Armenian bishop, Maku.[31]

Roman Revival *c.500–c.640*

Whereas the Armenian political experience in the fifth century had been one of increasing Persian pressure, in the sixth century, by contrast, it was one of Roman revival, in which the Roman emperors asserted and extended their control. Already in the late fifth century Zeno had created the office of count of Armenia, to supervise the princes of Inner Armenia, (that is, the former 'Roman' kingdom, annexed in 390, with the Arsacids in Carenitis, the Bagratunis in Syspiritis (Sper) and the Mamikoneans in Acilisene), though the precise extent of this count's authority is uncertain. In the lands annexed in 387, the five hereditary southern princes, known as satraps, had been replaced, except in Balabitene, as punishment for

---

[30] Raes, 1947; Lages, 1971.
[31] Thompson, 1946.

supporting a rebellion, and by 502 the satrapies had lost their immunity from taxation. Next the frontier was strengthened by Anastasius (491–518), prompted by the Persian invasion of 502, in which only Edessa had proved to be adequately defended. Theodosiopolis was expanded and given new walls, and at Melitene some refortification was undertaken, after 515. The fort of Citharizon in Asthianene was begun, probably, by Anastasius though it was completed by Justin I (518–27), to hold the northern end of one of the Taurus passes.

Even greater changes came with Justinian I (527–65). For Justinian embraced a massive programme of imperial restoration which entailed reconquest of the West besides defence, and necessitated provincial, military and financial reorganization, and much building. In Armenian lands military reorganization followed the reopening of war by Persia, desperate for money, in 527 and the failure of the Roman offensive of 528. Justinian abolished both the office of Count of Armenia and the title of Satrap. The satraps' territories were set, with Armenia I, Armenia II and Pontus Polemoniacus, under a *magister militum*, the highest military rank of the empire, with five dukes beneath him. The military centre was transferred north from Melitene to Theodosiopolis, and the line of defence moved east from Satala-Melitene to Theodosiopolis-Martyropolis. Martyropolis had been founded, or refounded, c. 410 by Bishop Marut^{c}a who endowed it with bones of martyrs killed by Shapur II of Persia. Satala was provided with new walls and at Theodosiopolis, Melitene and Martyropolis, Anastasius' walls were completed and improved. Justinian also, deciding not to fortify the city of Bizana, or Leontopolis, built another, Justinianopolis to act as capital. Some scholars suggest that the place selected was the ancient Urartian site at Altıntepe.[32]

Justinian also addressed Armenian civilian life.[33] In 536 he created four provinces. The first, Armenia I comprised Inner Armenia, part of the former Armenia I, including Satala and two other cities, and two cities from Pontus Polemoniacus. Justinianopolis was its capital and its governor held proconsular rank. The Armenian-born Acacius was appointed to this post but was killed by the Armenians not long after. The second province comprised the rest of former Armenia I, with additions. The third, Armenia III, was the former Armenia II. Its capital was Melitene and its count, an Armenian, Thomas, had military powers. (The office of duke was discontinued.) Armenia IV comprised the satrapies, Sophanene, Anzitene, Sophene, Asthianene and Balabitene and it included Martyropolis and Citharizon.

[32] The suggestion regarding Justinianopolis is reported in Sinclair, 1989a, p. 532. Procopius, *Buildings*, III, v, 13–15 says Justinianopolis was built in the place called Tzumina. Tzumina was at or near Altintepe. For Procopius' consistent exaggeration of Justinian's building, and crediting of earlier work to Justinian's reign, see Croke and Crowe, 1983.
[33] Adontz–Garsoïan, 1970, pp. 127–54, and also Hewsen, 1992, pp. 22 (map III) 18 and 25 (table) for provincial organization.

Justinian was not only an administrative innovator but also a legal reformer and a grasping financier. Inheritance was one of his major concerns and he decreed that Armenian customs should fall into line: women were to have rights of inheritance in cases of intestacy, which were probably normal for the Armenian aristocracy. Adontz regarded this order as an attempt to undermine Armenian princely power by fragmenting princely landed wealth.[34] Justinian followed it with the introduction of a tax of 400 pounds of gold. The result was rebellion, in 538, by the three princely families of former Inner Armenia. In 539, after their Arsacid leader John was slain, the Armenian rebels, led by John's son-in-law Vasak, probably a Mamikonean, asked Persia for aid, thereby contributing to the outbreak of another Roman–Persian war.

But the trouble-makers soon deserted Persia and the elite of the region were absorbed into Justinian's empire. The Bagratunis and Mamikoneans seem to have ceased to be important there after Justinian's reign. John's two sons served Justinian in Libya, where one, Artabanes, played a leading role between 541 and 545. Artabanes' participation, in 548, in an unsuccessful conspiracy in Constantinople was probably due to personal as much as to political reasons, the empress Theodora having thwarted his desire to marry a niece of Justinian. The conspiracy itself is certainly suggestive of particularly Armenian opposition to his deeds. It was organized by Artabanes' kinsman Arsaces, who had been punished for treacherous negotiations with Persia, and who was, apparently, provoked by John's death, by the taxation and occupation of his fatherland and by the enslaving and scattering of the Arsacids. But opposition to Justinian's expensive policies was not confined to the Armenians, and our source, the contemporary historian Procopius, in true classical tradition, uses speeches to express his own views as much as his perception of the views of the speakers. The declarations of the disgruntled Armenians to the Persians in 539 served Procopius as a vehicle for a general denunciation of Justinian's rule.[35]

Persian Armenia, combined with Iberia, Albania, Atropatene and Siwnik[c] in one administrative unit, meanwhile remained relatively unchanged. Sometimes the *marzpan* was an Armenian prince. Vahan Mamikonean was succeeded, early in the sixth century, by his brother, for four years. Mzhēzh Gnuni held the office 518–48. Mzhēzh's main problem came from the north, whence there had been an invasion in 515–16 and another in 527. Persian jurisdiction in Armenia extended to the church, just as it did elsewhere in Persian dominions, and Persian policy seems now to have been to detach Armenia from her Christian neighbours.[36] An eleventh-century Georgian treatise on the separation of

[34] Adontz–Garsoïan, 1970, p. 153.
[35] Procopius, *History of the Wars*, VII, xxxii and II, iii 32–54.
[36] Garsoïan, 1984, pp. 235–42.

the Georgians and the Armenians, sometimes attributed to the ninth-century Iberian katholikos, Arsen, and which draws on a seventh-century source, suggests that pressure from King Khosrov I (531–79) caused the Armenians, despite the dissent of the bishop of Siwnik^c and four northern colleagues, formally to separate from the Roman church at the 555 Council of Duin. Persia's encouragement of such separatism is more easily apparent in the events of the early seventh century. The katholikos Abraham (607–10/11 or 615) was elected in 607 at a council summoned by Smbat Bagratuni, an Armenian high in the favour of Khosrov II (591–628) and formerly (595–602) *marzpan* in Hyrcania, south-east of the Caspian Sea. Abraham was to rival John of Bagaran, an imperial appointee installed about 592 in opposition to the katholikos Moses II (574–604) and currently at Theodosiopolis. Smbat and Abraham tried, unsuccessfully, to persuade the Iberians to abandon communion with the empire and according to the tenth-century Armenian katholikos John V, the council of 608/9 at which Armenia separated from the Iberian church was also ordered by Smbat.[37]

These ecclesiastical events were related to the shifts in political fortune which had recently occurred. Rome had made peace with Persia in 561 but at a price and on condition that from 572 she would pay Persia an annual subsidy. Justin II (565–78) however was anxious to cancel this subsidy, especially since Persia was representing it to other people as tribute. He had been encouraged in 571 by a Turkish offer to join in an attack on Persia, but it was the Armenians of Persian Armenia who fortuitously provided him with a *casus belli*. In 572, just after the cessation of Siwnik^c to Persia and under the leadership of Vardan Mamikonean, they rebelled, after the Persian *marzpan* Surēn (564–72) had killed Vardan's brother Manuēl and, despite the objections of the Katholikos whose palace he seems to have taken over, built a Zoroastrian fire temple in Duin. Though Surēn was killed, and the palace and fire temple burnt, the rebellion failed. Vardan and the Katholikos fled to Constantinople. An Iberian rebellion meanwhile fared no better. So Justin seized this opportunity to engineer church union, to hold back the Persian subsidy, and to fight Persia, with Armenian allies, alleging religious provocation. His forces raided Arzanene, which had refused to support the rebellion.

For some sixteen years however Rome made little headway. In 573 Justin lost Dara and went mad. In 576 Khosrov invaded Armenia and sacked Melitene. In 577 Rome was defeated in Armenia. In 578 the future emperor Maurice (582–602) ravaged Arzanene, took thousands of prisoners and the fort of Aphum, but failed to capture Chlomaron, that is ancient Tigranocerta. In 580, and at the request of its princes, Persia abolished the kingship of Iberia. In 581 Maurice's offensive against

37 John Katholikos, *History of the Armenians*, XVII, 13, trans. Maksoudian, 1987, p. 96.

Ctesiphon failed. And in 582, 583, 585 and in 586, when Chlomaron was besieged but again not taken, there were yet further campaigns in Arzanene.

The tide only turned in 588. The Iberians petitioned the emperor for a king, and were granted Vakht͚ang I's grandson as 'presiding prince'. Then in 589 the Persian shah Hormizd's general Bahram (Vahram) Chobin, infuriated by the shah's insults after he had suffered a Roman defeat, rebelled against him, seemingly intending to enthrone Hormizd's son Khosrov II (591–628). When Khosrov fled, Bahram made himself king, and, according to the late seventh- or eighth-century Armenian historian 'Sebēos', offered the Armenians a restoration of their kingship and of their former territory in return for their support. They refused.[38] It was the Roman Empire which was to profit from Bahram's difficulty. The emperor Maurice restored Khosrov, and his reward was about half of Armenia. In 591 the Roman frontier was advanced, to run from Tiflis to just east of Bitlis, passing just west of Artaxata, Duin and Garni.

This Roman advance prompted yet another imperial provincial reorganization.[39] The ancient Armenian lands of Sophanene, Arzanene and Commagene now became Fourth Armenia, or Upper Mesopotamia, which consequently included Citharizon and Arsamosata. The existing Armenia I became Greater Armenia. Rome's newly acquired territory was grouped into Deep, Lower and Inner Armenia. Armenia III became the new Armenia I. Armenia II was retained. The former Armenia IV became Justiniana, retaining five of its six principalities, but not its former capital, Martyropolis. Martyropolis, betrayed to Persia in 589, and where Khosrov set up an inscription, once attributed to King Pap, commemorating the recovery of his dominions, was restored to Rome.

The Roman Empire's expansion proved however to have some disadvantages for the Armenians. One was ecclesiastical. Church union was established in 591 but then there was a schism. Katholikos Moses severed relations with the bishops of Roman Armenia whereupon Rome established an anti-katholikos, John, at Awan just across the frontier. There was also the emperor's policy of settling Armenians in Thrace, and recruiting Armenians to fight the Avars in the Balkans. Contingents under Musheḷ Mamikonean and under Sahak Mamikonean fought there. Unfortunately this recruitment was not popular with all Armenians. There was therefore some emigration into Persian territory, encouraged by Khosrov who offered gifts and emblems of rank and distinction. There may also have been an unsuccessful rebellion against Maurice, led by Smbat Bagratuni, the future *marzpan* of Hyrcania, though some

---

[38] Sebēos, *History of Heraclius*, III, trans. Macler, 1904, pp. 19–21.
[39] For detailed discussion and maps, Hewsen, 1992, maps III, IV, pp. 18–19, 24–7, 150–2, 153–4, 158, 162–3, 204–5, 212.

scholars, following the early seventh-century Greek historian Theophylact Simocatta rather than the later Armenian 'Sebēos', prefer to date this before the redrawing of the frontier, to 589.[40]

Nevertheless Roman control was seriously threatened only after the coup of 602 in which Maurice was executed. Then Khosrov, avenging his adopted father, recouped his losses with interest. He took Theodosiopolis (whose inhabitants were later deported), Satala and Citharizon in 607/8, Melitene in 612 and Jerusalem (with the True Cross) in 614. Rome's situation was eventually retrieved by the emperor Heraclius (610–41) who for six years made Armenia his base. In 623 Heraclius even destroyed the fire temple at Gandzak (Shīz), capital of Atropatene, one of Persia's greatest. In 627 the ruling prince of Iberia, a Persian ally, was killed and Heraclius installed another, retaining, for Rome, the Armenian–Iberian frontier regions, including Cholarzene. In 628 Khosrov II was deposed and Heraclius made peace with his successor, Kavad-Shiroe, stipulating that the Cross be returned.

The omens for Rome in the 630s were auspicious. The frontiers were restored. Roman Armenia was supervised first through Mzhēzh II Gnuni, Heraclius' commander-in-chief there from 628 to 635, and then through prince David Saharuni, and Persian Armenia through Varaztirots[c] II, son of Smbat Bagratuni, who had been fostered at Khosrov's court. Albania, whose kingship Persia had abolished early in the sixth century, was secured by Heraclius' appointment, in 628, of a presiding prince sympathetic to his religious policy. The Chalcedonian problem was addressed, by the emperor and the patriarch of Constantinople, Sergius, with the formulation of a doctrine of a single energy in Christ (Monenergism). They had some success in Egypt and Syria, and in Roman Armenia church union was established at a council in Theodosiopolis in 632–3. Unfortunately, disagreement elsewhere led to the imperial pronouncement, in 638, of another doctrine, that of a single will (Monothelitism), instead. This was to cause more trouble than Monenergism had, and in all quarters.

Literature, Art, Architecture *c.*570–640

The events of the later sixth and the early seventh century naturally affected the development of Armenian scholarship, historical literature, art and architecture. The so-called 'Hellenizing school' of Armenian writers and translators was founded in about 570 in Constantinople and flourished there until about 730. It produced translations, mainly

---

[40] Theophylact Simocatta, *History*, III, viii, 4–8, trans. Whitby, M. and Whitby, M., 1986, pp. 83–4; for dating, Whitby, M., 1988, pp. 127 and n. 55, 291 and n. 24.

of philosophical works, faithfully reproducing the original Greek syntax. Their purpose was probably to help Armenians studying the originals in Constantinopolitan schools. One of this school's members was David the Invincible, a Neoplatonist philosopher associated in later traditions with Mesrop's circle. He belonged to the school of Olympiodorus of Alexandria, where for a time he was head of the school. He was responsible for four major works in Greek, composed by him directly or, possibly, compiled by a pupil on the basis of lecture notes, which were used for centuries in Armenia as an introduction to philosophy and were also influential, later, in Byzantium and the Arab world.[41]

As for those who remained in Armenia, some justified events by referring to or inventing historical precedent, as had been done in the fifth century. Ecclesiastical politics required changes, in geographical locations and in points of doctrine, within the 'received' version of Armenia's Christian past, to bring it into line with the present. One of the several surviving versions of Agathangelos' *History* seems to derive from some time between 604, when Maurice's anti-katholikos John fled from the Persians to Theodosiopolis, and 610, when he was imprisoned. The very place where John resided appears in this version as the site of Gregory's mass baptism of Armenians, presumably to compensate for the fact that John's rival controlled the holy sites of Valarshapat. This western version of 'Agathangelos' was later recopied to help Katholikos Ezr (630–41), ally of Heraclius.[42]

Our most important text is the *History of Vardan and the Armenian War* by Ełishē, which became the classic account of the 450–1 rebellion. Its date has been much discussed, but the surviving version seems likely to be late sixth-century.[43] Its composition may be related to the 572 rebellion, its purpose to justify and inspire those involved in the ensuing war. Ełishē's version of the 450–1 revolt gives the clergy a leading role, justifies armed resistance and emphasizes martial martyrdom even more than had the account of Lazarus of Pᶜarp. Thus the clergy urge resistance even before the rebellion begins, and they question Vardan about his apostasy before sanctioning his leadership. The priest Łewond tells the warriors that the clerics wish to join in the attack instead of, as in former times, merely praying in the camp.[44]

Thomson, in his study of the *History*, emphasizes: that there are numerous verbal parallels between Ełishē's text and the Armenian version of the Syriac *Acts of the Persian Martyrs*; that the *History*'s set-piece speeches focus on Old Testament figures who fought for their country and people, instead of on early Christians who suffered torments for their

---

[41] Kendall and Thomson, 1983.
[42] van Esbroeck, 1971a.
[43] Thomson, 1982b, pp. 22–9 for dating; pp. 9–21 motives and themes. Frendo, 1985.
[44] Thomson, 1982b, pp. 3–9, and pp. 114–15, 165 for Ełishē, III, V.

faith; and that Eḷishē uses terms with connotations of martyrdom whenever the Armenians face the Persians in battle.[45] In the vision, seen by a chief magus newly converted to Christianity, of the ascent to Heaven of Vardan and numerous soldiers who died at Avarayr, his message is even more explicit. Eḷishē's heroes treat Persian promises of religious freedom as cunning deceits rather than genuine solutions, whereas the deserter Vasak of Siwnik[c] and his party accept them. The 'traitors' could have been portrayed very differently, as statesmen. But so that everyone may curse him and not lust after his deeds, Eḷishē emphasizes Vasak's bad end, denounced by all, his body thrown out as carrion.[46]

The historical literature of Armenian resistance was complemented just as the Scriptures were, by images decorating churches. Lucy Der Manuelian's studies of sculptural images on steles and in and on churches have highlighted significant differences from Byzantine, Coptic and Syrian art. Armenian monuments often depicted historical and secular Armenian characters, as, she believes, exemplars; earlier martyrs who had already made the choice as spelt out in Gregory's *Teaching*, or contemporaries who were currently making it. Their images evoked the concept of salvation through individual effort. Such effort might be death for the faith, as in the case of Manuēl, Lord of the Amatunis, who died in 389. His portrayal in a hunting scene, itself having connotations of the afterlife, at the sixth- or early seventh-century church of Ptḷni is suggestively close to images of Christ, angels and apostles. The effort might also be patronage of a church, as in the case of Kohazat, prince of Siwnik[c], whose portrait at a church at Sisian, probably completed in 691, is located at the point where the cupola, symbolizing Heaven, rises. Little, if any, art was purely decorative. Even the birds which decorate a sixth-century Armenian commemorative mosaic pavement in Jerusalem had a purpose, representing the souls of the dead.[47]

Despite the axe they ground against Persia however, ecclesiastical artists did not reject all aspects of Persian culture. The four Ējmiatsin miniatures, dated to sometime in the sixth–seventh centuries prior to 640, show familiarity with contemporary Persian art and practice, especially in the treatment of dress and stance in the representation of the Adoration of the Magi.

Architectural works include many carved steles, probably sepulchral and often associated with churches. Like many of the churches themselves, they are difficult to date precisely. The churches, which are numerous, vary in size, several single-naved churches being less than 9 yards long. They show a variety of designs, especially in the seventh century, behind which may lie not merely artistic creativity but also, perhaps, technical advance, changes in liturgical requirements, and, possibly,

---

[45] Thomson, 1982a and 1982b, pp. 11–21, esp. 20, 14, 17–18.
[46] Eḷishē, VII, VI, trans. Thomson, 1982b, pp. 198–202 (vision); 190–1 (Vasak's end).
[47] Der Manuelian, 1982.

Plate 7   The Adoration of the Magi (sixth–seventh century) from the Ējmiatsin Gospel, Erevan, Matenadaran, no. 2374, fo. 229.

doctrinal affiliation. Thus an apparent preference in the seventh century for more space and annexes may reflect liturgical need. In the same period some churches were built, or modified, to have three windows in the altar apse instead of just one and some specialists have hitherto accepted Érémian's argument that this feature reflected a Chalcedonian allegiance.[48]

[48] Érémian, 1971, accepted by the majority of specialists according to Donabédian, 1983, p. 8 of text and 1991a, p. 141. Mathews 'Observations on the Church of St. Hripsime', (Study IV in Mathews, 1995) disagrees, including a challenge to Érémian's dating of the windows in this church which is crucial to the argument.

Of the known churches the earliest were rectangular basilicas, with one or three naves. Five such buildings, with three naves, fairly certainly predate the 640s. Of these, those at Aḷdzkᶜ and Kᶜasaḷ (the Holy Cross) are fourth-century, that at Ereruᵏᶜ, which shows signs of Syrian influence, and those of Ashtarak and Eḷvard are sixth-century. The latter two were probably built by Katholikoi Nersēs II and Moses II. Some underground martyria, of several types, have been preserved, including the mausoleum (c.442) of Mesrop at Ōshakan, an Amatuni village, and the late fifth- or early sixth-century mausoleum traditionally associated with Saint Vardan and Tachat Gntᶜuni, at Zovuni in Gntᶜuni territory. The Armenians also built domed churches, a preference to which the ancient tradition of symbolizing and representing Heaven in domed ceilings may have contributed.[49] The late fifth-century church of St Sergius at Tekor, built by Sahak Kamsarakan and consecrated by John Mandakuni, Vahan Mamikonean's cathedral at Ējmiatsin (Vaḷarshapat), Katholikos Komitas's (610/11 or 615–28) smaller church of Hṙipᶜsimē, built nearby in 618, and the anti-katholikos John's cathedral of Awan, of about 600, are all domed with a central plan.

Design variations[50] included the number of apses as well as other aspects. The church of the Mother of God at Crviz (c.500), with a cruciform perimeter, has a central plan and is the earliest example of a church with four apses. A later one is the small church of the Holy Cross at Tᶜordan, founded by the emperor Heraclius c.625. Nersēs Kamsarakan's small church of St Anania at Alaman, built in 637, and Katholikos Christopher's church at Korhan, c.630 had three apses. Armenians built single-apsed cross-shaped churches, four-apsed square ones, four-apsed ones with galleries, and churches planned as crosses within perimeters, that is with four vaulted wings extending from the central cupola and with corner rooms in the angles. To this last category belong David Saharuni's cathedral at Mren, finished 639–40, and Katholikos Ezr's churches of St John at Bagawan and St Gayianē at Ējmiatsin. The category of hall-shaped churches with a cupola, which includes the church at Ptḷni, was concentrated in Amatuni territory in Ayrarat.

To the aesthetic impact of the churches a variety of media contributed. Besides the design there was the building material, namely different coloured tuff-stone. Sculptural decoration, of both churches and steles, comprised geometric and plant motifs, vine scrolls, birds, animals, portraits and scenes. Representations of the Virgin, Christ, saints and laity were more common than those of biblical scenes. At least some churches had decoration in mosaic, for a few fragments of mosaics have been

---

[49] For this contribution (without particular relevance to Armenia), Lehmann, 1945, criticized by Mathews, 1982a. McVey, 1983, discusses the literary evidence for the association of the Christian dome with cosmology in the sixth-century Hagia Sophia of Edessa.

[50] Categorized in Thierry and Donabédian, 1987 and 1989.

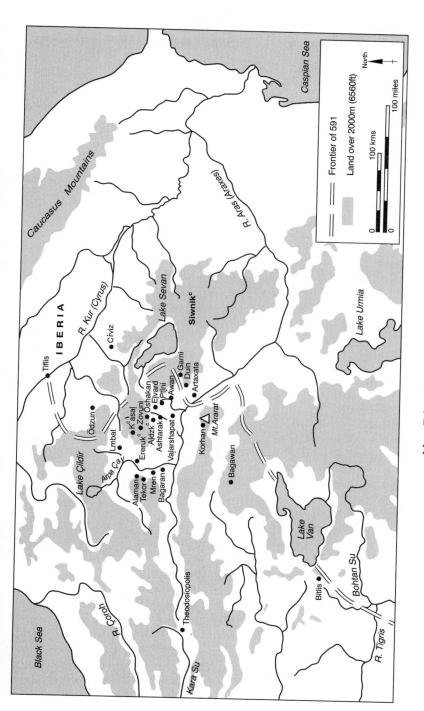

Map 7.3 Armenian churches

Plate 8   The south-west façade of the early seventh-century Church of St Hŕipᶜsimē at Vaḷarshapat

discovered. To judge by Vrtᶜanēs Kᶜertᶜoḷ's defence of images and modern scientific analysis,[51] churches also normally had frescoes. A few fragments of frescoes have survived at Mren and Lmbatavankᶜ and elsewhere.

The motives for building churches must have varied. Probably the katholikoi felt professionally obliged to build. For the aristocracy, building was an opportunity to display the donor's and his family's wealth and piety, and church decoration an opportunity not simply to inspire fellow Christians but also to recall their own great deeds: in short, to build was to make a statement about fitness to rule, whether in a small locality or the country at large. In addition, inscriptions reveal that church building was thought to help ensure salvation. The building itself was conceived as

[51] Kotandjian, 1991.

a kind of intercessor for the donor and for those he associated with his gift.[52] At Mren, where Nersēs Kamsarakan was joint patron with David Saharuni, an inscription records that the cathedral was built for the salvation of the souls of the Kamsarakans. Its intended audience will have included God, His angels and His saints in Heaven.

Ecclesiastical building, perhaps the greatest glory of Armenian culture, is an index of economic prosperity as well as of stability and of piety. Roman coins reached Armenia but the currency of trade in Armenia was Sasanian, and Sasanian coins, many minted in Nakhchawan and Duin, circulated throughout. Duin became a trading centre. Artisans lived there and Jewish, Syrian and Persian merchants visited. According to Procopius, Duin received goods from India, from practically all the nations of Persia and from some under the Romans.[53] The huge amount of unwoven silk which, according to Procopius's near-contemporary, the late sixth-century Gallo-Roman writer Gregory of Tours, Armenian rebels offered to the emperor in 572,[54] may have been booty from Duin.

The emperor Heraclius' achievements should have inaugurated a golden age. Armenians had weathered Persian persecution and much warfare, Roman–Persian relations were peaceful, Roman–Armenian relations close, the problem of Christian doctrine was, for a while, solved, and the building of churches was proceeding apace. Unfortunately a little-observed storm cloud on the horizon was about to break. The prophet Muhammad died in 632, and his followers emerged from Arabia to change the history of the world.

---

[52] Der Manuelian, 1984, pp. 104–5.
[53] Procopius, *History of the Wars*, II, xxv, 3.
[54] Gregory of Tours, *The Histories*, IV, 40.

8

Arab Rule and the Revival of Kingship, c.640–884

Neither Byzantium (as modern historians call the Roman Empire from around this date) nor Persia was prepared in the 630s for armies from Arabia, fighting in the name of Islam. With startling rapidity Arab forces conquered Persia, at Qadisiyya in 637, and Byzantine Syria, Mesopotamia and Egypt. In Armenia, however, the establishment of Arab rule took several decades. In the eighth century this rule was oppressive, but its gradual relaxation in the ninth culminated in the re-establishment of an Armenian monarchy, in the hands of the Bagratuni dynasty.

The Arab–Byzantine Struggle, 640–c.700

The initial Arab conquest of Armenia may be summarized as follows, though the tangled information in the sources has provoked disagreements, especially regarding chronology. The Arabs first invaded in 640. They captured Duin but then retired, with booty and thousands of captives. This was a raid rather than a conquest, but another invasion followed and by 652 the Arabs had, despite resistance, gained control. In 652/3 they made a treaty with the Persian-raised and Byzantine-appointed *sparapet*, Theodore Ṙshtuni, granting him authority, under their own sovereignty, over Armenia, Iberia, Albania and Siwnikᶜ. Neither Katholikos Nersēs III (641–66) nor, naturally enough, the Byzantine emperor Constans II (641–68) supported Theodore's coming to terms, and so they joined forces against it. Constans dismissed Theodore, but neither his military action nor his attempt to unite Armenia and Byzantium doctrinally succeeded in retrieving the situation. His *Typos*, issued in 648 to end Christological disputes, had been badly received and church union rejected at an Armenian church council in Duin in 648/9,

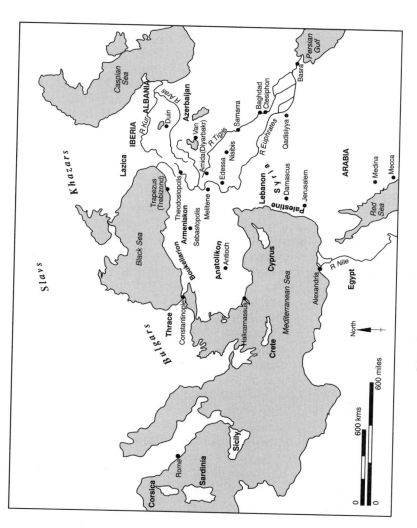

Map 8.1   Europe and west Asia

and there was now hostility in Armenia to Nersēs' abandoning his former opposition to union. And in 654 the Arabs captured Melitene, Theodosiopolis and Duin. It was only war within the Caliphate which caused them to retire, with Theodore, to leave Armenia to Byzantium. Constans appointed Hamazasp Mamikonean (654/5–8), nominated by Nersēs and the princes, as Prince of Armenia, that is, presiding prince, and Hamazasp refused to pay the tribute due the Arabs. But in 661 the Arabs invaded again and an assembly of the princes accepted their overlordship.

Why? It is often suggested that dislike of imperial Chalcedonianism and of religious persecution explains the early Byzantine losses to the Arabs, since the territories in question were Monophysite areas. Yet some scholars have disputed this explanation for the fall of Syria and Egypt[1] and it is just as questionable with regard to Armenia. Theodore's treaty after all provoked both disapproval and opposition. In the (seventh- or eighth-century) *History* by 'Sebēos' it is designated a covenant with death and a treaty with Hell,[2] and Constans' assembly in Theodosiopolis, which followed it, was well attended. Furthermore, as we shall see in Chapter 10, the Armenians were not uniformly anti-Chalcedonian.

It is more likely that surrender, heretic or not, to the enemies of Byzantium was a pragmatic attempt to avoid being ravaged, underpinned by a belief that Arab domination would prove temporary. The prevailing interpretation was that the Arab scourge was a divine punishment for sin, and especially for heresy, and, perhaps, a sign that the end of the world was near. Thus the Patriarch of Jerusalem combined opposition to imperial doctrine with belief, in 634, that Christian victory would follow repentance.[3] Such an expectation, that Arab conquest would not be permanent, is understandable. The Arabs were unknown as a world power but familiar as raiders, and recent events, namely the emperor Heraclius' Persian war, had proved that conquest could be followed by reconquest. Until it came, life had to go on. The terms the Arabs had offered Theodore were favourable: three years breathing-space; then the payment of tribute (probably what could be considered 'surplus' for it was to be 'what you wish' but given under oath),[4] probably a lighter burden than Byzantine tax; Armenia would not be occupied or garrisoned; Christianity would not be threatened; military service would not be required in Syria, though 15,000 cavalry were to be maintained and made available, and no aid was to be given to the Arabs' enemies; Arab help against Byzantine invasion was promised.[5]

---

[1] Jones, 1959; Moorhead, 1981a.
[2] Sebēos, *History of Heraclius*, XXXV, trans. Macler, 1904, p. 132.
[3] Kaegi, 1969.
[4] Sebēos, XXXV, Macler's translation (1904, p. 133) is amended by Mahé, 1993, p. 474 n. 154.
[5] Sebēos, XXXV, trans. Macler, 1904, p. 133.

And Byzantine recovery did indeed become a real possibility in the 680s. The period 681–2 brought the Arabs civil war in the Caliphate, and Iberian and Armenian rebellion. In 684 and 689 plague swept from Basra, through northern Mesopotamia and Syria, to Egypt, its effects worsened by extreme weather conditions in 683/4, 686/7 and 689. And in 685 the emperor Constantine IV (668–85), after beating the Arabs off from Constantinople, defeating them in Asia Minor, and threatening Syria, gained from Caliph Abd al-Malik (685–705) an annual tribute of horses, slaves and gold, amounting to more than a fifth of the taxes of Syria.

This propitious context encouraged Byzantium to resume her attempts to revover Armenia. Church union was established in 689, after a council at Theodosiopolis, and Nersēs Kamsarakan (689–93) was appointed presiding prince. There was a possibility of an alliance with the powerful Khazars, across the Caucasus, who had been allies in the past, during Heraclius' reign. They were now, like Byzantium, foes of the Arabs. In 681 the Khazars' underlings, the Huns of the north Caucasus, had attacked Albania. The Albanians had then, in consultation with the Armenian Katholikos and the (Arab-appointed) presiding prince of Armenia, Gregory Mamikonean (661–85), sent them a bishop on a peace mission.[6] Despite his success as a missionary, there had followed another Hun attack in 685, in which Gregory died. A Khazar–Byzantine rapprochement would have been logical,[7] and that it was expected is suggested in an apocalyptic text purporting to prophesy the end of the world, which was probably translated from Greek into Armenian at the end of the seventh or early in the eighth century. Its prophesy implies an anticipation that the Arabs would shortly be destroyed by the emperor, presumably either Justinian II (685–95 and 705–11) or the Armenian Philippicus Bardanes (Vardan) (711–13), assisted by the Khazars.[8]

But instead of pursuing a decisive victory and a full recovery of her lost territory, including Armenia, Byzantium allowed herself to be bought off. In 689, for a large tribute and a half share of the taxation revenue of Cyprus, Armenia and Iberia, Justinian II concluded a ten-year peace and removed what had been a serious threat to the Caliphate in Syria, namely the Mardaites, who, numbering many thousands, had occupied part of Lebanon since 669. This retreat could be considered a major tactical error, especially since it was followed by a deterioration of relations. Byzantium was provoked when papyrus made for her began to carry Islamic inscriptions, and the Arabs likewise – after Justinian, in 692, asserted his own religious position on his coins. Justinian's gold and silver

---

[6] Moses Daskhurants'i, *History of the Albanians*, II, 36, 38–45, trans. Dowsett, 1961b, pp. 150, 152–71, and cf. his p. 150, n. 1.
[7] For Khazar–Byzantine relations, Noonan, 1992.
[8] *The Vision of Enoch the Just.*

coinage now bore the image of Christ as Pantocrator (an innovation) with a plain cross behind; his own image, also with a cross; and, in some cases, the title, applied to Justinian, of servant of Christ. Both Christ and the Cross, as the sign of Christianity and of imperial victory, were objectionable to Arab authorities whose domains the coinage would reach and the whole must have seemed aggressive. In 692 Justinian was accused of breaking the 689 treaty, perhaps because he had moved some Cypriots to Asia Minor. Byzantium attacked, but was heavily defeated.

These events, combined with Byzantium's increasing preoccupation with the Bulgars in the Balkans, encouraged the Armenians, led by Smbat Bagratuni, the presiding prince appointed in 693, to submit to the Arabs. A subsequent Byzantine military intervention was unsuccessful and Armenia was lost. At the end of the seventh century the Arab province of Arminiya was formed, comprising Iberia and Albania as well as Armenia (except for Aldznik^c (classical Arzanene) and Korduk^c (Corduene)), under an Arab governor, the *ostikan*. There were Arab garrisons at Duin, the *ostikan*'s base, and at Theodosiopolis, and heavy taxation was imposed.

Arab Rule and Armenian Response, c.700–c.800

The eighth century brought Armenians financial burdens and religious repression, and it saw rebellion and migration in response. In their resistance Armenians were most often led, as they had been in the fifth-century struggles against Persia, by the Mamikoneans, but Mamikonean pre-eminence was increasingly threatened by the Bagratunis, who by and large were more conciliatory towards the Arabs. By c.800 it had gone for ever.

The cycle of demand, protest, punishment began early. The armed resistance of 703 and 705 was led by Smbat Bagratuni. Despite Byzantine backing, it failed, and Smbat settled, with his nobles, in Lazica. In response, in 705 the Arabs assembled many princes in two churches, at Nakhchawan and Khram, and burnt them. Some captives were executed, others deported. Repression subsequently eased, many exiles, including Smbat, returning home, but respite was only temporary. In 716–17 Arab–Byzantine war brought to Armenia an Arab force which wrought much devastation. Armenian Christianity was at least potentially threatened by the anti-Christian trend of some of the Caliphs' religious policies. Umar (Omar) II (717–20) began a policy of conversion to Islam in Syria, and, according to one source, forbade Christians to show their crosses.[9] Yazid II (720–4) ordered Christian images to be torn down. Hisham

---

[9] Constantelos, 1972; King, G. R. D., 1985.

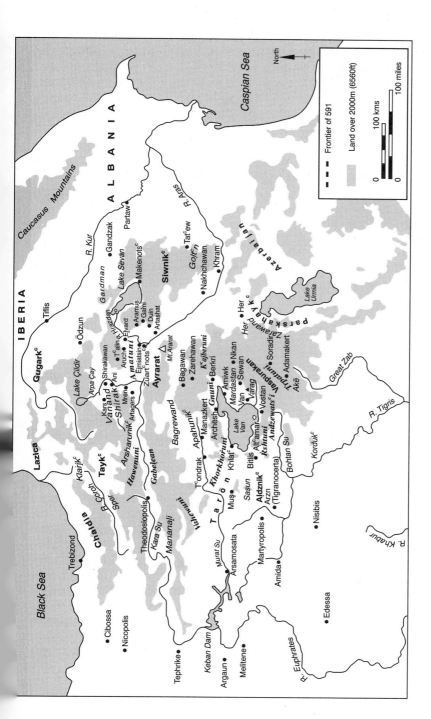

Map 8.2 Armenia

(724–43) encouraged conversion in the frontier zones. Yazid's order was implemented in Armenia, where crosses too were uprooted. And financial pressure was increased. Hisham took a census and changed levies per household to levies per head and on property, both land and cattle. Some of the treaties made in the early 740s between local rulers and Hisham's governor (732–44) the future caliph Marwan II (744–50) stipulated an annual supply of slaves.

These stimuli provoked a second Armenian rebellion to threaten in 745 and to break out in 747/8, while the Caliphate was being weakened by internal war. The rebels were led, not by the presiding prince, Ashot Bagratuni (appointed by Marwan in 732), but by Gregory Mamikonean. Byzantine help was anticipated but the rebellion had already failed by the time the emperor, Constantine V (741–75), attacked Melitene and Theodosiopolis.

The aftermath was another round of oppression, revolt, oppression. The Arab grant to maintain the Armenian cavalry, whose resumption after a three-year lapse Ashot had secured, was discontinued. The Abbasids, who had replaced the Umayyad Caliphs in 750, tightened the financial screw by not only increasing taxation, but also making money dues more important. Furthermore, as dues in kind they required fish and luxury goods rather than corn. Armenia was unable to pay the taxes in coin imposed by Caliph al-Mansur (754–75). And her suffering was exacerbated by Khazar invasions in 762 and 764. The canons of the 768 Council of Partaw show how the church had been affected: some bishops had been prevented from attending, church property had been sold, what peasants had previously paid to monasteries was now going to the *nakharar*s, women were raped by heathens, captives reduced to eating impure meat.

A second Mamikonean revolt followed in 774–5. It began with the killing of two financial officials and a military victory at Bagawan. This early success encouraged almost all the *nakharar*s to join the rebellion. They swore an oath of unity and a force of, apparently, 5,000 obliged Theodosiopolis to surrender. But at Archēsh many peasants were cut down and in a second battle the Armenians who had taken Theodosiopolis, outnumbered, were massacred. So Arab pressure continued. Under Harun al-Rashid (786–809) Arab settlement in Armenia increased, Arab emirates were founded on lands of dead or migrant princes,[10] efforts were made to convert Armenians to Islam, episodes of financial extortion were visited on the church, and the tax upon Arminiya was heavy: 13 million dirhams annually, plus 20,000 pounds of fish (from the River Araxes and Lake Van), twenty carpets, 200 mules, thirty falcons and 580 pieces of cloth.

By *c*.800, Arab rule had not only provoked rebellions, but it had also inspired many Armenians to move to Byzantine territory and service. A

[10] Ter-Ghewondyan, 1976.

group of over 12,000 is recorded to have settled near the border of Pontic Chaldia.[11] Of such migrants the most outstanding individual is Tachat Andzewats^c i. He moved west about 760, served the emperor Constantine V against the Bulgars, and became *strategus* of the Boukellarion theme (that is, the governor, with civil and military powers, of a province in which soldiers were settled on the land). Like Artawazd Mamikonean, *strategus* of the Anatolikon theme, Tachat was a leading general in Byzantium's eastern campaigns against the Arabs, in the 770s and early 780s. Indeed Tachat's desertion of the regent Irene in 782, provoked by Irene's purge of commanders and officials, forced Byzantium to pay the Arabs tribute. Tachat's final office, in reward from the Arabs, was the command of Armenia. Other Armenians too played a part in late eighth-century Byzantine politics, likewise in opposition to Irene. In 790 the army of the Armeniakon theme, led by Alexius Musele, refused to swear loyalty to her and instead proclaimed her son Constantine VI (780–97) as emperor. It subsequently enthroned Alexius after Constantine, in 791, readmitted Irene to government, and was defeated only in 793.[12]

Armenian Revival, c.800–84

The years immediately following the 774–5 rebellion were hard, but conditions eased in the first half of the ninth century. Arab sources record that the taxes of Arminiya in this period came to about 4 million dirhams, a fact which suggests that financial exactions had diminished, though the patriarchate was impoverished when, despite the resistance of Katholikos Joseph (795–806), it lost substantial estates at Artashat (classical Artaxata). The office of presiding prince, in abeyance since Tachat's death, was revived in 804 and entrusted to a Bagratuni, another Ashot. Subsequently Ashot had some success against the Arab emirs, including the dynasty which had taken Duin in the time of the Byzantine emperor Leo V (813–20). Ashot's power did indeed cause the *ostikans* some disquiet but this disquiet was soothed after his death when his sons, the *sparapet* Smbat and the Prince of Armenia, Bagarat, partitioned his domains (826). Then in 830 Smbat, Sahak of Siwnik^c and certain *azat*s joined the emir Sawada (Sewada) in revolt against the *ostikan*, and in 850 Bagarat and his nephew Ashot Artsruni defeated the emir of Arzn, when he tried to collect tribute for the *ostikan*. This rebellion was not nearly so easily defeated as the eighth-century revolts had been. The second army sent to suppress it, in 852, led by the Turk Bugha, took three years to do so.

[11] Lewond, *History*, 42, trans. Arzoumanian, 1982b, p. 149.
[12] For this and Tachat, Arvites, 1983, Tritle, 1977.

In the short term, the results of this show of spirit were unfortunate. Muslims living in Armenia, who had guided Bugha, seized their opportunity for territorial aggrandisement when leading Armenians were taken to the Caliph's new capital of Samarra, founded in 836. There the Caliph demanded the captives' conversion to Islam and few refused. One who did was the *sparapet* Smbat, who had been promised the rule of Armenia for helping Bugha. But from 858/9 the princes were allowed home, and thereafter internal economic weakness and the increasing strength of Byzantium led the Caliphs to be conciliatory.

The longer-term consequence of the revolt was that Smbat's son Ashot was able to amass great power. Spared captivity, he exploited opportunities opened by others' absence, and he was undaunted by their return. Ashot acquired new lands, for example parts of Gugark[c] (Gogarene) (before 876) from his sister's Iberian Bagratuni husband; subjugated other princes; and made judicious marriage alliances. In 862 the Caliph appointed him *ishkhan* of *ishkhan*s (Prince of Princes), and gave him the authority of an *ostikan* thereby entrusting him with the taxes. He remained on good terms with both his powerful neighbours, staying neutral in the wars between the Arabs and the Byzantine emperor Basil I (867–86). Basil himself claimed descent from the royal Armenian Arsacids, to whom the Bagratunis had been coronants, and in 875, according to the thirteenth-century Armenian writer Vardan, at Basil's request, Ashot sent him a crown.[13] Ashot had, admittedly, some trouble with local emirs. The emirs of Partaw and Manazkert plotted against him and he besieged Manazkert in 884. According to the emperor Constantine VII (913–57) Ashot actually gave Khlat[c], Archēsh and Berkri to Manazkert,[14] itself under his dominion, though some scholars doubt this.

Ashot followed his accumulation of power with the acquisition of royal status, granted by both Arab caliph and Byzantine emperor, and it is possible that such status had long been one of his conscious objectives. The 862 Council at Shirakawan, called to consider Byzantine proposals for church union and held by the Katholikos in Ashot's presence, may have been intended to reunite Christian Caucasia, thereby to advertise both Ashot's piety and the extent of his control, and so to gain Byzantine approval and Arab respect.[15] (As it turned out, although his council rejected Byzantium's proposals, it tolerantly decreed that persons who thought that Chalcedon did not accord with the first three ecumenical councils should anathematize it, whereas those who did not, should not.) Armenian inscriptions from Sewan, in 874, and from Garni, in 879, refer to Ashot and his wife as king and queen respectively. It was only in 884 that the Caliph, petitioned by the heads of the Artsruni and the two

[13] Vardan, *Historical Compilation*, 45, trans. Thomson, 1989, p. 186.
[14] *De Administrando Imperio*, ch. 44, 1.1–23 and v. II *Commentary*, ed. Jenkins, 1962.
[15] Maksoudian, 1988–9.

Siwnian houses, granted Ashot his royal title. The Byzantine emperor followed suit.

Power and its Foundations

Armenian society in 884 was, naturally, in some respects very different from what it had been in 640. The restoration of a monarchy after 456 years in abeyance had not been the only change. The internal balance of power had shifted, and especially after the failure of the 774–5 revolt it had increasingly become concentrated in a few hands. By 884 the Bagratuni, Artsruni and the two Siwnian houses far outstripped in importance those other of the ancient families which still survived.

Of these four it was the Bagratunis who held the crown, yet in about 800 it was perhaps the Artsrunis, based in Vaspurakan east of Lake Van who were the most powerful. They had heroism and resilience to their credit, for they had offered resistance to Arab penetration: two of their leaders had been killed in the process in 762 and two more martyred in 786. It is even possible that none of their number, in contrast to other families, joined in the trend of migration in response to the difficulties of the times. Their power in the ninth century can be gauged from the number and identity of their supporters. About twelve other aristocratic families were represented in Ashot Artsruni's train when he went to the help of Bagarat Bagratuni in 850.[16] Several Armenian families make their last appearance in history as Artsruni subordinates. They include the Apahunis, who, having been dislodged by the emirs of Manazkert, moved to Vaspurakan in the mid-ninth century; the Gabeḷeans, Kᶜajberunis and Trpatunis who last appear in the mid-ninth century; the princes of Akē and the Hawenunis who last appear at the beginning of the tenth century; and the Vahewunis who last appear in 906.[17] Andzewatsᶜi property passed to the Artsrunis about 867 when the last prince bequeathed it partly to his infant son and partly to Gregory-Derenik Artsruni, only for it all to pass to another Artsruni, Gurgēn Apupelch, who married his widow.[18] The failure of the 850 rebellion was a blow to Artsruni power but not a fatal one. Whilst Ashot was held captive in Samarra his relatives continued fighting Arabs. After he returned home, he himself recovered Varag, and his son Gregory-Derenik reconquered Slig (by Mount Varag) and gained some control over Her and Zarawand.

[16] Thomas Artsruni, *History of the House of the Artsrunis*, II, 6, trans. Thomson, 1985, p. 176.
[17] Toumanoff, 1963, pp. 199 (Apahunis), 220–1 (Gabeḷeans), 206 (Kᶜajberunis), 221 (Trpatunis), 197 (Akēatsis), 221 (Hawenunis), 215 (Vahewunis).
[18] Ibid., pp. 198–9.

The third Armenian power block in the middle of the ninth century was Siwnik^c. Little is discernible of the deeds of its rulers in the eighth century, but in the early years of the ninth its prince, Vasak, allied with Babik, the leader of some sectarians in Azerbaijan, the Khurramites who rebelled against the Caliph in 816/7. In 821 the allies expelled the emir Sawada from Siwnik^c. But this useful alliance failed to survive Vasak's death, also in 821. Babik proceeded to ravage Siwnik^c, killing thousands and burning the monastery of Makenots^c. The princely family subsequently split into two branches. One was the line of Vasak's son, Sahak, who joined Sawada in rebellion against the *ostikan* in 830. It was down the other that the superior status of prince of Siwnik^c was to pass, with a brief interruption when Sahak's grandson Vasak Gabuṙn, with the help of his father-in-law, Ashot Bagratuni (the future king), acquired it, retaining it until his death in 859. Yet a third branch of the family had meanwhile expanded into Albania, through a marriage with the daughter and heiress of Varaz-trdat, last prince of Gardman, presiding prince of Albania, after his murder in 822.

As these families had risen to greater eminence so others had declined. Their decline followed naturally from the financial difficulties and migrations of the eighth century and especially from the consequences of the failure of its rebellions, particularly that of 774–5. For the anciently pre-eminent Mamikoneans the 774–5 rebellion's failure had been a catastrophic final straw. They had already lost most of their lands, now they lost Tayk^c (mostly to the Bagratunis, partly to Iberia). They did retain Bagrewand but this was annexed by Ashot Bagratuni in 862, after the death of Gregory Mamikonean, a Byzantine sympathizer, apparently at Ashot's hands.[19] The appearance of the Mamikoneans as potentates near Arsamosata and in Sasun in the eleventh century suggests that they had retained some lands there.[20] By 884 some of the greatest names of the seventh century were of little account. The Kamsarakans, Khorkhoṙunis and Sahaṙunis were no longer among the powerful. The Gnunis had moved to Tayk^c after 775, and they last appear in history about 914. Ṙshtuni had ceased to be a name to conjure with a little earlier. Some families like the Aṙaweḷeans, Aṙaweneans, Dashtakarans, Dimak^{c}seans, and Spandunis seem not to have survived the seventh century, others, like the Bagratuni house of Goḷt^{c}n (classical Colthene), which last appears in the 730s, to have met their end in the eighth. By 800 the number of houses and of the dynasties to which they belonged were, according to Toumanoff, only twenty and twelve respectively, as opposed to thirty-five and twenty-two in *c*.500.[21]

---

[19] Ibid., pp. 209–10.
[20] Conversely, they may have returned to Tarōn after its annexation (966) by Byzantium.
[21] Toumanoff, 1963, pp. 206–7 (Kamsarakans), 208–9 (Khorkhoṙunis), 214 (Sahaṙunis), 205 (Gnunis), 213 (Ṙshtuni), 199 (Aṙaweḷeans and Aṙaweneans), 220 (Dashtakarans), 204 (Dimak^{c}seans), 221 (Spandunis), 215 (Vanand), 203–204 (Colthene), 227–29 (statistics).

The foundations of the extensive power which the Bagratuni, Siwnian and Artsruni dynasties[22] enjoyed in 884 were property, people and propaganda. The properties were of various kinds, one of which was land. For the Bagratunis the early ninth-century presiding prince Ashot had purchased the Kamsarakan lands in fertile Ayrarat, and retrieved Tarōn, which they had briefly lost after 775. The advantages of Tarōn and of the Ayrarat domains were their relative flatness, and suitability for agriculture. Another Bagratuni, grandson of the presiding prince who had been appointed in 732, and husband of an Iberian princess, established a branch of the family in Klařjkᶜ (Cholarzene) in the Iberian–Armenian border zone in the late eighth century. It acquired all of Taykᶜ and its Ashot I (813–30) was made presiding prince of Iberia by the Caliph, and given the title of Curopalate by the Byzantine emperor. In Siwnikᶜ the princes enjoyed the protection offered by the mountains beyond Lake Sevan. Artsruni territory included previously Ṙshtuni (anciently Urartian) lands, and some Amatuni lands which were acquired after 775. From their seventh-century territories the Arstrunis had expanded around Lake Van, coming into conflict with the emirs of Berkri in the north, and dislodging the Bagratunis in the south. The seventh-century territories themselves, centred on Adamakert (modern Başkale), were sheltered by mountains. The Arstrunis thus combined easily defensible refuges with lands vulnerable to Arab attack, offering them both security and opportunities to demonstrate valour and rally support.

A second type of property upon which the powerful depended was forts, or castles, essential as storehouses, refuges, and bases, for control of routes, for war and for government. Always important in Armenia, their importance had been enhanced, partly because Arab military power, though superior to that of the Armenians in open battle, was most often deployed in raiding, in campaigning to avenge an offence, or in enforcing payment of tribute, and partly because of the immigration of Arab settlers. In the eighth century, heroes, in their heroism, depended on forts. Thus Gagik Artsruni retreated from Arab attack to Nkan, whence he raided the frontier of Azerbaijan, and where he resisted siege for a year. He was captured, in c.772–3, only after the besiegers began negotiations.[23] Warfare in the ninth century is recounted, in the histories written in the early tenth by Thomas Artsruni and John Katholikos, largely in terms of possession of fortresses. In Thomas's illuminating account of the followers of Ashot Artsruni, the rebel of 850, wanting him to surrender to Bugha they told Ashot that the fortresses were not adequately prepared or provisioned for defence, and they told Bugha that if the Artsrunis turned their many fortresses to their advantage they would cause him great

---

[22] Ibid., pp. 201–3, 214, 199–200, for brief history and territorial vicissitudes.
[23] Łewond, 32, trans. Arzoumanian, 1982b, pp. 126–7.

trouble.[24] A number of citadels on the south of Lake Van were the basis of the Artsrunis' defence of their western frontier in the ninth and early tenth centuries.[25]

Urban sites, which as we shall see, were dominated by the Arabs, had by contrast little to do with Armenian aristocratic power. One indication of their mismatch is that the seventh-century churches, except in Duin and Vaḷarshapat and perhaps Gaṙni, where there is a church built either by the seventh-century Katholikos Nersēs III or in the eleventh century, are not closely related to towns. Some late ninth- and early tenth-century Siwnian churches however were near trade routes which are recorded by Arab geographers.

Besides lands and castles, potentates also needed movable treasure. It was for fear that the Arabs would find his treasure, buried in a barrel under his house, and thereby reduce his power to nothing that Vasak Artsruni denounced the rebel Ashot before the Caliph. That lavish gifts from leaders were expected, and that they created, in theory, obligations of support, is suggested by Ashot's speech to his followers who wanted him to surrender. For in his reproach it is emphasized that he had regularly let them 'plunder' his treasures. The role that treasure could play in politics is underlined in the story of another Artsruni betrayal, that of Ashot's son Gregory-Derenik by his nephew Hasan, to whom Gregory-Derenik had entrusted the fort of Sewan, containing much treasure. Hasan dreamt of power, namely of assembling forces, forming cavalry, calling everyone to support him and giving gifts to great lords, and the fulfillment of his dreams depended on his possessing the treasure.[26]

As these tales make plain, aristocratic power depended as much on people as it did on property, and the people upon whom it depended may be considered under three headings: outsiders and superiors, kinsmen, and subordinates. From the seventh through to the ninth century a determining factor in the Armenian political scene was Arab policy and action, or inaction. On the plus side, despite some Arab hostility, the *nakharar*s seem to have retained their traditional rights, and neither state territorial ownership, observable elsewhere in the Arab world, nor the system of assignment of an *iqṭāᶜ*[27] were significantly extended into Armenia. (The *iqṭāᶜ* has been a matter of debate, but seems to have been the assignment of tax revenue of particular land to a soldier or official in order to prevent him from becoming directly associated with the land itself.)[28] Particular family fortunes were significantly affected by

---

[24] Thomas, III, 2, trans. Thomson, 1985, pp. 203, 202.

[25] Thierry, M., 1976.

[26] Thomas, II, 6, III, 2, III, 20, trans. Thomson, 1985, pp. 180 (Vasak), 202–3 (Ashot), 286–7 (Hasan).

[27] Canard (translating Ter-Ghévondian), 1986.

[28] Cahen, 1953; Irwin, 1978.

Arab patronage. In the seventh century, appointment as Prince of Armenia enhanced an individual's status considerably. For the prince, though obliged to organize military aid for the caliph, lacking the rights of the Arsacid kings and, apparently, actually chosen by *nakharar*s in council, was nevertheless governor and involved in collecting the tribute.[29] The Arab-appointed Gregory Mamikonean's wife, Helen, is actually termed queen in a tenth-century source.[30] The later preference of the Arabs to appoint the Bagratunis, perhaps out of suspicion of the Mamikoneans' power and their loyalty to Byzantium, contributed to the Bagratunis' ousting the Mamikoneans from pre-eminence. Indeed the Armenian rebellion of 747 has some elements of a Bagratuni-Mamikonean power struggle. Its leader, another Gregory Mamikonean, had been exiled for opposition when Ashot Bagratuni had been made prince in 732. One source attributes Gregory's revolt to a wish to depose Ashot,[31] and Ashot himself only reluctantly fell in with the rebels' plans and then deserted them, for which act they blinded him. The ninth-century balance was likewise swung by the Arabs in the Bagratunis' favour, with the appointment, in 804, of another Bagratuni prince, and this time it may have been a wish to check Artsruni power which, partly, explains it.

The support of kinsmen for each other could not always be guaranteed, yet it is clear that co-operation and the acknowledgement of obligations, between close kin at least, were expected. This may explain why in 852 Bugha arrested, and fought, not only the leading rebels but also their kinsmen. The elimination of an enemy's kinsmen was more likely to prevent future trouble than was the taking of hostages, though this too could work. Mushel Mamikonean had not joined the transfer of allegiance from Arabs to Byzantium in 654 because four of his sons were hostages. An ethic and perhaps a reality of kin solidarity in Siwnikᶜ may be inferred from the retention, or renaissance, there of family ownership of lands, which itself may be inferred from donation texts, dating from the middle of the ninth century onwards, incorporated in the *History* written in the thirteenth century by Stephen Orbeıean.[32] The *azat*s who attested donations by princes and by their close kin may have been agnatic kinsmen, whose consent to the donations was required.[33]

Cases in which one kinsman failed to help another do not all necessarily disprove the hypothesis that solidarity was a norm. For matters

[29] Ter-Ghévondian, 1966.

[30] Moses Daskhurantsᶜi, II, 38, trans. Dowsett, 1961b, p. 153.

[31] Łewond, 21, 25, 26, trans. Arzoumanian, 1982b, pp. 113–14, 117–18, 119, for Gregory's exile, return, motive for revolt.

[32] In western Europe ninth-century charters appearing in thirteenth-century confirmations or compilations are usually not authentic. In Armenia many donation texts survived as inscriptions *in situ* (cf. above ch. 7 pp. 164–5). Stephen asserts that he was quoting inscriptions.

[33] Périkhanian, 1968.

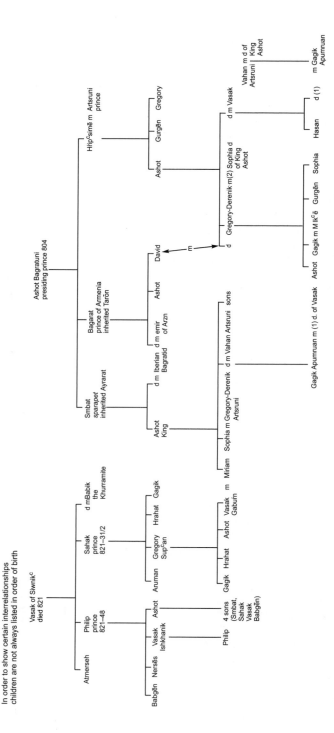

Figure 8.1 Partial genealogical table: the Artsrunis, Bagratunis and Siunians in the ninth century

might be complicated by an individual's having obligations, perhaps of differing force, which conflicted. In 878 Gregory-Derenik Artsruni established David Bagratuni as prince of Tarōn, imprisoning the rightful prince, David's brother Ashot, like David his first cousin once removed. One of his reasons was that David was his brother-in-law. David presumably seemed likely to be an easier neighbour. In this situation the Prince of Princes Ashot remained quiescent. He was first cousin to the two rival brothers but father-in-law of Gregory-Derenik. When Gregory-Derenik was himself captured, by Hasan, Ashot abandoned the siege of Manazkert to secure his son-in-law's release.[34] Hasan's own career paradoxically reveals both that kinsmen had positive expectations of each other and that they might be cruelly betrayed. Hasan's uncle Gregory-Derenik had entrusted the captive Ashot of Tarōn and the fort of Sewan to him when he was only fifteen. He had managed to imprison Gregory-Derenik by enticing him to visit, by feigning illness. Following his wrathful uncle's release Hasan regained Sewan by taking captive for him another rebel, Hasan's own brother-in-law. This man himself later seized the fort and gave it back to Hasan again.[35]

Bloodfeud is just as much an expression of family cohesion as is patronage,[36] and bloodfeud seems still to have obtained in Armenian aristocratic society. The clearest evidence lies in the career of Gurgēn Apupelch Artsruni. While the rebel Ashot Artsruni was in Samarra, Gurgēn refused a suggestion of Ashot's brother to partition Ashot's lands between them. His refusal was partly to avoid offending the Caliph who had just invested Ashot and his son Gregory-Derenik with the Artsruni principality and partly because his father had been killed by the brothers' father. When, later, Gurgēn had an opportunity to kill Gregory-Derenik, the offender's grandson, in vengeance, Gregory-Derenik expected that he would take it. But Gurgēn, for 'love of Christ', did not, and the two addressed each other as 'son' and 'father'.[37] This behaviour looks similar to the institution of adoption, by pronouncing a formula such as 'you are my daughter', known among some Caucasians in the nineteenth century. In one Caucasian tribe a murderer could consecrate himself to his victim at the grave to form a fictitious relationship

[34] Thomas Artsruni, III, 20, trans. Thomson, 1985, pp. 287–8.
[35] Ibid., 20, 22, trans. Thomson, 1985, pp. 284, 286–9, 295, 298.
[36] For anthropological appraisals of bloodfeud, Evans-Pritchard, 1940; Campbell, J. K., 1964 esp. ch. VIII, 'The Family as Corporate Group', (pp. 185–212); Beattie, 1964, ch. 9 'Social Control: Political Organisation' (pp. 139–164), ch. 10 'Social Control: Law and Social Sanctions' (pp. 165–81) esp. pp. 148, 150, 175–6; Gluckman, 1965, ch. III 'Stateless Societies and the Maintenance of Order' (pp. 81–122) esp. pp. 111–14 for significance in medieval European history. For bloodfeud in early medieval Frankish Gaul, Wallace-Hadrill, 1962. For feud in western Europe and the church's involvement therein, Geary, 1994, ch. 7 (pp. 125–60) esp. pp. 145–150 and, for an introduction to the literature, note 52 pp. 145–6.
[37] Thomas Artsruni, III, 14, trans. Thomson, 1985, pp. 265–7, 269.

which would presumably gain him the rights of blood kinship.[38] Gurgēn subsequently did assume a fatherly role towards Gregory-Derenik when he protected him from the Prince of Princes, Ashot, who took him prisoner in 862. Gurgēn engineered both Gregory-Derenik's release and his marriage to Ashot's daughter. The feud was not however completely resolved. In 895 Gurgēn asked Gregory-Derenik's son for part of Vaspurakan, especially the capital of Řshtunik^c (Vostan) the site of his father's murder, 'regarding it as the blood price'.[39]

The powerful could be promoted or baulked by caliphs and emperors, sustained or betrayed by kinsmen, and they also had to reckon with fellow Armenians of lesser individual influence. The structure of ninth-century society naturally differed somewhat from that of earlier centuries. The change of use of the words *ishkhan* and *nakharar* in the Armenian sources, *ishkhan* after the 770s seemingly representing a position and status superior instead of equivalent to that of *nakharar*, reflects the concentration of power in a few families. Yet the ninth-century princes still needed *nakharar* support, as is shown by the inability of Ashot Artsruni in 852 to resist Bugha, because his *nakharar*s did not agree with him.[40] As for *azat*s and *řamik*s, their role in the ninth century was much as it had been in the Arsacid period. The *azat*s, who had their own troops, provided most of the military strength of their superiors. Most of the references to the ninth- and early tenth-century *azat*s in the Artsruni *History* (comprising the work of Thomas Artsruni and of his continuator) occur in a military context. Bands of *azat*s are associated with Ashot Artsruni, his son and grandsons. When, for example, in about 900 Gagik Apumruan usurped Vaspurakan, the emir of Amida (Diyarbakır) welcomed the supporters of the rightful princes as brave and powerful men, 'especially because they had often acquired a victorious reputation'. They were *azat*s.[41] The *řamik* served as cavalry and defended forts. They participated in political life, as indicated by their attendance at King Ashot I's funeral,[42] and in their inclusion (with bishops, monks, princes, lords and *azat*s) in the early tenth-century king Gagik Artsruni's discussion of building plans for Ałt^camar (Aghtamar) on Lake Van.[43]

These gradations of power, and differentiations of roles involved control of territory, inherited status and, probably, tenurial obligation, yet we should not think entirely in terms of a neat and tidy social pyramid. It is possible that Armenian princes were attended by men who corresponded,

[38] Luzbetak, 1951, p. 58.
[39] Thomas Artsruni, III, 14, 22, trans. Thomson, 1985, pp. 270–1, 297.
[40] John Katholikos, *History of the Armenians*, XXV, 38, trans. Maksoudian, 1987 p. 119. For detail, Thomas Artsruni, III, 2, trans. Thomson, 1985, pp. 200–04.
[41] Thomas Artsruni, III, 22, trans. Thomson, 1985, pp. 298–9.
[42] John Katholikos, XXX, 8, trans. Maksoudian, 1987, p. 130.
[43] Thomas Artsruni, (Continuator), IV, 7, trans. Thomson, 1985, p. 356 and cf. his p. 332 n. 1 for differing editorial enumerations of the chapters of the anonymous continuators.

to some degree, with the *comitatus* of Germanic societies, a body of noble men attending a leader for purposes of war, distinct from the mass of troops.[44] It may be that the circumstances of Arab rule had provided the conditions for such an institution to flourish. Whereas the possibly seventh-century 'Sebēos' recorded a number of individuals serving Persia or Rome, in or outside Armenia, the probably late eighth-century Lewond's account of eighth-century events concentrated by contrast on Armenians making their careers inside Armenia, depending upon military power. Such persons include Sahak and Hamazasp Artsruni who met the Arab enemy with a few men in 762: Artawazd Mamikonean who gathered troops in considerable numbers in 774. Prince Ashot Bagratuni, whose *nakharars* accompanied him and the governor Marwan on campaign against the Khazars: and Gagik Artsruni, who after the deaths of his two brothers, gathered the local *nakharars* and their cavalry and raided from Nkan.[45]

The clearest examples of the existence and importance of the personal following lie like those of bloodfeud within the career of Gurgēn Apupelch in the 850s and 860s. Having begun as a follower of the prince of Vaspurakan Ashot Artsruni, he acquired renown during Ashot's captivity. He fought Byzantine forces in Sper, defeated the individual whom the Artsrunis who remained at liberty had elected as prince, removed Muslims living in Vaspurakan, and trounced the army Bugha sent against him. He was appointed prince (presumably of Vaspurakan) by Bugha, he was invited to enter Byzantine service and he was eulogized throughout the land. His retinue had grown with his success: in Sper he had forty warriors but when he encountered Bugha's army in Vaspurakan and when in 862 he marched from Tarōn to Ŕshtunik[c] to rescue Gregory-Derenik he had 400.[46]

There might of course be kinship bonds between the followers of a great lord. The Artsruni trains in the 850s included Gregory Gnuni with six *harazat* (related) men and Artawazd Ĕntruni with seven, several Varazhnunis, Vahewunis, and Amatunis. Loyalties might survive over several generations, as in the case of the Amatunis,[47] whether for reasons of kin solidarity, continuing friendship, tenurial obligations or political imperatives.

Besides property and people, propaganda, which simultaneously justifies achievements and reflects aspirations, was a third buttress of power. What survives from the period 610–884 was composed for the

---

[44] See below ch. 10 pp. 247–8.

[45] Lewond, 30, 34, 22, 32, trans. Arzoumanian, 1982b, pp. 124–5, 129, 114, 126–7.

[46] Thomas Artsruni, II, 6, III, 13, 14, trans. Thomson, 1985, pp. 176, 179, 258, 262, 264, 270; Laurent, 1922.

[47] Thomas Artsruni, II, 6, III, 4, and III, 20, 24, trans. Thomson, 1985, pp. 176, 213 (850s), and 291, 301 (Amatuni support for Ashot's son and grandsons).

Bagratunis. Moses of Khoren's *History of the Armenians*, which begins at the beginning, that is with Adam the first man, is dated by most scholars to the late eighth century, despite Moses' claim to have been one of the fifth-century circle of Patriarch Sahak and the scholar Mesrop. Their reasons include the text's anachronisms, its use of sources later than the fifth century, and authorial interests which seem to reflect later eighth-century developments.[48] Moses was concerned to explain the origins of Armenian aristocratic families and since such a concern might be the nostalgic interest of an antiquarian in something which is in decline it may reflect their decline. But Moses' main purpose was to exalt the Bagratunis and to justify their new late eighth-century position as the leading family. Behind his claim that he was writing at the request of 'Sahak Bagratuni',[49] presumably meant to be the *marzpan* of 482, may lie a real Bagratuni patron. In pursuit of his aim Moses falsely represents the Bagratunis as having been, by the mid-fifth century, prominent in Armenian affairs for many centuries,[50] for example making the Christian apostle Thaddaeus's first Armenian convert a Bagratuni,[51] and he portrays Bagratunis as consistently loyal to friends and steadfast in religion. He effectively erases the actual pre-eminence in Armenia's history of the Mamikoneans and, conveniently, ends his account just before their most heroic period, the second half of the fifth century.

The Bagratuni family also propagated a prestigious, false, genealogy. Moses is the first writer to ascribe them a Hebrew origin, that is an origin among God's chosen people.[52] A Georgian annalist writing between *c.*790 and *c.*800 took this further, asserting that the Bagratunis were descendants of the Old Testament king David.[53] This of course made them distant kinsmen of Jesus Christ. A sculptured relief of Ashot I of Iberia shows David interceding with Christ for Ashot, Ashot offering a church to Christ in return for a blessing.

The Church: Politics and Problems

Throughout the seventh and eighth centuries the Church had retained a leading role in politics. In the seventh century for example, Nersēs III had instigated Byzantium's appointments of Theodore Ṙshtuni and Hamazasp Mamikonean to oversee Armenia, and the mission to the Huns was,

---

[48] Thomson, 1978, pp. 7–8, 49–52, 56–61; Toumanoff, 1963, pp. 330–6; Adontz-Garsoïan, 1970, pp. 368–71.
[49] Moses, I, 1, trans. Thomson, 1978, p. 65.
[50] Thomson, 1978, pp. 29–31, 40, 46, 58–60.
[51] Moses, II, 33, trans. Thomson, 1978, p. 170.
[52] Ibid., I, 22, trans. Thomson, 1978, pp. 110–11.
[53] Martin-Hisard, 1984; Toumanoff, 1963, pp. 326–9.

probably, a political move. At a sensitive moment, after the 703 revolt, Katholikos Eḷia (703–17) conciliated the caliph Abd al-Malik when the Albanian patriarch turned to Chalcedonianism. Eḷia denounced him, and the princess who supported him, stressing that he had come to an agreement with the Byzantine emperor,[54] and replaced him at a synod in Partaw in 704. Katholikos John of Ōdzun (717–28) followed Eḷia's example, insuring independence by impressing the Arabs with Armenian loyalty and rectitude. The 726 Council of Manazkert was a joint enterprise between the Armenians and the Syrian church which was subject to the Arabs. It terminated Armenia's union with the Byzantine church. According to a later source, John expelled the 'Greek' party, at the Caliph's orders, arousing a protest from Emperor Leo III (717–41).[55] The Council's chief concern however was to re-establish good relations between the Armenian and Syrian churches, which it did with the condemnation of the errors of Julian of Halicarnassus, and agreement to differ on some liturgical matters. John's earlier measures, in the canons of his 719/20 Duin Council, to curb drunkenness in bishops, clergy and laymen, may have been meant not merely to improve standards but also to impress the, theoretically, teetotal Muslims. His compilation of a book of canon law in 720 was perhaps meant in part to prevent Armenian disputes either reaching Arab courts or suffering Arab interference. He certainly seems to have impressed the Caliph (Umar) with his glamorous attire and discourse and he obtained tax exemptions for clergy and church property.

John's accomplishments had political implications but it would be unfair to question his religious sincerity. His work was essentially to forge the Armenians into a people of God, attacking shortcomings and heresy (notably in two treatises, *Against the Docetists* and *Against the Paulicians*) and promoting improvements. In his 719 synodal oration for example he urged the extension of the Sunday vigil and liturgical uniformity, a matter addressed in the Council's canons. The organization, into a canon, of hymnodic material, which had proliferated in the seventh century, was probably the work of his contemporary, Stephen of Siwnikᶜ. The establishment of the canon of the Old Testament was yet to come, at the Council of Partaw in 768.

Just as it had done in the fifth century the church maintained a favourable attitude towards war, though soldiers were regarded as unfit to be given authority in the church or church property, as they clearly were (by laymen) according to the Albanian katholikos Symeon in 704.[56] Lewond's account of the two eighth-century Mamikonean rebellions offers a number of illuminating details. In both the *nakharar*s confirmed

---

[54] Moses Daskhurants‘i, III, 5, trans. Dowsett, 1961b, p. 191.
[55] Vardan, 38, trans. Thomson, 1989, p. 180.
[56] Moses Daskhurants‘i, III, 11, trans. Dowsett, 1961b, pp. 200–1.

their union with an oath.[57] In the second rebellion, almost as if they had learnt their lesson from Ełishē's account of the 450 revolt, the heroes of the last battle perceived themselves to be fighting for their church as well as for country and nation.[58] The *nakharar*s had earlier been encouraged by a visionary monk, who prophesied the return of 'the sceptre of the kingdom' and exhorted them daily.[59] The rebels were accompanied into battle by clerics carrying Gospels, candles and incense, and they were assisted, according to enemy informants, by a multitude of angels fighting in human form.[60] And though the Armenians lost, Łewond's audience could nevertheless rejoice. For in an earlier account, of the executions of the clerics of the church of St Gregory (probably the monastery of St Gregory at Bagawan), Łewond explains that those who are crucified with Christ will reign with Him, while the wicked will ultimately receive their just rewards.[61]

Thomas Artsruni's account of the early 850s resistance to Bugha has similar elements. When Gurgēn Artsruni's army was attacked, after the battle line was arranged, 'the deacons offered benedictions', 'the priests raised up the holy gospel and their banner – the holy cross', and the choir sang the song of victory over Pharoah. Both priests and heavenly hosts took part in the battle 'for it was a spiritual battle' 'for the holy churches and the people of God'.[62] In another passage the Albanian prince Apumusē claims that slaying enemies of God is 'great piety', citing four particular Old Testament examples and the Israelites in general as parallels.[63]

Such accounts as these scarcely represent the exact truth. They drew on earlier sources, Thomas, for example, owing much to Ełishē, and they reflected later authorial attitudes. Yet because they also drew on memories and because they were written for patrons it is unlikely that they entirely misrepresent the attitudes of the protagonists concerned. They certainly reveal the interpretations which the authors and their associates wished to be accepted. The church sanctioned armed struggle even when there was no immediate religious provocation, and insurgents used Christianity to justify their cause.

Ecclesiastical problems in the period of Arab rule included lay encroachment, low and declining standards, and, naturally, secular sins. The 645 Duin Council attests and attempted to curtail some aristocratic abuses – lodging in monasteries with cavalry, minstrels and dancing girls, dismissing monks, infringing ecclesiastical immunity from tax. The 704 Partaw Council complained of usurpation of property and of authority in

---

[57] Łewond, 26, 34, trans. Arzoumanian, 1982b, pp. 120, 132.
[58] Ibid, 34, trans. Arzoumanian, 1982b, p. 136.
[59] Ibid., trans. Arzoumanian, 1982b, pp. 131–2.
[60] Ibid., trans. Arzoumanian, 1982b, p. 137.
[61] Ibid., 7, trans. Arzoumanian, 1982b, p. 58.
[62] Thomas, III, 4, trans. Thomson, 1985, pp. 213–14.
[63] Ibid., 10, trans. Thomson, 1985, p. 243.

the church, especially by soldiers, cavalrymen and tax-collectors. The 768 Council as we have seen also attests ecclesiastical losses. The 645 canons stipulate that bishops should supervise monasteries but it also attests that they were themselves not immune from faults: they could not be relied upon to avoid violence, greed and encroachment on others' dioceses. The phenomenon of aristocratic control of monasteries surfaces in the tale of Vahan of Goḷtᶜn. Raised a Muslim, while hostage in Damascus, Vahan converted to Christianity after returning home around 719. Sought by the authorities he found shelter only in a monastery in Shirak, but was expelled after six months at the behest of the lady of the province, lest he ruin his benefactors as well as himself.[64]

The problems and deficiencies of monastic establishments are not the whole story of monasticism. Vahan had found hospitality in several monasteries before he returned to the Caliphate, to be beheaded in 737. Sayings of the fourth- and fifth-century Egyptian Desert Fathers, though first collected in an Armenian version in the twelfth century, were excerpted earlier, including during the eighth century. The selections suggest very respectable aspirations, towards contemplation, virginity, humility and solitude, towards monks fighting, as soldiers and martyrs, their thoughts and desires.[65] There was a large community at Makenotsᶜ in Siwnikᶜ in the 780s. There is no evidence for nunneries as such, but there are examples of well-connected women undertaking a monastic life. The sister of John of Ōdzun's contemporary, Stephen of Siwnikᶜ, was a recluse, though not so secluded that she could not give music lessons from behind a screen.[66]

Some snippets of information suggest that some monasteries and churches may have been wealthy even in the times of troubles. The monastery of St Gregory at Bagawan, when plundered, possessed glorious and precious vessels which had been given by kings, princes and nobles. Unfortunately the date of this event is uncertain, very early eighth century according to Ḷewond, in the late 780s according to John Katholikos.[67] A 783 inscription at Tᶜalin suggests monastic estate management, recording the digging of a monastic canal. Village clergy seem not to have held hereditary ecclesiastical properties any more and these properties

---

[64] Vahan's story is recounted by Artawazd, Abbot of Erashkhavorkᶜ, whose *Martyrdom of Saint Vahan of Colthene* is to be found in *Armenian Texts (Sopᶜerkᶜ Haykakankᶜ)* (22 vols, Venice, 1853–61) vol. 13 (1854).

[65] Leloir, 1968, 1974a, 1974b. The concept of monks as martyrs and soldiers was traditional, Malone, 1950, esp. pp. 91–111 for martyrdom and monastic life conceived as spiritual military service, and p. 60 for the later Church Fathers' concept of virginity as a species of martyrdom.

[66] Stephen Orbelean, *History of the House of Sisakan*, XXXI, trans. Brosset, 1864, I, p. 85.

[67] Ḷewond, 7, trans. Arzoumanian, 1982b, p. 58, and Arzoumanian's p. 164 where he states 699 to be the date, following another source's dating of the perpetrator's arrival in Armenia rather than Ḷewond's reference to the Caliph. John Katholikos, XXIV, 1–9, trans. Maksoudian, 1987, pp. 114–15 and his Commentary.

seem to have passed to monasteries.[68] Tat^cew, seat of the Siwnian bishops, had become very wealthy by 884. Bishop David purchased a village, in 839, from Prince Philip, and acquired half another by exchange; in 844 Philip gave the village of Tat^cew, Prince Hrahat another village; Bishop Solomon was given another in 867, gained another in 877 by exchange, and purchased another property in 881.[69]

But the wealth of Tat^cew was part of the ninth-century Armenian revival. While Arab domination was stronger, the glories which the seventh-century church had enjoyed had not continued. It was not that the wars which occurred between 640 and 700 had themselves dealt a fatal blow to Armenian culture, though the Armenians did complain in a letter to Constans II in 648 that Arab invasions had caused a decline in religious learning.[70] In this context, the career and brief autobiography of Anania of Shirak are instructive. Born between 595 and 600, Anania left his native Ayrarat for Theodosiopolis, then moved south, probably to Martyropolis, to study for six months with a mathematician, and then north to study for eight years, probably in the 620s, in Trebizond, under Tychicus who attracted pupils even from Constantinople. There were no mathematical books available in Armenia, nor anyone capable of teaching him.[71] Anania composed a variety of works, and some scholars believe that they were parts of a single exposition of knowledge, for use in the education of theologians, which has not survived in its entirety. His *Geography*, based on a work by Pappus of Alexandria, was composed before 636.[72] His *On Weights and Measures*, reworking a text of Epiphanius of Cyprus (*c*.315–*c*.403), included the Persian and Armenian systems. He also wrote a discourse about Easter and Christmas, and works of cosmography, astronomy, chronology and mathematics. In the 660s Anania was asked by Katholikos Anastas (661–7) to compose a perpetual calender of ecclesiastical feasts, both movable and fixed, but Anastas' death prevented its adoption. Anania taught for a while in Armenia but found his pupils lazy and arrogant, prematurely taking students of their own and so bringing him into disrepute. Popular legend later portrayed him as a scholar of the occult, exiled, his books banned.

The eighth-century church lacked such scholars, though learning did not entirely cease. In the early years Gregory, bishop of the Arsharunis, wrote a commentary on the Lectionary for Vahan Kamsarakan. Bishop Stephen of Siwnik^c, killed in 735 by a loose woman whom he had reprimanded, worked in Constantinople with the Armenian 'Hellenizing'

[68] Canard (translating Ter-Ghévondian), 1986.
[69] Stephen Orbelean, XXXIX, XL, trans. Brosset, 1864, I, pp. 123–7, 130–2.
[70] Sebēos, XXXIII, trans. Macler, 1904, p. 122.
[71] Berbérian, 1964, (French translation of text); Hewsen, 1992, pp. 273–5 for discussion.
[72] The Armenian section is based on local information and some research, possibly involving archival material, Hewsen, 1992, pp. 32, 59A, 249, and for full discussion of authorship, date and sources, his Introduction.

school and specialized in Biblical exegesis. In translating, into Armenian, the (probably early sixth-century) mystic works of Pseudo-Dionysius the Areopagite he was helped by the Byzantine emperor Leo III's consul and attendant David. His contemporaries Katholikos John and the Syrian patriarch Athanasius established a monastery on the Armenian–Syrian border where boys might learn Syriac and Armenian and works of the Fathers might be translated, but this venture failed after their deaths.

Of the historical works composed between 640 and 884 the most problematic is the anonymous text which was discovered in 1842. Its discoverer, Shakhat^cunean, identified it as the *History of Heraclius* by Bishop Sebēos, which is referred to by later Armenian historians, and thought Sebēos to be the Sebēos, bishop of the Bagratunis, who attended the 645 Duin Council. Subsequent scholars, concerned by the work's tripartite nature (focussing first, in the part nowadays known as the *Primary History*, on some fourteen generations of legendary history, second on the Artaxiad and Arsacid periods, and third on the late fifth century onwards), argued differences of authorship between the parts. In 1949 Malkhasian reasserted authorship of the whole by Sebēos. In 1958 Abgarian argued persuasively that the text is not Sebēos's lost *History*. And discussion of its authorship has continued.[73] It is even possible that even the third part of the text, though its narrative concludes in 661, was put together in the eighth rather than the seventh century. One indication is that it is not a unified construction. It combines a sympathetic account of Muhammad, as one who lead his people back to the true religion, with vehemently anti-Arab passages.[74] More important is that Arab dominion is identified as the fourth world empire prophesied in the Old Testament book of Daniel.[75] In another text, seemingly a short excerpt though not a literal quotation from the real Sebēos, this fourth is identified as the Persian monarchy.[76] The conviction of 'Pseudo-Sebēos' that Arab power was a permanency suggests that he wrote in an eighth-century context. Nevertheless Pseudo-Sebēos's work is especially valuable for the information it provides about late sixth- and seventh-century Roman–Persian wars, Armenian involvement therein, and the early Arab period. Oral tradition must have contributed to his information about the Bagratunis. The tale of the rebel Smbat Bagratuni first defeating bear, bull and lion in the Constantinopolitan arena then being spared at the prayer of the empress, and feasted,[77] was surely in the minstrels' repertoire.

[73] Frendo, 1985, includes a brief résumé.
[74] Sebēos, XXX, and XXXII, XXXIV, XXXV, trans. Macler, 1904, p. 95 and pp. 104–5, 129–30, 132.
[75] Ibid., XXXII, trans. Macler, 1904, pp. 104–5.
[76] Mahé, 1984, p. 227.
[77] Sebēos, X, trans. Macler, 1904, pp. 37–39.

Eighth-century writers later than Pseudo-Sebēos were Pseudo-Moses of Khoren, Armenia's 'Father of History' who glorified the Bagratunis, and, perhaps, the *vardapet* Łewond. Łewond's patron was 'Shapuh Bagratuni' brother of Ashot and so was either the Shapuh who was brother of the presiding prince Ashot who died in 826,[78] or the Shapuh who was the brother of the later king. Łewond's history covers 632–788. It incorporates a lengthy epistle, purportedly from the Byzantine emperor Leo III to Caliph Umar II, answering questions which had been put about Christianity.[79] This epistle may actually have been composed in reply to a letter written by a Muslim in Syria about 885–900, or may even be an original Armenian composition (rather than an Armenian translation from Greek) of the eleventh to thirteenth centuries.[80] A smaller scale work than these is an anonymous history of the Hŕipᶜsimean nuns, composed about 800. There was clearly an interest in literature and theology. The Patriarch of Jerusalem commissioned an explanation of the Chalcedonian faith for the Armenians and this led to a theological debate at Ashot Bagratuni's court, and at his instigation, between the author and the Syrian scholar the deacon Nonnus of Nisibis in 817. Ashot's son Bagarat Bagratuni subsequently asked Nonnus for a commentary on the Gospel of St John, which Nonnus provided, in Arabic, around 840. Its exposition of the divinity of Christ may have been intended specifically to buttress the faith of orthodox Christians, and provide ammunition for use in debate, in the face of criticism by Muslims or heretics. It was translated into Armenian in about 856.

The eighth century is marked by a decline in building, and this is partly attributable to the Umayyads' opposition to Christian construction or restoration, and partly, naturally, to economic difficulties and political distractions. Before 700 architecture had flourished. Katholikos Nersēs III is known as 'the Builder'. His greatest work was the congregational church of the heavenly host, Zuartᶜnotsᶜ, which was founded between 643 and 652, and was part of his palace complex near Ējmiatsin. Lavishly decorated with sculpture, four-apsed with galleries, its design is related to some Syrian and north Mesopotamian churches and it accommodates the Byzantine liturgy. The presiding prince Gregory Mamikonean likewise built a palace, beside the church which he and his wife founded, c.665, at Aruch. Gregory was also associated with the unusual church at Zōravar near Ełvard, which had a radiating plan with eight wings and apses. And there were other later seventh-century churches, for example Nersēs

---

[78] Łewond, Colophon, trans. Arzoumanian, 1982b, p. 150, and for the identification his pp. 41, 196 (n. 3).
[79] Łewond, 13–14, trans. Arzoumanian, 1982b, pp. 70–105 and for discussion his pp. 42–7.
[80] See Gaudeul, 1984, for the 885–90 suggestion; Gero, 1973, pp. 153–71 for the suggestion of the later date; Mahé, 1993, pp. 491 n. 311 for criticism of Gero's suggestion.

Plate 9   The khach^{c}k^{c}ar of Prince Gregory Atrnersehean from the village of Mets Mazrik, 881.

Kamsarakan's church of the Mother of God at T^{c}alin, c.690, and Prince Kohazat's and Bishop Joseph I's St John at Sisian, founded between 670 and 689, probably completed in 691. There was by contrast almost no building in the eighth century. There are assertions in literary sources that Katholikos John and Katholikos David I (728–41) built churches at Ōdzun and Aramus but their validity has been questioned.[81]

Like political independence, architecture revived, slowly, in the ninth century. Bagarat Bagratuni of Tarōn built a domed church in Muş at great expense.[82] In Vaspurakan the church of the Holy Cross of Aḷbak was

[81] Thierry and Donabédian, 1989, pp. 70–1, 561, 68, 81.
[82] Thomas Artsruni, II, 7, trans. Thomson, 1985, pp. 186–7.

founded sometime between *c*.670 and 859. This church is probably the church of St Ējmiatsin at Soradir, whose (poor) building is either later seventh-century or early ninth-century.[83] The illuminated Gospel presented in the early tenth century by King Gagik Artsruni's wife, Mlk^cē, to the monastery at Varag was completed in 862, at an unknown scriptorium but probably for an Artsruni patron. Its illustrator used as a model a 'classicizing' manuscript, perhaps one brought to Armenia in the fifth century. In Siwnik^c two churches (the Apostles and Mother of God) were built on an island in Lake Sevan, by Princess Miriam in 874. Khach^ck^c-ars, that is steles bearing a carved cross, perhaps in part a manifestation of the cult of the Cross, began to be erected. Queen Katranidē's, at Garni, of 879, is one of the earliest.

Literary, architectural and artistic patronage was one aspect of the laity's behaviour with which the church could be pleased, but there were of course others, besides aristocratic encroachment, which caused concern. Lay transgressions included traditional mourning practices, such as those which had been condemned by the Church Fathers, as shown in Thomas Artsruni's continuator's account of the reactions, after Gregory-Derenik's murder, of his widow and bodyguard, of nobles, labourers and artisans. These reactions included wailing, breast-beating, the wearing of black and of ashes on the head.[84] Clerical admonition, to recall the mourners to the fear of God, is also mentioned, and this may by now have become an integral part of the ritual, to mark its end. Some other lay sins were political necessities. Marriage with infidels, stigmatized by the 768 Council as worse than fornication and adultery, and condemned in the first Armenian penitential and law code, both of twelfth-century date,[85] could not be avoided. Thus daughters of the 770s rebel Mushel Mamikonean and of Bagarat of Tarōn were married off to Arab emirs and Vasak of Siwnik^c's daughter wed (by 821) Babik the Khurramite. Conversion to Islam was another danger. Quite apart from the occasional overt pressure on Christians to convert there was also the insidious pressure of social contacts with Muslims. Christian counter-attack was impracticable because apostasy from Islam and attacks on Islam were punishable by death. Bagarat's view that apostasy from Christianity, if insincere and forced, was harmless, was not the official one. Thomas Artsruni regretted that the returning apostates remained outside canonical regulations and committed further sins. He conceded that deathbed repentance might save Ashot from torments in the after-life, but he had doubts. He was sure that such a sinner would not 'enjoy the wedding with the bridegroom'.[86]

[83] Thierry and Donabédian, 1989, pp. 170, 577.
[84] Thomas, Anonymous Continuator, trans. Thomson, 1985, pp. 328–31 and see his p. 325, n. 1 and p. 332 n. 1 for difficulties regarding Book and Chapter numbering.
[85] For text and translation of *Penitential*, Dowsett, 1961a; for code, Mkhit^car Gosh (edns 1880, 1975).
[86] Thomas, III, 18, trans. Thomson, 1985, pp. 280–1.

The methods whereby sins might be atoned for included penance and other, traditional ones. Vahan Kamsarakan, recipient of Bishop Gregory's commentary on the Lectionary, lived as an anchorite after a military career. Animal sacrifice, with prayer for remission of the donors' sins, was practiced. Donation, other peoples' (the beneficiaries) prayers and salvation are explicitly connected in some Siwnian charters. Sometimes female donors acted for the benefit of husbands and sons. To make salvation secure, (Siwnian) records of 839, 867, 877 and 910 threaten that offenders against the grants will answer to God for the donors' sins. The 867 grantor adds the sins of her parents and husband.[87]

The Paulician Heretics

For probably most of the period 640–884 the church had the further problem of the Paulicians. Their history and doctrine, recounted in ninth-century Greek sources and, more briefly with regard to the history, by Katholikos John of Ōdzun, has suffered differing reconstructions.[88] What is certain is that between the 660s and the early ninth century they were active in the Armenian frontier zone, and had Armenian leaders (except for Symeon-Titus, their leader from 685 to 688). They were at Mananaḷi, (between Theodosiopolis and Erzincan) in the middle of the seventh century but about 655 they moved (for reasons unknown) to Cibossa near Coloneia in Lesser Armenia (a natural stronghold, probably one of Mithridates of Pontus's forts). There their leader Constantine-Silvanus was executed by imperial authorities in about 682 and then, or later, during the Byzantine emperor Leo III's reign (717–741), some Paulicians found Arab support and established themselves at 'Jrkay', probably the neighbourhood of the Bitlis river, south-west of Lake Van.[89] Further persecution in the reign of Justinian II caused a flight from Cibossa to Episparis (site unknown) led by 'Paul', the heretics' leader from about 688 until about 717. Paul established a dynastic right of leadership and it is not impossible that it was after him that the orthodox called the heretics 'Paulicians'. The Paulicians were condemned in Armenia at the 719 Duin Council. Their leader Gegnesius-Timothy was denounced to Leo III, but hoodwinked Leo's patriarch and then fled to Mananaḷi, by now Arab territory. The date of this episode is disputed, so no connection with the Duin Council can be established.

[87] Stephen Orbelean, XXXIX, XL, XLIV, trans. Brosset, 1864, I, pp. 124–5, 131–2, 130, 140–1.

[88] Astruc et al., 1970; Aucher, 1834, pp. 78–107; Garsoïan, 1967a; Lemerle, 1973; Loos, 1974a.

[89] Huxley, 1984.

With regard to Paulician doctrine, John of Ōdzun, whose testimony deserves more respect than it has sometimes received, accused Paulicians, amongst other things, of rejecting images and the Cross, of detesting Christ, of parodying the Eucharist, and of practices suggestive of surviving Zoroastrianism,[90] for example beseeching the sun. In addition, the ninth-century Greek sources allege, amongst other things, that the Paulicians credited the creation of matter to a god other than the heavenly father, espoused a docetic Christology (maintaining that Christ did not have a real body whilst He lived as a human, but only an apparent one), and rejected the Old Testament and the ecclesiastical hierarchy.

The Paulicians were dangerous because they were enthusiastic to recruit. Much of John's treatise against them answers Paulician criticisms of the orthodox, to counter Paulician evangelization. Against their charge of idolatry he stressed that divine power entered into churches, crosses, images and altars through consecration, and that it was through this that they performed miracles. John also emphasized that both the Creation and the miracles recounted in the Old Testament were works of God, who was pleased to inhabit inanimate materials.

This early eighth-century opposition must have weakened Paulicianism and further setbacks followed. In the mid-eighth century many Paulicians were executed by the Arabs for trying (for reasons unknown) to leave Mananaḷi. 'The sons of sinfulness' who joined Gregory Mamikonean's revolt (747) and whose presence, Ḷewond says, destroyed unity, may have been Paulicians.[91] Gregory, who went after the revolt to Theodosiopolis, may be the same Gregory who arrested some Paulicians in Episparis. Their leader Joseph fled, to the far off Antioch of Pisidia. And there were Paulicians amongst the transportees whom the Byzantine emperor Constantine V moved from Melitene and Theodosiopolis to the Balkans in 756. But Paulician numbers increased after Iconoclasm was temporarily defeated in Byzantium in 787, for disappointed iconoclasts were attracted by a sect which shared their rejection of images.

It is perhaps not surprising that Paulicianism proceeded to change. In the early ninth century it passed to Greek leadership and to military action. Sergius-Tychicus (800/1–4/5) refounded the sect, provoked a schism and gained many converts. Persecuted by the Byzantine emperors Michael I (811–13) and Leo V (813–20) (and later by the regent Theodora (842–56)), Sergius' disciples fled to (Arab) Melitene and were given Argaun, nearby, by the emir. Raids on imperial territory proved enriching, but later some Paulicians, under Carbeas, wanting independence, moved north to Tephrike (Divriği). They continued fighting, sometimes in

---

[90] Russell, 1987, p. 530, n. 11 and pp. 537–8 provides translation of passages which may reflect a survival of Zoroastrianism, itself the subject of his ch. 16, 'Children of the Sun' (pp. 515–533), in which John's evidence is discussed (pp. 518, 520, 522–4).
[91] Ḷewond, 26, trans. Arzoumanian, 1982b, p. 120 and his p. 180 (n. 5, 6 to ch. 26).

alliance with the Arabs. But in 872 the Byzantine emperor Basil I defeated Carbeas' successor, his nephew and son-in-law Chrysocheir, whose raids had been for Byzantium a major problem, and in 878 Tephrike fell. Many fled, some probably to strengthen a new Armenian heresy, T'ondrakianism, so called because its founder, Smbat, originally from Zarehawan, had worked in T'ondrak. The T'ondrakians had been massacred sometime in the mid-ninth century by the emir of Manazkert. If (king) Ashot did indeed give territory to Manazkert as Constantine VII claimed, it may have been in recompense for the emir's eschewing Melitene's patronage of troublemakers.

Exactly what had made Paulicianism attractive is unclear. It had permeated the upper classes and it had its own hierarchy, so it was hardly a peasant protest against 'feudalism'.[92] Garsoïan's interpretation, that Paulicianism was a survival of early Christianity, until the ninth century Adoptionist and iconoclast rather than dualist,[93] is undermined by the eighth-century Paulicians' rejection of the Cross and of the Eucharist. For contemporary Byzantine iconoclasts revered both. Lewond's, and the eleventh-century Stephen Asoḷik's historical works, drawing ultimately on the propaganda of the iconoclast Leo III, present Leo as a new Moses who in 717 caused Arab besiegers of Constantinople to drown by the power of the Cross.[94] Under Constantine V iconoclasts taught that the Eucharist was the true image of Christ.

Cities and Commerce

In the seventh century Duin became a centre of glass-making, and the volume of trade passing through Armenia increased as war in Mesopotamia disrupted more southerly routes. But Armenia's economy declined in the eighth century, since internal conditions were disturbed and poor, and because there was another shift of trade routes, this time to avoid Arab–Byzantine and Arab–Khazar wars in eastern Anatolia and in the Caucasus. Matters did not improve until the last quarter of the eighth century. In the reign of the caliph al-Mahdi (775–85) a discovery of silver relieved poverty and frontier dues were abolished. Urban life revived, but it was in Arab hands. Duin, although the majority of its population remained Armenian, had already become very much an Arab city. Katholikos David I (728–41) had left because he was 'annoyed' by its non-Christian population.[95] The choice of Partaw (Bardaa) for the 768 Council may have been for the same reason. Duin was after all the

[92] Garsoïan, 1971b.
[93] Garsoïan, 1967a, e.g. pp. 227, 230; 1971b.
[94] Gero, 1973, pp. 37, 39.
[95] John Katholikos, XXIII, 3, trans. Maksoudian, 1987, p. 112.

ostikan's base, though from 789 it shared this honour with Partaw. Arabs also held Melitene, which they had refortified in 757, Theodosiopolis (reconquered from Byzantium in the 750s) and Arzn. The towns of Khlat^c, Archēsh, Berkri and Manazkert were regarded by Byzantium's Constantine VII in the mid-tenth century as effectively Arab territory.[96] Emirate territories rarely included much land outside cities.

Just as towns revived so too did commerce. Trade between eastern Europe and the Islamic world, via the Caucasus, began in the period 775–800 when Arab–Khazar wars ceased. This route itself was not Armenian, but coin circulation suggests that in the ninth century Armenia had links with many parts of the Arab world. The two main Armenian routes passed through or by Nakhchawan, Duin, Ani and Theodosiopolis, and through or by Her, Van, Berkri, Archēsh, Manazkert, Khlat^c, Bitlis and Martyropolis. When trade increased in the tenth century it was the latter, sourthern route, which could be controlled throughout by the emirs, which developed first.[97] Probably the most famous exports were Armenian carpets, of which Theodosiopolis was a centre of production. Merchants were widespread. Indeed, Babik the Khurramite and some companions once disguised themselves as commercial travellers to escape capture.[98] It was merchants who retrieved the corpse of Gregory-Derenik Artsɾuni, murdered by the emir of Her in 887.[99]

The coronation of Gregory-Derenik's father-in-law, Ashot Bagratuni, as king, marked a revival of political independence coinciding with economic growth, artistic renaissance and a triumph of religious orthodoxy. It remained to be seen whether Ashot's successors would retain or lose leadership of the Armenians.

---

[96] *De Administrando Imperio*, ch. 44 l.13–115.
[97] Ter-Ghewondyan, 1976, pp. 139–40.
[98] This is recorded by two Arab writers, al-Mutahhar b. Tahir al-Maqdisi and al-Mas^c-udi. Extracts from their works are translated into French in Canard's 1980 revision of Laurent, 1919, pp. 372–3 and pp. 374–6 in App. II 'La Révolte de Bâbek' (pp. 357–81).
[99] Thomas Artsruni, III, 20, trans. Thomson, 1985, p. 291.

9

Kings and Migrants, 884–c.1071

The establishment of Ashot Bagratuni as king in 884 proved to be little more than icing on a cake made by his own good management and baked by courtesy of his neighbours. Bagratuni kingship ultimately neither united Armenians nor preserved them from the twin perils of the eleventh century, the annexation policy of Byzantium and the aggression of the newly appeared Seljuk Turks. These Turks, originally from central Asia and Muslims, were to establish themselves in Iran, Mesopotamia and Azerbaijan, and from these regions invade Armenian lands.

One explanation of Armenia's failure to develop into a powerful country is that Ashot's Armenia was not a nation-state. She lacked some of the governmental institutions, especially a legal system controlled by kings, which were to be essential to state formation in Western Europe.[1] Though the historian John Katholikos asserts that, as king, Ashot did pass many laws, concerning noble houses, cities and villages, this claim cannot be taken at face value. For John was following a literary model, Moses of Khoren's account of King 'Valarshak'.[2] Not until 1184 was there a written Armenian law code, compiled by Mkhit^car Gosh. King Ashot worked not through a bureaucracy but through his kin. The office of Prince of Princes (*ishkhan ishkhanats^c*) continued, held successively by Ashot's sons Smbat and (under Smbat) David, and by Smbat's son Ashot, but what it involved is not recorded. It was King Ashot's brother Abas and son Smbat who held his extended frontiers in the north. It was his marriage alliances which facilitated influence in Siwnik^c and Vaspurakan.

[1] Of those polities which were to become nation-states only Wessex, in England, had achieved this as early as the late ninth century.
[2] John Katholikos, *History of the Armenians*, XXIX, 7, trans. Maksoudian, 1987, p. 128 and his commentary p. 273 pointing out the debt to Moses, *History of the Armenians*, II, 6 and 7 (trans. Thomson, 1978, pp. 135–9).

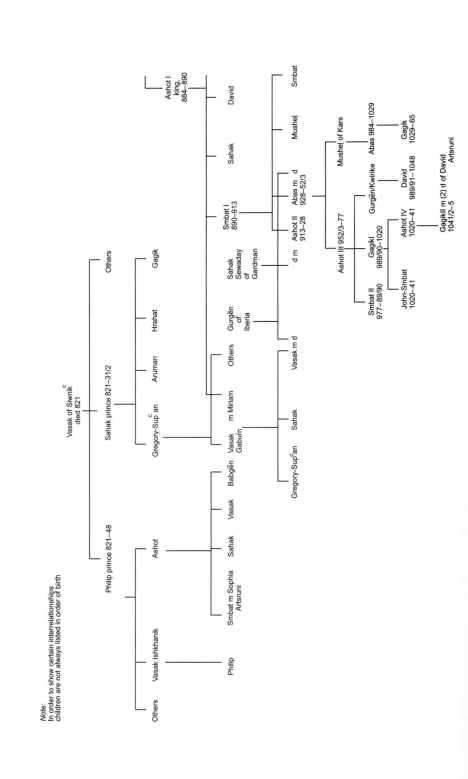

Note:
In order to show certain interrelationships
children are not always listed in order of birth

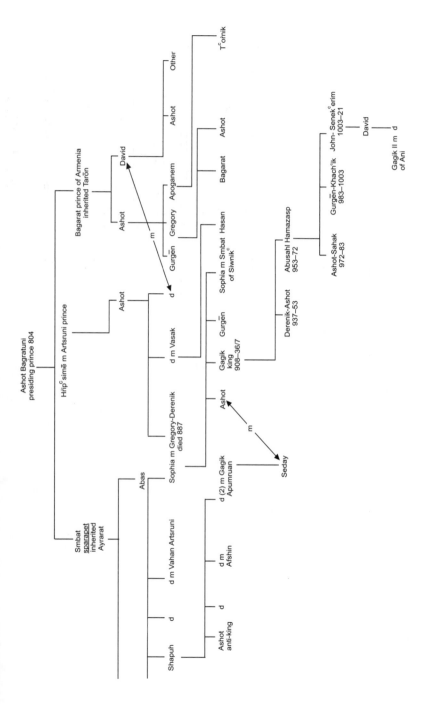

Figure 9.1 Partial genealogical table: Artsrunis and Bagratunis in the tenth and eleventh centuries

Although his son-in-law Gregory-Derenik Artsruni of Vaspurakan did begin to reject Ashot's advice,[3] after Gregory-Derenik's assassination Ashot made his (own) grandson, Gagik Apumruan, regent, retrieving him from an Artsruni prison. Gagik's marriage to a granddaughter of Ashot, accomplished by the mid-890s, may have been made then.

Secondly, ninth- and tenth-century Armenians also lacked an inspirational, unifying ideology, such as the empires of Rome and Sasanian Persia had enjoyed. Kingship may have been perceived as a personal, non-exclusive honour, for two of Ashot's junior contemporaries, Gregory-Derenik, and David of Tarōn, seem also to have assumed a royal title. Their contemporary, Thomas Artsruni, refers to each as king.[4] This is, admittedly, only three times in all, and possibly an aberration, but in David's case there is some confirmation from the Byzantine emperor Constantine VII (913–57). Constantine's account of recent Tarōnite history refers to David as *Arkaikas*, which is a diminutive of *ark^cay*, Armenian for 'king'.[5] By the end of the tenth century there were five Armenian kingdoms, three Bagratuni (Ani, Kars and Loṙi), one Artsruni and one Siwnian.

The Early Bagratuni Kings

The royal Bagratuni pre-eminence had declined quite quickly. In the reign of Smbat I (890–913), the causes were the intrinsic power of the Artsrunis, Arab patronage, Byzantine revival, and Smbat's personal mishandling of friends and allies. Admittedly Smbat did deal successfully with rebellion by his uncle Abas and with failure by two Arab governors of Duin, in 892/3, to pay taxes, and he extended his frontiers and influence in the north. But Tarōn was effectively lost. Taken in 895 by the emir of Amida (Diyarbakır) and Arzn and recovered in 898 by Gregory Bagratuni, cousin of its deprived prince, Tarōn revolved thereafter in the Byzantine orbit, its princes receiving invitations to Constantinople, titles, a subsidy and a house.

Smbat's major troubles were provoked by the Caliph's governors of Azerbaijan, ambitious for greater power, and were compounded by his own alienation of the Artsrunis. They began when the governor Afshin (appointed in 889, and whose duty regarding Armenia was to forward

---

[3] John Katholikos, XXVIII, 5–7, trans. Maksoudian, 1987, p. 127.

[4] Thomas, III, 20, trans. Thomson, 1985, pp. 292 and 283, 284 (where Thomson translates *ark ^cay* as ruler).

[5] *De Administrando Imperio*, ch. 43 1. 28 and v. II. *Commentary* ed. Jenkins, 1962, where the identification of Arkaias as David's son, rather than as David, is preferred and the ruler (*ark ^cay*) of Thomson, 1985, p. 284 is taken to be David's brother Ashot, which is also the interpretation of Brosset's 1874 French translation.

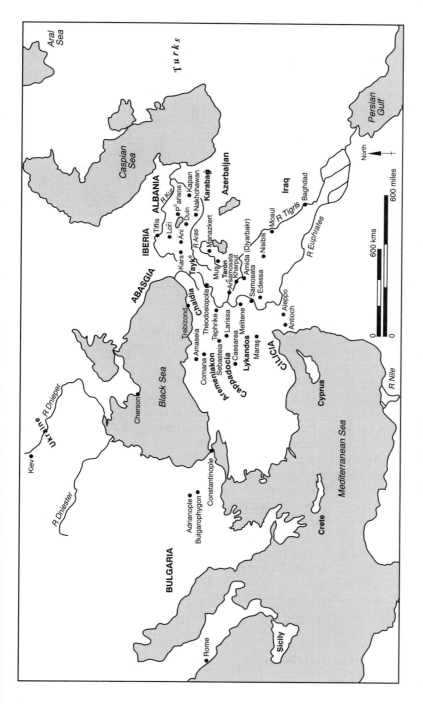

Map 9.1   *The east Mediterranean and west Asia*

the taxes to the Caliph) reacted suspiciously to Smbat's making, early in his reign, a treaty with Byzantium. Only temporarily soothed, Afshin took Duin in 894. Smbat, worried by Afshin's friendly relations with the late Gregory-Derenik's son Ashot Artsruni of Vaspurakan, incited Gurgēn Apupelch who, as we have seen, had a grudge of bloodfeud against the Artsrunis, and Gagik Apumruan to dispossess Ashot and his two brothers. In defence, Ashot obtained troops from Afshin, but the three brothers were nevertheless taken captive. Though Smbat disapproved of this, according to the contemporary historian John Katholikos,[6] yet he did nothing to help them. The brothers' supporters then went to Diyarbakır. When its emir fought Smbat over the matter of Tarōn, Smbat's ally Gagik Apumruan defected and led Smbat to defeat. Gagik was killed soon after, by Ashot Artsruni's brother, also called Gagik, whom he had lately freed. The outcome of all this was that Afshin was encouraged to attack Armenia. In 897 he took Kars, removing Smbat's queen, other noble women, and its treasure. Then he acquired Smbat's son, nephew and niece as hostages and a bride. He subsequently attacked again, not only Smbat's territory, but also Vaspurakan, where he appointed governors, in Van and Vostan, and exacted tribute.

A brief respite followed Afshin's death in 900 but it was soon squandered. The Caliph released Smbat from the authority of the new *ostikan*, Afshin's brother Yusuf, and tribute was reduced. The breach with the Artsrunis was healed. Smbat's success, in about 902, against the emirs of Manazkert who had reneged on their financial and military obligations to him, and the peace which was then made owed much to Ashot Artsruni. Smbat rewarded Ashot with Nakhchawan, over which he, Smbat, had acquired some kind of suzerainty. And Ashot proceeded to reconcile King Smbat with Prince Smbat of Siwnik[c] to whom the king had previously entrusted Nakhchawan, and who would have liked to keep it, thereby preventing an alliance between Prince Smbat and the resentful Yusuf. But the king proceeded to jeopardize Artsruni support when he provoked Ashot's successor Gagik. Smbat restored Nakhchawan to Siwnik[c] after Ashot's death in 904 and, jealous of Gagik's success in recapturing the long-lost fort of Amiwk, bribed its commander to surrender it to him and then required a high price of Gagik for its return. Smbat also antagonized another powerful figure, Atrnerseh (Adarnase). Atrnerseh had restored the monarchy of Iberia in 888, and, by 899, had been crowned by Smbat. He subsequently lost much of his territory to Constantine of Abasgia (modern Abkhazia), and Smbat, shortly after Constantine attacked Gugark[c] in about 904, annoyingly crowned him too.

The results were disastrous. When Yusuf rebelled against the Caliph, Smbat was faced with financial demands from both parties, and his

[6] John, XXXIV, 7–8, trans. Maksoudian, 1987, p. 145.

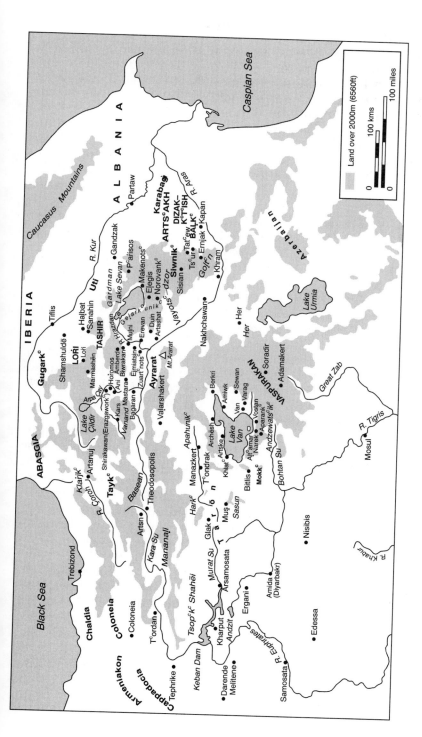

Map 9.2 Armenia

consequential exactions irked his *nakharars*. In 907 one of them joined
Atrnerseh in a murderous plot. In 908 Yusuf crowned Gagik Artsruni as
king, both wanting vengeance on Smbat. In 909 Yusuf devastated Siwnikᶜ, which was cut off from royal territory by Arab enclaves at Duin,
Nakhchawan, and Golṭᶜn. In Golṭᶜn, previously part of Vaspurakan,
Yusuf allowed the establishment of an emirate, with the fort and district
of Ernjak, wrested from Siwnikᶜ in 914, for its support. In 910 Yusuf and
Gagik campaigned against Smbat. Although Gagik subsequently, secretly,
came to terms, and Gregory of Tarōn lobbied the Caliph, King Smbat lost
support and incurred hostility. So he surrendered to Yusuf. It was his
crucifixion, in 913, which saved his reputation. Armenia's trials however
went on. Yusuf himself continued campaigning, martyring persons who
refused conversion to Islam. Armenia's Byzantine and northern neighbours joined in her pillage and there was unrest, disunity and famine.

The recovery which followed was brought about only with Byzantine
help, negotiated by Katholikos John. Unity between Armenians, Iberians
and Abasgians was recommended by the Byzantine patriarch Nicholas.[7]
King Ashot II, already crowned by Atrnerseh of Iberia, was invited to
Constantinople, whence he returned with an army in 915. This Byzantine
push against the Arabs was marked also by the creation of a new Byzantine theme, Lykandos, between Caesarea and Melitene. Its fort had been
rebuilt in 907–8 by an Armenian warrior Melias.[8] Melias was possibly a
Varazhnuni, had perhaps once been in the service of the grandson of the
Ashot of Tarōn whom Gregory-Derenik Artsruni dethroned in 878, had
certainly been in Byzantine service at the battle of Bulgarophygon in 896,
and was subsequently leader of a band of Armenians, including three
Mamikonean brothers. After being implicated in a (Byzantine) rebellion
they had taken refuge in Melitene whence they successfully asked the
emperor Leo VI (886–912) for immunity and for employment in the
Cappadocian frontier regions. Melias attacked Maraş (Germaniceia) in
915 and, with Byzantium's general John Curcuas (Domestic of the eastern
Schools), who came from the Armeniakon theme and was likewise of
Armenian descent, Melitene in 925–6.

The restored Ashot II's reign avoided extremes, both of success and
failure. For a while he did well. The Siwnian princes were submissive. His
cousin, another Ashot, who was crowned by Yusuf as another rival king,
was a problem, but with the aid of the Katholikos the two periodically
came to terms. And after Yusuf was imprisoned by the Caliph in 919,
Ashot II was recognized as King of Kings. He established friendly relations with the governor of Duin. He also repressed rebellions, by the
prince of Uti, by the Gntᶜuni keepers of the fort of Shamshuldē in

---

[7] Ibid., LIV, 1–15, trans. Maksoudian, 1987, pp. 189–191.
[8] Dédéyan, 1981b for Melias's career.

Gugark^c, by his own brother Abas and Abas's father-in-law (Gurgēn of Iberia), and by his own father-in-law, Sahak Seway the prince of Gardman. He took Sahak's territory and he annexed Geḷark^cunik^c in Siwnik^c.

But Ashot's good fortune did not last. Vasak Gnt^cuni offered Shamshuldē to Gurgēn of Iberia. Ashot managed to keep it, but he failed to suppress a further rebellion in Uti. Worse was that Nasr, a subordinate of Yusuf's to whom Yusuf, released in 922 but bought off by Gagik Artsruni, entrusted Armenia, resumed Yusuf's offensive. Babgēn and Sahak of Siwnik^c, who were at odds over territory, he lured to imprisonment having posed as a friendly intermediary. Katholikos John's fort, Biwrakan, was pillaged in 923 and other patriarchal property seized. War was waged on Ashot by Nasr's deputy and on the Siwnian captives' brother, Smbat, by Nasr himself. Meanwhile Ashot's blinding of his father-in-law and brother-in-law had, according to John Katholikos, made everyone lose confidence in him.[9] Furthermore, he had undermined his friendship with Byzantium. In 922 Byzantium had, unsuccessfully, attacked Duin. Ashot had sided with Duin, perhaps out of his resentment, which the emperor Constantine VII attests,[10] of Byzantium's paying a stipend to Gregory of Tarōn, and perhaps in retaliation for Byzantine collaboration with the governor of troublesome Uti, who had had dealings with John Curcuas.

By the mid-920s, it was only King Gagik Artsruni who offered strength, security and reliability. Gagik, with his brother Gurgēn, had extended Artsruni power, northwards towards Mount Ararat and south to the basin of the Bohtan Su. In about 923–4 the Katholikos left Ashot's court for Gagik's. And by 925 Byzantium had transferred the title *Archon* of *Archons*, Greek equivalent of Prince of Princes, from Ashot to Gagik.

Political Society, 884–c.925

The superiority of Gagik Artsruni's vision and strength to those of his Bagratuni contemporaries may be gauged from three vehicles of Artsruni propaganda, none of them matched by the Bagratunis. These are the history undertaken by Thomas Artsruni for Gagik's father, the panegyric of Gagik written by a contemporary continuator, and the remarkable church of the Holy Cross which Gagik built on Alt^camar between 915 and 921.

What Thomas did, despite claiming to be a careful scholar, was, first, to exalt Artsruni history just as Moses of Khoren had, earlier, exalted the Bagratunis'.[11] Thomas distorts Moses' account of Armenia's early history

---

[9] John, LX, 33–4, trans. Maksoudian, 1987, p. 212.
[10] *De Administrando Imperio*, ch. 43 1. 107–17.
[11] Thomson, 1984b.

by editing out some Bagratuni material and by inserting Artsruni details, for example making the first Armenian Christian, who according to Moses had been a Bagratuni, an Artsruni.[12] In his treatment of the 451 rebellion he emphasizes the martyrdom of an Artsruni, whose absence from Ełishē's account Thomas explains by asserting that Artsruni details had been deleted by a contemporary heretic bishop with a grudge.[13]

Thomas's second achievement was to suggest that the mid-fifth- and ninth-century situations were comparable and that the Artsrunis were the new Mamikoneans. Ashot Artsruni's son and grandsons must have delighted in Thomas's portrayal of Ashot as an unprecedented hindrance to Arab power and dominion.[14] Thomas's account of the period after about 850 is strongly influenced by Ełishē, particularly in the use of imagery, in remarks about Armenian disunity and its effects, and in the use of the term *nahatak* with its connotation of 'martyr'.[15] Ashot and his fellows in one battle are 'like brave *nahataks*', and through him 'much valour of *nahatak*dom' was accomplished. Thomas was willing to use these terms despite believing that Ashot's fate in eternity was open to question.[16] The heroic warrior on the make, Gurgēn Apupelch Artsruni, who eventually died from a fall from his horse,[17] Thomas considered to be the equal of *nahataks*, and his struggles against the invaders as 'of a martyr' using a word (*martirosakan*) which more explicitly denotes what we might regard as martyrdom in the ordinary sense. Gurgēn expended blood for his native land, and soul and body for the saints and believers, 'in order to preserve them safe and unsullied'.[18] A slightly later worthy was Shapuh Akēatsʿi, who liberated booty and captives from invaders who had seized them; he apparently showed 'much bravery of *nahatak*dom', and being wounded 'died a martyr's death' (both *martirosakan* and *nahatak*dom are used), 'for the sake of Christ's sheep'.[19]

At Altʿamar the sculpted decoration of the church exterior incorporates the Artsruni martyrs of 786, Hamazasp and Sahak, and King Gagik himself, with a nimbus on his head, offering his church to Christ. Other scenes include David and Goliath, and Samson and the Philistine. The designer was implying that Gagik was comparable to victorious Old Testament heroes and hence that adherence to Gagik was both righteous and profitable. According to Gagik's panegyricist, his new palace was

---

[12] Thomas, I, 6, trans. Thomson, 1985, pp. 110–11 and his n. 1 for comment.

[13] Ibid., II, 2, trans. Thomson, 1985, pp. 147–8.

[14] Ibid., 5, 6, trans. Thomson, 1985, pp. 174, 176–83.

[15] Thomson, 1984a, 1985, pp. 46–51, 197 n. 5, 206 n. 1, 235 n. 8, 249 n. 1.

[16] Thomas, II, 6, II 5 and III, 18, trans. Thomson, 1985, pp. 177, where *nahatak* is translated as 'hero', 174 where 'notable deeds of valour' is the translation, and pp. 280–81.

[17] John Katholikos, XXXIV, 31, trans. Maksoudian, 1987, p. 147.

[18] Thomas, III, 13, trans. Thomson, 1985, p. 257.

[19] Ibid., 29; Thomson, 1985, p. 323, translates the first phrase as 'exhibited many acts of prowess'.

equally awe-inspiring, with domed halls, and pictures, of Gagik and his entourage, and of minstrels, dancing girls, armed men, wrestlers, lions and other animals and birds.[20] The Bagratunis matched neither the splendour nor the volume of Artsruni building. Their ecclesiastical foundations between about 875 and 925 were only about half those of Gagik and his brother Gurgēn, and about a quarter of the Siwnians'.

Though the Artsruni historians and John Katholikos describe only a few aristocratic careers in any detail, the most important institutions of political society are nevertheless identifiable. The continued importance of feud, as ideal and reality, is revealed for example by Thomas Artsruni's continuator. He records that there was no-one to avenge the murdered Gregory-Derenik because his sons were very young, that his widow forbade the opening of her palace windows until one of them should have undertaken to avenge him, and that God allowed (King) Gagik to slay Gagik Apumruan, whom the continuator implicates in the murder, in vengeance.[21] Feud might be resolved by marriage, by adoption and by compensation, as well as by retaliation. Bloodless resolution necessitated negotiation. Clerics, professionally interested in peace, and perceptible, being outsiders, as objective, were often mediators. Other intermediaries must have been mutual kinsmen, with obligations to, and influence over, both parties.

Such relatives included married women and such women must often have participated in negotiations involving bloodfeud. This was one aspect of their political role. That highly placed women could wield power is clear from the Siwnian charters. These charters attest ownership, purchase, bequest and donation of properties by some such women, though women are never portrayed in ecclesiastical sculpture as donors, as men often are. Women's lands probably came from their husbands rather than from their fathers, unless their fathers lacked male heirs. That married aristocratic women (for example the wives of King Smbat and of Smbat and Ashot of Siwnik^c, this Ashot's mother, and King Smbat's daughter-in-law) had a value and role beyond the purely sentimental and personal may perhaps be implied by the practice of the Arabs of taking them hostage. Female intercession was probably usually too private to reach the historical record, but it may explain why it was Gagik Artsruni rather than his elder brother Ashot who killed Gagik Apumruan. For Ashot's wife was the victim's daughter. Such intercession is however sometimes directly attested. When Ashot captured his treacherous kinsman Hasan, it was not Hasan's brother but his mother, Ashot's aunt, who negotiated, refusing to surrender Sewan. She was rightly distrustful of Ashot, who guaranteed Hasan's safety with an oath, but blinded him after receiving the fort.

[20] Thomas Artsruni (Continuator), IV, 7, trans. Thomson, 1985, pp. 357–8.
[21] Thomas (Continuator), between III, 29 and IV, 1, IV, 2, trans. Thomson, 1985, pp. 328, 330, 334–5.

The great Armenian potentates were all related. Kinship ties were constantly regenerated by marriages, and quite convoluted ones could be formed. For the eighth- and ninth-century Armenian church was more generous than was the Byzantine in its rules,[22] restricting marriages to relatives only up to, and including, the fourth degree of kinship (first cousins were thus forbidden to marry). But there seem to have been some slight differences between the great families in their structures of loyalties. The behaviour of the Bagratunis towards each other suggests that within their family emphasis was on direct descent rather than shared blood. Sons appear more reliable than brothers, uncles, nephews and cousins. The bond between son-in-law and father-in-law could resemble that between son and father. John Katholikos commented that Ashot II had been adopted by his father-in-law through his marriage.[23] Ashot's brother Abas supported his own father-in-law against Ashot in 918. And there is a case of an illegitimate Bagratuni being as important as legitimate ones. Gregory of Tarōn, when courted by Byzantium, sent his bastard son Ashot to Constantinople, probably between 898 and 900, where Ashot received a title. After Gregory's death, Ashot acted with his half-brother against their cousin Tᶜoṙnik. Tᶜoṙnik bequeathed his land to the Emperor, to avoid his cousins obtaining it. (They arranged an exchange.)[24] There are no comparable references to bastards of other families, but the evidence is, admittedly, very limited.

Siwnian behaviour by contrast suggests a greater emphasis on consanguinity. The *azat* witnesses in the charters may imply the common ownership of land by the agnatic kin.[25] There were certainly multiple interests in lands. Vayotsᶜ-dzor and other lands passed from Vasak Ishkhanik to his brother Ashot and then to Vasak's son as co-heir with Ashot's four sons. There may have been some joint patronage of churches. The church of Eḷegis was apparently built, in 929, at the order of Smbat, his wife and his brother.[26] But there was also some partition of territory. Nasr had exploited the resentment of Prince Babgēn following a partition.

It is less easy to categorize the Artsrunis. Over three generations fathers, sons, and brothers maintained amicable relations, fathers-in-law and sons-in-law less so. Gregory-Derenik's lands were divided into three, his eldest son, Ashot, taking the principate and the greatest share, and redivided after Ashot's death, when Gagik, the second son, took the principate.

---

[22] Dauvillier and De Clercq, 1936, pp. 136–9, 144–5 for Byzantine and Armenian rulings respectively.

[23] John, LX, 4, trans. Maksoudian, 1987, p. 208.

[24] *De Administrando Imperio*, ch. 43 1. 49–54, 163–88 and v. II *Commentary* ed. Jenkins, 1962.

[25] Périkhanian, 1968.

[26] Stephen Orbelean, *History of the House of Sisakan*, L, trans. Brosset, 1864, I p. 151.

The society beneath the greatest potentates retained its earlier structures. There were the *nakharar*s, whose lack of accord with him forced
King Smbat to give his son and nephew as hostages and his niece as bride
to Afshin (*c*.897). There were *dzeṙnasun* ('brought up by hand', or
protégé) men,[27] perhaps a retinue. Gregory-Derenik was mourned by
his, a youthful bodyguard distinct from the army of *azat*s.[28] It was the
protégés of Vasak Gnt^cuni who held the fort of Shamshuldē while Vasak,
in about 920, negotiated with Gurgēn of Iberia, refusing to admit either
Gurgēn or King Ashot II until Vasak returned, and surrendering to Ashot
only after a siege. There were the humblest soldiery, the *ṙamik*, distinct, to
judge by references to non-*ṙamik*s, from the rest of the common people.
*Ṙamik*s and non-*ṙamik*s attended the funeral of Ashot I. When King
Gagik gathered money in 922, it was from his relatives, *azat*s, *ṙamik*s
and non-*ṙamik*s.[29]

Urbanization

The early tenth-century Armenian elite retained its traditionally non-
urban character. Thomas Artsruni was suspicious of city life, describing
populous Duin in 893 as 'teeming with commerce and all kinds of impur-
ity'.[30] Seldom did potentates have urban bases. Biwrakan, near Erevan,
where John Katholikos built his church of St John, was a village. The later
capitals of Ani and Kars were in his time still primarily fortresses. John
called them forts, and they functioned as such. King Smbat used them to
store treasure. Kars sheltered Smbat's wife from Afshin. Even Erazgawork^c
(also called Shirakawan), which Smbat made his capital, appears in John's
text as a fortified village.[31] There were nevertheless some urban aristocratic connections. John called Bagaran a 'town'.[32] Van, Adamakert and
King Gagik's fortified complex of streets, residences, gardens and palace,
complete with storehouses and harbour on Alt^camar, were termed cities by
the Artsruni historians.[33] But the concept of a good king, at least as held by
Thomas Artsruni's continuator, paid no attention to cities, emphasizing

---

[27] Used in Agathangelos, *History of the Armenians*, 131, of clients (of the Arsacids) and
in Elishē, *History of Vardan and the Armenian War*, VII, of servants; trans. Thomson,
1976, p. 143 and 1982b, p. 244 where he translates as 'domestic' and his n. 10.
[28] Thomas Artsruni, (Continuator), trans. Thomson, 1985, pp. 328–29.
[29] John Katholikos, XXX, 8, LXIV, 20–1, trans. Maksoudian, 1987, p. 130 (funeral), and
p. 219 (Gagik).
[30] Thomas, III, 22, trans. Thomson, 1985, p. 293.
[31] Garsoïan, 1987, pp. 77–8 and n. 69 for these capitals and terminology.
[32] John, XXX, 6, trans. Maksoudian, 1987, p. 130 and his 'Glossary of Feudal Terminology' p. 309.
[33] Thomas Artsruni, III, 22, IV, 10, IV, 8, trans. Thomson, 1985, pp. 296, 365, 359.

instead the fortification of hill summits and fortresses to serve as refuges.[34] The family base of eleventh-century Ani's great general, Vahram Pahla-wuni was the old fort of Amberd, fortified in the eleventh century by Vahram himself. There was a three-storeyed castle, a bathhouse and two secret passages leading to the river, besides an aqueduct. Vahram also built a church there, in 1026. Anti-urban attitudes were tenacious, echoed in comments, written between 1072 and 1087, by the historian Aristakēs of Lastivert regarding the Turkish sackings of Artsn and Ani in 1048 and 1064: Artsn had ceased to be a centre of piety, the *ishkhan*s had become slaves to money, there was injustice in Ani, usury, and disregard for and exploitation of the poor.[35]

Nevertheless, the tenth century was a period both of urban expansion and of an increased association between royalty and towns. Duin, despite the 893 earthquake, after which its Arab character was accentuated, increased in commercial importance. Woollens, silks, other textiles and goldwork were manufactured. New towns arose: unfortified Artsn (with a mixed population) near Karin (Theodosiopolis), Loṙi, built by David of Tashir (989/91–1048), Kars and Ani. In the late tenth century Ani's enclosed area was trebled, with new walls. Ani was about 400 acres with a population of perhaps 50,000–100,000. There had also been urban growth in the formerly Armenian Sophene by 956. Three cities which had not existed in *c*.600 are mentioned in an account of an Arab raid in 956.[36]

Towns depended on trade, traffic increased as routes further south were disrupted by wars, and the major beneficiaries were Armenian kings. Royal interest is suggested by Smbat I's defence, to Afshin, of his Byzantine treaty, referring to obtaining items desirable to Afshin and the Caliph and to clearing the way for Muslim merchants.[37] The later king-doms are related to commercial intersection points. On Artsruni Lake Van and its towns centred three major routes. By the late tenth century Bagratuni Ani eclipsed Duin as a commercial centre. Kars (like Artsn) profited from land and sea traffic. Artanuj in Klaṙjk[c], seat of the Iberian Bagratunis, connected Armenia, Iberia and Abasgia with Byzantine Tre-bizond. Armenia imported luxury products and arms, and exported natural resources, such as wood, arsenic and agricultural produce, and textiles, such as carpets and silks. Artashat (classical Artaxata) was a centre of the dye industry, producing a valuable red. Some exports how-ever signified tax, not trade. In *c*.907–8, Smbat, pressed for tribute, ordered the collection of one-fifth of all herds of horses and cattle and

[34] Ibid., IV, 6, trans. Thomson, 1985, p. 353.
[35] Aristakēs of Lastivert, *History of the Armenians*, XII, XXIV, trans. Canard and Berbérian, 1973, pp. 63–4, 120–4.
[36] Howard-Johnston, 1983, pp. 253–61 esp. p. 258.
[37] John Katholikos, XXXI, 3–6, trans. Maksoudian, 1987, p. 138.

of flocks of sheep. In 922 King Gagik paid silver, gold, moveables, horses, mules and gifts. An Arab tribute list of 955 envisages some payment in kind.[38]

The Church

Whilst wealth supported kings, the Church offered them authority and eternal peace. John V and the Artsruni historians perceived their society as a new Israel. Admittedly, the Artsruni *History* seldom asserts this explicitly, but it does say that Gagik reigned 'like Josiah over a new Israel'.[39] All three authors cite numerous Old Testament parallels, and Biblical prophecies as being fulfilled in Armenia. To them, God's will and anger were constantly at work. The sources suggest that kings were normally consecrated, and it may be that their authority was thought to depend on their consecration. Gagik Artsruni's biographer, the continuator of Thomas Artsruni, was concerned because Gagik, having been crowned by a Muslim, had not been consecrated by the Church. He thought it necessary to say that Gagik's anointing 'was invisibly performed by the Holy Spirit'.[40] Church councils were held in royal residences, at Kapan in 958, at Shirakawan in 967/8 and at Ani in 969 and 1038. Katholikoi moved as power shifted. John V, who had returned the katholikosate to Duin, moved it to Vaspurakan in 923–4. It was transferred to Argina sometime between 948 and 967 and to nearby Ani in 992. The katholikos was usually a royal nominee, and could be vulnerable. For oath-breaking, John V excommunicated Ashot Artsruni, but merely reproved his king. John's three successors were from the family of the Ṙshtuni, Artsruni subordinates. Ełishē I (936–43) was deposed by King Derenik-Ashot (937–53).

Prelates played an overtly political role, often as intermediaries. Ashot II, wishing to dissuade his father-in-law from war, sent a bishop to remind him of his earlier oath of peace. Katholikos Peter (1019–58) surrendered Ani to Byzantium in 1045. Katholikoi sanctioned oaths despite the fact that oath-swearing was forbidden in the Bible. John V was involved in procuring oaths several times, for example Ashot Artsruni's oath not to harm his captive cousin Hasan. Oaths could be supported by the most powerful of ecclesiastical weapons, for excommunication might follow oath-breaking and the sign of the Cross and relics might be used in oath-swearing. Oaths seem normally to have been written, not merely spoken, and there are references to their being sealed. Ashot II and his

---

[38] The list is translated and the tributaries identified in Minorsky, 1953.
[39] Thomas Artsruni, III, 14, and IV, 11 for Gagik, trans. Thomson, 1985, p. 265 and his n. 3, and p. 366.
[40] Thomas Artsruni, (Continuator), IV, 3, trans. Thomson, 1985, p. 348.

father-in-law sealed an agreement with the cross and with the intercession of the cross, a phrase which could mean swearing over a cross or relic of the True Cross. When they nevertheless came to war Ashot attached his opponent's deed 'to the mantle of the Cross' carried before him.[41]

By the tenth century the cult of relics was established, though it was restrained by comparison with Byzantium and especially western Europe. Its modesty was perhaps partly due to the decline in ecclesiastical productivity and in monasticism under Arab domination. For the cult of relics in Christendom depended in part on active promotion, through the dissemination of miracle tales, by their associates. There is little to suggest that relics of contemporary Armenian martyrs were treasured. John Katholikos does record that the soil on which King Smbat's blood had dripped had healing qualities,[42] but Thomas Artsruni's references to relics are restricted to early ones. Though it is possible that our sources' coverage was meant to educate, rather than to record current practice, it seems that the earlier the relic the better. John acquired a twig from a tree planted by the Illuminator, and refers to the bones of the saints buried at T^cordan as treasures. Siwnian Tat^cew had relics of Peter and Paul, other apostles, pontiffs and martyrs. The very best were relics of the True Cross. The church of the Mother of God at Aparank^c was built for one given by Basil II, installed in 983. Abḷḷarib Pahlawuni's church of the Redeemer in Ani of 1036 was for another, also from Constantinople.

The intimate association between kings and clerics extended also, as earlier, to war. Katholikos Ełishē and groups of priests are recorded as contributing to victory for King Gagik Artsruni in 937 through prayer, Ełishē lowering his hands only after victory was achieved, through the intercession of Gregory the Illuminator.[43] In 1040 David of Loṙi took bishops, priests and monks, each armed only with a cross and Gospels, into battle against the emir of Duin.

In return for such support the church acquired wealth. The evidence is abundant. To monasteries Gagik Artsruni gave not only estates but also treasures, horses, mules, cattle and sheep.[44] In Siwnik^c princely grants were many and lavish. Gregory-Sup^can for example made Makenots^c a grant which included five vineyards at Erevan, livestock, fish at Boḷashēn and what seems to be river revenues.[45] Tat^cew received substantial donations, including villages, in both the tenth and the eleventh centuries. Inscriptions on the walls of churches in Ani record gifts of shops and land, of treasures of gold, silver and jewels, made between 994 and 1041.

[41] John Katholikos, LX, 6, 29, trans. Maksoudian, 1987, pp. 209, 211.
[42] John, XLIX, 16, trans. Maksoudian, 1987, p. 177.
[43] Thomas Artsruni, (Continuator), IV, 9, trans. Thomson, 1985, pp. 363–4.
[44] Ibid., 3, trans. Thomson, 1985, p. 350.
[45] Stephen Orbelean, XXXVII, trans. Brosset, 1864, I pp. 110–11. In the reading used by Brosset the word river, *get*, appears as part of the first proper name, and hence is not translated. The word is separate in Emin's 1861 edition (p. 131).

The katholikos Peter had 500 prosperous villages in his charge. After Peter's death the Byzantine Emperor removed his treasure to Constantinople, and tried, unsuccessfully, to persuade Peter's successor to pay tax before allowing him to leave Constantinople to reside in present-day Darende, west of Melitene. Some scholars believe that peasants were more harshly exploited by the church than by the laity, and certainly Tat^cew suffered rebellions. The inhabitants of the fort of Ts^cur which, with its territories, had been granted to Tat^cew, attacked Tat^cew in 915. Some monks were killed, the monastery pillaged, the bishop and others fled. Prince Smbat expelled and punished the rebels, destroyed the fort, confirmed Tat^cew's possession and restored the bishop. Another revolt began in 930. This one centred on the village of Aweladasht and was put down by the bishop. There was a third in the 990s, again at Ts^cur. This time the bishop was killed and the revolt put down by troops sent by King Vasak from Kapan.

Since great wealth could be had, there must have been competition for endowments. Such competition explains the *History of Tarōn*. This was purportedly written in the fourth century by Zenob of Glak, and purportedly continued in the seventh by Zenob's thirty-fifth successor as bishop of Tarōn, John Mamikonean. Beginning with Gregory the Illuminator and ending in the mid-seventh century, it focuses on events in and near the monastery of Glak, or Innaknean, whose first abbot Zenob is purported to have been. But Avdoyan[46] has shown that the *History* was actually composed between 966 and 988, its final three sections, and possibly some editing, being added before 1220, its purposes to deprive Ējmiatsin and Duin of their pre-eminence and to acquire patronage for Glak, in reality a relatively new foundation. There is no corroborative evidence for the monastery's existence before the end of the tenth century. To enhance Glak's cause the tenth-century writer makes Glak Gregory's first foundation, and its abbot Zenob the first bishop of Tarōn. The power of St Karapet (John the Baptist), whose relics Glak possessed, is a major theme, illustrated by miracle stories. A number of them involve supernatural help in war. Their inclusion was presumably to hint at potential returns on investment in order to attract aristocratic donation. There is also rather more explicit encouragement. Gregory is told by a correspondent to advise princes to be charitable. Some ascetics pray that anyone who has made liberal gifts from their sinful wealth be delivered from tribulation, and a voice from Heaven assents.[47]

Patronage involved art and architecture as well as estates. Splendid works combined debts to earlier and contemporary traditions, both native and foreign, with originality. King Gagik Artsruni's church on

---

[46] Avdoyan, 1993, pp. 25–48.

[47] Pseudo-John Mamikonean, *The History of Tarōn*, trans. Avdoyan, 1993, pp. 60, 117–18.

Plate 10   Sculpted decoration on the exterior of the south wall of the early tenth-century Church of the Holy Cross on the island of Aḷtᶜamar, Lake Van.

Aḷtᶜamar, designed by the architect Manuēl, was lavishly decorated, externally with five bands of sculpture and internally with frescoes, though one scholar has dated these frescoes to 1002–21.[48] Artisans are recorded as having come to Gagik's court from all countries[49] and a number of influences are identifiable: Byzantine iconographic types, possibly the mosaics, now lost, of the residence of Basil I, Palestinian art, Sasanian art and Abbasid court art, itself partly influenced by Turkish traditions. In plan, the church is a variation on the seventh-century St Ḥripᶜsimē, as is the church at Soradir which was perhaps the Holy Cross of Aḷbak where Artsruni princes were buried.[50] In its decoration Gagik's church has many elements of originality. The detail of an angel watching the Creation of Eve is unique to its frescoes.[51] The subjects of its sculpture – including prophets, apostles, saints, evangelizers, martyrs, bird, animal and plant life – and their purpose, to instruct as well as to embellish, are not original. But the amount of its sculpture and the scope and variety of its programme are unique. There have of course been differing interpretations of its meanings. The most recent[52] is that the south wall illustrates

[48] Grishin, 1985.
[49] Thomas Artsruni (Continuator), IV, 7, trans. Thomson, 1985, pp. 356–7.
[50] Thierry and Donabédian, 1989, pp. 170, 577.
[51] Mathews, 1982b, p. 251.
[52] Davies, 1991.

Plate 11   The apostle James and another apostle, from an interior wall painting on the north side of the main apse of the early tenth-century Church of the Holy Cross on the island of Aḷtᶜamar, Lake Van.

confrontation between good and evil, warns of doom and judgement, and offers an assurance of the eventual triumph of good; the east presents Paradise regained; the north resumes the theme of conflict; the west, featuring Gagik's presentation of the church to Christ, proclaims the power of the Life-giving Cross, the four crosses here meant as allusion to the four in the famous vision of St Gregory. The interior is a renewed Paradise. Its paintings trace the Creation of Adam and Eve, their sin, and the Redemption offered by Jesus, and encourage Christians to remain steadfast should they be persecuted.

The most important Siwnian church was at Tatᶜew. Dedicated, uniquely for the period, to Peter and Paul, some of whose relics the bishop had acquired, it was built between 895 and 906 by Bishop John, funded by him and by several princes. Its paintings, commissioned by

John's successor Jacob, were consecrated in 930. Those surviving include the Nativity and the Resurrection of the Dead for the Last Judgement. They are remarkable for their West European affinities, which confirm the record that Jacob procured Frankish painters, at enormous expense.[53] In Bagratuni Ani the most important monuments were by the architect Trdat. Smbat II (977–89/90) commissioned a cathedral. Halted by Smbat's death, it was finished in 1001. Trdat then built St Gregory for Gagik I (989/90–1020), finished, probably, about 1005. Its decoration included a large statue, now lost, of Gagik holding a model of the church. A major architectural development was the *gawit^c*, a type of porch in front of a church, originally a memorial building though subsequently used for meetings, study and prayer. It first appears in Siwnik^c in 911. The innovative *gawit^c* of the church of St John, built in 1038 at the monastery of Horomos by King John-Smbat of Ani (1020–41), seems the archetype for late twelfth- and thirteenth-century *gawit^c*s.[54]

Yet over a fifth of late ninth- and early tenth-century monuments recall seventh-century building. They include John V's church at Biwrakan, Smbat I's at Erazgawork^c, founded *c*.892, King Abas's Holy Apostles at Kars, built in the 930s (modelled on Mastara, though its drum is different), and Gagik I's St Gregory, modelled on Zuart^{c}nots^c. Such architectural conservatism was perhaps a natural consequence of the near cessation of ecclesiastical building in the eighth and much of the ninth centuries. Other possibilities are that schooling in tradition as well as technique was necessary for artistic confidence, and that conservatism was an assertion of ecclesiastical continuity and of the comparability of present and past patrons.

Illuminated manuscripts include the famous Ējmiatsin Gospel, with sixth-century ivory covers and four seventh-century miniatures at the end, produced at Noravank^c in Siwnik^c, in 989. The Gospel of King Gagik of Kars (1029–65), which survives in a mutilated form, had more than 227 miniatures, including portraits of Gagik himself. It was produced between 1045 and 1054, possibly to mark Gagik's assumption of the title King of Kings after the Byzantine annexation of Ani in 1045. The combination of foreign influence and independent interpretation is apparent, as also in the Mulṇi Gospel, dated between 1050 and 1075.

Secular patrons were not exclusively kings and queens. The father of Vahram Pahlawuni, who died in 982, built a church of St Gregory at Ani, Vahram himself a church at Amberd (in 1026), and a monastic

[53] Stephen Orbelean, XLIX, trans. Brosset, 1864, I p. 150; Thierry, N. and Thierry, M., 1968.

[54] Thierry, J.-M., 1980, ch. III, 'Le jamatoun Saint-Jean', (pp. 15–48) esp. 'Datation' (pp. 45–8).

Plate 12   *The mid-tenth-century Church of the Holy Apostles, Kars*

complex at Marmashēn, and his nephew Gregory Magistros founded or restored at least three churches. Gregory's kinsman Abllarib's church at Ani may have been designed by the great architect Trdat.

Glorious books and buildings marked the partnership of kings and church and they testified to piety. But they were also monuments to sin. The inscriptions at Ani record the traditional expectation of masses in recompense for generosity. Abllarib, in 1040, stipulated that the office be celebrated in his two new chapels, St Stephen's and St Christopher's, Friday for his mother and sister respectively and Saturday in St Stephen's for his father. An inscription of 1041 stipulated six offices yearly in four chapels, adding that anyone usurping the property should be answerable for the donor's sins.[55] The Armenian who commissioned the Gospel of Adrianople, copied in 1007, did so 'as a memorial' to his, his parents' and the nation's souls, and requested prayers for forgiveness for his own, his wife's, parents' and sons' sins.[56] Such arrangements had the additional advantage of perpetuating the memory of the deceased. Less permanently ostentatious was the lavish charity of Ashot III of Ani (952/3–77) to the poor and sick, to expiate his sins,[57] probably commensurate with his power, which, as we shall see, was great.

Donation was perhaps a more attractive option than penance. The suggestion of Smbat I's uncle Abas that if Mashtots^c became Katholikos (897) there should be no confession of sins[58] implies an elite dislike of penance, and there are few recorded cases. Private penance had developed by the tenth century, but how recently is unclear. By the eleventh the Armenians had become idiosyncratic in their practice. The Syrian Orthodox patriarch John X (1064–73), writing to Katholikos Gregory II (1066–1105), condemned the Armenian custom of the priest's reading out a long list of sins, to which the penitent was to confess as appropriate. He also, like another polemicist, complained about lengthy exclusions from communion.[59]

Anxiety about salvation is one of the factors which, historically, have contributed to monasticism. In Siwnik^c, Tat^cew, whose monks eventually numbered about a thousand, became a centre of scholarship, and other houses were restored or founded. The spate of Armenian foundations in the 930s and 940s was a continuation of the late ninth-century revival. They were not, as often suggested, the work of refugees fleeing eastwards from imperial persecution.[60] For there was no such persecution. Like the monastery founded by Katholikos Mashtots^c on the island of Sewan, the new houses followed the rule of St Basil of Caesarea. They included Narek, on Lake Van, founded in 935, and Hoṙomos, where Bagratuni kings were buried from 977 onwards. In the kingdom of Tashir, Sanahin and Haḷbat, whose churches, Haḷbat's probably by Trdat, were founded by the wife of Ashot III in 966 and 976, thrived. Sanahin's buildings were augmented in the mid-eleventh century by Queen Hṙanush. Like penance, however, Armenian monasticism was to attract criticism. John X criticized superiors buying positions and treating monks as slaves, monks

[55] Basmajian, J., 1922–3 and 1931, nos 16 and 18, and Uluhogian, 1992, p. 399 n. 27 for a different version of no. 16 (following *Corpus Inscriptionum Armenicarum* I 1966 (no. 97)) which is followed here.

[56] Janashian et al., 1967.

[57] Stephen Asoḷik, *Universal History*, III, viii, trans. Macler, 1917, p. 39.

[58] John Katholikos, XXX, 53, and XXX, 69, 70, for Mashtots ^c recommending it, trans. Maksoudian, 1987, pp. 135, 136.

[59] Nau, 1912; Mingana, 1931.

[60] Maksoudian, 1990–1.

taking the habit when they wished, without the saying of office or prayers over them, and the eating of meat.[61]

Literature and Scholarship

Literature and scholarship flourished at both elite and popular levels. There was some cultural interaction between Arabs and Armenians, as the reference by Thomas Artsruni's continuator to friendship between Gregory-Derenik and the emir of Her suggests.[62] Some tenth-century Arab authors record a few Armenian legends. Thomas Artsruni, who relates Muhammad's early life in more detail than did his predecessors, is the first Armenian historian to assert that Muhammad was a pupil of a heretic Christian monk, a legend also found in Islamic tradition.[63] Arab medicine was known, and influenced Armenian vocabulary, either directly or through Syrian intermediaries, like the Syrian physician at Gagik I of Ani's court.[64] The Arab literary device of rhymed prose was used by Gregory Magistros.

Several histories were written. Shapuh Bagratuni's, now lost, covered the eighth and ninth centuries and the accomplishments of his father King Ashot I. Katholikos John V wrote a *List of Katholikoi* and, in the early 920s, his *History*, from the Flood to 923–4, concentrating on the reigns of Smbat I and Ashot II, unfortunately for us giving no more than five precise dates.[65] John was asked to write this by (unidentified) kings. He hoped his audience, 'kings, princes, leaders and commanders' would learn from his account, and 'come to your senses'.[66] His experiences allowed him to form an overview of Armenian society and its political weaknesses. But he depended heavily in his early sections on earlier historians and, though his most recent commentator denies it,[67] he was partial. Artsruni and Siwnian history receive only slight attention. The dedication of the church of Tatᶜew, attended by King Smbat and Gagik Artsruni as well as himself, could have been exploited, as an example of Armenian unity, to inspire potentates to see unity as an ideal, but it is not even mentioned. His coverage reflects disunity without challenging it. John seems more concerned about family than about 'national' unity, about war between the two King Ashots than about the coexistence of an

---

[61] Nau, 1912.
[62] Thomas Artsruni, (Continuator), trans. Thomson, 1985, pp. 326–7.
[63] Thomson, 1979–80, 1985, p. 36, and 1986a.
[64] Greppin, 1986; Vardanyan, 1982; Scarborough, 1986–7 (p. 242).
[65] Maksoudian, 1987, pp. 25–52 for John's literary works, p. 51 and n. 23 for lack of dates.
[66] For the request to write, John's Preface, 2, 3, 4, and 'A Separate Discourse Commemorating His (Yovhannēs's) Name', 4, trans. Maksoudian, 1987, pp. 63, 234; for his hopes, 'A Separate Discourse...', 1, trans. Maksoudian, pp. 233–4.
[67] Maksoudian, 1987, pp. 48–9.

Artsruni with a Bagratuni kingdom. Political disunity is not coherently presented as a cause of ill fortune but rather as an aspect of it.

Thomas Artsruni's *History of the House of the Artsrunis*[68] moves rapidly from the Creation to the mid-ninth century AD, and thereafter slowly, with detail, to the accord and achievements of Gagik and Gurgēn Artsruni after the death of their brother Ashot. Thomas's continuator, writing at Gagik's request, began not there but with Gagik's father, Gregory-Derenik, thereby duplicating some of the coverage. There are slight differences between the two writers' accounts, but their outlook is much the same and the continuator refers to Thomas's work as if it were his own. Thomas used a variety of earlier sources, both Armenian and non-Armenian, but was most indebted to Moses of Khoren and Elishē. He is the first Armenian historian to include apocryphal stories about Old Testament figures.

There are three late tenth-century three-part histories. Moses Daskhurantsʿi's *History of the Albanians*[69] was composed, probably, in the 980s, perhaps by the Moses cited last in its list of Albanian patriarchs. Western Albania had become a kingdom in about 880, its capital Pʿaṙisos, and one of the *History*'s interests is in justifying Albanian independence from the Armenian church, perhaps inspired by the interference of Katholikos Anania in the 950s. He had cited historical precedent.[70] Ukhtanēs, Armenian bishop of Sebasteia (*c.*970–985),[71] wrote for his former teacher, abbot Anania of Narek. Ukhtanēs covered, first, the period from Adam to Tiridates IV. His third, lost, section treated the conversion of the Tsad (Chalcedonians), either their conversion to Christianity or their recent abandonment of Chalcedonianism. His second section recounted the early seventh-century separation of the Georgian from the Armenian Church. Ukhtanēs' interest was perhaps a defensive reaction stimulated by late tenth-century Byzantine expansion and also by Georgian pre-eminence and pressure on Armenia, both of which were to encourage the growth of Chalcedonianism among Armenians. Stephen Asoḷik of Tarōn's *Universal History*[72] began with the Old Testament and concluded in 1004 AD. The third, most useful, part begins with Ashot I's kingship. Stephen is lucid and, unusually, gives precise, often accurate, dates, using the Armenian era.

Another late tenth-century writer was Gregory of Narek (*c.*950–1010). Priest, teacher, kinsman of Abbot Anania (likewise a scholar, and who wrote against the Tʿondrakian heretics), and son of bishop Khosrov of Andzewatsʿikʿ (who wrote a commentary on the liturgy, probably for use in monastic schools), Gregory was familiar with some Greek theological

---

[68] Thomson, 1985.
[69] Dowsett, 1961b.
[70] Akopjan, 1987, reviewed by P. Donabédian, 1988–9 (pp. 492–3 for Moses).
[71] Arzoumanian, 1985; Kolandjian, 1986.
[72] Macler, 1917.

writings. He wrote religious treatises, including one against the Paulicians, and poetry. His most famous work, the *Book of Lamentations*,
completed in 1002, is a collection of prayers together comprising a poem
about the wretchedness of the soul, confessing mankind's sins but trusting
in salvation.

In the eleventh century the philhellene Armenian known as Gregory
Magistros was celebrated in Constantinople. A religious debate there
with a Muslim prompted Gregory to compose a version of the Bible in
Armenian verse. Like cultivated Byzantines, Gregory could write letters
whose style and imagery makes them almost incomprehensible. He also
translated two dialogues of Plato and the *Elements* of Euclid into Armenian. Gagik II of Ani was another learned layman. He defended Armenian
religious doctrine in Constantinople in 1065.

At popular level there was oral tradition, some of which passed into
written form. An anonymous collection of tales, once suggested to be the
(lost) history of Shapuh, contains ninth- or tenth-century material concerning the Roman emperors Maurice and Heraclius, and post-twelfth-
century material about (earlier) Artsruni personages.[73] The fraudulent
History of Tarōn contains elements from oral tradition, like the cutting
off of enemy noses, 24,000 on one occasion. A complaint in it that an
impious prince gave some monastic estates to a *gusan* reflects both the
continuing importance of minstrels, and, of course, ecclesiastical disapproval of them.[74]

Yet despite this, by now traditional, disapproval, the church may
have contributed to the Armenian national epic, *David of Sasun*.[75]
This is a collection, first written down in 1873, of tales which go
back to the tenth century. It recounts the history of David's family over
four generations, Sasun, its setting, symbolizing Armenia. The epic has
much in common with other, non-Armenian, oral and epic traditions,
but it also reflects Armenian history, especially in its third and most
important part, concerning David himself. In a general sense David
incarnates the heroes who fought foreign tyranny, and more particularly
there are reminiscences of seventh- and eighth-century Armenian experiences, of Bagarat of Tarōn's resistance, of Bugha's invasion, and, in
some characters' names, of real persons, Theodore Řshtuni and King
Gagik Artsruni.

David of Sasun was a popular epic. In some respects it embodies what
were probably popular attitudes. Thus war is blamed on foreign kings,
their armies are felt to prefer peace, and resistance is the task of Armenian
leaders rather than of their people, for they fight alone. And the cycle has

[73] Thomson, 1988–9.
[74] Avdoyan, 1993, Introduction, p. 39, translation, pp. 137, 110.
[75] Shalian, 1964, Kudian, 1970, for English translations; Feydit, 1964, for French; Der
Melkonian-Minassian, 1972, for detailed study.

been seen as testimony to a pre-Christian religion surviving at popular level, either paganism or Zoroastrianism.

But it has also been argued[76] that *David of Sasun* contains much Judaeo-Christian imagery, belongs in a Judaeo-Christian ideological framework, and was actually crafted to recount and promote the triumph of Christianity over Zoroastrianism. Thus for example the virgin mother of the first (twin) heroes is reminiscent of the Virgin, one story recalls a theme in the baptismal rite, David embodies elements of the biblical Moses and David. The Mithraic elements, in this argument, are used actually to demonstrate the superiority of Christianity. Thus for example Great Mher, by keeping a pact to sleep with another man's wife, embodies Mihr's character as guardian of oaths, but in Christian terms commits sin. The resulting son proves the arch-foe of Sasun. The epic had, it is suggested, ecclesiastical, or, since they ruled Tarōn and claimed Davidic ancestry, Bagratuni patronage.

Ecclesiastical Problems

The Church had two major problems. One was Tᶜondrakianism which had grown considerably since its ninth-century beginnings, in Tᶜondrak in Apahunikᶜ. Tᶜondrakianism, reinforced by Paulicians after the fall of Tephrike, combined an Adoptionist theology (a view that Christ in His humanity was the Son of God only by adoption, whereas Christ in His divinity was the Son of God by nature), with hostility to ecclesiastical hierarchy, sacraments and the cult of the Cross. It had spread by 1000 to Mananaḷi (formerly Paulician) and to Vaspurakan. Early eleventh-century Tᶜondrakians[77] included noble ladies and a prince, Vrvēṙ in Mananaḷi. The bishop of Harkᶜ was also accused, perhaps erroneously, of Tᶜondrakianism. Amongst other things this bishop taught that prayers for the dead, masses and animal sacrifice were of no help to sinners who died without doing penance. Twice a synod tried to curb him, but the *ishkan*s of the *gawaṙ*, thinking him pious, protected him. He subsequently became a fugitive after a disillusioned disciple informed against him to the Katholikos. Prince Vrvēṙ too was difficult to combat. He engineered the imprisonment of bishops who took action against him, temporarily avoiding condemnation by the judge sent by the Byzantine emperor, and was treated lightly, because his brother was an *ishkhan* known to the emperor, even when exposed. In Tarōn and Vaspurakan, both under Byzantine rule in the mid-eleventh century, the governor, Gregory Magistros, endeavoured, between 1051 and 1054, to expunge

---

[76] Alishan, 1985–6.
[77] Aristakēs of Lastivert, XXII, XXIII, trans. Canard and Berbérian, 1973, pp. 108–20.

T^condrakianism, but it was to survive in Tarōn into the nineteenth century.

The second major problem was tension arising from the growth of Chalcedonianism in Armenia. The 862 Council had recommended toleration and there are a number of indications that Chalcedonianism had many adherents. In a letter to Ashot, the Byzantine patriarch Photius claimed that the 'Taronites' of Fourth Armenia were 'orthodox'.[78] Chalcedonian sympathies seem to have been particularly strong in Siwnik^c and Vaspurakan. One *alumnus* of Siwnian Makenots^c, Katholikos Mashtots^c, had been excommunicated by his predecessor, Katholikos George for removing 'the difference' between anti-Chalcedonians and Chalcedonians.[79] He contemplated going to Constantinople for his consecration[80] and to discuss religious questions. His kinsman and disciple John V was likewise tolerant. John's refusal to visit Constantinople himself was due only to fear of criticism, and he did make a long visit to the Chalcedonian Atrnerseh of Iberia.[81] The two chief bishops of Siwnik^c and Albania resisted the efforts of the katholikos Anania (946–68) to make them give up Chalcedonianism for ten years, until 958–9 when they died. Anania had the support of King Abas, who forbade marriage with dyophysites, on pain of death, and he himself required that former Chalcedonians be rebaptised.[82] Katholikos Vahan I (968–9), who was actually deposed on suspicion of Chalcedonianism, was the son of a Siwnian prince and had trained and worked in Siwnik^c. And the rebellions against Tat^cew may, as they have sometimes been interpreted, have been protests against 'heresy'. As for Vaspurakan, King Gagik had initiated discussion with Byzantium about church union (after 930); Anania of Narek had Chalcedonian leanings; and Khosrov, bishop of Andzewats^cik^c was excommunicated by Katholikos Anania in 955 for challenging his authority over other bishops. Khosrov himself was respectful towards Rome and saw the Armenian church as part of the universal church.[83] Anania's moving his seat from Alt^camar could have been related to doctrinal disagreement, for the deposed Vahan found sanctuary in Vaspurakan and Vahan's replacement, coming to admonish king and exile, was imprisoned.

As T^condrakianism had been, though indirectly, Chalcedonianism was strengthened by Byzantine expansion. There was some persecution of

---

[78] Photius, Letter 284, lines 3194–7, in ed. Laourdas and Westerink, 1985, also Darrouzès, 1971, pp. 146 (French translation) 147 (Greek text). Darrouzès dates this letter, and Photius' letter to the Katholikos, to around 862. The authenticity and chronology of Photius' Armenian correspondence are problematic. For a résumé of views, and discussion, Mahé, 1993, pp. 492–6, Canard's 1980 revision of Laurent, 1919, pp. 344–56.

[79] John Katholikos, XXX, 38, trans. Maksoudian, 1987, p. 133.

[80] Mahé, 1993, p. 497.

[81] John, LV, 7, for fear, trans. Maksoudian, 1987, p. 198, and his pp. 18–20 for discussion of John's attitude.

[82] Mahé, 1993, pp. 507–9, 510.

[83] Cowe, 1991, pp. 10–13; Mahé, 1993, pp. 509–10.

anti-Chalcedonians, beginning in the late tenth century. In 986 priests were arrested and Bishops Sion and John of Sebasteia and Larissa pressed into 'conversion' in Sebasteia and the Armenian katholikos Khach^{c}ik admonished by its metropolitan. In 1063 or 1064 the emperor Constantine X, whose position was complicated by the 1054 Papal-Byzantine schism, ordered the persecution of Syrian and Armenian 'heretics'. More importantly, Byzantium had created Chalcedonian bishoprics in her annexations. It is to these we should now turn.

Byzantines, Bagratunis and Turks: Revival, Decline and Annexation, c.925–1071

After restoring Ashot II Byzantium had continued her Arab offensive. She attacked Duin, though unsuccessfully, in 927/8; Khlat^c, Berkri and other towns, which had recovered independence after Smbat's death, in 931; took Melitene (which she subsequently repopulated with Syrian Orthodox) in 934; took eastern Andzit in 937; and took Arsamosata, which was to become by 951/2 capital of a small province, in 937–9. Byzantium's aim was command of the southern east–west route through Armenia, and of the Ergani Pass. Perhaps as a riposte, an (Arab) emir, unidentified in our (Artsruni) source,[84] invaded Armenia as far as Duin in 937, and there was a raid by a subordinate of the governor of Iraq. They were defeated, respectively by King Gagik Artsruni, and by Atom Andzewats^{c}i in 937/8.

Thereafter Byzantium, the Armenian Bagratunis and their Iberian kinsmen all consolidated their positions. Byzantium reconquered Theodosiopolis in 949 and acquired command of the Ergani Pass sometime between 956 and the early 970s. The Armenian Bagratuni king Abas (928–52/3) defeated an invasion from Abasgia, blinding its leader who had sent a message ordering that his (Abas's) cathedral at Kars be consecrated according to the Chalcedonian rite. The Iberian Ashot II, son of King Atrnerseh, expanded his territory, acquiring upper (south-west) Tayk^c after the death of Gurgēn II of Tayk^c (918–41) and Armenian Basean in about 952. Basean was bestowed on Ashot by Byzantium, but, according to Constantine VII, Iberian rights here and near Theodosiopolis were contended.[85]

It was under Ashot III (952/3–77) that the glory of the Armenian Bagratunis revived. Byzantium was preoccupied with the Hamdanids, who controlled the territory between Mosul and Aleppo, their capital, and with the emir of Manazkert, who by 952 had reasserted independ-

---

[84] Thomas Artsruni, (Continuator), IV, 9, trans. Thomson, 1985, p. 362.
[85] *De Administrando Imperio*, ch. 45 l. 99–175 and v. II *Commentary*, ed. Jenkins, 1962.

ence and taken the strategically important Khlat^c, Archēsh and Artskē. Vaspurakan was declining. Derenik-Ashot (937–53) had been briefly captured by the emir of Her; Ashot-Sahak (972–83) was to lose the northern banks of Lake Van to the emir of Diyarbakır in about 980, and to suffer attack from the emir of Golt^cn. Arab Azerbaijan was suffering internal disputes. The omission of Ashot III from a list of tributaries of the ruler of Azerbaijan, composed in 955 and recorded by the Arab writer Ibn Hauqal,[86] suggests that his kingdom had now broken free of Azerbaijani dominion, for Ashot's predecessors, Ashot II and Abas are listed; they had owed (together) 2,000,000 dirhams with 200,000 remitted. Ashot III may also have taken Duin from the Sallarids (who ruled there 941–87), and held it between 957 and 966. He transferred his capital from Kars to Ani, whither the katholikos followed.

The figures in the 955 list suggest that the Bagratunis were now the richest of the Armenian rulers. Derenik-Ashot and his brother Abusahl Hamazasp (953–72) of Vaspurakan together owed a tribute of 100,000 dirhams. Vasak of Vayots^c- dzor in Siwnik^c owed 50,000 dinars (750,000 dirhams) plus offerings. Three other potentates, two from Albania, owed, respectively, 300,000 dirhams plus some offerings, 200,000 dirhams, and 100,000 dirhams plus offerings and horses to the value of 50,000 dirhams.

Ashot III was not daunted even by the resumption of Byzantine expansion. In 966 the emperor Nicephorus II Phocas (963–9) acquired the estates of the two grandsons of Smbat I's contemporary, Gregory of Tarōn, in exchange for others, probably in Chaldia. In 968 Bardas Phocas, *dux* of Chaldia and Coloneia, working, probably, from Tarōn, took Manazkert. In 974 or 975 the emperor John I Tzimisces (969–76), himself Armenian, came to Muş. Ashot earlier assembled all the Armenian princes and, apparently, an army of 80,000 in response to Byzantium's victories just south of Armenia. He provided 10,000 men and provisions for John's campaign against the Arabs, and was rewarded with 30,000 dahekans, 2,000 slaves, 10,000 horses and 1,000 mules.[87]

But the domination of Bagratuni Ani was soon challenged. In 961/2 Ashot had granted, under pressure, Kars, Vanand and a royal title to his brother Mushel. In about 972 he had given Shamshuldē and Tashir-Dzoraget in Gugark^c to his son Gurgēn/Kwirike. This became a kingdom

---

[86] Minorsky, 1953.
[87] Matthew of Edessa, *History*, paragraphs 17–21, trans. Dostourian, 1993, pp. 27–33. The source for Ashot's reward is a corrupt and incomplete passage in Matthew's rendering of a letter from John to Ashot, corrected and reconstructed by N. Adontz in his 'Notes arméno-byzantines' (first published in *Byzantion* 1934 and 1935) reprinted in Adontz, 1965, pp. 137–95. The letter is discussed pp. 141–46. Adontz's correction is accepted in Yuzbashian 1973–4 pp. 144–5 and n. 26. Dostourian's translation (p. 33) of the passage (Matthew, para. 21) follows Adontz only in part, though the rejection of Adontz's additions is not explained in the notes (p. 291).

in 982. And, sometime between 961 and 997 Smbat II of Vayotsᶜ-dzor proclaimed himself king.

Between 975 and 1000 the leading potentate in the region was an Iberian Bagratuni, David of Taykᶜ. David brought Smbat II of Ani and his uncle Mushel of Kars to terms, Smbat having taken up arms against Mushel in the late 970s. David and the king of Iberia rallied Smbat, King Abas of Kars and troops of the princes of Vaspurakan, Siwnikᶜ and Albania in about 988 in the two Iberians' defence against King Bagarat of Abasgia. Bagarat was grandson of the Iberian king and David's adoptive son and heir and his current hostility to them had perhaps been provoked by David's rapprochement with the encroaching Byzantium. David had helped Byzantium against the rebellion (976–9) of Bardas Sclerus, which had been based in Kharput and supported by Gregory and Bagarat of Tarōn and by the prince of Mokkᶜ. The emperor Basil II (976–1025) had re-established good relations with the prince of Mokkᶜ, giving a relic of the True Cross to the monastery of the prince's deceased uncle, at Aparankᶜ, in 983. To David Basil had granted territory, including Theodosiopolis and Basean and, seemingly for David's lifetime only, Arab Harkᶜ and Apahunikᶜ which David subsequently conquered, in the 990s.

After David the most prominent leader was Gagik I of Ani (989/90– 1020). Like Abas of Kars, Bagarat of Iberia, and Bagarat's successor Gurgēn, Gagik joined in defending David's conquests. For himself Gagik established control of Duin and, through his marriage to the heir of its king Vasak VI who died in 1019, of much of western Siwnikᶜ, subdued Goltᶜn, and also acquired the submission of David of Tashir-Dzoraget (989–1048).

But Basil II had designs on Armenia and the way to complete Byzantine annexation was opened when David of Taykᶜ changed his will, in about 990. Its exact terms are unknown, but it favoured Byzantium, due probably to Basil putting pressure on David after David helped Bardas Phocas in his rebellion of 987–9, and to David being disillusioned with his adoptive son Bagarat after the war between them. In 1000/1 Basil came to claim his legacy. At that time King Gagik stayed aloof but others met and were submissive towards the emperor. Since problems elsewhere prevented Basil removing Bagarat from territory which each considered his own the two rivals parted apparent friends. Next Basil looked to Vaspurakan. In 1018, when he refortified Theodosiopolis, the support he had earlier promised to the Artsruni king Gurgēn-Khachᶜik (983– 1003) seemed needed. For Vaspurakan was attacked that year, probably by some group from Azerbaijan, rather than the Turks, as the Armenian sources have it, and again in 1020.[88] In about 1019 and 1021 Prince David Artsruni and his father King Senekᶜerim-John (1003–21)

---

[88] Identification of the attackers as the Turks is incompatible with the other evidence for early eleventh-century Turkish history. Turkish pressure seems to have begun in 1029. Cahen, 1968, pp. 67–8.

exchanged their domains for lands and office in Cappadocia, removing to Sebasteia with 14,000 men, and their women and children.[89]

In 1021–2 Basil went to war for his inheritance from David of Tayk^c. His adversary now was George I, king (1014–27) of a powerful and recently united Georgia. For Bagarat, who had ruled north-eastern Tayk^c and other lands, had inherited first Abasgia, in 978 through his mother, and then Iberia, in 1008 through his natural father, and he had seized Klarjk^c in 1011. George refused to relinquish to Basil the lands which Basil had conceded to Bagarat. The outcome of their clash was that Byzantium acquired southern Tayk^c and Basean and established the theme of Iberia, with its capital at Theodosiopolis, thereby blocking Georgian expansion into Armenia.

Byzantium next claimed the kingdom of Ani, currently divided between Gagik I's sons, John-Smbat and Ashot IV. In 1022 John-Smbat, as penalty for having supported Georgia, bequeathed his lands to Byzantium. Ashot and Smbat died in 1040 and 1041, and then the emperor Michael IV (1034–42) tried to take possession. Michael met resistance and Ashot's young son, Gagik II, acceded to the kingship, despite the ambitions of the regent, Sargis, to do so himself. But he did not last long. In 1044 Constantine IX (1042–55) attacked Ani and persuaded the emir of Duin to do likewise. Disregarding warnings to the contrary, Gagik accepted an invitation to Constantinople and he was imprisoned. His grandees then contemplated turning for help to Bagarat IV of Iberia and another ruler, perhaps David of Lori. But in 1045 the katholikos Peter surrendered Ani to Byzantium.

The last Byzantine annexation, that of the kingdom of Kars, followed submission of Kars to the Turks in 1064. Kars joined Ani in the Iberian theme. Like the Artsrunis before them, the kings moved to Cappadocia, most probably accompanied by their nobility. Gregory Magistros is known to have followed his king to Constantinople and exchanged his estates for ones in Mesopotamia.

The interest of the Byzantine annexations lies in the attitudes and the consequences to which they gave rise.[90] The histories of Tayk^c and Ani reveal some hostility to annexation at the time, and this was shared later, after the Turkish conquests, by some Armenian historians. Thus the late eleventh-century Aristakēs of Lastivert bewailed the dispersal and exile of Armenians and their abandonment of their land,[91] and the twelfth-century Matthew of Edessa believed Armenia was left abandoned and unprotected, its brave leaders replaced with eunuchs.[92] Certainly

---

[89] Thomas Artsruni, (Continuator), IV, 12, trans. Thomson, 1985, pp. 370–1; Dédéyan, 1975, pp. 52–3, 58–9, 78–82 for Vaspurakan and Artsruni family.

[90] Arutjunova-Fidanjan, 1980a and 1980b.

[91] Aristakēs, Epilogue, trans. Canard and Berbérian, 1973, pp. 130–1.

[92] Matthew, para. 109, trans. Dostourian, 1993, p. 96, where it is numbered as II, 13.

Byzantium did use Armenian resources for non-Armenian problems and her non-Armenian problems caused difficulties in Armenia. In 1041 Michael IV used troops from Sebasteia, Tarōn and Vaspurakan against rebellion in Bulgaria, and Balkan matters contributed to Turkish victory over Ani in 1064. The annexations may in their turn, by weakening Armenian defence, have contributed to Byzantium's own decisive defeat by the Turks at Manazkert, in 1071, (when the emperor Romanus (1068–71) was briefly captured). After this battle Armenia was lost, and a new era began.

Resentment of annexation was not, however, universal. In the south, resistance was minimal and attitude to its architect, Basil II, very favourable. Gregory of Narek's (*c.*950–1010) *History of the Holy Cross at Aparank^c*, intended for the elite of Vaspurakan, begins with a panegyric of Basil II.[93] Matthew of Edessa characterized Basil as illustrious, merciful, just and saintly.[94] And the author who continued the Artsruni history to the mid-twelfth century regarded Basil as a benefactor who offered safety from the Turks on generous terms.[95] Westward migration was not actually forced on Armenians by Byzantium, but happened partly because of fear of the Turks and partly because of the strength of personal ties to Armenian leaders and to kin.

Nor was Byzantium's treatment of the Armenians unfavourable. First, migrant Armenian leaders appear to have assumed the role of *strategoi* of themes.[96] The Artsrunis were given the district of Sebasteia, including the former Paulician site of Tephrike, Larissa, and, for a time, Caesarea. Initially they had about 17,375 square miles, most of it good land, reaching down to Melitene. Gagik of Ani's initial holding was small, but later he acquired more, including the lands of David Artsruni, his second wife's father, who died without male heirs in 1036. Gagik of Kars received Tzamandus, Amaseia and Comana in Pontus, Larissa and Caesarea. Second, Byzantine rule in Armenia was initially successful. (Arab) Berkri and Archēsh were taken. The commander of Archēsh was, admittedly, defeated in 1045–6 by a Turkish force coming up from Mesopotamia. But when the Turks ravaged Vaspurakan in 1048, having overrun many other areas, they were defeated by Vaspurakan's governor, with the governor of Ani. These two, with the Armenian Gregory Magistros from Mesopotamia and the Georgian prince Liparit, faced a second invasion in 1048. Even Byzantium's defeat at Capetrus near Artsn, was not the end. And third, annexation did not bring rule by aliens. The *strategus* of Melitene in 1047 was descended from T^cornik of Tarōn. When the provinces of Vaspurakan and Tarōn were combined into one in 1051

[93] Mahé, 1991.
[94] Matthew, paras 24, 53, trans. Dostourian, 1993, pp. 34–5, 49.
[95] Thomas Artsruni, (Continuator), IV, 12, trans. Thomson, 1985, p. 370.
[96] Dédéyan, 1975, pp. 86–90 for the organization of areas settled on Armenians.

they were entrusted to Gregory Magistros, previously *dux* of Mesopotamia. Catacalon Cecaumenus, governor of Ani and Iberia from late 1045, was of Armenian origin. His family originated from Tayk^c and he had property in the theme of Coloneia. Bagarat, governor of Ani under Constantine X Ducas (1059–67), belonged to the same family.

Nevertheless the new Byzantine system was not sufficiently well established to cope with the Turks, who brought Armenia much economic and political disruption. One indication of the former is provided by analysis of pigments used in illuminated manuscripts: by *c.*1050 artists in the region of Melitene no longer used gold, or the expensive ultramarine, made from Afghan lapis lazuli.[97] In 1054, 1057 and 1059 respectively Kars, Melitene and Sebasteia were sacked. In 1064 Loṙi and Kars submitted and Ani fell. In 1067 Caesarea was sacked. Between then and 1071 Cappadocia was troubled regularly.

The Bagratuni period had seen Armenian kingdoms proliferate, and learning, art, architecture and religious life, in both approved and deviant forms, flourish. These developments had been facilitated by economic growth and by the dynamics of the international situation. The coming of the Turks changed everything.

[97] Cabelli and Mathews, 1984.

10

Armenians and Europe, to c.AD 1100

Despite their geographical position and their entanglement with Assyrians, Urartians, Persians, Arabs and Turks, both ancient and early medieval Armenians have a European significance. It is not only that their origins were western and their language Indo-European. It is also that Armenians contributed to western life, in the Christian period particularly. Some of their contributions were more spectacular, and some are more certain, than others, and some have been overstated and need qualification, yet these too still deserve to be noted. Furthermore, Armenians had important elements in common not only with Christian Byzantine society, but also with Germanic peoples who established kingdoms in Rome's western provinces, becoming Christian and, in different degrees, partially Romanized, yet retaining, like Armenians, their warrior character. A reader familiar with, say, seventh- and eighth-century England, will recognize old friends in Armenia, and conversely Armenian phenomena may occasionally be illuminated by consideration of English parallels. Identification of European links and similarities is not of course intended to be either a complete delineation of the character of the Armenians, or a denial of its individuality. Armenians had both eastern and western affinities, and, besides, a whole is more than the sum of its parts.

The truth of Armenian involvement in European history and culture considered on a large scale is undeniable. As a frontier region between the western and eastern powers, Armenia was important to, and affected by, Rome and Byzantium, besides Parthia, Sasanian Persia and the Arab Caliphate. Byzantium's failure effectively to use Armenia as a buffer against the Seljuk Turks, and her defeat by the Turks at Manazkert in 1071 contributed to her losing her multinational, imperial character, and much of her international power and status. Manazkert was a milestone in European as much as in Asia Minor history. As for culture, Armenia had, in antiquity, like many other lands to both east and west, shared in Hellenistic culture; then, like others to west and south, suffered Roman expansion and enjoyed Christian conversion. Armenian Christians thus shared with many other Christians a common heritage. They also had common concerns and experiences: a conviction that sin and heresy would provoke divine punishment in this world, and so have political and military consequences; tensions and compromises between Christianity and society; religious and psychological problems posed by Christian suffering at the hands of non-Christians; these were common to all early medieval Christian societies.

On a subordinate level the hypothesis that 'Armenians were Europeans' involves first and foremost their interest in the west, their physical presence there, and the degree of political and cultural influence they had therein.

Armenians West of Armenia

Significant Armenian involvement in western society occurred only in the Christian period, though some scholars have thought that Urartian influence had reached as far west as Etruria and Greece, perhaps through the movement of refugees, or perhaps through trade. It now seems however that Urartian exports and artistic influence have been greatly exaggerated. The Armenians who came to the west varied, of course, in status, and travelled for different reasons. King Tiridates I's visit to the emperor Nero in AD 66 belongs in the context of Roman–Parthian rivalry and diplomacy. Some Armenians came as high-ranking representatives of (east) Roman and Byzantine imperial power. The pious eunuch general, Narses, who in 552 completed Justinian I's reconquest of Italy, and who was the last person to enjoy an official triumph in Rome, in 554, was Armenian. The exarch of Ravenna between 625 and 644, commemorated in the church of S. Vitale, was another Armenian, possibly a Kamsarakan. Yet another was the *strategus* of Lombardy who in 892 issued a privilege for the monastery of Monte Cassino. Basil II's governor in Thessalonica in the early 990s, who died in 995 in the war with Samuel of Bulgaria, was the former rebel Gregory of Tarōn. The governor of Philippopolis whom Basil appointed in 994 was, likewise, Armenian,[1] and he had an Armenian staff; one of them commisioned the Adrianople Gospels, copied by an Armenian scribe and illuminated by an Armenian artist in 1007.

There were also ecclesiastical visitors and settlers.[2] St Gregory of Pithiviers, in France, who died early in the eleventh century, was an

[1] Dédéyan, 1982, for Armenians in Byzantium.
[2] Dédéyan, 1979.

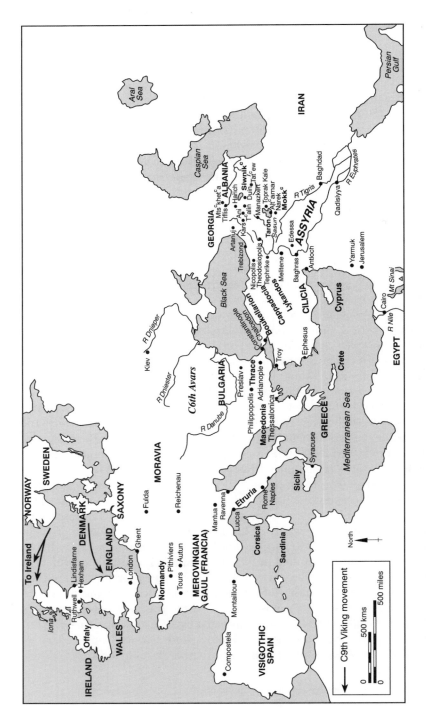

Map 10.1 Europe and west Asia

Armenian who had worked for the archbishop of Nicopolis. The St Macarius who died of plague at St Bertin in Ghent in Flanders in 1012, and whose body was elevated in 1067 before Philip I of France, hailed from the Armenian community in Antioch where he had been archbishop. Three Armenian bishops, Peter, Abraham and Stephen, are recorded by Icelandic sources as missionaries in Iceland in the eleventh century.[3] Their presence has been explained in terms of the connection between Harald, King of Norway (c.1047–66) and Constantinople, where Harald had served and where there was an Armenian community.

These are particular cases, few and far between in the hurly-burly of Europe. For more, though mostly anonymous, we should look amongst the many refugees, who fleeing war, political upheaval or religious persecution, came to western Europe from the east. The seventh-century Gallo-Roman Gregory of Tours records that an Armenian bishop, Simon, who had been a prisoner of the Persians, reached Tours in 591.[4] An early medieval Irish litany suggests that the monastery of Killeigh in County Offaly passed under Armenian leadership at about the same time. In the seventh century there was a particularly large eastern influx to Italy, in response to Arab conquests. The, formerly Latin, monastery 'called Renati' (meaning of Renatus) appears among the 'Greek' monasteries in Rome which are first referred to in the Acts of the Lateran Council of 649, as a 'monastery of the Armenians'. This community seems to have disappeared by 807, but there were Armenian immigrants elsewhere. The feasts of Gregory, Hṙipᶜsimē and Gayianē were being celebrated in Naples by the late eighth century. The monastery of Polirone (near Mantua) was home to the Armenian saint Symeon, who died in 1016, and who had, it seems, visited England, St Martin's tomb at Tours and the shrine of St James at Compostela in Spain.

Symeon himself is of course an example of the pilgrim. He had gone to Rome in 983, from the east. Accused of heresy, by spectators suspicious of his strange customs and language, he cleared himself with the help of a bishop who had happened to come to Rome from Armenia and who acted as interpreter. Other Armenian pilgrims included a Davin, who died in Lucca in Italy in 1050, and Katholikos Gregory II (1066–1105).

As an object of pilgrimage for all early medieval Christendom, Rome is one place where we can be sure that the chances of westerners meeting Armenians were reasonably continuous. Another, for the same reason, is Jerusalem, more anciently, nearly and naturally within Armenian horizons than was the further west. Interest in the Holy Land was continuous. The first Armenian attested to have visited it, Eutactus of Satala, did so in the 350s and is likely to have gone to Jerusalem. An account of two visits,

[3] Dachkévytch, 1986–7.
[4] Gregory of Tours, *The Histories*, X, 24.

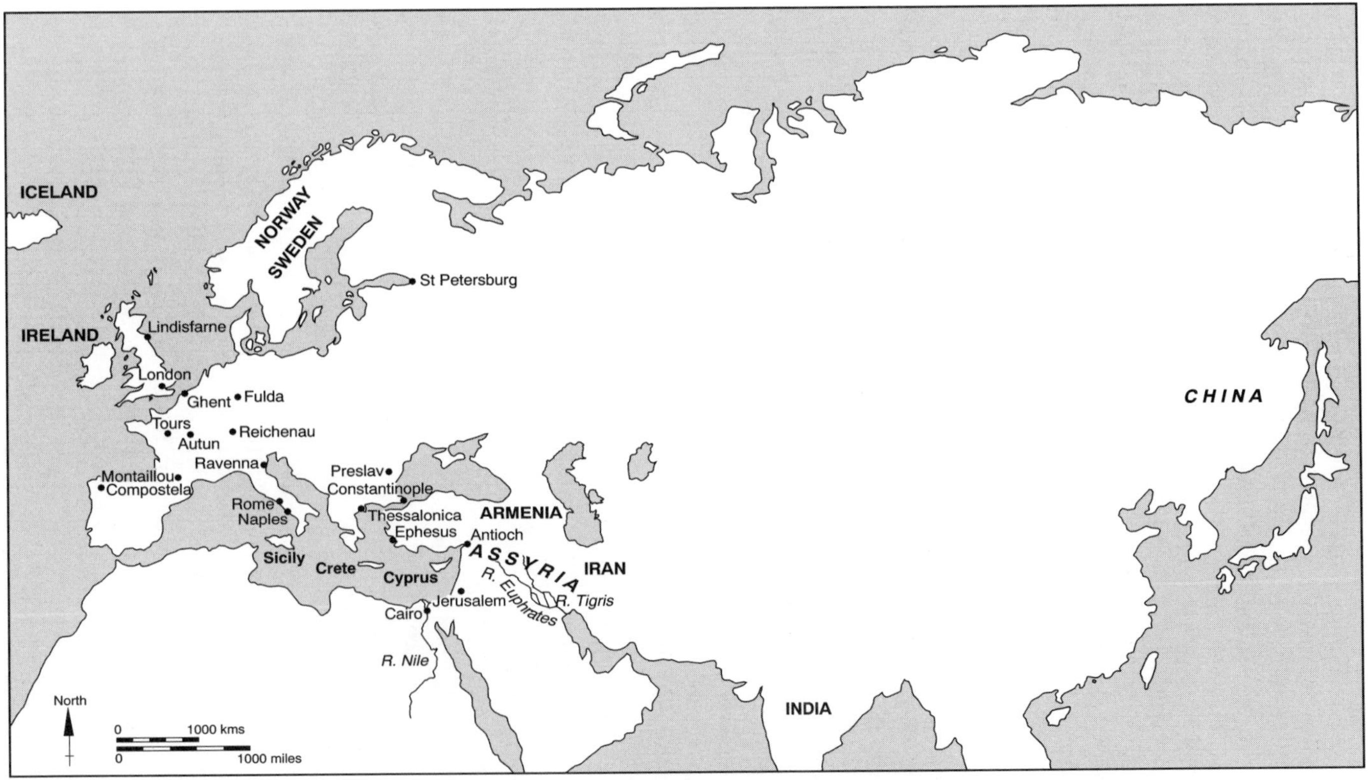

Map 10.2 Africa and Eurasia

each by a different Armenian hermit, probably in the 630s,[5] is incorporated in the tenth-century Moses Daskhurants^c^i's *History of the Albanians*. Inscriptions from the Sinai dating from the fifth century onwards suggest that Armenians were the second largest group to visit there. Armenians probably travelled to the Holy Land regularly, and in large groups. One source refers to a group of four hundred, soon after the year 428, another to one of eight hundred, in about 630.[6] Pilgrimage may have declined in the Arab period, but it revived later. Symeon and Davin had reached Rome via Jerusalem. Gregory II was in Jerusalem in 1099 when the western Crusaders arrived. The interests of Jerusalem pilgrims in enhancing their spiritual life included seeing the holy places and acquiring relics of them. They could also, because of the difficulties involved in the journey, regard their pilgrimage as a penitential exercise. Like many western Christians the Armenian katholikos Komitas (610–28), in a letter to Modestus, primate of Jerusalem, viewed Armenian pilgrimage in this light.[7]

The Holy Land harboured Armenian residents as well as Armenian pilgrims. In Palestine they were numerous in the Greek Lavra of St Sabas, and in the monastery of Theodosius at Deir Dossi in the fourth century. In Jerusalem the presence of an Armenian (religious) community is suggested by several panels from mosaic pavements with Armenian inscriptions which have been found. Two date from the fifth century and the others may be only slightly later. One inscription is 'to the memory and for the salvation of all Armenians' but the others commemorate individual Armenians, some of whom were buried nearby. That there was some, later, Armenian belief in a significant Armenian presence in Jerusalem may be implied from a dubious list of seventy monasteries and a number of churches founded in Jerusalem and its environs by Armenians in the fourth century, some still in existence and some fifteen still under Armenian control in the seventh century. This list was written purportedly by an Armenian monk Anastas Vardapet, in the seventh century and it is thought to be apocryphal.[8] The details might be wishful thinking, but their gist is not inherently implausible. The Armenian religious community in Jerusalem was to have a long history, and it made itself felt. The calendars of the Armenian and Greek churches sporadically (twelve times

---

[5] Stone, 1986, favours the 630s for the first on the grounds of territorial information in the text. (The second hermit travelled three years after the first's return.) A previous suggestion was c.660. For Moses, II, 50 see Dowsett, 1961b, pp. 181–2.
[6] Stone, 1986. According to Samuel of Ani and two other sources, after the formal separation of the Armenian Church from communion with Chalcedonians, Katholikos Nersēs II forbade Armenians to visit Jerusalem. This claim may or may not be true (see Garitte, 1952 p. 171). Modestus of Jerusalem (see below n. 7) alludes to the resumption of Armenian pilgrimage but not to what caused its interruption, (which may well have been the recent Roman–Persian wars). Sebēos, *History of Heraclius*, XXV, trans. Macler, 1904, p. 70)
[7] Sebēos, XXV, trans. Macler, 1904, pp. 73–6.
[8] Sanjian 1969a.

between AD 570 and AD 2071 inclusive, but not at regular intervals) yield different dates for Easter. From the early twelfth century there were outbreaks of violence, during the Easter period, when the dates clashed, and there may well have been on the previous occasions, though there is no documentary evidence for them.

Besides Armenian visitors, refugees, pilgrims and voluntary residents west of Armenia, there were also Armenian transportees. For some Roman and Byzantine emperors used transportation to deal with economic, military and political problems, and many Armenians were involved. Tiberius II (578–82) apparently moved 10,000 to Cyprus in 578. Constantine V settled Armenians in Thrace. Leo IV apparently moved some 150,000, including Armenians, to Thrace, and some 1,000 soldiers, probably Armenians, to Sicily. Armenians were settled in Crete in 961. Basil II moved more, to Macedon, in 988.[9]

Armenians and Byzantine History

That there were Armenians, of varying backgrounds, in the territory of the east Roman (Byzantine) Empire in Late Antiquity and the early Middle Ages is undeniable, and hence it follows that they were involved in its history. The nature and significance of their connection, however, is less certain, though some scholars have attributed to Armenians an important role in Byzantine war, leadership, culture and government.

Armenia certainly contributed to the empire's military might. She was an important source of recruits for Justinian I, and perhaps the principal one for Maurice and for Heraclius after the Balkan provinces were lost to Slavs and Avars late in the sixth century. Armenians were involved in major campaigns in Crete in 911, 949, and 960, in Italy in 934, and in the Balkans in 971 and 986. And on the eastern frontier the Armenian Melias and the theme of Lykandos which he governed defended Byzantium and promoted her conquest of Arab lands.

It is certain also that some Armenians reached the highest level of Byzantine society. The number of (identifiable) Caucasian individuals in imperial service was greater after 811 than before and it rose during the ninth and tenth centuries to a height of twenty-four. It has been concluded that between c.582 and c.959 Armenians were in the majority at court and in the forces, where they were '25% or more' in the ninth and tenth centuries.[10] Some Armenians founded great families. It has been estimated that almost all the tenth-century Byzantine provincial nobility, and a large proportion of its finest troops, were of Armenian stock, that most of the twenty great Anatolian families which emerge in eleventh-century

[9] Toumanoff, 1971; Charanis, 1963.
[10] Toumanoff, 1971, p. 131 for percentage.

Byzantium had Armenian origins, and that about 10 per cent of Byzantium's approximately 340 'aristocratic' families in the eleventh and twelfth centuries were 'Armenian'.[11]

Such conclusions might make Byzantium seem like an annex of Armenia. But some qualification is needed. We cannot date the immigration of all the 'Armenian' families exactly, and sometimes the evidence for their origins is questionable. An Armenian personal name, for example, qualifies an individual for inclusion by Toumanoff in his list of Caucasians in imperial service, but Toumanoff himself notes that the deduction of Armenian origin from an Armenian name seems precluded in two cases, that of the house of Boilas, because of this family's apparent Bulgarian origin, and that of the house of Phocas, taken by some earlier scholars to be Armenian, because of what seems definite evidence of western origin. This house, Toumanoff concludes, had been Armenianized through marital alliances.[12] The choice of personal names can reflect fashion, or calculation, and their repetition may express family rather than ethnic consciousness.

Within Byzantium's intellectual leadership the Armenian element was most marked in the ninth-century cultural revival. The patron Caesar Bardas, and the scholars Patriarch Photius, Patriarch John the Grammarian (837–45) and Leo the Philosopher were Armenian.

The greatest position of leadership in Byzantium was of course that of the emperor, and some of the greatest emperors have also been credited with Armenian origins. Maurice is one, but the counter-arguments, in his case, seem overwhelming.[13] His Armenian origin appears only in late Armenian and in late Greek sources. In the latter case at least it is explicable in terms of the contemporary Armenian population in Cappadocia, which is where Maurice really came from and a consequential failure to distinguish Armenia from Cappadocia in the past. The Armenian origin of Heraclius, however, is likely. His father, also named Heraclius, was born in the region of Karin. One interpretation of a remark by 'Sebēos' is that Heraclius was descended from the Arsacids, but a Mamikonean origin is also possible, for Heraclius is the equivalent of Vahagn, a name favoured by the Mamikoneans.[14] Basil I, known as the Macedonian, was also, probably, of Armenian stock. According to one Byzantine source, he spoke Armenian as a first language. Explicit claims of Arsacid descent were made by his family and friends, in the funeral oration delivered by his son Leo VI, and also in his biography, whose author may have been his grandson Constantine VII.[15] The biographer suggests

[11] Jenkins, 1981, p. 66; Bryer, 1981, p. 92; Kazhdan, 1984.
[12] Toumanoff, 1971, pp. 156, 134–5.
[13] Goubert, 1940.
[14] Toumanoff, 1971, pp. 135–6 (n. 98), 157–8.
[15] Tougher, 1994; Adontz, 1934a.

that Basil's reign fulfilled a prediction of the fifth-century Armenian katholikos Sahak, that one day an Arsacid would rule the Roman Empire. And according to the thirteenth-century Armenian historian Vardan, the bishop of Tarōn more or less assured Basil that he was this prophesied king.[16] The exact truth is probably less glamorous. There are signs of scepticism in Leo VI's account of Basil's royal descent and his family might have been merely an impoverished branch of the Mamikoneans.[17]

What is clear is that Basil was interested in promoting his lineage. Sahak's 'prediction', which included the eventual restoration of the ecclesiastical patriarchate to Gregory the Illuminator's family, has been shown to emanate from Basil's circle. Its interpolation into the history by the fifth-century Armenian Lazarus of Pᶜarp has been concluded to have been made at Constantinople at the time of Basil's accession.[18] In these genealogical inventions the 'Armenian' Byzantine patriarch Photius may have played a part. Some association is certainly suggested by the biographer of Ignatius, Photius' rival for the patriarchate. He asserts that Photius, whilst in (temporary) exile, invented a genealogy connecting Basil and Tiridates, thereby regaining Basil's favour.[19] It is even possible that Photius himself was regarded, like Basil, as a fulfilment of Sahak's prophecy. Photius could have claimed, with some justification, to be a member of the family of Gregory, whose cult he may have promoted. An Armenian text attributes to Photius the translation of some relics of Gregory, miraculously discovered in Constantinople, to its greatest church, Hagia Sophia,[20] where Basil arranged for him (Gregory) to be pictured in mosaic. Basil's claims, and his sending to Ashot Bagratuni for a crown, given that the Bagratunis had been the royal Armenian Arsacids' coronants, must have been meant to impress his descent not just on Byzantines but also on Armenians, and thereby to encourage Armenians to be submissive. Basil's biographer tellingly alludes to the Armenians' ancient devotion to the Arsacids.[21]

The influence which the presence of Armenian stock in the empire's greatest families had upon the direction of Byzantine government however was probably less than has sometimes been claimed. Only in the case of Heraclius is the evidence strong. Shahîd has argued that Heraclius' assumption in 629 of the title βἀσιλεύſ, often seen as a significant landmark in the decline of the Latin and the rise of the Greek element in the empire's polity and culture, was to a considerable extent for reasons connected with Heraclius' involvement in Armenia. Since Heraclius

---

[16] Vardan, *Historical Compilation*, 45, trans. Thomson, 1989, p. 186.
[17] Adontz, 1934a, pp. 245, 255–9.
[18] Adontz, 1933b, 1934a; Der Sahaghian, 1911.
[19] Adontz, 1934a, p. 233.
[20] Van Esbroeck, 1971b.
[21] Adontz, 1934a, p. 237.

spent six years here in pursuit of his Persian war and since his reign could be regarded as a period of 'Christianization', Shahîd believes that Heraclius must, as a result, have reminded Armenians of Tiridates the Great, and also that his new title marked Heraclius' resumption of the Armenian, possibly (if he was an Arsacid) his ancestral, kingship.[22] It has also been asserted that Heraclius' policies were dominated by Armenian concerns:[23] that Heraclius made sacrifices in religious dogma in his attempts to heal the rift between Chalcedonians and anti-Chalcedonians because he needed Armenian support in his campaigns: and that his presentation of the Persian war as a religious one, to free the holy places and to recapture the True Cross, was designed to appeal to Armenians, and indeed reflected his own Armenian outlook. His promise to his troops of the martyrs' crown and of eternal life is also susceptible to this interpretation.

In other imperial and elite cases however Armenian descent had less import. The evidence to support the assertion that Heraclius' successors were influenced by their Armenian origin is that they paid careful attention to Armenia, but this attention can be more simply explained, by Armenia's very real importance. Whether Basil's dynasty was significantly influenced by its Armenian roots has been acknowledged as not determinable.[24] The sophisticated scholar Photius has been deemed 'Hellenized'.[25] The generally absorbing power of Byzantium, from which Armenians within the empire cannot have been entirely exempt, may be seen in the case of Eustathius Boilas whose will survives. His family was thoroughly Byzantinized, but his ultimate origin was perhaps Bulgar, his own original home Cappadocia, and the estates he was granted were in the region of Artanuj in the Armenian–Iberian border zone.[26]

As for changes and developments within Byzantium, Armenian impact upon them is not easy to evaluate. There was a contribution to religious tension. For the Armenians were sometimes an obstacle, though not the only one, to Imperial attempts to heal the internal rift created by the Council of Chalcedon, a problem which lasted well into the seventh century. It is also not impossible that there was an Armenian contribution to eighth-century Byzantine Iconoclasm, since opponents of image worship are attested in Armenia in the early seventh century. On the other hand the origins and significance of Byzantine Iconoclasm have generated differing interpretations and they are explicable without giving major importance to Armenian factors. There had for example been opposition to images throughout the early church.

---

[22] Shahîd, 1972.
[23] E.g. Grégoire, 1946.
[24] Charanis, 1963, p. 35.
[25] Ibid., p. 28.
[26] Vryonis, 1957.

Armenian influence has also been associated with two very important elements in Byzantine government and society, namely the theme system (in which the soldiers of the province's army were settled on the land) and feudalism. The first was the mainstay of Byzantine organization, and its origins and date of introduction have suffered considerable debate. There is little evidence and it is only comparison and chronology which suggest an Armenian contribution. There are two points of comparison: first, like the Byzantine governors of themes, Armenian princes combined civil and military functions; second, there is a parallel in the development of the meaning of both Greek θέμα and Armenian *gund*, from 'military contingent' to 'geographical-administrative division'. As for chronology, Armenian *gund* had acquired its second meaning by 555,[27] and an Armenian 'origin' for the theme system would tie in with its appearance in Byzantium in Heraclius' reign, if indeed it did appear then. But these arguments are easy to challenge. A different suggestion for example is that Byzantium borrowed the term θέμα from the Avars, and that it was her contact with them which stimulated the development of the new system.[28] It may even be that it was not a deliberately planned system, but one which slowly evolved, from a beginning in the second half of the seventh century.[29]

Finally, we have the historiographically thorny issue of feudalism. The view that Armenian movement into and influence in Byzantium in the eleventh century probably played a crucial role in the development of feudalism in eleventh- and twelfth-century Byzantium has been commonly held.[30] But it ought not to be maintained. First, some scholars, working on other medieval societies, have suggested that historians have understood the terms 'feudalism' and 'feudal system' so variously as to have deprived them of any useful meaning at all. 'Feudalism' as pointed out by Elizabeth Brown,[31] is a construct devised in Europe in the seventeenth century, the 'feudal system' an early essay in comparative jurisprudence. Consequently neither the application of these terms to Armenian society nor any general comparison of it to western society which involves asserting that the western society is 'feudal' should be considered illuminating in itself. They may of course have had much in common, but their similarities must be precisely identified, and their inner workings detailed.[32] However, the assertion that late antique and medieval Armenian society itself was feudal, has been almost *de rigeur* in secondary literature, though not the more convincing for its repetition. One example is the supposition that the Armenians who moved to Cilicia in the

[27] Garsoïan, 1980.
[28] Howard-Johnston, 1984.
[29] For this view and a résumé of others, with references, Haldon, 1993 and 1995.
[30] E.g. Bryer, 1981, pp. 88–92.
[31] Brown, E. A. R., 1974, and also Reynolds, 1994.
[32] Cf. above ch. 5 pp. 97–98.

late eleventh century took 'feudalism' with them. As Edwards has noted, modern comments regarding their 'feudal system' in Cilicia are not supported by textual evidence and most often derive from examples of an earlier 'feudal system' in Armenia.[33] The Armenian aristocracy and its monarchy in Cilicia did in fact change under external influences as western Crusaders established themselves nearby in the twelfth century. Relations between Cilicia and the Norman principality of Antioch (1098–1268) were particularly close, and by the Armenian Leo II's reign (as prince 1187–98, as king 1198–1219) the influence of western 'feudalism' on Cilician elite society is apparent.[34]

Armenians and Western Culture

That there was an Armenian contribution to the actual structure of Byzantine government and society seems doubtful, that there was one to western heresy and art a little more certain. Bulgarian Bogomilism, a heresy whose date of origin is not entirely clear, but which is generally thought to have become a problem in Bulgaria by the 930s, was both to infect Constantinople and also to contribute to the emergence of Catharism in the late twelfth-century Rhineland and France. Bogomilism was itself very likely influenced by Armenian Paulicianism. There are some similarities of doctrine, and the historical context suggests some contacts. Paulicianism reached the Balkans, partly, as a tenth-century Byzantine chronicler noted, through the mid-eighth-century emperor Constantine V's transporting Armenians from Melitene to live there.[35] Subsequent movements of both people and frontier, in the context of frequent Byzantine–Bulgarian hostilities, will have facilitated the heresy's reaching Bulgaria itself. Given their history, some at least of the heretics are likely to have been active in recruitment and they may even have been reinforced. Basil I's ambassador to the Paulicians of Tephrike in 868–9, Peter of Sicily, discovered that they were planning to send missionaries to Bulgaria.[36] The surviving reply of Pope Nicholas I (858–67) to the 106 lost questions put to him by Bulgaria's first Christian monarch, Boris, in 866,[37] reveals that there were Armenians teaching in Bulgaria even before then. These need not, of course, necessarily have been Paulicians. But Boris had asked which, of the different teachers available, he ought to obey, and for guidance on particular isses. Some of Nicholas's replies

[33] Edwards, 1983a, pp. 35–6.
[34] Dédéyan, 1989.
[35] Theophanes, *Chronographia*, I p. 429; Garsoïan, 1967a, pp. 122–3 and n. 38.
[36] Peter of Sicily, 5, text and trans. Astruc et al., 1970, pp. 8, 9; Lemerle, 1973, pp. 19–21 for comment.
[37] Sullivan, R.E., 1994, (1966); Mayr-Harting, 1994.

concern points regarding which Paulicians and non-Paulicians would certainly have differed, such as the sign of the Cross, and baptism, which involve the sanctification of matter. Unfortunately the exact purpose of Boris's questions is not clear. It is unknown whether they reflect puzzlement about differences of opinion in Bulgaria, or simple ignorance, or a desire for a written authoritative statement with which to impress his subjects.

As for art, although the overall conclusion of Strzygowski, in his monumental work of 1918, that Armenia played a formative role in the architecture of Christendom, is not now accepted, a number of Armenian–western links are nevertheless identifiable and explicable. For amongst the Armenian transportees and refugees who came to the west there were probably at least some artists and craftsmen. If they were able to ply their trade, they must have worked in their old style unless and until re-educated. There were, most likely, some Armenian artefacts in their baggage which could have kept the memory of this style alive. We might expect some impact in Bulgaria, and it has been suggested that one of her most important churches, the so-called Round Church at Preslav (dated to *c.* 900), owes a great deal to Armenian inspiration.[38] There are certainly no surviving parallels for this church in contemporary Byzantine architecture, though it is recorded that Basil I, a few years earlier, built a similar one in Constantinople.[39] But it is also likely that the Preslav church was influenced from a quite different direction, by the western, Carolingian, emperor Charlemagne's palace church at Aachen[40] in present-day Germany, which was completed in the very early ninth century and to which it bears some resemblances. For there was a great deal of contact between Carolingians and Bulgarians in the ninth century.

Another, though tentative, suggestion is that the development of early Irish and Anglo-Saxon free-standing sculptured crosses owes something to the Middle East.[41] Some resemblances to pre-Arab Armenian works in Armenia, namely steles at Ōdzun, (these were probably carved by a Georgian sculptor), and fragments of steles at Harich and T꜀alin, are discernible. Like the western crosses these are carved on four sides and include figures within a frame. The fragments may even be fragments of crosses. One channel through which Armenian influence reached England may have been the Irish monastery on Iona (off the coast of Scotland) which itself hugely influenced seventh-century Anglo-Saxon Northumbria. It has been argued that there was an Armenian influence on Virgin

[38] Boyadjiev, 1978.
[39] Mango, 1986, pp. 173–4.
[40] Hoddinott, 1983. Scholars of the Carolingian world relate Charlemagne's palace chapel to the (earlier) church of S. Vitale at Ravenna and not to Armenian tradition.
[41] Der Nersessian, 1978, p. 68; Cramp, 1966, p. 5; Richardson, 1984, notes parallels and suggests development from a common heritage.

and Child iconography in eighth-century Iona.[42] There is some similarity between a panel on the eighth-century Northumbrian Ruthwell Cross and a scene on an exterior wall of a late sixth-century church at Mts'khet'a, capital of Iberia in the fourth century, though this has been explained as parallel development.[43] Some decorative fragments from Hexham in Northumbria are reminiscent of strips of decoration on Armenian churches.[44]

Some Armenian traits in the art of the west must have come with Armenian individuals, but some may have followed contacts and perhaps acquisition of artefacts, made initially in Italy, especially in Rome, where Armenians were not the only foreigners. There were a number of English there in the late seventh and early eighth centuries, and in the ninth and tenth centuries the western emperors, first the Carolingians and then the Ottonians, were heavily involved in Rome. Such contacts might explain two tantalizing glimpses of Armenian interplay with the culture of the far west. There is the Latin–Armenian glossary of ninety words (including days, numbers, sacred things, and some parts of the body) found at the end of an early tenth-century Autun (in France) manuscript of letters of St Jerome.[45] And there are the paintings consecrated at Tat'ew in Siwnik' in 930, which had been commissioned from Frankish artists by its bishop Jacob, and which have affinities to the art of some great German monasteries, for example Fulda and Reichenau.[46]

Another, indirect, source of Armenian styles must have been Constantinople. For although only a fraction of Byzantine architecture survives, it is clear that in the late ninth, late tenth and the eleventh centuries several imperial churches were built under the influence of Armenian design. Basil I's round church was one, Constantine IX's church of the monastery of St George of Mangana another.[47] The most famous Armenian work of the period which still survives is of course that done on the dome of the church of Hagia Sophia, itself one of the greatest monuments of Byzantine civilization, after it was damaged in an earthquake in 989. The dome's restoration was planned and begun by Trdat, the great architect of the kingdom of Ani who, it seems, just happened to be in Constantinople at the time.[48]

It is less easy to see Armenian influences in western literature, though Armenian elements have been perceived by some scholars in the medieval Greek epic poem *Digenis Akritas*. These elements include echoes of ninth-century Paulician history and of the ninth- to tenth-century *strate-*

---

[42] MacLean, 1991.
[43] Neuman de Vegvar, 1987, pp. 308–9, n. 116.
[44] Cramp, 1966, pp. 4–5 and n. 14, 17.
[45] Hewsenian, 1960; Weitenberg, 1982.
[46] Thierry, N. and Thierry, M., 1968.
[47] Mango, 1986, pp. 174, 127–8.
[48] Donabédian, 1991b, pp. 99–101.

gus Melias, toponyms and personal names. And late ninth- to early tenth-century Armenian Paulician 'authorship' and transmission has been inferred.[49] But the current, convincing, consensus is to deny that Armenian echoes are either loud or significant. *Digenis Akritas* was shaped probably early in the twelfth century, in Constantinople or in Pontus or Cilicia, and has much in common with the folklore of other societies.[50] Nor is it certain, though it has been suggested, that an ancient version of the Armenian *David of Sasun* was one source of the German *Nibelungen*. There are similarities, particularly at the beginning and end, but there are also important differences, in narrative and characterization. If Armenian epic did impinge on German culture it was probably in the twelfth century, when the German emperor Frederick Barbarossa went east on crusade.[51]

Armenian-European Parallels: Problems, Perceptions and Peculiarities

The study of early medieval Armenian history shares some of the problems which bedevil it with that of European history of the same period. One example is omission and imprecision in written sources. Another, more important, is that early historians shaped and interpreted their material, leaving us artificial pictures rather than disinterested recollections of the past. The applicability to Armenian authors of such a warning, commonplace, if not always heeded, in studies of medieval western writers has been emphasized by Robert Thomson in his annotated translations of the major Armenian historical texts. His criticism has had a hostile reception in some quarters[52] but its validity is not thereby diminished.

It is to a European rather than a non-European context that Armenian historiography belongs. This is true despite the apparent implication to the contrary in the *History* of Moses of Khoren, in Armenian tradition the 'Father of History' – that is, despite his emphasis on Anatolian and Iranian elements in Armenian history and culture. Moses emphasizes these by claiming to have used Persian archive material; stressing the kinship of Armenian and Parthian royalty; suggesting similarities between their societies; and presenting history in a manner reminiscent of Iranian epic tradition. But the pre-Islamic Iranians had no historiographical tradition, whereas Greeks and Romans, and Jews, did. The context in which Moses portrayed Armenian history is the Judaeo-

---

[49] Especially by Adontz, Grégoire, Bartikian; cf. Bartikian in Beaton and Ricks, 1993.
[50] Essays in Beaton and Ricks, 1993.
[51] Amsler, 1978–9.
[52] E.g. comment in D. M. Lang, 1979, and 1980, reviews of Thomson, 1978. For his approach and reaction, Thomson, 1982b, pp. vii–viii.

Christian one provided by the Bible, that is the history of the world beginning with Adam. Moses traced the ancestry of Armenian legendary heroes back to the only survivors of the biblical flood, to Noah and his family. He also used the Bible for specific information and for parallels with Armenian history, and he often modelled descriptive passages or elements within them on biblical ones. He made a similar, and extensive, use of two works which were of seminal importance in the development of western historiography, the first-century Jewish Josephus' *Jewish Wars*, and the fourth-century Greek Eusebius' *Ecclesiastical History*. Moses' real debt to these far exceeds what is implied by the sparsity of his explicit references.[53]

When the same questions are posed of Armenian and western societies, it is not only the problems involved which are similar. Sometimes the answers are too. It seems that most, if not all, early medieval Christian societies developed self-images with elements of the Old Testament about them, though particular emphases, nuances and consequences differed in different societies. For example, the belief that God would inflict punishment in this world, not just the next, is connected to this attitude, and in Byzantium, in whose conceptual world the Old Testament played a dominant role, the Iconoclast movement was related to it. In Armenia, Ełishē's interpretation of the 450 revolt is modelled on the Old Testament books of the Maccabees, and John Katholikos and Thomas Artsruni too were strongly influenced by the Old Testament in their presentation of their subject matter. This presentation probably reflected both their own perception of their society and its events, and also, in part, that of their patrons and audience. Such presentation and perception is paralleled in England, Merovingian Gaul and Visigothic Spain. A self-image as a New Israel is also discernible among Syrian Christians. One element in such images was divine sanction for warfare. The religious preparation and strengthening, by religious means, of Armenian armies and war leaders is paralleled, perhaps even surpassed, in Byzantium, where it is particularly well-documented from the ninth century, in Visigothic Spain and in Carolingian Francia.[54] But whereas west European kings, stimulated by Old Testament kings and by Roman emperors as their two role models, issued written law codes, sometimes more for propaganda than for practical purposes, Armenian kings did not. The scholar who compiled a code in 1184, for the Katholikos of Albania, found this neglect surprising, as we might too. He included Armenians' acceptance of the law of foreign overlords among possible explanations.[55] We might emphasize that codification is not a prerequisite for effective law and order where a

[53] For Moses as historian, and his use of sources, Thomson, 1978, pp. 8–56.
[54] McCormick, 1986, pp. 245–52 for Byzantium, p. 308 for Spain, pp. 344, 347, 357–8, 385 for Francia.
[55] Mkhit ᶜar, 1880, pp. 16–17.

society is small and personal, and has long tradition and ecclesiastical canons to draw on. And since medieval law-giving both expressed and enhanced the legislator's authority, the lack of a code may reflect aristocratic resistance to central control.

With some westerners Armenian Christians had in common an especial veneration of the Virgin Mary and of the Cross. The cult of Mary is particularly interesting. It reached different places at different times, not being widely promoted in Gaul for example until the twelfth century. But in the eastern churches it was established early, and the decisions of the Council of Ephesus in 431 contributed to its growth. Mary's popularity in Armenia is revealed in the dedication of many churches to her both in the seventh and in the late ninth and early tenth centuries. In these later years she seems to have been the most popular saint, having more, almost a third of new dedications, than others did. Mary was likewise especially honoured in Byzantium and in England. In Byzantium she had come, by the late sixth century, to be seen as the special protectress of Constantinople. Whether Armenia influenced Byzantium or vice versa is a different matter. In England Mary's cult was promoted by contact with the late seventh-century papacy, and it flourished especially during the tenth-century Reformation.

As for the Cross, its veneration in Armenia is clear, in, for example, its association with Gregory the Illuminator's victories over pagans, and in King Gagik Artsruni's church at Alt͑amar and in the honour paid to its relics in the tenth and eleventh centuries. For many Christians the Cross had martial associations. In Byzantium it became very much a symbol of Imperial victory, especially over non-Christian enemies, and the Imperial battle standard was a gilded cross containing a relic of the True Cross. Further west the Visigoths in the seventh and the Franks in the mid-ninth century likewise followed the Cross into battle. Pope Nicholas advised the Bulgars to do the same.[56] There may have been some Armenian influence in this development, given that in the 620s the emperor Heraclius had lent his Persian war a religious dimension by stressing the objective of regaining the relics of the True Cross, which the Persians had taken from Jerusalem, and given his Armenian connections. In western Europe, the eastern festival of the Exaltation of the True Cross was introduced to Rome by Sergius I (687–701), one of a series of popes of eastern origin. Again Roman influence promoted veneration in England, discernible in various sources, including vernacular poetry.

At a more mundane level, it is not surprising that similar disciplinary problems worried different early medieval churches. That of drunken clergy, for example, which troubled the eighth-century katholikos John

---

[56] McCormick, 1986, pp. 247, 308, 358 for Byzantines, Visigoths and Franks; and Mayr-Harting, 1994, p. 17 for Nicholas and the Bulgars (referring to q. 33 of Nicholas I, *Papae Epistolae* M.G.H. Epp. VI, no. 99, pp. 568–600).

III, appears in almost exactly contemporary Anglo-Saxon legal and penitential texts. The complaints of Bede, and others, about Northumbrian
and Mercian monasticism, suggesting that some eighth-century Anglo-
Saxon monasteries were practically indistinguishable from (secular)
aristocratic households, are not a world apart from the Duin canons'
complaints in 645 about monasteries suffering noble encroachment, minstrels and dancing girls.

Whereas in its religious life the early medieval Armenian aristocracy
had much in common with Byzantium as well as with Germanic Europe,
its secular life bore in some respects a closer similarity to the ancient
Iranian and the Germanic than it did to the Byzantine. The minstrel
tradition, saga and oral poetry so entrenched as even to invade the
cloister, was common to Iranian, Germanic and Armenian societies.[57]
Kings and war leaders desired their own great deeds, like the history of
their dynasty, to be recorded and recounted in poetry as soon as possible.
The minstrel acted as entertainer, news reporter and publicist. Another
common institution was bloodfeud, a judicial process to deal with murder, injury and dishonour, which differs, as anthropologists have shown,
from generalized recourse to violence or from individual or family ani-
mosity and grudges. Bloodfeud is discernible in late antique and early
medieval Armenia, just as it is in Germanic Europe, for example in
Merovingian Gaul and in Anglo-Saxon England. The Armenian Arsacids
yearned to exact vengeance for their kinsmen from the Sasanians. Armenian Christianity accommodated feud. That bloodfeud was also part of
Iranian society can be seen from the *Shah-nama* or *Epic of the Kings*, the
historical tradition of Iran written in verse by Firdausi, who died, probably, between 1020 and 1025. True, the Iranians had a system of written
law and law courts, as evidenced by the Sasanian legal tract, but the law,
and probably also the courts, dealt predominantly with property. As in
western Europe the right to feud in appropriate cases may have been
maintained.

A third area of comparison concerns great men and their entourages.
One particular piece of Armenian evidence is reminiscent of evidence
from the first-century Roman writer Tacitus and the Old English poem
Beowulf, of debated date, both used by historians of seventh-century
England in discussion of the *comitatus* (warband, retinue) as a major
institution within its royal and aristocratic society. As reported by the
historian Thomas Artsruni, the mid-ninth-century Prince Ashot Artsruni's
speech reproaching his disloyal followers, who intended to surrender
him, emphasizes the generosity, protection and affection that he had
afforded them.[58] It is not dissimilar to the reproach directed, in *Beowulf*,

---

[57] For England, Wormald, 1978; for Iran, Boyce, 1957.
[58] Thomas Artsruni, *History of the House of the Artsrunis*, III, 2, trans. Thomson,
1985, pp. 202–3 and his pp. 52–7 for comment on princely responsibilities and rewards.

by the loyal Wiglaf to the men who have deserted King Beowulf, that Beowulf's care and generosity have been wasted.[59]

There are, certainly, difficulties attached to this suggestion that the institution of the warband, or something like it, was known in Armenia but they are not overwhelming. One objection is that there is no particular term in the Armenian texts for such a retinue. Yet it is not necessarily true that, where there is no technical name for an institution, the institution itself did not exist or was of no importance. Old English similarly lacks a standard technical term. There is no routinely used technical term for 'retinue' even in *Beowulf*. But the Armenian historians writing in the early tenth century do use terms which appear to refer to distinguished fighting men who were especially close to their leader – 'brought up by hand', 'familiars', 'his own' – in appropriate contexts.

Another difficulty is that, whereas in the case of the Anglo-Saxon *comitatus* historians have evidence for it from very different sources, the same is not true of Armenia. Yet there are parallels nearby. Asian nomads provide one. During the ninth-century, the Bulgarian monarch had, according to Browning, an 'entourage' of warriors, 'whom he maintained', 'whose loyalty to him was a personal one', who appear in memorial inscriptions as *threptoi anthropoi* (kept men), and who offer some parallel to the unfeoffed household knights of early Norman society.[60] The Arab world offers further parallels. In a study of Umayyad clientage, Crone has remarked on the *qawm*, 'a general's personal recruits, usually from within his own tribal group', including both ordinary and more distinguished retainers, '*aṣḥāb* or companions', 'the general's most trusted men'. In one anecdote is 'an undeniable whiff' of the Anglo-Saxon style 'warlord and gold-giver whose followers would faithfully repay him in battle and avenge his death'.[61] In the early tenth century the *ghulam* system was introduced; in this, men, often only a few hundred, fought in bands, having been recruited by a leader who was seen as a sort of father figure and was responsible for their pay and employment, and their first responsibility was to each other rather than to their sovereign or their ultimate paymaster.[62]

Armenian–European Divergences

There were, of course, differences as well as similarities between Armenia and western Europe in the development of Christianity, in the experiences, practices and expectations of its adherents and in their fate.

---

[59] *Beowulf*, ll. 2864–91.
[60] Browning, 1975, pp. 125–6.
[61] Crone, 1980, pp. 55–6.
[62] Kennedy, 1986, p. 206.

The most obvious is that the Armenian church refused to recognize the Council of Chalcedon, whose creed was normally the official doctrine of the Byzantine church, and was always accepted by the Roman Papacy. A striking difference is the lack of evidence, after the fifth century, for the existence in Armenia of religious houses for women, whereas in England, Francia and Ottonian Saxony both female communities and powerful abbesses could be found. Another is that whereas there are indications that in the western church, between 600 and 1000, salvation was generally felt to be difficult for individuals other than monks and nuns to attain, there may in Armenian society, at least in the ninth and tenth centuries, perhaps have been a rather more optimistic attitude. Der Manuelian's study of sculptural images between the seventh and fourteenth centuries indicates that Armenians were less concerned than Europeans were with frightening Last Judgement images. They also neglected the kingly and remote aspect of Christ, and instead seemed to emphasize that Christ was ever-present.[63] Similarly, the Genesis frescoes at Alt͏ʿamar suggest, according to one interpretation, a God closely involved in the Creation, and merciful, rather than a remote and severe one, underpinned by a 'peculiarly Armenian reading of . . . Genesis'.[64] A fourth difference is that Armenian historians between the seventh and early tenth centuries do not suggest that there was much expectation of tangible supernatural intervention in events. In this respect Armenians had more in common with their Muslim neighbours than with their western co-religionists. In Muslim literature divine involvement is a more distant affair than it is in west European or Syriac literature or in that of demon-ridden Byzantium.[65]

Most striking is Armenian ethnic, political and cultural longevity, scarcely paralleled in European history. By 1065 there had been an independent 'Armenia' albeit of varying extent and form, for nearly thirteen centuries (since 189 BC), despite having been both buffer and theatre of war between neighbouring powers and suffered temporary subservience and oppression. The Armenian sense of national identity has survived even longer than did 'Armenia'.

Armenian Identity in the Early Middle Ages

To the survival of a sense of Armenian identity several factors contributed. The geography of Armenia helped resistance to would-be conquerors, and hindered their consolidation as much as it did Armenians' political unity. In general terms the sharing of a language may contribute

[63] Der Manuelian, 1984.
[64] Mathews, 1982b, pp. 249, 252–3.
[65] Kennedy, 1986, p. 351.

to internal and external perception of national identity. And after Armenian became a literary language, in the early fifth century, Armenians had a literary heritage of which they could be proud, and they could partake of prestigious Christian culture without losing their separate identity. Other aspects of their long history meant that, unlike, say, early Franks and Bulgars, they did not have to regard their neighbours' culture and institutions as superior to their own.

A common theme in Armenian historiography has been a connection not only between national identity and Christianity but also between national identity and Christology. The first, with its suggestion that Christianity ultimately unified at least some Armenians and hindered foreign assimilation or elimination, is convincing. Tiridates IV's conversion was due, partly, to hopes of this. Persian and Arab attempts to eradicate Christianity were resisted. The impression of a Christian–national link was fostered in the fifth and sixth centuries by Agathangelos and by Ełishē, whose works became classics of Armenian historiography. Agathangelos depicted Gregory the Illuminator as the model for the church leaders who were the leaders of society after the abolition of the monarchy. Ełishē's purpose in writing about the 450 rebellion was undoubtedly to stimulate religious enthusiasm, bravery and unity against a foe. For him, Christianity, the Church, ancestral culture and being Armenian were all bound up together. And his viewpoint was, it seems, promoted, perhaps mendaciously, by refugees from Armenia at the court of the Roman emperor Justin II (565–78). They claimed religious motivation for the 572 rebellion against Persia, probably to enhance their standing in Constantinople and to give Justin an excuse to support them in what may have been simply a political, national, movement. For the Armenian 'Sebēos' does not offer us a religious interpretation and two reliable Greek accounts suggest that Persia denied religious interference.[66] Ełishē's position was also taken up in the early tenth century by Thomas Artsruni.

The significance of the Armenian church's rejection, for most of our period, of the dyophysite Christological doctrine (that Christ had two natures) propounded by the 451 Council of Chalcedon, and hence of church union with Rome and with Byzantium, is doubtful. Armenian identity and Armenian anti-Chalcedonianism have often been seen as closely related, expressing, cloaking and protecting one another, anti-Chalcedonianism and anti-Byzantine feeling going together.

But there are difficulties about such views. The general thesis that ancient heresies were national or social movements in disguise has been challenged, even, some might consider, refuted.[67] As for the particular

---

[66] Frendo, 1985.
[67] Jones, 1959; Moorhead, 1981a.

case of Armenia some scholars have concluded that the anti-Imperial aspect of the Armenians' original rejection of Chalcedon was not nationalist and deliberate, but an accidental consequence of a genuine difference of theological opinion.[68] And the ambitions of dissenters in general were for the imperial authorities to accept and enforce their own dissenting views. This is neither political nor cultural separatism.

Second, doctrinal and political disagreements and allegiances did not always dovetail neatly. Sometimes of course, political expediency caused them to appear to do so. Persian pressure rather than Armenian free will may have lain behind the Armenian Church's separations, in 555 and (about) 608 from the Churches of the Roman Empire and of Iberia. When Katholikos Eḷia (703–17) denounced to the Caliph the Albanian patriarch who had turned to Chalcedonianism, and the princess who supported him, emphasizing that he had made an agreement with the emperor, and implying political overtones,[69] he may have been communicating the literal truth, but he may also have been, to put it cynically, currying favour with Arab overlords. To drag politics into a doctrinal debate must often have seemed a useful way of strengthening one's position if not one's argument, and both the truth and the sincerity of protagonists' assertions are elusive.

Thus the Armenian katholikos Abraham, in his letters to the Iberians early in the seventh century, expressed surprise that they should both profess to be loyal to the Persian king and also communicate with the Roman church. His correspondent naturally denied their incompatibility.[70] A letter of 648 in 'Sebēos'' text, explaining to Emperor Constans II that the Armenians could not accept his doctrinal position, but never dispatched, addresses Constans respectfully and includes profession of loyalty.[71] Doctrinal disagreement and political co-operation were easily combined. Theodore Ṙshtuni's coming to terms with the Arabs met disapproval. The ending, in 726, of the brief union (established in 689) between the Byzantines' and the Armenians' churches, did not inhibit political rapprochements in the eighth century. Byzantine help was anticipated in the rebellion of 747, and many Armenians entered imperial territory and service.

Politics can be a dirty business and it may be that what seems, judged strictly, to be inconsistent, might seem, judged realistically, to be inevitable and insignificant. But a third reason for denying that Armenian national identity was guarded by the anti-Chalcedonian church is that Armenians were not in fact united under an anti-Chalcedonian banner. Chalcedonianism and the desire for church union were undoubtedly

[68] Sarkissian, K., 1965.
[69] Moses Daskhurants ͨi, III, 5, trans. Dowsett, 1961b, p. 191.
[70] Kojababian, 1977, pp. 112–13.
[71] Sebēos, XXXIII, trans. Macler, 1904, pp. 114–29, 138; Mahé, 1993, p. 473.

opposed, and ultimately vanquished, in the seventh century, in 726, in 862 and in the mid-tenth century especially, but they were just as much part of the tradition of Armenian Christianity as were their opposites.

We are handicapped by the practice, not, of course, confined to Armenia, of victors destroying opponents' writings. The writings of the Albanian patriarch deposed by Katholikos Ełia, for example, were thrown into a river.[72] But the continuing existence of Armenian Chalcedonians, significant in numbers and/or strength and influence, can be deduced from a variety of evidence, both direct and indirect.

Some of it, certainly, is disputable. According to Érémian, whose suggestion some specialists have accepted, the building of three windows in the apse, instead of the usual single one, in several seventh-century churches, results from a Chalcedonian allegiance.[73] Yet fashion, diplomatic compromise or coercion may have played a role, and a challenge to Érémian's dating of the earliest of such windows undermines the argument as a whole. From the proposition that Monophysites were averse on doctrinal grounds to figural representation, particularly of Christ, in religious art it would follow that there were Chalcedonian sympathies where such representations occur. But this proposition has been challenged and in Armenia we find non-Chalcedonian church leaders, Vrtᶜanēs Kᶜertᶜoł and John III, defending figural representations. Curiously it is also true that in the tenth century some Armenians did explicitly associate images with Chalcedonianism. When the katholikos Vahan was deposed in 969, he was accused of trying to renew the errors of the Council of Chalcedon by introducing images into the church. The justification for such an association is not clear, but perhaps the role of middle Byzantine church decoration in stimulating emotion and heightening the liturgical experience made it a natural one. The paintings in the church at Tatᶜew, including Heaven, the prophets, apostles and pontiffs, were so well done that one could not, apparently, tell which were artificial colours or living beings.[74]

The existence of a 'Chalcedonian' party is more explicitly attested by the production, in Armenian, of Chalcedonian literature and of anti-Chalcedonian tracts whose purpose must have been, in part, to persuade members of the 'party' to abandon it. Of the former, only a little survives. The so-called *Narratio de rebus Armeniae*, surviving only in a Greek translation, was composed about 700 to relate Armenian–Byzantine ecclesiatical relations from a Chalcedonian point of view.[75] On the other side, amongst others, we can count two (one lost) of the three

---

[72] Moses Daskhurantsᶜi, III, 7, trans. Dowsett, 1961b, p. 193.
[73] See above, ch. 7 p. 161 and n. 48.
[74] Stephen Orbelean, *History of the House of Sisakan*, XLIX, trans. Brosset, 1864, I, p. 150.
[75] Garitte, 1952.

parts of the history by the late tenth-century Ukhtanēs, bishop of Sebas-teia and the *Root of Faith* by his contemporary, Anania of Narek. They complement our sources' more direct references to Chalcedonianism in tenth-century Armenia.

Chalcedonian sympathies were not a new development in the tenth century. The 862 attempt to restore church union (ended in 726) is a complex issue, for there are uncertainties about the negotiations; for example, scholarly opinion as to authenticity and the exact date of all the Byzantine patriarch Photius' letters about union has varied, Byzantine authors are almost completely silent about them, and nor are they men-tioned in the early tenth-century *Histories* by John Katholikos or Thomas Artsruni. But they are mentioned by the eleventh-century Stephen Asoḷik and it is generally agreed that they are to be associated with Photius and the future king Ashot Bagratuni. The outcome was neither union nor its unequivocal rejection, but toleration (in Armenia). Photius seems to have resumed discussion in about 881. As we have seen, Chalcedonianism was subsequently particularly strong in Siwnikᶜ and Vaspurakan, and the issue was a sensitive one and caused some tension. It was fear of criticism which prevented John from visiting Constantinople, and perhaps it was the same concern, a desire to avoid provoking scandal and division, which explains his omission of the Photius–Ashot negotiations, and Thomas's continuator's omission of the ones undertaken by King Gagik. Thomas himself criticizes Gagik's original choice of the Saving Name as the dedication of one of the churches he built, seeming to think it had Chalcedonian implications and terming Gagik 'not rightly inclined to the faith'.[76] Gagik opted for Peter instead, a relatively unusual choice, found also in Siwnikᶜ with a church built sometime after 885 by Princess Miriam, and at Tatᶜew, where the dedication is to Peter and Paul. The context, the Siwnian preference and the association of Peter with the Papacy suggest that Gagik's choice was not an insignificant one.

Finally, neither the maintenance of a sense of Armenian identity, nor its assertion, nor even the assertion of Armenian independence were ruled out by the sharing of doctrine or by the choice, for church dedications, of honorands whose veneration was shared with other Christians rather than of narrowly national ones. That they were not emerges most clearly in the case of King Gagik's Vaspurakan. Whereas Tatᶜew's St Peter's and St Paul's paintings resembled German ones, Gagik's palatine church of the Holy Cross was far from an example of cultural subordination to the west, drawing as it did on a number of artistic influences and having many elements of originality. Then there are the legends that two of the twelve apostles, Thaddaeus and Bartholomew, had worked in Armenia, which made it possible to assert that the Armenian church was an

---

[76] Thomas, III, 29, trans. Thomson, 1985, p. 318 and his n. 6.

apostolic foundation and an autonomous church. The assertion, citing both apostles, was first made explicitly by the katholikos John in the *History* which he wrote at Gagik's court. John's use of Bartholomew is of particular interest since the locations of legends about Bartholomew in Armenia are the border zones of Vaspurakan and in Siwnik^c. One of Bartholomew's functions was, probably, to lend extra glory and status to the new kingdom of Vaspurakan and its dynasty. Probably at a lower level too, the Chalcedonian element in the Armenian church seems to have remained and felt just as 'Armenian' as its opponents, well into the eleventh century. Armenian Chalcedonians were characterized by bilinguilism and trilinguilism, used Armenian rites and traditions, and avoided merging, or identification, with their Georgian and Greek co-religionists. Thus though these co-religionists pressed Armenian Chalcedonians to celebrate the litugy in Georgian or Greek, the late tenth-century Chalcedonian David of Tayk^c preferred an Armenian translation he commissioned, from Arabic, and the late eleventh-century prince Gabriel of Melitene is described by the twelfth-century historian William of Tyre as Greek by religion, Armenian by race, language and custom.[77]

Christianity had played an important role in the forging of a sense of national identity, and it was to foster it after 1071. A related factor was pride in heritage, and a particular perception of the past. This too was to sustain Armenian national identity in the centuries, mostly weary, to come.

[77] Arutjunova-Fidanjan, 1988–9 and 1991.

11

The Third Millennium, 1071 to the Present

The two major landmarks in Armenian history after the Byzantine annexations and the Seljuk victory at Manazkert in 1071 are the twelfth- to fourteenth-century kingdom in Cilicia, and the genocide of 1915 in the Turkish Ottoman Empire. The recent collapse of the Soviet Union, which engendered new prospects and attitudes for Armenians at home, in their newly independent republic, and abroad, may prove to be a third.

The Aftermath of Manazkert

After 1071 Armenia itself was controlled by the Seljuks, but much previously Byzantine territory nearby was controlled by Armenians. The most notable of these was Philaretus, once *strategus* at Romanopolis in Sophene, who effectively dominated Cilicia and north Syria between 1072 and 1086. Philaretus played some part in the deaths of two of his rivals, T'oṙnik Mamikonean of Sasun, who refused Philaretus' summons to submit, and Gagik of Ani, though it was on Byzantine orders that Gagik died, in about 1077. The others, only the Artsruni brothers, Atom and Abusahl, since Gagik of Kars had died in 1069, died, without his help, soon after.

Philaretus had many compatriots amongst his subjects, for the Seljuk conquest had inspired large-scale migration. Edessa, which he took in 1077, and Melitene were full of refugees. Antioch, offered to Philaretus by the troops of the deceased Armenian governor, Vasak, son of Gregory Magistros, was, by 1098, about one-third Armenian. Samosata, in the twelfth century, housed Armenian clergy and Armenian heretics, (Arewordik^c or sun worshippers, probably Zoroastrians). Most of the

Armenians will have been from southern Armenia. From the north many migrants went to Tiflis, and some to the Ukraine.

Despite this context of disruption, some Armenian scholarly culture continued. Katholikos Gregory II (1066–1105) *Vkayasēr*, brother of Vasak of Antioch, who resigned his position rather than live under Philaretus, had Greek and Syriac acts of the martyrs translated into Armenian. John Sarkawag (died 1129) studied philosophy. The *vardapet* Aristakēs of Lastivert wrote, between 1072 and 1087, a history covering 1000–71. Their near-contemporary the monk-priest Matthew of Edessa wrote a three-part chronicle covering the years 952–1136, whose third part, and its continuation, to 1162, by Gregory the Priest, are particularly valuable for their evidence regarding western Crusader activity in the region.

Armenians in the Time of the Crusades, 1097–1375

1   *Cilicia and Armenia before the coming of the Mongols, 1097–1220*

A complete assessment of the Armenian kingdom of Cilicia would involve careful consideration of the western Crusaders and of the Papacy, which lie outside the scope of this book. Put briefly, the Crusaders appeared in the area in 1097, soon took over several places which had Armenian populations, including Jerusalem, Antioch and Edessa; their lords and military orders (the Templars, the Teutonic knights and the Hospitallers) subsequently had much to do with Armenian rulers in Cilicia, and the Papacy negotiated repeatedly with the Armenian-Cilician church about union.

Two major Armenian principalities had been established in Cilicia in the late eleventh century. The founder of one, Ruben, had served both Philaretus and Gagik of Ani, and he was perhaps related to Gagik. The Rubenids had two external problems, Byzantine attempts to control them, and Crusader ambitions, but from their base at Vahka they extended their domination over their rivals the Hetᶜumids (whose base was further west, at Lambron), some towns, and a coastal outlet. The first to attain effective independence was Tᶜoros II (1148–68).

Cilician Armenia's rapprochement with Rome is perhaps best explained by its general political context, papal approval seeming a precondition of western military and political friendship and support. An embassy was sent to the Papacy in 1145. The orthodoxy of the Byzantine church's Christology was recognized in 1179, at the Synod of Hṙomkla, seat of the Katholikosate since Gregory III (1113–66) had acquired it, *c.*1150, from the countess of Edessa. And an agreement with Rome to implement union followed in 1198. At this time Prince

Leo II (1187–1219) and the Crusaders needed each other's support against Saladin, Muslim conqueror of Jerusalem, which had been a (Latin) Crusader kingdom between 1099 and 1187.

Another part of this deal was that Leo acquired royal status, thereby becoming King Leo I. He was crowned in Tarsus on 6 January (the date the Armenian church celebrates both Epiphany and Christmas together) 1198, anointed by his Katholikos, his crown sent by the Roman (western) emperor Henry VI and presented by the archbishop of Mainz. His new status was recognized by Byzantium, and the unity of the new kingdom was eventually ensured by the marriage, in 1226, of his heiress, Isabel, to the son of Constantine of Lambron, King Het^cum I (1226–70).

Leo I's Cilicia was rich and cultured. The Armenian occupation was predominantly non-urban, the capital, Sis, an unwalled village, but it benefitted from west–east trade. Leo struck his own coins, the first Armenian coins since the Artaxiads', granted rights to Italian merchants from Venice and Genoa, and rebuilt, in 1206, the harbour of Korikos, second port of the kingdom after Ayas.

Cilicia's relations with her Latin neighbours were close. Her coinage bore similarities to that of the early Crusader rulers. Her aristocracy and monarchy, under Norman influence, became more 'feudal'. There were various marriage alliances, one of whose consequences was entanglement, in 1201–19, in succession disputes over Antioch, which later fell under Armenian domination. There had also been marriages with Jerusalem, where an Armenian presence and interest continued. Katholikos Gregory III had attended councils there, in 1136 and, after a Latin church council in Antioch in 1139, in 1140 or 1141. The Armenians' position in Jerusalem even weathered its Muslim conquest. For Saladin trusted the Armenians more than he did the Greeks or the Latin Christians, who retained domination of the Holy Places until 1291, and he guaranteed Armenian security, property and freedom of worship.

There were also reciprocal Cilician–Crusader cultural influences. Nearly two-thirds of the castles of Cilicia are 'Armenian', and through them and through the churches associated with them there may have been an Armenian input into west European architecture. The reverse, European influence on Armenian culture, is apparent in literature and in the excellent and distinctive miniature painting, in illuminated manuscripts, which constitutes most of Armenian Cilicia's surviving art. The western image of the Lamb of God appears in the 1166 Gospels from the school of Hřomkla, and in those made at Skewřa in 1193 for Nersēs of Lambron (died 1198) and his brother. It was used by Nersēs as his personal symbol. This Nersēs, great-nephew of another, the poet, theologian and philosopher, Katholikos Nersēs the Gracious (1166–73), and brother of Katholikos Gregory III, was archbishop of Tarsus, and a scholar. He collaborated with a monk of Antioch on a translation of what had for several centuries been the dominant monastic Rule in the west, the Rule of St Benedict of Nursia. He produced a translation of the *Ecloga* of the Byzantine emperor Leo III, perhaps hoping that Cilician Armenians, currently lacking a written law code, would use it. He also wrote a commentary on the liturgy, itself enriched by his own and by Katholikos Nersēs' and Katholikos Gregory II's work.

The highlights of Armenia proper were likewise phenomena of the later twelfth century onwards. In the eleventh, the Seljuk conquerors had allowed local rulers to continue in return for submission and taxes. An Artsruni offshoot lingered in Vaspurakan, sheltered at Amiwk and Alt͑a-mar, its memory preserved in the updating of the Artsruni history in the mid-twelfth century. The kingdoms of Tashir, conquered only in 1113, of Balk͑ in Siwnik͑, and the two Albanian kingdoms, Dizak-K͑tish and Arts͑akh, survived, the latter three in amalgamation. In 1071 the king of Dizak-K͑tish was bequeathed Balk͑ by his brother-in-law Gregory. His kingdom subsequently passed by marriage to Arts͑akh. Arts͑akh itself had become a kingdom by 1000, held by descendants of the presiding prince who had been murdered in 822. In the thirteenth century it began to be known as Karabağ. Mountainous Karabağ in the twentieth century has been a bone of contention between Armenia and Azerbaijan. Yet in general the domination of Armenia by a nomad people, not all obedient to their central government, must have been destructive, just as it was further west, where annual raids led to economic, administrative and ecclesiastical disruption.

The twelfth century however brought major changes. The Seljuk empire, the Sultanate of Rum, with its centre at Iconium, disintegrated. The Albanian kingdoms and the Armenians to their north-west eventually fell under the sway of Georgia, whose Queen Tamara (1184–1213), whose armies included Armenians, defeated the Sultan in 1204. New families were then established in Armenia, under the overlordship of the Zak͑arean dynasty, some ancient, others genuinely new. The Orbeleans, a branch of the Mamikoneans who had settled in Georgia in the late ninth century, and who held there the position of commander-in-chief in the eleventh and twelfth centuries, settled in Siwnik͑. Ani grew increasingly wealthy from the much improved trade which passed through Armenia to the Black Sea, where Trebizond had become the Byzantine capital after Constantinople fell to the Crusaders in 1204, and where there were Genoese and Venetian merchants.

With this political and economic revival came a cultural revival. Notable buildings were erected, in Ani for example, where the rich merchant Tigran Honents͑ endowed his church of St Gregory, decorated with frescoes by Georgian painters, with estates and precious objects in 1215. The monastery of Gełard, which had been deserted since the early tenth century, was revived by the Zak͑areans and is still active in the late twentieth century. Samuel of Ani (born *c*.1100) wrote a chronicle, ending *c*.1180, and Mkhit^car of Ani, at the end of the twelfth and beginning of the thirteenth centuries, wrote a *History*, of which only part survives. The literary revival was however predominantly a phenomenon of eastern Armenia. The first to attempt some codification of Armenian law was the *vardapet* David of Gandzak (died 1140), in his early twelfth-century *Penitential*. The second, Mkhit^car Gosh (*c*.1130–1213), from the city of Gandzak, produced a code in 1184 at the request of the katholikos of Albania. Mkhit^car also wrote a short Albanian chronicle, its surviving version ending in 1162, and he founded a monastery and school at Nor Getik, in 1213 named Goshavank^c after him.[1]

2 Armenians and Mongols, 1220–c.1300

The thirteenth century saw the establishment of a new world power, the empire of the Mongols, from which in some respects some Armenians benefited. The Mongols first defeated Armenian and Georgian forces in 1220, and they completed the conquest of Armenia after three further invasions, the last 1236–44, taking Ani and Kars in 1239, Karin in 1242, and defeating the Seljuk Sultan in 1244.

In Armenia itself, the great families surrendered, and retained their property. Some of them made Mongol marriage alliances, worked in Mongol administration, visited and joined the Mongol court. They gave lands to the church, in some cases, perhaps to prevent their acquisition by Mongols and to avoid taxation. For from the mid-1250s the church enjoyed exemption, though this theory was not always put into practice. But Mongol rule also had negative effects, on economy, society and religion. Severe taxes, imposed in 1243, led to attempted rebellion in 1248/9 and to harsh punishment. Imperial reorganization in 1256 put Armenians under the control of Iran, and brought new Mongol groups to the area. Military service could take Armenians far from home. Another rebellion, again heavily punished, occurred in 1259–61. In addition, Armenians inevitably became entangled in Mongol rebellions, rivalries and disunity, and there were sporadic outbreaks of local religious persecution.

Yet for Cilicia, now threatened by the rising power of the Mamluks of Egypt, the Mongols proved providential. A Cilician-Mongol alliance was established. And Cilician prosperity increased. For not only did the Mongol empire offer extensive commercial opportunities, but the Mamluk conquest of the Holy Land made Cilicia an obvious base for western

---

[1] For chronicle, Dowsett, 1958; for laws, Mkhit ^car Gosh, in T ^corosyan (ed.), 1975, and Bastameants (ed.), 1880.

merchants. In Armenia proper however the increased trade had a mixed effect. Erzurum was a major station, and both the growth of Tabriz, and a shift of routes southwards, benefited the Van region. But it destroyed Ani, a city in the twelfth century, a village in the sixteenth, a ruin in the eighteenth.

Prosperity and international contacts in turn invigorated culture. In Cilicia the school of Hṙomkla continued to flourish, producing the distinguished and inventive artist Tᶜoros Ṙoslin, who undertook six Gospel books between 1256 and 1268. He developed narrative illustration, often using scenes from daily life, and he introduced typological references in illustration of Gospels. In some of his work the influence of French and Italian art and of some Franciscan ideas is apparent. Some western influence is also detectible within a group of 'royal' manuscripts whose illustrators are anonymous. The Gospel of Prince Vasak (brother of Hetᶜum I), illuminated some time between 1268 and 1284, possibly by Tᶜoros Ṙoslin, is one of the first Armenian manuscripts to incorporate the allegorical Tree of Jesse. A Gospel for Vasak's brother, Archbishop John, illustrated in 1287, draws from French miniature painting of the first half of the thirteenth century, and John's scriptorium at Gṙner, established by 1263, was influenced by Italian art. Royal manuscripts contained pictures of the donors and of their families which suggest that they were not merely offering their manuscripts to Christ, like other donors depicted in other manuscripts, but rather giving their whole life up to divine protection.[2]

The output in Armenia proper includes the Erzincan Bible of 1269, the first known Armenian illustrated Bible. Its artist drew on Byzantine and western prototypes for iconography, and his style shows some influence of Cilician art. Manuscript illumination in Vaspurakan revived in the late thirteenth century in a number of local schools. Their materials betray a lack of money but their illumination is lively and interesting, drawing on daily life, for example weaving. Some compositional characteristics are common to some rugs and to some manuscript illumination. Building continued, in Siwnikᶜ and in Artsᶜakh for example under the patronage of the ruling dynasties. And khachᶜkᶜars were approaching their best, the decoration becoming more elaborate, and openwork sculpture used.

Scholarship, especially history, also continued, in eastern Armenia. From Nor Getik there came the *vardapet* Kirakos of Gandzak (1203–71). Briefly captured, and used as a secretary, by the Mongols (in 1236), Kirakos wrote a two-part history, the second, longer part, an important source for the period 1220 onwards. Vardan of the East (*c.* 1200–71) wrote an *Historical Compilation* (proceeding from the Creation to 1267), a brief geography, a grammar, biblical commentaries and hymns. Bishop

[2] Der Nersessian, 1978, pp. 148–50.

Stephen Orbelean's (died 1304) *History* of Siwnik^c included an account of its geography and many quotations of inscriptions. He was the first to make extensive use of such material. A copy of the Artsruni *History* was made at Stephen's request in 1303 at Aḷt^camar. Another historian was the monk Mkhit^car of Ayrivank^c (1222–91) whose abbreviated universal history ends in 1289.

Cilician scholarship too included historical work. Abbot Gregory of Akner (who died about 1335) wrote *The History of the Nation of the Archers*, covering 1229/30–73. A chronicle of events in Cilicia and nearby, 951–1273, which is attributed to Constable Smbat (1208–76) elder brother of King Het^cum is probably not, in its surviving form, by Smbat,[3] but is based on his work. It was continued to 1331 by another anonymous writer. There were also legal advances. Smbat, having already translated parts of the *Assizes of Antioch* for use in Cilicia, revised Mkhit^car Gosh's law code in 1265. The penitential text, the *Advice on Confession*, which is attributed to the *vardapet* Moses, and was written before 1305, drew on some western ideas as well as on Armenian tradition.

3 Decline, c.1285–c.1400

Armenian decline was mostly a fourteenth-century phenomenon, though the glory days were already under threat in the later thirteenth. The kingdom of Arts^cakh was terminated in 1266 with the execution of its king. The Mamluks were not checked: they defeated the Mongols and their Cilician allies, invaded Cilicia, forced a disadvantageous peace in 1285, imposed heavy tribute and punished default. They had taken Crusader Acre in 1291, and they captured Armenian Hṙomkla in 1292, forcing the Katholikosate to move to Sis. They took Ayas in 1337. Meanwhile in the Mongol Empire Islam had become the official religion in 1304, soon afterwards religious persecution became a matter of policy, and the empire itself was to disintegrate in the second half of the fourteenth century. There was a series of ruinous invasions of Armenia between 1357 and 1403. Tens of thousands of Armenians were transported as slaves, Ayrarat was devastated and Van pillaged and razed, though its walls survived, in 1387. By 1400 much of Armenia had passed to a Turkmen dynasty, the Kara Koyunlu (the Black Sheep), first established there only a century before.

Cilician policy in these years was to strengthen the Cypriot and Papal alliances. King Leo I had begun the close involvement with Cyprus through his second marriage. Franciscan and Dominican teachers had

---

[3] Dédéyan, 1980.

established a presence in the late thirteenth century, the Franciscans in Cilicia, where they had a convent at Sis by 1289, and the Dominicans in Armenia proper. Het^cum II (acceeded 1289 and died 1307, having reigned and resigned three times) converted to Catholicism and took the Franciscan habit. There were often envoys from king and katholikos at Avignon, the papal residence from 1309 to 1376. In 1341 Pope Benedict XII (1334–42) requested a proclamation of union. This request was granted by a synod at Sis, whose exact date is uncertain and which also refuted 117 criticisms of Armenian teaching and practice. These criticisms indirectly reflected both the unpopularity of union, and the fact of resistance to it, in Cilicia, Armenia and elsewhere. In Jerusalem for example the Armenians had refused to accept the pro-Latin canons of a synod of 1307 and in 1311 the Mamluk Sultan of Egypt recognized the Armenian patriarch of Jerusalem as independent within his sultanate.

But neither Rome nor Cyprus could save Cilicia. In 1375 the Mamluks brought the kingdom, which had passed by marriage to the (French) Lusignan family of Cyprus in 1342, to an end, taking the royal family captive, and occupying the capital, Sis.

The state of fourteenth-century culture was less depressing than was its political context. The last great Cilician artist was the prolific Sargis Pitsak, who sometimes worked at Sis, but mainly at Drazark. In Armenia, T^coros of Tarōn worked at the monastery of Gladzor, between 1307 and 1346. His work shows some western influence, especially of thirteenth-century French art. Building work too continued for a while. The church of the White Virgin (Spitakawor), for example, was completed in 1321. This is decorated with sculptures, including depictions of the donors. Nor did learning suddenly disappear. Abbot Esayi of Nich^c made Gladzor a 'second Athens'. Gregory of Tat^cew (*c.*1346–1410), who taught philosophy and theology, was familiar with Greek and Latin authors and with western scholastics. Between 1320 and 1350 a number of western works, by authors such as Thomas Aquinas, were translated into Armenian. And Latin influence on the Armenian Bible can be seen with the incorporation of the modern Latin chapter divisions which had been devised by the English archbishop Stephen Langton (died 1228).[4] But a sign of the times was the abandonment of Goshavank^c in the mid-fourteenth century, an abandonment which lasted until the seventeenth.

The Twilight Years, *c.*1400–*c.*1828

Armenian institutions and communities limped into the modern world enfeebled if not shattered. Their church, in the fifteenth century, was not

---

[4] Smalley, 1941, for Langton and chapter divisions.

united. In the Holy Land, Mamluk religious intolerance and financial demands caused the Armenian community to decline. In Armenia, ancient aristocratic society was by the sixteenth century almost completely destroyed. The Mamikoneans had lost their hold in Siwnik[c] early in the fifteenth century, and southern Armenia was now ruled by two Turkmen dynasties, the Black and the White Sheep, the White based at Diyarbakır, the Black at Van. Only the descendants of the Siwnian dynasty remained. Such local leaders, not all of princely origin, enjoyed a new, all-purpose, title of *melik*, maintained castles, had about 1,000–2,000 infantry, had sovereign rights over their subjects, and collected taxes, transferring much of their income, as tribute, to their overlords. There were four *melik*doms in Karabağ (and a fifth established in the seventeenth century) and eight in Siwnik[c] established in the middle of the fifteenth century by the Black Sheep (Kara Koyunlu) as buffer territories.[5]

Outside Armenia, Armenians became established, in the late medieval and early modern periods, in a great variety of places: Cyprus, Italy, the Ukraine, Russia, the Crimea, Romania, Poland, Mongolia, China, Transylvania and India. Those who remained at home were to be troubled by three great powers: Turkey (the Ottoman Empire), Persia and Russia.

The Ottoman Turks' empire rose out of the wrecked Sultanate of Rum. Then they took Constantinople, thereby ending the Byzantine Empire, in 1453; they defeated the White Sheep, who were then controlling Persia, Armenia and Mesopotamia, in 1473, gained Armenia in the 1510s and 1530s, and destroyed Mamluk rule, thereby acquiring the Holy Land, in 1516–17.

The effects of Ottoman rule over Armenians varied from place to place. The Turks' non-Muslim subjects were grouped by religion into *millet*s, which retained their own laws, the members obeying their head, and their heads being responsible to the government. Armenians initially fell under the jurisdiction of the sees of Ējmiatsin, Alt[c]amar, Sis and Jerusalem, and of the Armenian patriarchate of Constantinople, established by Sultan Mehmed II in 1461. Then in 1863 this patriarchate was formally recognized, by the Ottoman government, as the Armenians' sole representative.[6] In Armenia itself, the devastated southern lands were repopulated with Kurds. Unfortunately the Muslim Kurds often pillaged the Armenians and they found no redress from the authorities. In the Holy Land, Sultan Selim I guaranteed, in 1517, Armenian possessions and Armenian ecclesiastical rites and institutions from disturbance. But custodianship of the Holy Places was always to be a matter of rivalry and sometimes, due to legal expenses and bribery, of expense. The Armenians' first rivals were the Greek Orthodox, who had been granted the same concessions as

---

[5] Hewsen, 1972, 1973–4.
[6] Bardakjian, 1982.

them, and with whom they shared the major shrines. The rivalry could sometimes assume an international character, Orthodox Russia supporting the Greek Church, Catholic European powers the Latin. In 1847 for example, the Latin patriarchate of Jerusalem was revived with French backing.

Once the Ottoman Empire had been established, some revivals were possible. Inevitably Armenia resumed a position as the battleground of great powers. Turkish wars with Safavid Persia began early in the sixteenth century, but in 1639 the two powers agreed upon Turkish authority over western Armenia and Persian authority over eastern Armenia. Another revival was that of western contacts. In the seventeenth century Capuchins and Jesuits attempted to promote Roman Catholicism in the Ottoman Empire. Since apostacy from Islam was punishable by death, their prime targets were the Turks' Christian subjects, whose own ecclesiastical authorities opposed them, sometimes enlisting governmental support. Such opposition had a financial besides a religious cause, the *millets*' tax being fixed, regardless of their size. A third revival was of Armenian hope for foreign aid against Muslim masters. Louis XIV of France was first targeted, by the Katholikos of Cilicia, in 1663. Pope Innocent XI, the Elector Palatine and Peter the Great of Russia were canvassed, from Armenia, in 1699.

For some time it was Persia which offered Armenians the best opportunities. Across the river from the Persian capital, Isfahan, was New Julfa, whither the Persian Shah Abbas I (1587–1629) had removed the population of the border town of Julfa on the Araxes in 1604. New Julfa had a population of 30,000 in 1620. Armenian merchants were entrusted with the silk trade, establishing a trading network which reached as far as western Europe, Scandinavia and India, and many became wealthy. But these happy conditions did not last, and by 1700 persecution and taxation were stimulating emigration. Many went to India, where Armenian merchants were favoured by Indian rulers and prospered. In 1686 Armenians made the agreement with the British East India Company which gave Britain a monopoly on the transport of goods.

Armenian art was, naturally, affected by all these political developments, as it reflected the origins, conditions and contacts of the communities who produced it. Crimean work, for example, generally exhibited a Cilician or Byzantine style, and at Constantinople Greek and Russian icon painting was influential. In Armenia, the schools at Van and Khizan were influenced by Persian Muslim illumination. At New Julfa, art profited from international connections and from the attraction to it of Armenian artists from elsewhere, so Persian, Chinese and European influences are discernible. The printing of Armenian books was related to the eastern communities and to their trading interests, the books themselves intended for a merchant market. The first was printed in

Plate 13   The Gates of Paradise, from a Gospel of 1587 illustrated at Julfa, the John Rylands University Library of Manchester, Arm. 20, fo.8.

1641 in New Julfa, and in 1666 the printer Oskan produced a Bible, in Amsterdam. The first press in Armenia itself, established at Ējmiatsin, in 1771, was financed by a merchant from India.

The next major political development was the extension of Russian authority into Armenia. In 1722 Persian Armenia suffered invasion by Peter the Great (1682–1725) and rebellion led by David Bek, an Armenian from Georgia. David, using the fort of Tat^cew as his base, established a principality, from four *melik*doms. The results were Turkish invasion and the division of Persia's territory between Russians and Turks in 1724. David's principality subsequently fell, to the Turks, in 1730. Russian aggression revived under Catherine the Great (1762–96) and Alexander I (1801–25). Russia annexed the Crimea in 1783, eastern Georgia in 1801, and the rest of Georgia by 1804, and she gained Karabağ by treaty with Persia in 1813. Persia withdrew from Armenia entirely in 1828, when the Russian–Persian frontier was fixed at the Araxes. Russia's further acquisitions came from Turkey.

It was in the later eighteenth century that the T^condrakian heretics, not mentioned in Armenian sources after the fourteenth century, reappeared. There was a revival, around Karin, in the 1770s, and T^condrakian migrants from Turkey are attested in Ark^cweli in Russian Armenia in 1837. A copy, made in Tarōn in 1782, of their manual, *The Key of Truth*, was discovered in 1838. Its text has been thought by some scholars to go back to the ninth century,[7] but its doctrine differs in some significant respects from that of the medieval T^condrakians.

Awakenings, Dreams and Nightmares: *c*.1820–1918

The nineteenth century saw Armenia attract the attention of other westerners, besides Russians. Commercial contacts existed already, but now American missionary work and European scholarly research helped to spread western ideas among Armenians and information about Armenian matters among westerners.

American Protestant missionaries targeted the Ottoman Empire, and so, like their Catholic predecessors, the Ottomans' Christian subjects, in 1831, with a mission to Constantinople. An Armenian Evangelical Church was established in 1846 and by 1908 Protestantism had over 15,000 communicants, over 40,000 adherents, fifty-four educational establishments and 130 churches.[8]

Western scholarly investigation was often connected with the European diplomatic presence. Major discoveries began with the suggestion, in the

---

[7] Conybeare, 1898a; Garsoïan, 1967a, for résumé and discussion.
[8] Mirak, 1983, p. 24.

1820s, of a French scholar, J. Saint-Martin that the city which, according to Moses of Khoren, Queen Semiramis had built at Van, should be searched for. A German scholar, Schultz, discovered cuneiform inscriptions at Toprak Kale, and his copies reached Paris, despite his murder by bandits in Kurdistan. Armenia also benefited from European interests in biblical and in ancient history, since these subjects led the interested to the civilizations of Assyria and Persia and these in turn involved Armenia. After French and British endeavours, in the 1840s and 1850s, uncovered Assyrian monuments, Henry Layard, seeking further Assyrian antiquities, copied cuneiform texts from the cliff at Van. The British Museum subsequently commissioned excavations at Van, under the supervision of Layard's assistant, Rassam, in the late 1870s. The remains of a temple were found, and from 1880 the Urartian of the inscriptions was deciphered and translated, in which achievement the Oxford professor A. H. Sayce played a leading role. French translations of Armenian historical works were published in Paris and in St Petersburg between 1836 and 1876. English translations of the Tᶜondrakian *Key of Truth* and of the liturgy were published, in Oxford, in 1898 and 1905, and a catalogue of the British Museum's 143 Armenian manuscripts, in 1913, all by F. C. Conybeare.

Contemporary conditions in Armenia became known in the west from Armenian exiles, from official reports, and also from a stream of publications of western travellers. And as a consequence of the later

Plate 14   The town of Van in the mid-nineteenth century, east side, from C. Texier, Description de l' Arménie, la Perse, et la Mésopotamie 2 vols, (Paris, 1842–52)

nineteenth-century accounts, relief and pressure groups were established, for example the Friends of Armenia, formed in London in 1897. By 1897 they were sorely warranted.

The Ottoman Empire had been declining throughout the nineteenth century and it was particularly threatened by the percolation within it of western ideas of nationalism and liberty. The repercussions for Armenians of both these trends (themselves exemplified in the Balkan revolts of 1875), and of western, especially Russian, interests, had initially been favourable, but ultimately they were fatal.

The Armenians began the nineteenth century with the reputation of 'the loyal community'. They proceeded to increased freedom of expression and educational opportunities, and, consequently, to the rise of an intellectual class, imbued by the 1880s with patriotic and nationalistic sentiment. Their progress followed developments in intellectual culture and scholarship in Russian Armenia and in Europe, at the Benedictine Mkhit^{c}arist monasteries in Venice and Vienna. (The first was established by Abbot Mkhit^{c}ar, originally from Sebasteia, in 1715, the second in 1811, from an earlier house in Trieste itself established in 1773.) It was also a response to external challenge. The American missionaries had inaugurated the first long-running Armenian periodical, a monthly, in Smyrna, in 1839, and had promoted education, including female education, founding girls' boarding schools in 1845 and 1864. In sum, a variety of stimuli engendered a renaissance of Armenian intellectual life within and outside the empire. The patriarchate of Jerusalem, for example, founded a printing press, in 1833, three educational establishments and a monthly periodical, *Sion*. In Constantinople, *Masis*, whose founder was a major influence on later writers, began publication in 1852. Some ninety periodicals were founded between 1840 and 1870, though few lasted. *Bazmavep*, founded in Venice in 1843, proved the most enduring, still published, though retitled, today.

Whereas the emphasis in the 1860s was on journalistic activity, in the 1870s it was on education. In 1878 Patriarchal agents of enquiry recommended a national educational effort, and in 1880 the three main educational pressure groups, founded in 1871, 1876 and 1877, amalgamated. Soon afterwards, with financial help from Armenians outside Turkey, almost every community with some hundred families had a school. And as editions of Armenian historical works were published in Venice, Moscow, Paris, Jerusalem, St Petersburg and Valarshapat, education and journalism inspired in Turkish Armenians an incipient nationalism.

Their feelings were fired also by consciousness of better conditions in Russian Armenia. There, Russian troops and officials provided secure borders, internal stability, and protection for middle-class Armenians, who dominated the urban economy, from exploitation by a contemptuous and envious Georgian nobility. There too, Armenians were allowed to settle in formerly Muslim areas. They enjoyed an increasing prosperity, educational revival and dynamic publications.

In all the circumstances it was natural for Armenians to seek to improve the Armenian lot in Turkey. It was not that Turkish Armenians uniformly suffered atrocious conditions, though certain restrictions, for example exclusion from military and governmental service, did apply to them all. Erzurum, with a large Armenian population, was prosperous, Van one of the most important fortified sites in the empire. In Constantinople, where there were about 250,000 Armenians in 1851, Armenians had always been reasonably well-off and some, indeed, had been powerful. For Turkish officials, who had to collect their own salaries together with the taxes which they were responsible for gathering, were often dependent on Armenian bankers. Such bankers could, consequentially, be influential outside the *millet*, and since the same bankers often financed the patriarchate, they were also very powerful within it.

Conditions were worst in Armenia itself, partly because of Kurdish–Armenian problems. Muslims could apply to Muslim courts, where non-Muslim testimony was originally disallowed, and after 1854, when allowed, usually discounted. Christians were forbidden to bear arms, so self-defence was difficult. Additionally, Christians were subject to more taxes than were Muslims. The governmental demands were heavy and the farming of taxes effectively increased them. And fourthly, Armenians had to give free winter quarters to the Kurds. These problems caused suffering, fear, and emigration to Russia, all recorded by western observers.

Early on, Armenian dreams were of constitutional reform, later they were of better conditions in the east. The former, paradoxically, was more disadvantageous to the Armenian establishment than to the Ottoman government. After a general reform of 1839, forbidding bribery, establishing salaries for officials, regulating taxation and promising freedom of worship and civil equality, the influence of the Armenian bankers declined. So too did that of the church. For Catholic and Protestant Armenians became separate *millet*s in 1831 and 1850, and in 1863 the Armenian National Constitution was approved. This gave the *millet* a democratic, representative system of government, by a National General Assembly, dominated by the laity. But subsequently the Turkish regime itself was targeted. The Assembly took up petitions and complaints. Specific reforms were requested, in 1872 and 1876, but to no avail.

Matters were complicated by the entanglement of foreigners, which provoked an expectation of active interference, and in consequence, Armenian trust and boldness and Turkish suspicion and repression. Russia was involved, as also were the powers of western Europe, especially Britain, concerned about the balance and the inclinations of the powers of the east. Unfortunately for Armenians western humanitarian concerns were concentrated on Balkan Turkey, and British policy was to strengthen Turkey against Russia.

The most fateful western intervention followed the Russian–Turkish Treaty of San Stefano of 1878. This treaty had required Turkish reforms in territory where Armenians lived and whence Russia was to withdraw, to be implemented prior to Russian withdrawal. In the revised version, the Treaty of Berlin, implementation of reform and protection of Armenians from Kurds and Circassians was instead to follow Russian withdrawal, and to be periodically reported to the signatory western powers. The force of the requirement was thereby lost. It was the major role played by Britain in the negotiations leading to the revisions which caused some British people to feel, later, a particular duty to help the Armenians.

It was now that Armenian dreams began to turn into nightmares. The Ottoman government tarried, Britain preferred diplomacy to force, and the West found Balkan issues more important than Armenian ones. Consequently both Turkish and non-Turkish Armenians founded revolutionary groups. The two most important were the socialist Hunchakian Revolutionary Party, formed by Russian Armenians in Geneva in 1887, and the Armenian Revolutionary Federation, or Dashnaktsᶜutᶜiwn, which emerged in 1891, and was based in Tiflis. Dashnaks wanted freedom within the Ottoman Empire, Hunchaks independence from it. Both groups were prepared to use terrorism.

This development alarmed Russia as well as the Turks. Russia was now moving away from liberalism and reform, her authorities perceiving national feeling and socialism as dangers to empire and government. Policies of Russification and repression were being introduced, and revolution and repression proved mutually stimulating. Armenian schools were closed in 1884, despite resistance. Reopened, under closer supervision, in 1886, they were closed again in January 1896, in angry, suspicious response to some Armenians in Europe seeking British assistance following massacres in Turkey in 1895–6. Societies and libraries were closed, and references in print to the Armenian people or nation forbidden, in 1898. Nicholas II (1894–1917) took over management of church property in 1903, provoking violence and then retaliatory, Tatar, violence against the Armenians in 1905.

The miseries of 1895–6 which had indirectly provoked this Russian hostility were the responsibility of the perpetrators, but considered chronologically they were caused by the Armenian revolutionaries. In 1890 there had been a near-riot, begun by a Hunchak, in Constantinople. In 1893 revolutionaries had posted seditious placards. In 1894 peasants in Sasun, encouraged by two Hunchaks, had refused to pay the tribute traditionally demanded by local Kurds in addition to government taxes. This refusal led to weeks of slaughter. In 1895 a demonstration in

Constantinople was violently suppressed, and another, small, incident led to the massacre of about 1,000 in Trebizond, to be followed by massacres in a number of other cities. In 1895–6 there was rebellion at the town of Zeytun, (in the mountains near Maraş), in 1896 the Ottoman Bank in Constantinople was seized, briefly, by Dashnaks, and again violence followed. Western ambassadors protested, the USA safeguarded American personnel and property, and relief work was undertaken, but otherwise no western support for Armenians, except more schemes for reform, was forthcoming.

Many Armenians now saw emigration as their best option, despite its attendant expense and difficulty. Some 20,000 went to Russia in 1892–3; 12,500 to the USA between 1891 and 1898; 51,950 (some from Russia) to the USA between 1899 and 1914.[9]

Yet hopes for Armenia were to be revived, and dashed, twice more. In 1908 the Committee of Union and Progress, known as the Young Turks, forced the Sultan to concede constitutional reform. There was a slight decline in emigration and some encouragement felt in the USA to return home. But the possibility of rebuilding Armenia was short-lived. The Young Turks adopted pan-Turkism, the policy of Turkicization of Ottoman subjects. Some 20,000 people in Adana, Cilicia, were massacred in 1909, purportedly to prevent an imminent Armenian uprising. Muslim refugees from the Balkans were resettled on Armenian lands. More auspiciously, in February 1914 the government agreed on another reform scheme.

There were by then about 1.5 million Armenians in Russian Armenian territories, which included Kars and Erevan. Their number in Turkey is harder to establish. Ottoman government statistics and some modern Turkish scholars acknowledge only 1,295,000 Armenians, including 660,000 in the six provinces which lay in historic Armenia, comprising 17 per cent of those provinces' people. But the figures compiled, in 1912, by the Armenian patriarchate in Constantinople were 2,100,000 and 1,018,000 respectively, suggesting that the Armenian population of the six provinces was 38.9 per cent, as against 25.4 per cent Turks and 16.3 per cent Kurds.

The First World War brought a second prospect of a new world. Since Russia sided with Britain, and Turkey joined their foe, Germany, the other western powers no longer wished to strengthen Turkey. Their politicians could now afford humanitarianism and were glad to denigrate the Turks and to express commitment to the oppressed subjects, hoping to justify their cause to their own people, and to gain support in Turkey. Early in 1915 Turkey was disastrously defeated by Russia with whom, of course, she shared a frontier in Armenia. Genocide followed. It is not

---

[9] Mirak, 1983, pp. 45, 290.

surprising, given previous Armenian agitation, earlier threats, real or imagined, from outsiders, and the current participation of Russian and diaspora Armenians in fighting for the Allies, that the Turkish government was suspicious of Armenians. But even more important was the Ottoman Empire's continuing decline and hence its search for a new identity. By 1912 it had lost nearly 20 per cent of the population, and over 33 per cent of the territory which it had incorporated in 1908.[10] Retaining only a toe-hold in Europe, it had become an Anatolian, Muslim, and shocked state. Not only did the Armenians now stand out as an apparently deviant, and dangerous, minority, but the possibility of one day losing eastern Anatolia to Armenian nationalism was one of a fatal blow certainly to the power of Turkey, and perhaps even to the state itself. It seemed necessary both to deny Armenians independence and to claim their homeland as the homeland of the Turks. These factors, present though less marked twenty years earlier, may also have contributed to the violence of the later 1890s.

Following the Russian victory in 1915 Armenians serving in Ottoman forces were demobilized and organized into labour groups, in the February, and then massacred in the April. It had been ordered that Armenians be moved out of the regions near the war front. But it is probable that few deportees were anticipated to arrive at their destinations, which were the Syrian desert and Mesopotamian valley, and that those who did were expected to survive the inhospitable terrain and hostile tribesmen only briefly. Furthermore the deportations were not actually confined to frontier regions. They developed into large-scale massacres. Some evidence, whose authenticity has been disputed, suggests that the central government had decided to exterminate the Armenians, and had issued orders accordingly. Estimates have varied, but it seems that about 1 million people were killed. April 24, the date of the arrest of the leaders of the Armenian community, is Armenian Martyrs' Day.

The Armenians' situation was next complicated by the Russian Revolution of 1917. Amid the ensuing turmoil, the Allies' Caucasian front collapsed, the Russian Armenians opposed the Turkish advance, their Republic of Armenia declared independence in May 1918, and Turkey granted some 3,861 square miles of territory by treaty in June 1918. And Armenians hoped for yet more from the Armistice, which ended the First World War in November 1918; for further territory and for security from the Turks. The Allies, whom they had supported, had repeatedly promised these things.

But, as so often this century, though understandably, the victors were ceasing hostilities before concluding their work, and they proved unable to resume it later. First, the unprecedented slaughter of this war left the

[10] Melson, 1986, pp. 71–3.

western powers lacking money, men, and nerve to enforce their wishes; second, their interests lay further south than Armenia; third, their own rivalries and the political considerations which had obtained in the nineteenth century resurfaced.

It was, consequently, possible neither to protect Armenians in Turkey, nor to guarantee the borders of any new Armenian state.

Armenians in the Modern World

1 The mid-twentieth century

The frontiers of the new Armenia took some time to be resolved. In 1919, at the Paris Peace Conference, Britain proposed borders running from Lake Sevan to the Cilician coast, incorporating Trebizond and a Black Sea coastal stretch to its west. It left Karabağ (where Armenians were the majority, though they were outnumbered by Muslim Azerbaijanis in the province of Elizavetpol to which Karabağ belonged), theoretically provisionally, under Azerbaijani control. In Turkey, meanwhile, Armenians remained insecure, with thousands massacred in 1920 and some 50,000 emigrating in 1921.

The question was finally settled in 1920. First, the Treaty of Sèvres, in August, granted the Armenian Republic a territory somewhat smaller than the 1919 proposal, its exact borders, adjudicated by President Woodrow Wilson of the USA, announced in November. But there was no-one willing or able to enforce these terms. In September Turkey had invaded Armenia and in early December, by the Treaty of Alexandropol, Turkey allowed to Armenia a much smaller territory, some 10,425 square miles, keeping Kars for herself, while Azerbaijan gained the disputed Nakhchawan and Zangezur. Before it was ratified however the Bolsheviks took over Armenia's government. The border was finally fixed by further treaties in March and October 1921. Then in December 1922 Armenia was incorporated in the Union of Soviet Socialist Republics. (For the Republic in relation to modern states see chapter 1 map 1.1)

There were a number of postscripts to these events. The year 1923 was another landmark. The newly secularized Republic of Turkey now enjoyed western favour. Powerless to intervene, its missionaries tempted by the prospect of converting Muslims, and its government by Turkish oil and other resources, the USA sought Turkish friendship and a favourable image of the Turks in the American press. By the treaties of Lausanne the Allies drastically revised the Treaty of Sèvres and abandoned the Armenians. Armenian humanitarian needs, naturally, remained. Some 400,000 had fled Turkey to the Caucasus, and between 300,000 and 400,000 to other places. There were some 200,000 refugees in the Near East. In September 1923 the Council of the League of Nations approved the settlement of 50,000 in the Soviet Republic of Armenia. But humanitarian needs were still entangled in political concerns. Some western governments offered aid, but Britain, fearing to 'fund' the Soviet Union, refused, and the scheme was abandoned in 1929. The Lausanne treaties' betrayal of Armenians had been softened by articles referring to minorities in Turkey, whose guarantor was the League. But they were not implemented. Some 30,000 Armenians were deported in 1929–30.

Other postscripts were ecclesiastical rearrangements, including the re-establishment of the katholikosate of Cilicia, in 1930, at Antelias near Beirut, and the independence of Jerusalem from Constantinople, and a revival of Armenian education and culture, facilitated by the establishment of Palestine and Syria as British and French mandates. Present-day Jerusalem houses some 4,000 Armenian manuscripts, the only larger collection being in Armenia at the Matenadaran, the library of ancient manuscripts at Ējmiatsin; a large library; and stunning artistic treasures including illuminated manuscripts, vestments and vessels.

After the Lausanne treaties it is the Soviet Union which has most affected twentieth-century Armenian matters. In 1938 some Armenian diasporan political parties, convinced that Armenia's safety was dependent on the Soviet Union, decided not to oppose the regime there. Yet it had already proved inimical to Armenian Christianity and Armenian nationalism. In the 1920s Christian worship had been allowed, but the church had been repressed and undermined in other ways. In the 1930s, under Stalin, there had been persecution and purges, the Katholikos murdered in 1938. On the other hand, Soviet rule had also seen industrialization and educational and cultural improvements. Soviet repression ceased during the Second World War (1939–45), to encourage the effort against Germany, and these positive trends continued, one example being the creation of the Armenian Academy of Sciences in 1943.

The Cold War, from 1947, caused both western powers and Soviet authorities to be unhelpful to Armenian ambitions, and it complicated relations between Armenians inside and outside the Republic. One example concerns the Republican and central Soviet authorities' attempt to repatriate Armenians to Armenia after the Second World War finished. Though some 150,000 were resettled, the Cold War ended the movement. In 1947 an Armenian assembly, with delegates from twenty-two countries, asked the United Nations, successor to the League of Nations, for either an extension of Armenian territory or the implementation of the 1920 Wilson boundaries. Nothing came of this, or of Soviet claims, made in 1945, to Kars and Artahan. American support for Turkey in 1947, and Turkey's joining NATO in 1952, both contributed to their abandonment in 1953. And in Armenia itself many of the recently repatriated persons had suffered in another purge, in 1949. It was only in the 1950s, under Khrushchev, that conditions began to relax.

A particular problem for diaspora Armenians was that the head of their church had to live with the Soviet regime, since he lived under it. Katholikos Vazgen I (1955–94), improved both internal conditions and relations with other churches, leading his katholikosate, in 1962, into the World Council of Churches. But he could not prevent the election of an anti-Communist, backed by the pro-western Dashnaks, to the katholikosate of Cilicia in 1956, and its consequence, schism. This schism was important because it was the Cilician katholikosate which had authority over the majority of Middle Eastern Armenians, many of whom lived in the Lebanon. Beirut was, after the Second World War, perhaps the major centre of Armenian culture outside the Soviet Republic.

2   The present day

Various later twentieth-century wars and conflicts caused many Armenians to leave the Middle East. Turkey's invasion of Cyprus in 1974, and the Turkish sector's declaring itself a republic in 1975; troubles in Iran, Egypt, Syria and Iraq; civil war in Lebanon, in 1958 and 1975, and very unsettled conditions there only a few years ago, have all stimulated migration.

Consequently there are now many Armenians in England, France, Canada, some South American countries and in the USA, where there are more Armenians than anywhere else outside the former Soviet Republic. There are few left in Turkey, where there were some 50,000, the majority in Istanbul, in 1984.[11] In England, Armenians are concentrated in Manchester, and in (Greater) London where there were some 10,000 at the beginning of the 1980s. In France, Armenians are concentrated in Paris, Lyons, and the ancient port of Marseilles, gateway to the New World. Paris, where a number of periodicals are published and Armenian studies taught at university level, is the centre for intellectuals. In the USA, where some of the earlier immigrants rose to riches, (in the Oriental rug business on the east coast, or in agriculture in California, an area popular with Armenians), many periodicals and charitable foundations have been nurtured. Armenian studies are taught in several universities and children instructed in the Armenian heritage in a number of Armenian day schools, Saturday schools and Sunday schools. The diaspora has generated many distinguished individuals, not all widely known as 'Armenian'; the American singer-actress and celebrity Cher is a case in point.

---

[11] The figure is an estimate of the Armenian patriarchate, cited by Takooshian (1986–7).

The Armenian Apostolic Church still guards Armenian national identity, with its own distinctive practices and calendar, though these are not everywhere observed, and its grip, like that of other Churches, has been loosened by the secularization of the modern era.

3   Armenian history

The study and interpretation of Armenian history have been much influenced by the experiences of the twentieth century, as one can see clearly in some Armenian, Turkish and Soviet writings.

Many Armenians have maintained an interest in their past, and of these some have shown a patriotic fervour in rejecting some modern scholarship. There was and is a conviction that the Armenians were the original inhabitants of much of historic Armenia[12] and the psychological appeal of this assertion is easily understandable. It buttresses the Armenian case against the Turks, whereas acknowledgement that Armenians were, like Turks, once newcomers, might raise the possibility that Armenian and Turkish 'rights' to Armenia were morally equal. The distant glories of Urartu and its forerunners compensate for modern miseries. And the symbol, in the diaspora, of the Armenian as exile is one element which nourishes consciousness of Armenian identity in people who are otherwise of different backgrounds and interests, and are often well integrated into non-Armenian communities.[13] It is also understandable that some modern analyses of unacknowledged literary debts, of invention and of distortion by medieval Armenian historians have been perceived as anachronistically and unfairly discrediting these early authors, given some Turkish treatments of Armenian history. The official Turkish denial of genocidal activity towards the Armenians evolved, perhaps, to avoid legal claims and international opprobrium which might prejudice Turkey's political, economic and military aims. There were some particular embarassments for Turkey in the late 1960s and in the 1970s. In 1965 diaspora Armenians commemorated the fiftieth anniversary of the 'deportations', in 1973 a survivor murdered two Turkish consular officials in California, the fact of the massacres was reiterated and denied in the forum of the United Nations, and there was some Armenian terrorist activity between 1975 and 1984.

Writers on the Turkish side have often deployed 'source criticism' of medieval Armenian historians and of modern western reports. Some have rewritten history. In their accounts, western reports of Turkish atrocities appear as exaggeration, or even deliberate untruth, and the 'limited' repression of Armenians as legitimate responses to terrorism and treach-

---

[12] See e.g. Kavoukjian (trans. Ouzounian), 1987.
[13] Talai, 1989, pp. 127–8 for the claim to be the homeland, p. 4 for symbol of exile.

ery. Such authors also deny Armenian national identity in history any reality and Armenian nationalism in the present any historical justification. Their arguments include the following:[14] Armenians were immigrants; they were never self-governing, their 'kingdoms' being merely vassalages and buffers formed by the (foreign) dominant states; Armenians were few, and, under Turkish rule, happy, lacking national feeling; nationalism was created partly by the church, disapproving the laicization and democratization of the *millet*'s administration in the 1860s, partly by the machinations of the western powers seeking the end of the Ottoman Empire, and partly by the propaganda and activities of Protestant missionaries and of foreign consulates; Armenian terrorists were encouraged by such agencies, wanted genocide against the Turks and committed atrocities; nowadays Armenians in Turkey are happy.

Another method of removing Armenians from Turkey's history has been to Turkicize, or to render anonymous, elements of the Armenian past which cannot be made to disappear. Two instances are the representation of the Bagratuni kings as Turkish in origin, and the inclusion of the Artsruni church on Aḷtᶜamar in guide books without acknowledgement of any Armenian connection.

Of course some elements of the past can indeed be made to disappear. Archives, photographic records and local reports suggest that material evidence of Armenian historical achievement has significantly diminished, due to lack of care and, sometimes, to deliberate destruction.[15] It is not long since some non-Turkish scholars whose research programmes and concern conflicted with officially approved Turkish representations found visiting Turkey to be rather difficult.

Urartian culture, by contrast, has escaped such treatments. Sites have been excavated, for example Çavuştepe and Altıntepe, and cherished. Of the holdings of the museum at Van, which houses blocks and steles, rock reliefs, jewellery, seals, statuettes, belts, helmets and other items, about 80 per cent are Urartian. Unauthorized treasure hunting has been discouraged. And in former Soviet Armenia both Urartian and Armenian sites have been studied. Excavations at Karmir-Blur and Duin for example began in 1939 and 1937, and some monuments, including the 'temple' at Garni, have been restored.

Such work has been more disinterested than was some Soviet historiography.[16] To take two instances, in the Soviet Union heretical movements tended to be interpreted as socio-economic protest, and nineteenth-century nationalism represented according to Stalin's views, as

---

[14] For résumé, Foss, 1992.

[15] This was brought to public attention in an article in the British newspaper *The Independent*, 18 March 1989.

[16] Though archaeological scholarship may likewise reflect political thinking. See Atkinson et al., 1996, and esp. Dolukhanov, 1996.

lacking historical foundation, its immediate legacy, resistance to socialist Russian rule, a treacherous disregard of the popular will.

The study of Armenian history and culture which began in the nineteenth century has continued and has been well served in recent decades. US Archive material on the 1915–18 genocides, and over 42,000 photographs relating to Armenian architecture, in seven volumes (though not widely accessible), are now on micro-fiche.[17] The monuments of eastern Turkey have been comprehensively surveyed.[18] A collection of Armenian inscriptions was published in 1913, and inscriptions from Ani and from the Republic have been published in a series of volumes, beginning in 1960, at Erevan, though sadly these are virtually inaccessible in the west.[19] Many manuscript colophons have been collected and published since 1950 and some translated.[20] The major manuscript collections are gradually being catalogued. An iconographical index is being compiled on computer.[21] There has been western–Soviet scholarly collaboration in the publication of some monuments.[22] The early medieval Armenian histories have been reprinted and translated into English in the USA and some medieval histories are available in other western European languages too. Armenian matters are now an object of academic study and publication in a number of countries. Several histories of the Armenians have recently been published, some brief and general, others longer and more detailed.[23]

In 1939 Adolf Hitler asked who nowadays still speaks of the annihilation of the Armenians? One hundred years after Gladstone's great speech, we must answer that of this and of their history many, around the world, are well aware.

Epilogue: The Future

The Republic of Armenia declared its independence in September 1991, having been part of the Soviet Union since December 1922. The Armenian National Movement had emerged in the late 1980s.[24] Its broader

---

[17] *Armenian Architecture*, 1985 onwards – Project Director V. L. Parsegian in *Atti del Quinto...*, 1991, pp. 243–7, reported vols 1–5, 7, containing over 30,000 photographs, were already issued, vol. 6 forthcoming, and about eighty European and US institutions held the collection. Vol. 7 covers the region outside the Republic of Armenia and Turkey.

[18] Sinclair, 1987, 1989a, 1989b, 1990.

[19] *Corpus Inscriptionum Armenicarum*, 1966, 1960, 1967, 1973, 1982, 1977.

[20] Sanjian, 1969b for English translation.

[21] Der Manuelian, 1991.

[22] The *Documenti di Architettura Armena* series, published Milan, 1970 onwards involved the Faculty of Architecture of Milan Polytechnic and the Academy of Science of the Armenian SSR. At the end of the Soviet period, in 1990, an American–Armenian Horom Expedition began investigations at the site of Horom, most notable for an Urartian fortification. Badaljian et al., 1993 and 1994.

[23] E.g. Bournoutian, 1993, and Dédéyan (ed.), 1982.

[24] Libaridian, 1991.

context was the disintegration of the Soviet Union, its immediate context the failure of the Soviet Union physically to protect Armenians, a failure which prompted some Armenians to reassess traditional policies and to incorporate more realism in their calculations.

Armenian criticism of the Soviet regime became public and outspoken in 1987, when there were demonstrations to do with environmental issues and more so after the eruption, in 1988, of Armenian–Azerbaijani violence in Mountainous Karabağ (Nagorno-Karabakh). The Armenian Karabağ Committee had at first concentrated on the Karabağ question but had soon moved to a broader programme, and in December 1988 its members were imprisoned, for six months.

After national elections, the Armenian National Movement formed the government of the Republic in August 1990. It renamed the Armenian SSR the Republic of Armenia and issued a Declaration, establishing independence as a goal. It also asserted the independence of its foreign policy and of regulation of its economic system, proclaimed a multi-party political system, guaranteed the use of Armenian as the state language and, after much debate, supported the goal of achieving international recognition of the 1915 massacres as an act of genocide. The Republic refused to sign the new Union treaty proposed by President Gorbachev in December 1990. It exchanged trade delegations and had high-level meetings with Turkey not long after the elections, without insisting on acknowledgement of the genocide as a pre-condition, or demanding 'Armenian' territory.

The major principle behind such activity was to rely on Armenia's own resources and tailor policy accordingly, rather than to wait for a champion and to pursue impossible dreams. Not surprisingly, not all Armenians have agreed with the ANM's stance. There remain distaste for Turkey, a belief that Turkey continues to be a threat, and the conviction that Armenia needs a protector. The three major Armenian political parties, active during the Soviet period only in the diaspora, and mainly in cultural and community work, returned home to take advantage of the new climate, and their responses were critical. Some more recently formed groups likewise dissented. The National Self-Determination Group (which began in 1965) for example seems to have felt that armed help from the United Nations and from the European Parliament, which recognized the Armenian genocide on 18 June 1987, were possibilities.

But the relative success of the new regime and the spirit of optimism it has promoted has prompted some calls in the diaspora for a reassessment of diasporan attitudes and institutions so that diasporan Armenians too can contribute to a new democratic nation-state. The past, with its fear of Turkey and bitter memories of the genocide, is not to paralyse the present and abort a future.

Bibliography

Abbreviations

CATRS   Classical Armenian Text Reprint Series ed. J. A. C. Greppin (Delmar, New York)
REArm   Revue des Études Arméniennes
ns   new series
os   old series

Primary Sources: Texts and Translations

Agathangelos, *History of the Armenians*, ed. G. Tēr-Mkrtchᶜean and St. Kanayeantsᶜ (Tiflis, 1909); repr. CATRS (1980); Arm. text and Engl. trans. of paras 259–715 as *The Teaching of Saint Gregory*, Thomson, 1970; of the rest, Thomson, 1976.

Anania of Shirak, *Autobiography*, French trans. Berbérian, 1964.

—— *Geography*, Engl. trans. Hewsen, 1992.

Anastas Vardapet, *List of Armenian Monasteries . . .*, text and Engl. trans. Sanjian, 1969a.

Appian, *Roman History*, Loeb Classical Library.

Aristakēs of Lastivert, *History of the Armenians*, ed. K. Yuzbashyan (Erevan, 1963); French trans. Canard and Berbérian, 1973. An Engl. version exists, Bedrosian, 1985a.

Arrian, *The Anabasis of Alexander*, Loeb Classical Library.

—— *Parthica* in ed. A. G. Roos, *Flavius Arrianus* v. II *Scripta Minora et Fragmenta* (Leipzig, 1967).

Beowulf, in *Anglo-Saxon Poetry* trans. and ed. S. A. J. Bradley (London, Melbourne and Toronto, 1982), pp. 411–94.

Canons: *Kanonagirkᶜ Hayotsᶜ* (*The Book of Canons of the Armenians*) ed. V. Hakobyan (2 vols) (Erevan, 1964, 1971) (with comm.).

Cassius Dio, *Roman History*, Loeb Classical Library.

Colophons, Sanjian, 1969b.

Constantine Porphyrogenitus, *De Administrando Imperio*, ed. G. Moravcsik and Engl. trans. R. J. H. Jenkins (rev. edn, Washington, 1967).

Corpus Inscriptionum Armenicarum, I, ed. Orbeli, *The City of Ani* (Erevan, 1966) (in Armenian).

II, ed. S. G. Barkhudarian, *Districts of Goris, Sisian and Kap^{c}an* (Erevan, 1960) (in Armenian).

III, ed. *idem*, *The Valley of Vayots^c-dzor; region of Ełegnadzor and of Azizbekov* (Erevan, 1967) (in Armenian).

IV, ed. *idem*, *Gełark^{c}unik^c* (Erevan, 1973) (in Armenian).

V, ed. *idem*, *Arts^{c}akh* (Erevan, 1982) (in Armenian).

VI, ed. S. A. Avagyan and R. M. Janp^{c}oladyan, *Region of Ijewan* (Erevan, 1977) (in Armenian).

David the Invincible Philosopher, *Definitions and Divisions of Philosophy*, Engl. trans. Kendall and Thomson, 1983.

David of Gandzak, *Penitential*, Dowsett, 1961a.

David of Sasun, French trans. Feydit, 1964; Engl. trans. Shalian, 1964, and Kudian, 1970.

Dionysius Barsalibi, *Against the Armenians*, text and Engl. trans. Mingana, 1931.

Ełishē, *History of Vardan and the Armenian War*, ed. E. Tēr Minasean (Erevan, 1957); repr. CATRS (1993); Engl. trans. Thomson, 1982b.

The Vision of Enoch the Just in S. Yovsep^{c}eants^c (ed.), *Collection of Uncanonical Writings of the Old Testament* (Venice, 1896), pp. 378–86 (in Armenian); Engl. trans. in J. Issaverdens, *Uncanonical Writings of the Old Testament* (Venice, 1901), pp. 309–23.

The Epic Histories (Buzandaran Patmut^{c}iwnk^c), ed. K^c. Patkanean (St Petersburg, 1883); repr. CATRS (1984); Engl. trans. Garsoïan, 1989.

Eznik, *De Deo* ed. and French trans. L. Mariès and C. Mercier, *Eznik de Kołb De Deo* (2 vols), (v. XXVIII, fascicules 3, 4 of the *Patrologia Orientalis*) (Paris, 1959).

The Epic of the Kings Shah-Nama the national epic of Persia by Ferdowsi trans. R. Levy (London, 1967).

The Sháhnáma of Firdausí, done into English by A. G. Warner and E. Warner, 9 vols (London, 1905–25).

Fragments of Greek Historical Texts, Jacoby, 1929.

Gregory of Tours, *The Histories* trans. L. Thorpe as *The History of the Franks* (Harmondsworth, 1974).

Herodotus, *The Histories*, Loeb Classical Library.

Inscriptions: Armenian-Basmadjian, 1931; Basmajian, 1920–21, 1922–23; *Corpus Inscriptionum Armenicarum*; Khatchatrian, 1974; Uluhogian, 1992: Urartian – Melikishvili, 1960: Assyrian – Grayson, 1972, 1975, 1976; Lanfranchi and Parpola, 1990; Lie, 1929; Luckenbill, 1926, 1927; Parpola, 1987; Pfeiffer, 1935; Starr, 1990; Waterman, 1930: Persian – Kent, 1953; King and Thompson, 1907: Greek – Jalabert and Mouterde, 1929: others – Clay, 1904; Cardascia, 1951; Grayson, 1975.

Jerome, *Letters* in ed. J. P. Migne, *Patrologia Latina*, 22, I, (Paris, 1854).

John X, Jacobite Patriarch, *Letter*, text and French trans. Nau, 1912.

John Katholikos, *History of the Armenians*, ed. M. Emin (Moscow, 1853); repr. (Tiflis, 1912) and CATRS (1980); Engl. trans. Maksoudian, 1987.

(Ps) John Mamikonean, *The History of Tarōn*, ed. A. Abrahamyan (Erevan, 1941); Engl. trans. Avdoyan, 1993.

John of Ōdzun, *Against the Paulicians*, Arm. text, Latin trans. Aucher, 1834 pp. 78–107.

Josephus, *The Jewish War*, Loeb Classical Library.

Justin, *Epitome* = *Epitoma Historiarum Philippicarum Pompei Trogi*, ed. O. Seel (Stuttgart, 1972).

Juvenal, *The Satires*, Loeb Classical Library.

The Key of Truth, Arm. text, Engl. trans. Conybeare, 1898a.

Khosrov Andzewatsᶜi, *Commentary on the Divine Liturgy*, Arm. text and Engl. trans. Cowe, 1991.

Koriwn, *The Life of Mashtots*, German trans. Winkler, 1994; Engl. trans. of mod. Arm. trans., Norehad, 1964.

Laws: Armenian-Mkhitᶜar Gosh; Persian-Bulsara, 1937.

Lazarus of Pᶜarp, *History of the Armenians*, ed. G. Tēr-Mkrtchᶜean and St. Malkhasean (Tiflis, 1904); repr. CATRS (1985); partial Engl. trans. Thomson, 1982b (appendix); complete Engl. trans. Thomson, 1991.

Ḷewond, *History*, ed. K. Ezean (St Petersburg, 1887); Engl. trans. Arzoumanian, 1982b.

Liturgy, Nersoyan, 1984.

Matthew of Edessa, *History*, ed. unnamed (Jerusalem, 1869); ed. M. Melik-Adamian, N. Tēr-Mikᶜayelian (Vaḷarshapat, 1898); Engl. trans. Dostourian, 1993.

Mkhitᶜar Gosh, *Law Code of the Armenians*, ed. C. Bastameants, *Mkhitᶜaray Goshi Datastanagirkᶜ Hayotsᶜ* (Vaḷarshapat, 1880); ed. Kh. Tᶜorosyan, *Girkᶜ Datastani* (Erevan, 1975).

Moses Daskhurantsᶜi, *History of the Albanians*, ed. M. Emin (Moscow, 1860); repr. (Tiflis, 1912); ed. V. Aṙakᶜelean (Erevan, 1983); Engl. trans. Dowsett, 1961b.

Moses of Khoren, *History of the Armenians*, ed. M. Abeḷean, S. Yarutᶜiwnean (Tiflis, 1913); repr. CATRS (1981); Engl. trans. Thomson, 1978; French trans. A. and J.-P. Mahé, 1993.

Narratio de Rebus Armeniae, Greek text, Comm. (in French) Garitte, 1952.

Peter of Sicily, *History of the Paulicians*, Greek text, French trans., Astruc et al., 1970.

Photius, *Epistolae et Amphilochia* vol. III ed. B. Laourdas, L. G. Westerink, (Leipzig, 1985).

—— *Letters*, Greek text and French trans., Darrouzès, 1971.

Pliny the Elder, *Natural History*, Loeb Classical Library.

Plutarch, *Lives*, Loeb Classical Library.

Polybius, *The Histories*, Loeb Classical Library.

Procopius, *Buildings*, Loeb Classical Library.

—— *History of the Wars*, Loeb Classical Library.

Sahak (St), *Canons*, Engl. trans. Conybeare, 1898b.

Sebēos, *History of Heraclius*, ed. K. Patkanean, *Patmutᶜiwn Sebēosi episkopi Heracln* (St Petersburg, 1879); ed. G.V. Abgarean, *Patmutᶜiwn Sebēosi* (Erevan, 1979); French trans. Macler, 1904; Italian trans., Gugerotti, 1990. An Engl. version exists, Bedrosian, 1985b.

Smbat, Constable, *Chronicle*, French trans. Dédéyan, 1980.
Sopᶜerkᶜ Haykakankᶜ (*Armenian Texts*), (22 vols) (Venice, 1853–61).
Stephen Asoḷik of Tarōn, *Universal History*, ed. S. Malkhaseantsᶜ (St Petersburg, 1885); French trans. Macler, 1917.
Stephen Orbelean, *History of the House of Sisakan*, ed. B. Emin Stepᶜanos Siuneatsᶜ Episkoposi, Patmutᶜiwn Tann Sisakan (Moscow, 1861); French trans. Brosset, 1864.
Strabo, *The Geography*, Loeb Classical Library.
Tacitus, *The Annals*, Loeb Classical Library.
—— *The Histories*, Loeb Classical Library.
Theophanes, *Chronographia* ed. C. de Boor (2 vols, Leipzig, 1883).
Theophylact Simocatta, *History*, ed. C. de Boor, re-ed. P. Wirth (Stuttgart, 1972); Engl. trans. Whitby and Whitby, 1986.
Thomas Artsruni, *History of the House of the Artsrunis*, ed. K. Patkanean (St Petersburg, 1887); French trans. Brosset, 1874; Engl. trans. Thomson, 1985.
Ukhtanēs, *History of the Armenians*, ed. (Vaḷarshapat, 1871); Engl. trans. Arzoumanian, 1985.
Vardan, *Historical Compilation*, ed. unnamed (Venice, 1862); repr. CATRS (1991); Engl. trans. Thomson, 1989.
Xenophon, *Anabasis*, Loeb Classical Library.
—— *Cyropaedia*, Loeb Classical Library.
—— *Oeconomicus*, Loeb Classical Library.

Secondary Sources

Abgarian, G. V. 1964, 'Remarques sur l'histoire de Sébéos', *REArm*, ns, 1: 203–15.
Adcock, F. E. 1937, 'Lesser Armenia and Galatia after Pompey's settlement of the East', *Journal of Roman Studies* 27: 12–17.
Adontz, N.-Garsoïan, N. G. 1970, *Armenia in the Period of Justinian. The Political Conditions Based on the Naxarar system*. First publ. 1908, trans. into Engl. by Garsoïan (Lisbon).
Adontz, N., 1933a, 'La portée historique de l'oraison funèbre de Basile I par son fils Léon VI le Sage', *Byzantion* 8: 501–13.
—— 1933b, 'L'age et l'origine de l'empereur Basile I (867–86)', *Byzantion* 8: 475–500.
—— 1934a, 'L'age et l'origine de l'empereur Basile I (867–86)', *Byzantion* 9: 223–60.
—— 1934b, 'Les légendes de Maurice et de Constantin V, empereurs de Byzance', *Annuaire de l'Institut de Philologie et d'Histoire Orientales* 2(1): 1–12.
—— 1946, *Histoire d'Arménie. Les origines du Xᵉ siècle au VIᵉ (Av. J. C.)* (Paris).
—— 1965, *Études Arméno-Byzantines* (Lisbon).
Aharonian, A. G. 1983, *Intermarriage and the Armenian-American Community: A Socio-Religious Study* (Shrewsbury, Mass,).
—— 1986–7, 'Armenian Intermarriage in the United States, 1950–1976', *Journal of Armenian Studies* 3(1–2): 103–10.

Akopjan, A. A. (Hakobyan, A. H.), 1987, *Albania in the ancient Graeco-Latin and Armenian sources* (in Russian) (Erevan).

Alexander, P. J. 1955, 'An Ascetic Sect of Iconoclasts in Seventh Century Armenia'. In K. Weitzmann (ed.) *Late Classical and Mediaeval Studies in Honor of Albert Mathias Friend, Jr.* (Princeton), pp. 151–60.

Alishan, L. P. 1985–1986, 'The Sacred World of *Sasna Tsrer*: Steps Toward an Understanding', *Journal of the Society for Armenian Studies* 2: 107–39.

Amsler, J. 1978–9, ' "Dawit^c de Sasun" et les "Nibelungen" ', *REArm* ns 13: 187–95.

Ananian, P. 1961, 'La data e le circostanze della consecrazione di S. Gregorio Illuminatore', *Le Muséon* 74: 43–73, 317–60.

Ananikian, M. H. 1925, *Armenian Mythology* (Boston).

Anderson, B. 1983, *Imagined Communities: Reflections on the Origin and Spread of Nationalism* (London and New York).

Arakelyan, B. 1968, 'Excavations at Garni 1949–50'. In V. P. Alekseev, *Contributions to the Archaeology of Armenia*, trans. A. Krimgold, ed. H. Field, (Peabody Museum, Cambridge, Mass.,).

Armen, G. and Artinian, V.-A. 1987, *Historical Atlas of Armenia* (New York) (in Engl. and Arm.).

Armenian Architecture, publ. by the Armenian Architectural Archives (Dr. V. L. Parsegian, Project Director). vol. 1, (with introd. K. Maksoudian, text L. Der Manuelian Zug, Switzerland, 1981); vol. 3 (1985); vols 2, 4, 5, 7. Microfiche. (Inter Documentation Company bv, Leiden).

Arutjunova-Fidanjan, V. A., 1980a *The Chalcedonian Armenians on the Eastern Frontiers of the Byzantine Empire* (in Russian, with English summary) (Erevan).

—— 1980b, 'Sur le problème des provinces byzantines orientales', *REArm* ns 14: 157–69.

—— 1988–1989, 'The Ethno-Confessional Self-Awareness of Armenian Chalcedonians', *REArm* ns 21: 345–63.

—— 1991, 'Les Arméniens chalcédoniens en tant que phénomène culturel de l'Orient chrétien'. In *Atti del Quinto...*, 1991, 463–77.

Arvites, J. A. 1983, 'The Defense of Byzantine Anatolia during the Reign of Irene (780–802)'. In S. Mitchell (ed.), *Armies and Frontiers in Roman and Byzantine Anatolia* (Oxford), 219–37.

Arzoumanian, Z. 1982a, 'A Critique of Sebēos and his *History of Heraclius*, A Seventh-Century Document'. In T. J. Samuelian (ed.), *Classical Armenian Culture*, (Univ. of Pennsylvania Armenian Texts and Studies 4) (Pennsylvania), 68–78.

—— 1982b, *History of Lewond, The Eminent Vardapet of the Armenians*, (trans., Introd. and Comm.). (Philadelphia).

—— 1985, *Bishop Ukhtanes of Sebastia, History of Armenia Part II History of the Severance of the Georgians from the Armenians*, (trans., Introd. and Comm.). (Fort Lauderdale).

Astruc, C., Conus-Wolska, W., Gouillard, J., Lemerle, P., Papachryssanthou, D., Paramelle, J., 1970, 'Les sources grecques pour l'histoire des Pauliciens d'Asie Mineure: Texte critique et traduction', *Travaux et Mémoires* 4: 2–227.

Atkinson, J. A., Banks, I., O'Sullivan, J. (eds) 1996, *Nationalism and Archaeology. Scottish Archaeological Forum* (Glasgow).

Atti del Quinto Simposio Internazionale di Arte Armena (1988) ed. Zekiyan, B. L. (Venice, 1991).

Aucher, J. B. (ed.) 1834, Domini Johannis Philosophi Ozniensis Armeniorum Catholici Opera (Armenian text, Latin trans.) (Venice).

Avdoyan, L. 1993, Pseudo-Yovhannēs Mamikonean, The History of Tarōn [Patmut͑iwn Tarōnoy]: Historical Investigation, Critical Translation, and Historical and Textual Commentaries (Atlanta).

Badaljan, R. S., Edens, C., Gorny, R., Kohl, P. L., Stronach, D., Tonikjan, A. V., Hamayakjan, S., Mandrikjan, S., and Zardarjan, M. 1993, 'Preliminary Report on the 1992 Excavations at Horom, Armenia', Iran 31: 1–24.

Badaljan, R. S., Kohl, P. L., Stronach, D., Tonikjan, A. V. 1994, 'Preliminary Report on the 1993 Excavations at Horom, Armenia', Iran 32: 1–29.

Banks, I. 1996, 'Archaeology, nationalism and ethnicity'. In Atkinson et al. (eds), 1996, 1–11.

Barb, A. A. 1963, 'The Survival of Magic Arts'. In A. Momigliano (ed.), The Conflict between Paganism and Christianity in the Fourth Century (Oxford), 100–25.

Bardakjian, K. B. 1982, 'The Rise of the Armenian Patriarchate of Constantinople'. In B. Braude and B. Lewis (eds) Christians and Jews in the Ottoman Empire (2 vols) (New York, London) vol. I, 89–100.

Barnett, R. D. 1963, 'The Urartian Cemetery at Igdyr', Anatolian Studies 13: 153–98.

Barnett, R. D. and Falkner, M. 1962, The Sculptures of Aššur-naṣir-apli II (883–859 B.C.) Tiglath-pileser III (745–727 B.C.) Esarhaddon (681–669 B.C.) from the Central and South-West Palaces at Nimrud (London).

Barrett, A. A. 1977, 'Sohaemus, King of Emesa and Sophene', American Journal of Philology 98: 153–59.

——— 1979, 'Annals 14.26 and the Armenian settlement of A.D.60', Classical Quarterly 29: 465–69.

Bartikian, H. 1968, 'Les Arewordi (Fils du Soleil) en Arménie et Mésopotamie et l'épître du catholicos Nersès le Gracieux', REArm ns 5, 271–88.

Bart͑ikian, H. M. 1986, 'The Religious Diplomacy of Byzantium in Armenia during the Tenth and Eleventh Centuries'. In D. Kouymjian (ed.), 1986, 55–62.

Basmadjian, K. J. 1931, Les inscriptions d'Ani, de Bagnaïr et de Marmachen (Paris).

Basmajian, J. 1920–1921, 'Les inscriptions arméniennes d'Ani', Revue de l'Orient Chrétien 22: 337–62.

——— 1922–3, Continuation from 1920–1921, ROC 23: 47–81, 314–44.

Beattie, J. 1964, Other Cultures. Aims, Methods and Achievements in Social Anthropology (London).

Beaton, R. and Ricks, D. (eds.) 1993, Digenes Akrites: New Approaches to Byzantine Heroic Poetry (Publications of the Centre for Hellenic Studies, King's College, London, 2) (Variorum) 13 Studies in English.

Bedoukian, P. Z. 1978, Coinage of the Artaxiads of Armenia (London).

Bedrosian, R. G. 1979, The Turco-Mongol Invasions and the Lords of Armenia in the 13–14th Centuries (Columbia University PhD) (New York) (Microfiche).

Bedrosian, R. 1983, 'The Sparapetut͑iwn in Armenia in the Fourth and Fifth Centuries', Armenian Review 36(2): 6–46.

—— 1984, '*Dayeakut͗iwn* in Ancient Armenia', *Armenian Review* 37(2): 23–47.

—— 1985a, trans., *Aristakēs Lastivertcʿi's History* (New York).

—— 1985b, trans., *Sebēos' History* (New York).

Berbérian, H. 1964, 'Autobiographie d'Anania Širakacʿi', *REArm* ns 1: 189–94.

Blockley, R. C. 1984, 'The Romano-Persian Peace Treaties of A. D. 299 and 363', *Florilegium* 6: 28–49.

—— 1987, 'The Division of Armenia between the Romans and the Persians at the End of the Fourth Century A.D.', *Historia* 36: 222–34.

Boyadjiev, S. 1978, 'Influences arméniennes dans l'architecture de l'église Ronde de Preslav'. In *Atti del Primo Simposio Internazionale di Arte Armena (1975)* (Venice), 35–52.

Bournoutian, G. A. 1993, *A History of the Armenian People* vol. I *Pre-History to 1500 A.D.* (Costa Mesa, Cal.).

Boyce, M. 1957, 'The Parthian Gōsān and Iranian Minstrel Tradition', *Journal of the Royal Asiatic Society*, 10–45.

Braude, B. and Lewis, B. (eds) 1982 *Christians and Jews in the Ottoman Empire: The Functioning of a Plural Society* (2 vols) (New York and London).

Braund, D. C. 1984, *Rome and the Friendly King: The Character of Client Kingship* (London and New York).

—— 1988, 'Client Kings'. In D. C. Braund (ed.) *The Administration of the Roman Empire, 241 B.C.–A.D. 193* (Exeter), 69–96.

—— 1994, *Georgia in Antiquity: A History of Colchis and Transcaucasian Iberia 550 BC–AD562* (Oxford).

Braund, S. H. 1989, 'Juvenal and the East: satire as an historical source'. In D. H. French and C. S. Lightfoot (eds) *The Eastern Frontier of the Roman Empire* (2 vols) (Oxford) vol. I, 45–52.

Brock, S. P. 1973, 'Early Syrian Asceticism', *Numen* 20: 1–19 (repr. in *idem*, *Syriac Perspectives on Late Antiquity* (London: Variorum, 1984)).

—— 1982, 'Christians in the Sasanian Empire: A Case of Divided Loyalties'. In S. Mews (ed.) *Religion and National Identity* (Studies in Church History, 18) (Oxford), 1–19.

Brosset, M. 1864, trans., *Histoire de la Siounie par Stéphannos Orbélian* (2 vols) (St Petersburg).

Brosset, M. F. 1874, *Histoire des Ardzrouni par le vartabied Thoma Ardzrouni* in *idem, Collection d'historiens arméniens* I (St Petersburg).

Brown, E. A. R. 1974, 'The Tyranny of a Construct: Feudalism and Historians of Medieval Europe', *American Historical Review* 79: 1063–88.

Brown, S. C. 1988, 'The Mêdikos Logos of Herodotus and the Evolution of the Median State'. In A. Kuhrt and H. Sancisi-Weerdenburg (eds) *Achaemenid History III: Method and Theory* (Leiden), 71–86.

Browning, R. 1975, *Byzantium and Bulgaria. A comparative study across the early medieval frontier* (London).

Bryer, A. 1981, 'The First Encounter with the West – A.D. 1050–1204'. In Whitting (ed.) 1981, 83–110.

Bullough, D. 1983, 'Burial, Community and Belief in the Early Medieval West'. In P. Wormald with D. Bullough and R. Collins (eds), *Ideal and Reality in Frankish and Anglo-Saxon Society* (Oxford), 177–201.

Bulsara, S. J. 1937, *The Laws of the Ancient Persians*, trans. with Introd., Gloss. and Ind. (Bombay).

Burney, C. A. 1957, 'Urartian Fortresses and Towns in the Van Region', *Anatolian Studies* 7: 37–53.

Burney, C. and Lang, D. M. 1971, *The Peoples of the Hills* (London).

Burney, C. A. and Lawson, G. R. J. 1960, 'Measured Plans of Urartian Fortresses', *Anatolian Studies* 10: 177–96.

Cabelli, D. E. and Mathews, T. F. 1984, 'Pigments in Armenian Manuscripts of the Tenth and Eleventh Centuries', *REArm*, ns 18: 33–47.

Cahen, C. 1953, 'L'évolution de l'iqtâ^c du IXe au XIIIe siècle: Contribution à une histoire comparée des sociétés médiévales', *Annales* 8: 25–52.

—— 1968, *Pre-Ottoman Turkey* (London).

Cameron, G. G. 1973, 'The Persian Satrapies and Related Matters', *Journal of Near Eastern Studies* 32: 47–56.

Campbell, J. K. 1964, *Honour, Family and Patronage* (New York and Oxford).

Campbell Thompson, R. and Mallowan, M. E. L. 1933, 'The British Museum Excavations at Nineveh, 1931–32', *Annals of Archaeology and Anthropology* 20: 71–186.

Canard, M. 1971, 'Les Impôts en nature de l'Arménie à l'époque ^cAbbâside', *REArm* ns 8: 359–63.

—— 1986, ''Les familles féodales d'Arménie et leurs possessions héréditaires' d'a Ter-Ghévondian'. (Translating part of Ter-Ghevondian, 1977). In Kouymjian (ed.), 1986, 89–104.

Canard, M. and Berbérian, H. 1973, trans., *Aristakès de Lastivert, Récit des Malheurs de la Nation Arménienne* (with introd. and comm.) (Brussels).

Cardascia, G. 1951, *Les archives de Murašû* (Paris).

Charanis, P. 1963, *The Armenians in the Byzantine Empire* (Lisbon).

Chaumont, M.-L. 1966, 'L'Ordre des préséances à la cour des Arsacides d'Arménie', *Journal Asiatique* 254: 471–97.

—— 1973, 'Chiliarque et curopalate à la cour des Sassanides', *Iranica Antiqua* 10: 139–65.

—— 1976, 'L'Arménie entre Rome et l'Iran I, Dès l'avènement d'Auguste à l'avènement de Dioclétien', *Aufstieg und Niedergang der römischen Welt* II.9.1. (Berlin and New York), 71–194.

—— 1985–8, 'A propos des premières interventions parthes en Arménie et des circonstances de l'avènement de Tigrane le Grand', *Acta Antiqua Academiae Scientiarum Hungaricae* (Budapest) 31: 13–25.

Clay, A. T. 1904, *Business Documents of Murashû Sons of Nippur Dated in the reign of Darius II (424–404 B.C.)* (Philadelphia) (The Babylonian Expedition of the University of Pennsylvania, Series A Cuneiform Texts, vol. 10).

Considine, P. 1979, 'A Semantic Approach to the Identification of Iranian Loan-words in Armenian'. In B. Brogyanyi (ed.), *Studies in Diachronic, Synchronic and Typological Linguistics: Festschrift for Oswald Szemerényi* (Amsterdam Studies in the Theory and History of Linguistic Science. Series IV – Current Issues in Linguistic Theory vol. 11) (2 vols) (Amsterdam), vol. I, 213–28.

Constantelos, D. J. 1972, 'The Moslem Conquests of the Near East as revealed in the Greek Sources of the Seventh and the Eighth Centuries', *Byzantion* 42: 325–57.

Conybeare, F. C. 1898a, *The Key of Truth. A Manual of the Paulician Church of Armenia* (Oxford). Armenian text, Engl. trans.

—— 1898b, trans., 'The Armenian Canons of St. Sahak, Catholicos of Armenia (390–439 A.D.)', *American Journal of Theology* 2: 828–48.

Cowe, S. P. 1991, *Commentary on the Divine Liturgy by Xosrov Anjewacᶜi*: trans. with an introd. (New York) (includes Arm. text).

Cramp, R. 1966, *Early Northumbrian Sculpture* (Jarrow Lecture 1965) (Jarrow).

Croke, B. and Crow, J. 1983, 'Procopius and Dara', *Journal of Roman Studies* 73: 143–59.

Crone, P. 1980, *Slaves on Horses: The Evolution of the Islamic Polity* (Cambridge).

Curtis, J. (ed.) 1988, *Bronzeworking Centres of Western Asia, c.1000–539 B.C.* (London and New York).

Dachkévytch, Y. R. 1986–7, 'Les Arméniens en Islande au XIᵉ siècle', *REArm* ns 20: 321–36.

Dagron, G., Riché, P., and Vauchez, A. (eds), 1993, *Histoire du christianisme des origines à nos jours 4: Évêques, moines et empereurs (610–1054)* (Desclée).

Dandamaev, M. A. and Lukonin, V. G. 1989, *The Culture and Social Institutions of Ancient Iran* (Cambridge).

Darrouzès, J. 1971, 'Deux lettres inédites de Photius aux Arméniens', *Revue des études byzantines* 29: 137–81. Greek text, French trans.

Dauvillier, J. and De Clercq, C. 1936, *Le Mariage en droit canonique oriental* (Paris).

Davies, J. G. 1991, *Medieval Armenian Art and Architecture: The Church of The Holy Cross, Aght'amar* (London).

Debevoise, N. C. 1938, *A Political history of Parthia* (Chicago).

Dédéyan, G. 1975, 'L'immigration arménienne en Cappadoce au XIᵉ siècle', *Byzantion* 45: 41–117.

—— 1979, 'Les Arméniens en Occident fin Xᵉ – début XIᵉ siècle'. In *Occident et Orient au Xᵉ siècle* (Publications de l'Université de Dijon, LVII) (Paris) 123–43.

—— 1980, *La Chronique Attribuée au Connétable Smbat*: Introduction, traduction, et notes (Paris).

—— 1981a, 'Les Arméniens en Cappadoce aux Xᵉ et XIᵉ siècles'. In *Le aree omogenee della Civiltà Rupestre nell'ambito dell'Impero Bizantino: la Cappadocia* (Galatina), 75–95.

—— 1981b, 'Mleh le Grand, stratège de Lykandos', *REArm* ns 15: 73–102.

—— 1982, 'Vocation impériale ou fatalité diasporique: les Arméniens à Byzance (IVᵉ–XIᵉ siècles)'. In Dédéyan (ed.), 1982, 269–96.

—— (ed.), 1982, *Histoire des Arméniens* (Toulouse).

—— 1986, 'Le peuplement Arménien aux frontières de la Cilicie aux IVe–Ve siècles'. In Kouymjian (ed.), 1986, 215–27.

—— 1989, 'Les listes "féodales" du Pseudo-Smbat', *Cahiers de Civilisation Médiévale* (Poitiers) 32: 25–42.

Dejiver, H. 1989, 'Equestrian officers in the East'. In D. H. French and C. S. Lightfoot (eds), *The Eastern Frontier of the Roman Empire* (2 vols) (Oxford), vol. I, 77–111.

Dilleman, L. 1962, *Haute Mésopotamie orientale et pays adjacents* (Paris).

Der Manuelian, L. 1982, 'Armenian Sculptural Images, Fifth to Eighth Centuries'. In Samuelian (ed.), 1982, 176–207.

—— 1984, 'Armenian Sculptural Images Part II: Seventh to Fourteenth Centuries'. In Samuelian and Stone (eds), 1984, 96–119.

—— 1991, 'The State of the Field of Armenian Art: ubi sumus/quo imus'. In *Atti del Quinto...*, 1991, 103–17.

Der Melkonian-Minassian, C. 1972, *L'Épopée populaire arménienne David de Sassoun: Étude critique* (Montreal).

Der Nersessian, S. 1944–1945, 'Une apologie des images du septième siècle', *Byzantion* 17: 58–87.

—— 1946, 'Image Worship in Armenia and its Opponents', *Armenian Quarterly* 1: 67–81.

—— 1978, *Armenian Art* (London).

Der Sahaghian, G. 1911, 'Un document arménien de la généalogie de Basile Ier', *Byzantinische Zeitschrift* 20: 165–76.

Diakonoff, I. M. 1984, *The Pre-History of the Armenian People* (trans. L. Jennings) (New York).

Documenti di Architettura Armena, 1970 onwards, series publ. Milan Polytechnic.

Dolukhanov, P. M. 1996, 'Archaeology and nationalism in totalitarian and post-totalitarian Russia'. In Atkinson et al. (eds) 1996, 200–13.

Donabédian, P. 1983, 'L'architecture religieuse dans l'Arménie du haut Moyen-Age', *Les cahiers de Saint-Michel de Cuxa* (Prades-Codalet) 14, (unpaginated).

—— 1988–9, review of Akopjan, 1987, *REArm* ns 21: 485–95.

—— 1991a, 'La sculpture architecturale dans l'Arménie préarabe: rapports extérieurs'. In *Atti del Quinto...*, 1991, 125–45.

—— 1991b, 'Le Point sur l'architecte arménien Trdat-Tiridate', *Cahiers archéologiques* 39: 95–110.

Dostourian, A. E. 1993, *Armenia and the Crusades: Tenth to Twelfth Centuries – the Chronicle of Matthew of Edessa* (trans., comm. and introd.) (Lanham, NY and London).

Dowsett, C. J. F. 1958, 'The Albanian Chronicle of Mxit^{c}ar Goš', *Bulletin of the School of Oriental and African Studies* 21: 472–90.

—— 1961a, *The Penitential of David of Ganjak* (ed. with an Engl. trans.) (*Corpus Scriptorum Christianorum Orientalium*, Scriptores Armeniacae 3, 4, vols 216, 217), (Louvain).

—— 1961b, trans., *The History of the Caucasian Albanians by Movsēs Dasxurançi* (London Oriental Series, 8) (London, New York and Toronto).

Edwards, R. W. 1983a, 'The Fortifications of Medieval Cilicia' (Dissertation, Univ. of California, Berkeley).

—— 1983b, 'Ecclesiastical Architecture in the Fortifications of Armenian Cilicia: Second Report', *Dumbarton Oaks Papers* 37, 123–46.

—— 1983c, 'Bagras and Armenian Cilicia: A Reassessment', *REArm* ns 17: 415–55.

Érémian, A. B. 1971, 'Sur certaines modifications subies par les monuments arméniens au VIIe siècle', *REArm* ns 8: 251–66.

Evans-Pritchard, E. E. 1940, *The Nuer* (New York and Oxford).

Feydit, F. 1964, *David de Sassoun: Épopée en vers, traduit de l'Arménien avec une introduction et des notes* (Paris).

—— 1986, *Amulettes de l'Arménie chrétienne* (Venice).

Foss, C. 1992, 'The Turkish View of Armenian History: A Vanishing Nation'. In Hovannisian (ed.), 1992, 250–79.

Freeman, P. and Kennedy, D. (eds) 1986, *The Defence of the Roman and Byzantine East* (British Archaeological Reports, International Series, 297) (2 vols) (Oxford).

Freeman-Grenville, G. S. P. 1993, *Historical Atlas of the Middle East* (New York).

Frendo, D. 1985, 'Sebēos and the Armenian Historiographical Tradition in the Context of Byzantine-Iranian Relations', *Peritia* 4: 1–20.

Frye, R. N. 1964, 'The Charisma of Kingship in Ancient Iran', *Iranica Antiqua* 4: 36–54.

—— 1972, 'Gestures of Deference to Royalty in Ancient Iran', *Iranica Antiqua* 9: 102–7.

Garitte, G. 1952, *La Narratio de Rebus Armeniae* (*Corpus Scriptorum Christianorum Orientalium* vol. 132. Subsidia vol. 4) (Louvain).

Garsoïan, N. G. 1967a, *The Paulician Heresy: A study of the Origin and Development of Paulicianism in Armenia and the Eastern Provinces of the Byzantine Empire* (Publications in Near and Middle East Studies, Columbia University, Series A, VI) (The Hague, Paris).

—— 1967b, 'Politique ou Orthodoxie? L'Arménie au quatrième siècle', *REArm* ns 4: 297–320. Repr. as Study IV in Garsoïan, 1985.

—— 1969, 'Quidam Narseus? – A Note on the Mission of St. Nersēs the Great', *Armeniaca: Mélanges d'études arméniennes* (Venice), 148–64. Repr. as Study V in Garsoïan, 1985.

—— 1971a, 'Armenia in the Fourth Century – An Attempt to Redefine the Concepts "Armenia" and "Loyalty"', *REArm* ns 8: 341–52. Repr. as Study III in Garsoïan, 1985.

—— 1971b, 'Byzantine Heresy, a re-interpretation', *Dumbarton Oaks Papers* 25: 87–113.

—— 1976, 'Prolegomena to a Study of the Iranian Aspects in Arsacid Armenia', *Handes Amsorya* 90, cols 177–234. Repr. as Study X in Garsoïan, 1985.

—— 1980, '*Gund*-Θέμα dans les sources Arméniennes'. In *Actes du XVe Congrès International d'Études Byzantines* (Athens), IV, 121.

—— 1981, 'The Locus of the Death of Kings: Iranian Armenia – the Inverted Image'. In R. G. Hovannisian (ed.), 1981, 27–64. Repr. as Study XI in Garsoïan, 1985.

—— 1982, 'The Iranian Substratum of the "Agatᶜangełos" Cycle'. In N. G. Garsoïan, T. F. Mathews and R. W. Thomson (eds), *East of Byzantium: Syria and Armenia in the Formative Period* (Washington), 151–74. Repr. as Study XII in Garsoïan, 1985.

—— 1983, 'Nersēs le Grand, Basile de Césarée et Eustathe de Sébaste', *REArm* ns 17: 145–69. Repr. as Study VII in Garsoïan, 1985.

—— 1984, 'Secular Jurisdiction over the Armenian Church (Fourth – Seventh Centuries)'. In *Okeanos: Essays Presented to Ihor Ševčenko on his Sixtieth Birthday* (*Harvard Ukrainian Studies* 7) (Cambridge, Mass.), 220–50. Repr. as Study IX in Garsoïan, 1985.

—— 1985, *Armenia Between Byzantium and the Sasanians* (London).

—— 1987, 'The Early Mediaeval Armenian City: An Alien Element?'. In *Ancient Studies in Memory of Elias J. Bickerman, Journal of the Ancient Near Eastern Society* 16–17 (1984–85 (1987)), 67–83.

—— 1988, 'Some Preliminary Precisions on the Separation of the Armenian and Imperial Churches. I: The Presence of "Armenian" Bishops at the First Five Œcumenical Councils'. In J. Chrysostomides (ed.), ΚΑΘΗΓΗΤΡΙΑ *Essays Presented to Joan Hussey on her Eightieth Birthday*, (Camberley), 249–85.

—— 1988–1989, ' "*T^cagaworanist kayeank^c*" *kam "Banak ark^cuni"*: Les résidences royales des Arsacides arméniens', *REArm* ns. 21: 251–70.

—— 1989, *The Epic Histories Attributed to P^cawstos Buzand (Buzandaran Pat-mut^ciwnk^c)*, (trans. and Comm.) (Harvard Armenian Texts and Studies, 8) (Cambridge, Mass.).

—— 1992, 'Quelques Précisions Préliminaires sur le schisme entre les églises byzantine et arménienne au sujet du concile de Chalcédoine. III Les évêchés méridionaux limitrophes de la Mésopotamie', *REArm* ns 23: 39–80.

Garstang, J. and Gurney, O. R. 1959, *The Geography of the Hittite Empire* (London).

Gaudeul, J.-M. 1984, 'The Correspondence between Leo and ^cUmar', *Islamo-christiana* 10: 109–57.

Geary, P. J. 1994, *Living with the Dead in the Middle Ages* (Ithaca and London).

Gero, S. 1973, *Byzantine Iconoclasm during the reign of Leo III with particular attention to the Oriental Sources (Corpus Scriptorum Christianorum Oriental-ium* vol. 346. Subsidia vol. 41) (Louvain).

Gignoux, P. 1976, review of Chaumont, 1973, *Studia Iranica* 5: 160.

Gluckman, M. 1965, *Politics, Law and Ritual in Tribal Society* (Oxford).

Godel, R. 1976, *An Introduction to the Study of Classical Armenian* (Wiesbaden).

Goubert, P. 1940, 'Maurice et l'Arménie, Note sur le lieu d'origine et la famille de l'Empereur Maurice', *Échos d'Orient* 39: 383–413.

Grayson, A. K. 1972, 1976, *Assyrian Royal Inscriptions* (2 vols), I From the beginning to Ashur-resha-ishi I (Wiesbaden), II From Tiglath-Pileser I to Ashur-nasir-apli II (Wiesbaden).

—— 1975, *Assyrian and Babylonian Chronicles* (New York).

Grégoire, H. 1946, 'An Armenian Dynasty on the Byzantine Throne', *Armenian Quarterly* 1: 4–21.

Greppin, J. A. C. 1986, 'Arabic Pharmaceutical Terms in Middle Armenian', *Annual of Armenian Linguistics* 7: 65–71.

Grigolia, A. 1962, 'Milk relationship in the Caucasus, its function and meaning', *Bedi Kartlisa* 41–2: 148–67.

Grishin, A. D. 1985, 'The Aght^camar wall paintings: some new observations', *Parergon* ns 3: 39–51.

Gugerotti, C. 1990, *Sebēos Storia* (Trans, introd. and notes). (Verona, Casa Editrice Mazziano) (in Italian).

Gulbekian, E. V. 1973, 'The Significance of the Narrative Describing the Traditional Origin of the Armenians', *Le Muséon* 86: 365–75.

Haldon, J. F. 1993, 'Military Service, Military Lands, and the Status of Soldiers: Current Problems and Interpretations', *Dumbarton Oaks Papers* 47: 1–67.

—— 1995, 'Seventh-Century Continuities: the *Ajnād* and the "Thematic Myth"'. In A. Cameron (ed.), *The Byzantine and Early Islamic Near East III States, Resources and Armies* (Princeton), 379–423.

Hamilton, B. 1961, 'The city of Rome and the Eastern Churches in the tenth century', *Orientalia Christiana Periodica* 27, 5–26. Repr. as Study I in *idem, Monastic Reform, Catharism and the Crusades (900–1300)* (London, 1979).

Hawkins, J. D. (ed.) 1977, *Trade in the ancient Near East. Papers presented to the XXIII Rencontre Assyriologique Internationale, University of Birmingham, 5–9 July, 1976* (London: British School of Archaeology in Iraq).

Herrenschmidt, Cl. 1976, 'Désignation de l'empire et concepts politiques de Darius Ier d'après ses inscriptions en vieux-Perse', *Studia Iranica* 5: 33–65.

Herzfeld, E. 1935, *Archaeological History of Iran* (London).

—— 1968, 'The Satrapies of the Persian Empire'. In *idem, The Persian Empire. Studies in Geography and Ethnography of the Ancient Near East* ed. from the posthumous papers by G. Walser (Wiesbaden), 298–349.

Hewsen, R. H. 1972, 'The Meliks of Eastern Armenia. A Preliminary Study', *REArm* ns 9: 285–329.

—— 1973, 'Caspiane: An Historical and Geographical Survey', *Handes Amsorya* 87, cols 87–106.

—— 1973–1974, 'The Meliks of Eastern Armenia II', *REArm* ns 10: 281–303.

—— 1975, '*The Primary History of Armenia*. An Examination of the Validity of an Immemorially Transmitted Historical Tradition', *History in Africa* 2: 91–100.

—— 1982a, 'Ptolemy's Chapter on Armenia: An Investigation of His Toponyms', *REArm* ns 16: 111–50.

—— 1982b, 'Ethno-History and the Armenian Influence upon the Caucasian Albanians'. In Samuelian (ed.), 1982, 27–40.

—— 1983a, 'Introduction to Armenian Historical Geography II: The Boundaries of Achaemenid "Armina"', *REArm* ns 17: 123–43.

—— 1983b, 'The Kingdom of Arc^cax'. In Samuelian and Stone (eds), 1983, 42–68.

—— 1984, 'Introduction to Armenian Historical Geography III: The Boundaries of Orontid Armenia', *REArm* ns 18: 347–66.

—— 1985, 'Introduction to Armenian Historical Geography IV: The Boundaries of Artaxiad Armenia', *REArm* ns 19: 55–84.

—— 1985–1986, 'In Search of Tiridates the Great', *Journal of the Society for Armenian Studies* 2: 11–49.

—— 1988–1989, 'Introduction to Armenian Historical Geography IV: The *Vitaxates* of Arsacid Armenia. A Re-Examination of the Territorial Aspects of the Institution (Part One)', *REArm* ns 21: 271–319.

—— 1990–1991, 'Introduction to Armenian Historical Geography IV: The *Vitaxates* of Arsacid Armenia. A Re-Examination of the Territorial Aspects of the Institution (Part Two)', *REArm* ns 22: 147–83.

—— 1992, *The Geography of Ananias of Širak (AŠXARHAC^cOY^c). The Long and the Short Recensions. Introduction, Translation and Commentary* (Wiesbaden).

Hewsenian, R. H. 1960, 'The Autun Glossary', *Armenian Review* 13 (3–51): 90–3.

Hoddinott, R. F. 1983, 'Ninth Century Bulgaria between East and West and an Archaeological Footnote'. In A. G. Poulter (ed.), *Ancient Bulgaria*. Papers presented to the International Symposium on the Ancient History and Archaeology of Bulgaria, University of Nottingham, 1981 (2 vols) (Nottingham), vol. II, 270–82.

Holt, P. M. (ed.) 1978, *The Eastern Mediterranean Lands in the Period of the Crusades* (Warminster).

Hovannisian, R. G. (ed.) 1981, *The Armenian Image in History and Literature* (Studies in Near Eastern Culture and Society 3) (Malibu, Cal.).

—— (ed.) 1992, *The Armenian Genocide. History, Politics, Ethics* (London).

—— (ed.) 1997a, *The Armenian People From Ancient to Modern Times*, vol. I *The Dynastic Periods: From Antiquity to the Fourteenth Century* (Basingstoke, London and New York).

—— (ed.) 1997b, *The Armenian People From Ancient to Modern Times*, vol. II *Foreign Dominion to Statehood: The Fifteenth Century to the Twentieth Century* (Basingstoke, London and New York).

Howard-Johnston, J. D. 1983, 'Byzantine Anzitene'. In S. Mitchell (ed.), *Armies and Frontiers in Roman and Byzantine Anatolia* (British Archaeological Reports International Series 156) (Oxford), 239–90.

—— 1984, 'Thema'. In A. Moffat (ed.), *Maistor. Classical, Byzantine and Renaissance Studies for Robert Browning* (Canberra), 189–97.

Hughes, M. J., Curtis, J. E., and Hall, E. T. 1981, 'Analyses of Some Urartian Bronzes', *Anatolian Studies* 31: 141–5.

Hultgård, A. 1982, 'Change and Continuity in the Religion of Ancient Armenia with Particular Reference to the Vision of St. Gregory'. In Samuelian (ed.), 1982, 8–26.

Huxley, G. 1984, 'The Historical Geography of the Paulician and Tondrakian Heresies'. In Samuelian and Stone (eds), 1984, 81–95.

Irwin, R. 1978, '*Iqṭāʿ* and the end of the Crusader States'. In Holt, (ed.) 1978, 62–77.

Isaac, B. 1990, *The Limits of Empire. The Roman Army in the East* (Oxford).

Jacoby, F. 1929, *Die Fragmente der Griechischen Historiker* vol. II Zeitgeschichte 2 (Berlin).

Jalabert, L. and Mouterde, R. 1929, *Inscriptions grecques et latines de la Syrie, I. Commagène et Cyrrheslique* (Paris).

Janashian, M. et al. 1967, *Armenian Miniature Paintings*, (Venice).

Jenkins, R. J. H. (ed.) 1962, *Constantine Porphyrogenitus' De Administrando Imperio. Volume II. Commentary* (London).

Jenkins, R. 1981, 'The Age of Conquest – A.D. 843–1050'. In Whitting (ed.), 1981, 61–82.

Jones, A. H. M. 1959, 'Were Ancient Heresies National or Social Movements in Disguise?', *Journal of Theological Studies* ns 10: 280–98.

—— 1971, *The Cities of the Eastern Roman Provinces* (2nd rev. edn, Oxford).

Kaegi, W. E. Jnr. 1969, 'Initial Byzantine Reactions to the Arab Conquest', *Church History* 38: 139–49.

Kavoukjian, M. 1987, trans. N. Ouzounian, *Armenia, Subartu, and Sumer. The Indo-European Homeland and Ancient Mesopotamia* (Montreal).

Kazhdan, A. 1984, 'The Armenians in the Byzantine Ruling Class Predominantly in the Ninth through Twelfth Centuries'. In Samuelian and Stone (eds), 1984, 439–51).

Kendall, B. and Thomson, R. W. 1983, trans., *Definitions and Divisions of Philosophy by David the Invincible Philosopher* (Univ. of Pennsylvania Armenian Texts and Studies 5) (Chico, Cal.).

Kennedy, H. 1986, *The Prophet and the Age of the Caliphates. The Islamic Near East from the sixth to the eleventh Century* (London and New York).

Kent, R. G. 1953, *Old Persian Grammar, Texts, Lexicon* (2nd edn, New Haven, Connecticut).

Khatchatrian, A. 1974, *Inscriptions et histoire des églises arméniennes* (Milan).

Khosdegian, G. 1982, 'Les colonies arméniennes des origines à la fin du XIIIᵉ siècle'. In Dédéyan (ed.), 1982, 390–409.

King, G. R. D. 1985, 'Islam, iconoclasm and the declaration of doctrine', *Bulletin of the School of Oriental and African Studies* 48: 267–77.

King, L. W. and Thompson, R. C. 1907, *The Sculptures and Inscription of Darius the Great on the Rock of Behistûn in Persia* (London).

Kojababian, G. 1977, 'The Relations Between the Armenian and Georgian Churches, According to the Armenian Sources (300–610)' (Oxford Univ. DPhil thesis).

Kolandjian, S. E. 1986, 'The Tenth Century Armenian Historian Uxtanēs: Was he bishop of Sebastia or Edessa?'. In Kouymjian (ed.), 1986, 397–413.

Kotandjian, N. 1991, 'Fresques arméniennes du VIIᵉ siècle d'après les monuments d'Arménie Soviétique'. In *Atti del Quinto...*, 1991, 367–380.

Kouymjian, D. (ed.) 1986, *Armenian Studies/Études Arméniennes in Memoriam Haïg Berbérian* (Lisbon).

Kristensen, A. K. G. 1988, *Who were the Cimmerians, and where did they come from? Sargon II, the Cimmerians, and Rusa I* (Copenhagen).

Kudian, M. 1970, *The Saga of Sassoun: the Armenian Folk epic; retold* (London).

Kuhrt, A. 1995, *The Ancient Near East c. 3000–330 B.C.* (2 vols) (London and New York).

Lages, M. F. 1971, 'The Most Ancient Penitential Text of the Armenian Liturgy', *Didaskalia* 1: 43–64.

Lanfranchi, G. B. 1983, 'Some new texts about a revolt against the Urartian king Rusa I', *Oriens Antiquus* 22: 123–35.

Lanfranchi, G. B. and Parpola, S. 1990, *The Correspondence of Sargon II, Part II: Letters from the Northern and Northeastern Provinces* (*State Archives of Assyria* 5) (Helsinki).

Lang, D. M. 1979, review of Thomson, 1978. In *Bulletin of the School of Oriental and African Studies* 42: 574–5.

—— 1980, review of Thomson, 1978. In *Armenian Review* 1: 109–10.

Laurent, J. 1919, *L'Arménie entre Byzance et l'Islam Depuis la Conquête Arabe jusque'en 886* (Paris). Rev. edn by M. Canard (Lisbon, 1980).

—— 1922, 'Un féodal arménien au IXᵉ siècle: Gourguen Ardzrouni, fils d'Abou Beldj', *REArm* os 2: 157–88.

Lehmann, K. 1945, 'The Dome of Heaven', *Art Bulletin* 27: 1–27.

Leloir, L. 1968, 'Essai sur la silhouette spirituelle du moine d'après la collection arménienne des apophtegmes', *REArm* ns 5: 199–230.

—— 1974a, 'Solitude et sollicitude: Le moine loin et près du monde selon les "Paterica" arméniens', *Irénikon* 47: 307–24.

—— 1974b, 'Les orientations essentielles de la spiritualité des Pères du désert d'après les "Paterica" arméniens', *Revue de Théologie et de Philosophie* 3rd series 24: 30–47.

Lemerle, P. 1964, 'Note sur les données historiques de l'autobiographie d'Anania de Shirak', *REArm* ns 1: 195–202.

—— 1973, 'L'histoire des Pauliciens d'Asie Mineure d'après les sources grecques', *Travaux et Mémoires* 5: 1–44.

Leroi-Gourhan, A. 1975, 'The Flowers found with Shanidar IV, a Neanderthal Burial in Iraq', *Science* 190: 562–64.

Leroy, M. and Mawet, Fr. (eds.) 1986, *La place de l'arménien dans les langues indo-européennes* (Louvain).

Libaridian, G. J. (ed.) 1991, *Armenia at the Crossroads: Democracy and Nationhood in the Post-Soviet Era: Essays, interviews and speeches by the leaders of the national democratic movement in Armenia* (Watertown, Mass.).

Lie, A. G. 1929, *The Inscriptions of Sargon II* (Paris).

Lieu, S. N. C. 1986, 'Captives, Refugees and Exiles: a Study of Cross-frontier civilian movements and contacts between Rome and Persia from Valerian to Jovian'. In Freeman and Kennedy (eds), 1986, 475–505.

Loos, M. 1974a, 'Deux publications fondamentales sur le paulicianisme d'Asie Mineure', *Byzantinoslavica* 35: 189–209.

—— 1974b, *Dualist Heresy in the Middle Ages* (Prague).

Luchaire, A. 1892, *Manuel des institutions françaises période des capétiens directs* (Paris).

Luckenbill, D. D. 1926, *Ancient Records of Assyria and Babylonia* vol. I (Chicago).

—— 1927, vol. II (Chicago).

Luzbetak, L. J. 1951, *Marriage and the Family in Caucasia* (Studia Instituti Anthropos vol. 3) (Vienna-Mödling).

Lynch, H. F. B. 1901, *Armenia: Travels and Studies* (2 vols) (London). Repr. Beirut, 1965.

McCormick, M. 1986, *Eternal Victory. Triumphal Rulership in Late Antiquity, Byzantium and the Early Medieval West* (Cambridge).

MacLean, D. 1991, 'Iona, Armenia and Italy in the Early Medieval Period'. In *Atti del Quinto...*, 1991, 559–73.

McLin, T. C. 1981, 'Just War in Byzantine Thought', *Michigan Academician* 13: 485–9.

McVey, K. E. 1983, 'The Domed Church as Microcosm: Literary Roots of An Architectural Symbol', *Dumbarton Oaks Papers* 37: 91–121.

Macler, F. 1904, trans., *Histoire d'Héraclius par l'évêque Sébéos* (Paris).

—— 1917, *Histoire Universelle par Étienne Asolik de Tarôn, traduite de l'arménien et annotée* Deuxième Partie, Livre III (Paris).

Magdalino, P. (ed.) 1994, *New Constantines: The Rhythm of Imperial Renewal in Byzantium, 4th–13th Centuries*. Papers from the Twenty-sixth Spring Symposium of Byzantine Studies, St. Andrew's, March 1992 (Aldershot, Hants and Brookfield, Vt).

Magie, D. 1950, *Roman Rule in Asia Minor to the end of the third century after Christ* (2 vols) (Princeton).

Maguire, E. D., Maguire, H. P. and Duncan-Flowers, M. J. 1989, *Art and Holy Powers in the Early Christian House* (Urbana and Chicago).

Mahé, A. and Mahé, J.-P. 1993, *Histoire de l'Arménie par Moïse de Khorène. Nouvelle traduction de l'arménien classique (d'après Victor Langlois) avec une introduction et des notes* (Paris).

Mahé, J.-P. 1984, 'Critical Remarks on the Newly Edited Excerpts from Sebēos'. In Samuelian and Stone (eds), 1984, 218–39.

—— 1988–1989, review of Feydit, 1986. In *REArm* ns 21: 552–54.

—— 1991, 'Basile II et Byzance vus par Grigor Narekacᶜi', *Travaux et Mémoires* 11: 555–73.

—— 1992, 'Une légitimation scriptuaire de l'hagiographie: la préface de Koriwn (443) à la *Vie de Mastocᶜ*, inventeur de l'alphabet arménien' *Mélanges Jacques Fontaine* I (Paris) 29–43.

—— 1993, 'L'église arménienne de 611 à 1066'. In Dagron et al (eds), 1993, 457–547.

Maksoudian, K. 1987, trans. and comm., *Yovhannēs Drasxanakertcᶜi History of Armenia* (Atlanta, Ga).

—— 1988–1989, 'The Chalcedonian Issue and the Early Bagratids: The Council of Širakawan', *REArm* ns 21: 333–44.

—— 1990–1991, 'A Note on the Monasteries Founded during the Reign of King Abas I Bagratuni', *REArm* ns 22: 203–15.

Malone, E. E. 1950, *The Monk and the Martyr. The Monk as the Successor of the Martyr*, (The Catholic University of America. Studies in Christian Antiquity no. 12) (Washington).

Manandian, H. A. 1965, *The Trade and Cities of Armenia in Relation to Ancient World Trade*, trans. into Engl. from the 2nd rev. edn, N. G. Garsoïan (Lisbon).

Manfredi, V. 1986, *La strada dei Diecimila. Topografia e geografia dell' Oriente di Senofonte* (Milan) (in Italian).

Mango, C. 1986, *Byzantine Architecture* (London).

Martin-Hisard, B. 1984, 'L'aristocratie géorgienne et son passé: Tradition épique et références bibliques, (viiᵉ–xiᵉ siècles)', *Bedi Kartlisa* 42: 13–34.

Mathews, T. F. 1982a, 'Cracks in Lehmann's "Dome of Heaven"', *Source* 1: 12–16. Repr. in *idem*, 1995.

—— 1982b, 'The Genesis Frescoes at Altᶜamar', *REArm* ns 16: 245–57.

—— 1995, *Art and Architecture in Byzantium and Armenia. Liturgical and Exegetical Approaches* (Aldershot, Hants. and Brookfield, Vt).

Mathews, T. F. and Wieck, R. S. (eds) 1994, *Treasures in Heaven: Armenian Illuminated Manuscripts* (New York).

Mayr-Harting, H. 1994, *Two conversions to Christianity: The Bulgarians and the Anglo-Saxons* (Stenton Lecture, 1993) (Reading).

Melikishvili, G. A. 1960, *Urartskie Klinoobraznye nadpisi* (*Urartian Cuneiform Inscriptions*) (Moscow) (Urartian texts, Russian trans.).

Melson, R. 1986, 'Provocation or Nationalism: A Critical Inquiry into the Armenian Genocide of 1915'. In R. G. Hovannisian (ed.), *The Armenian Genocide in Perspective* (New Brunswick and Oxford), 61–84.

Merhav, R. (ed.) 1991, *Urartu: A Metalworking Center in the First Millennium B.C.E.* (Jerusalem).

Meyendorff, J. 1970, 'Messalianism or Anti-Messalianism'. In *Kyriakon. Festchrift Johannes Quasten* II (Berlin), 585–90.

Mikirtitchian, L. 1959, 'Soviet Historiography of the Armenian Nation', *Caucasian Review* 9: 98–122.

Mingana, A. 1931, 'The Work of Dionysius Barsalibi Against the Armenians' (ed., with Engl. trans.), *Bulletin of The John Rylands Library, Manchester* 15 (2): 489–599.

Minorsky, V. 1953, 'Caucasica IV', *Bulletin of the School of Oriental and African Studies* 15: 504–29.

Mirak, R. 1983, *Torn between Two Lands: Armenians in America, 1890 to World War I* (Harvard Armenian Texts and Studies, 7) (Cambridge, Mass.).

Mitford, T. B. 1979, 'Cappadocia and Armenia Minor: Historical Setting of the Limes', *Aufstieg und Niedergang der römischen Welt* II. 7. 2. (Berlin and New York), 1169–261.

Moorhead, J. 1981a, 'The Monophysite response to the Arab Invasions', *Byzantion* 51: 579–91.

——— 1981b, 'The Earliest Christian Theological Response to Islam', *Religion* 11: 265–74.

Moosa, M. 1969, 'The Relation of the Maronites of Lebanon to the Mardaites and Al-Jarajima', *Speculum* 44: 597–608.

Mouraviev, S. 1980a, 'Les caractères daniéliens (identification et reconstruction)', *REArm* ns 14: 55–85.

——— 1980b, 'Les caractères Mesropiens (leur genèse reconstituée)', *REArm* ns 14: 87–111.

Muhly, J. D. 1988, 'Concluding Remarks'. In Curtis (ed.) 1988, 329–42.

Muscarella, O. W. 1970, 'Near Eastern Bronzes in the West: The Question of Origin'. In S. Doehringer et al., *Art and Technology* (Cambridge, Mass.), 109–28.

Mutafian, C. 1993, *Le Royaume Arménien de Cilicie XIIe–XIVe siècle* (Paris).

Narkiss, B. (ed.) 1979, *Armenian Art Treasures of Jerusalem* (New York).

Nau, F. 1912, ed. and trans., 'Lettre du Patriarche Jacobite Jean X (1064–73) au Catholique Arménien Grégoire II (1064–1105)', *Revue de l'Orient Chrétien* 7: 145–98.

Naval Intelligence Division 1942, 1943, *Geographical Handbook Series: Turkey* (2 vols) vol. 1 (Oxford).

Nercessian, Y.T. 1984, *Armenian Numismatic Bibliography and Literature* (Armenian Numismatic Society, Special Publication no. 3) (Los Angeles/Pico Rivera, Cal.). Abstracts in English and Armenian.

Nersoyan, H. J. 1985–1986, 'The Why and When of the Armenian Alphabet', *Journal of the Society for Armenian Studies* 2: 51–71.

Nersoyan, T. 1984, trans., *Divine Liturgy of the Armenian Apostolic Orthodox Church* (5th rev. edn London). Arm. text, Engl. trans., pref. and comm.

Neuman de Vegvar, C. L. 1987, *The Northumbrian Renaissance. A Study in the Transmission of Style* (Selinsgrove, London and Toronto).

Neusner, J. 1966, 'The Conversion of Adiabene to Christianity', *Numen* 13: 144–50.

Nock, A. D. 1932, 'Cremation and Burial in the Roman Empire', *Harvard Theological Review* 25: 321–59.

Nogaret, M. 1983, 'À Propos du Relief "Sassanide" de Boşat en Turquie Orientale', *Iranica Antiqua* 18: 221–32.

Noonan, T. S. 1984, 'Why dirhams first reached Russia: the role of Arab-Khazar relations in the development of the earliest Islamic trade with Eastern Europe', *Archivum Eurasiae Medii Aevi* 4: 151–282.

—— 1992, 'Byzantium and the Khazars: a special relationship?'. In J. Shepard and S. Franklin (eds) *Byzantine Diplomacy* (Aldershot, and Brookfield, Vt), 109–32.

Norehad, B. 1964, *The Life of Mashtots* (New York). Text of M. Abeḷean's 1941 modern Arm. trans., and Engl. trans. thereof. Repr. of Engl. trans. with Arm. text and Russian trans., Erevan, 1981.

Palmer, J. J. N. 1972, *England, France and Christendom 1377–99* (London).

Parpola, S. 1987, *The Correspondence of Sargon II, Part I Letters from Assyria and the West (State Archives of Assyria* 1) (Helsinki).

Parsegian, V. L., *Armenian Architecture* see *Armenian Architecture*.

—— 1991, 'The Armenian Architectural Archives Project (A status report)'. In *Atti del Quinto...*, 1991, 243–7.

Pecoroella, P. E. and Salvini, M. 1982, 'Researches in the Region between the Zagros Mountains and Urmia Lake', *Persica* 10: 1–46.

Périkhanian, A. 1968, 'Notes sur le lexique iranien et arménien', *REArm* ns 5: 9–30.

—— 1971a, 'Inscription araméenne gravée sur une coupe d'argent trouvée à Sisian (Arménie)', *REArm* ns 8: 5–11.

—— 1971b, 'Les inscriptions araméennes du roi Artachès', *REArm* ns 8: 169–74.

—— 1986, 'Sur le mot arménien *Buzand*'. In Kouymjian (ed.), 1986, 653–7.

Pettersen, A. 1984, '"To Flee or Not to Flee": An Assessment of Athanasius's *De Fuga Sua*'. In W. J. Shiels (ed.), *Persecution and Tolerance* (Studies in Church History 21) (Oxford), 29–42.

Pfeiffer, R. H. 1935, *State Letters of Assyria* (New Haven, Conn.).

Piotrovskii (y), B. B. 1967, ed. and trans. P. S. Gelling, *Urartu. The Kingdom of Van and its Art* (London).

—— 1969a, *The Ancient Civilization of Urartu* (London).

—— 1969b, trans. J. Hogarth, *Urartu* (London).

Porada, E. 1967, 'Of Deer, Bells and Pomegranates', *Iranica Antiqua* 7: 99–120.

Raes, A. 1947, 'Les Rites de la Pénitence chez les Arméniens', *Orientalia Christiana Periodica* 13: 648–55.

Reynolds, S. 1994, *Fiefs and Vassals: The Medieval Evidence Reinterpreted* (Oxford and New York).

Richardson, H. 1984, 'The Concept of the High Cross'. In P. N. Chatain and M. Richter (eds), *Irland und Europa: Die Kirche im Frühmittelalter* (Stuttgart, Klett-Cotta), 127–34.

Rush, A. C. 1941, *Death and Burial in Christian Antiquity* (Catholic University of America, Studies in Christian Antiquity 1) (Washington).

Russell, J. R. 1982, 'Zoroastrian Problems in Armenia: Mihr and Vahagn'. In Samuelian (ed.), 1982, 1–7.

—— 1986–1987, 'Some Iranian Images of Kingship in the Armenian Artaxiad Epic', *REArm* ns 20: 253–70.

—— 1987, *Zoroastrianism in Armenia* (Harvard Iranian Series vol. 5) (Cambridge, Mass.).

Samuelian, T. J. (ed.) 1982, *Classical Armenian Culture* (University of Pennsylvania, Armenian Texts and Studies, 4) (Pennsylvania).

Samuelian, T. J. and Stone, M. E. (eds), 1984, *Medieval Armenian Culture* (University of Pennsylvania, Armenian Texts and Studies, 6) (Chico, Cal.).

Sancisi-Weerdenburg, H. 1988, 'Was there ever a Median Empire?'. In A. Kuhrt and H. Sancisi-Weerdenburg (eds), *Achaemenid History III: Method and Theory* (Leiden), 197–212.

Sanjian, A. K. 1965, *The Armenian Communities in Syria under Ottoman Dominion* (Cambridge, Mass.).

—— 1966, '*Čřazatik* 'Erroneous Easter' – A source of Greco–Armenian Religious Controversy', *Studia Caucasia* 2: 26–47.

—— 1969a, 'Anastas Vardapet's List of Armenian Monasteries in Seventh-Century Jerusalem: A Critical Examination', *Le Muséon* 82: 265–92. (Text, trans. and discussion.)

—— 1969b, *Colophons of Armenian Manuscripts, 1301–1480* (Cambridge, Mass.). (Annotated selection in trans.)

Sansterre, J.-M. 1983, *Les moines grecs et orientaux à Rome aux époques byzantine et carolingienne (milieu du VIe s. – fin IXe s.)* (2 vols) (Brussels).

Sarkissian, K. 1965, *The Council of Chalcedon and the Armenian Church* (London).

Scarborough, J. 1986–1987, 'Medieval Armenia's Ancient Medical Heritage', *REArm* ns 20: 237–51.

Schahgaldian, N. B. 1979, 'The Political Integration of an Immigrant Community into a Composite Society. The Armenians in Lebanon, 1920–1974' (PhD Dissertation, Columbia University).

Schottky, M. 1989, *Media Atropatene und Gross-Armenien in hellenistischer Zeit* (Bonn).

Shahîd, I. 1972, 'The Iranian Factor in Byzantium during the Reign of Heraclius', *Dumbarton Oaks Papers* 26: 293–320.

Shalian, A. K. 1964, *David of Sassoun. The Armenian Folk Epic in Four Cycles, the original text translated with an introduction and notes* (Athens, Ohio).

Sinclair, T. A. 1987, *Eastern Turkey: an Architectural and Archaeological Survey* vol. I (London).

—— 1989a, vol. II (London).

—— 1989b, vol. III (London).

—— 1990, vol. IV (London).

—— 1994–1995, 'The Site of Tigranocerta. I', *REArm* ns 25: 183–254.

Smalley, B. 1941, *The Study of the Bible in the Middle Ages* (Oxford).

Solecki, R. S. 1971, 1972, *Shanidar* (New York and Toronto, and London).

Stancliffe, C. 1982, 'Red, white and blue martyrdom'. In D. Whitelock, R. McKitterick and D. Dumville (eds), *Ireland in Early Medieval Europe: Studies in Memory of Kathleen Hughes* (Cambridge), 21–46.

Starr, I. (ed.) 1990, *Queries to the Sungod: Divination and Politics in Sargonid Assyria* (State Archives of Assyria 4) (Helsinki).

Stone, M. E. 1986, 'Holy Land Pilgrimage of Armenians before the Arab Conquest', *Revue Biblique* 93: 93–110.

Stronach, D. 1967, 'Urartian and Achaemenian Tower Temples', *Journal of Near Eastern Studies* 26: 278–88.

Strzygowski, J. 1918, *Die Baukunst der Armenier und Europa* (2 vols) (Vienna).

Sullivan, R. D. 1970, 'Some Dynastic Answers to the Armenian Question: A Study in East Anatolian Prosopography', (PhD dissertation, University of California, Los Angeles).

—— 1973, 'Diadochic coinage in Commagene after Tigranes the Great', *The Numismatic Chronicle* 7th series, 13: 18–39.

Sullivan, R. E. 1994 (1966), 'Khan Boris and the Conversion of Bulgaria: A Case Study of the Impact of Christianity on a Barbarian Society'. First publ. 1966, repr. as Study IV in *idem, Christian Missionary Activity in the Early Middle Ages* (Aldershot, Hants and Brookfield, Vt).

Summers, G. D. 1993, 'Archaeological Evidence for the Achaemenid Period in Eastern Turkey', *Anatolian Studies* 43: 85–108.

Suny, R. G. 1989, *The Making of the Georgian Nation* (London).

—— 1993, *Looking toward Ararat: Armenia in Modern History* (Bloomington and Indianapolis).

Takooshian, H. 1986–1987, 'Armenian Immigration to the United States from the Middle East', *Journal of Armenian Studies* 3 (1–2): 133–55.

Talai, V. A. 1989, *Armenians in London* (Manchester and New York).

Ter-Ghévondian, A. 1966, 'Le "Prince d'Arménie" à l'époque de la domination arabe', *REArm* ns 3: 185–200.

—— 1975–1976, 'Les impôts en nature en Arménie à l'époque arabe', *REArm* ns 11: 313–21.

—— 1977, *Armenia and the Arab Caliphate* (Erevan) (in Russian).

Ter-Ghewondyan, A. 1976, *The Arab Emirates in Bagratid Armenia* trans. N. G. Garsoïan, (Lisbon).

Thierry, J.-M. 1980, *Le couvent arménien d'Hoṙomos* (Louvain–Paris).

Thierry, J.-M. and Donabédian, P. 1987, *Les arts arméniens* (Paris).

—— 1989, *Armenian Art* (New York).

Thierry, M. 1976, 'Notes de géographie historique sur le Vaspurakan', *Revue des études byzantines* 34: 159–73.

Thierry, N. and Thierry, M. 1968, 'Peintures murales de caractère occidental en Arménie: Église Saint-Pierre et Saint-Paul de Tatev (début du Xme siècle)', *Byzantion* 38: 180–242.

Thompson, E. A. 1946, 'Christian Missionaries among the Huns', *Hermathena* 67: 73–9.

Thomson, R. W. 1962, 'Vardapet in Early Armenian Christianity', *Le Muséon* 75: 367–84.

—— 1970, *The Teaching of Saint Gregory: An Early Armenian Catechism*, trans. and comm. (Cambridge, Mass.).

—— 1976, *Agathangelos, History of the Armenians*, trans. and comm. (Albany, NY).

—— 1978, *Moses Khorenats^{c}i, History of the Armenians*, trans. and comm. (Harvard Armenian Texts and Studies, 4) (Cambridge, Mass. and London).

—— 1979–80, 'Armenian Variations on the Baḥira Legend', *Harvard Ukrainian Studies* 3/4(1): 884–95.

—— 1982a, 'Eliśē's *History of Vardan*': New Light from Old Sources'. In Samuelian (ed.), 1982, 41–51.

—— 1982b, *E̦lishē, History of Vardan and the Armenian War*, trans. and comm. (Harvard Armenian Texts and Studies, 5) (Cambridge, Mass. and London).

—— 1982c, 'The Armenian version of Ps. Dionysius Aeropagita', *Acta Jutlandica* 27: 115–23. Repr. as Study XIV in Thomson, 1994.

—— 1984a, 'T^covmay Arcruni's Debt to Ełišē', *REArm* ns 18: 221–35.

—— 1984b, 'T'ovmay Arcruni as Historian'. In Samuelian and Stone (eds), 1984, 69–80.

—— 1985, *Thomas Artsruni, History of the House of the Artsrunik^c*, trans. and comm. (Detroit).

—— 1986a, 'Muhammad and the Origin of Islam in Armenian Literary Tradition'. In Kouymjian (ed.), 1986, 829–58.

—— 1986b, 'Jerusalem and Armenia'. In E. A. Livingstone (ed.), *Proceedings of the 1983 Oxford Patristic Conference* (Leuven), 77–91. Repr. as Study V in Thomson, 1994.

—— 1988–1989, 'The Anonymous Story-Teller (also known as "Pseudo-Sapuh")', *REArm* ns 21: 171–232.

—— 1989, 'The Historical Compilation of Vardan Arewelc^ci', *Dumbarton Oaks Papers* 43: 125–226.

—— 1991, *The History of Łazar P^carpec^ci* (Atlanta, Ga).

—— 1994, *Studies in Armenian Literature and Christianity* (Aldershot, Hants and Brookfield, Vt).

Tierney, M. 1996, The nation, nationalism and national identity'. In Atkinson et al. (eds), 1996, 12–21.

Tougher, S. F. 1994, 'The wisdom of Leo VI'. In Magdalino (ed.), 1994, 171–79.

Toumanoff, C. 1963, *Studies in Christian Caucasian History* (Georgetown).

—— 1969, 'The third-century Armenian Arsacids. A chronological and genealogical commentary', *REArm* ns 6: 233–81.

—— 1971, 'Caucasia and Byzantium', *Traditio* 27: 111–58.

Tritle, L. A. 1977, 'Tatzates' Flight and the Byzantine-Arab Peace Treaty of 782', *Byzantion* 47: 279–300.

Uluhogian, G. 1992, 'Les églises d'Ani d'après le témoignage des inscriptions', *REArm* ns 23: 393–417.

Van Esbroeck, M. 1971a, 'Un nouveau témoin du livre d'Agathange', *REArm* ns 8: 13–167.

—— 1971b, 'Témoignages littéraires sur les sépultures de Saint Grégoire l'Illuminateur', *Analecta Bollandiana* 89: 387–418.

Van Loon, M. 1977, 'The Place of Urartu in First-Millenium B.C. Trade'. In Hawkins (ed.), 1977, 229–31.

Vardanyan, S. 1982, 'Ancient Armenian Translations of the Works of Syrian Physicians', *REArm* ns 16: 213–19.

Vööbus, A. 1958, 1960, *History of Asceticism in the Syrian Orient* (2 vols) (Louvain).

Vryonis, S. Jr. 1957, 'The Will of a Provincial Magnate, Eustathius Boilas (1059)', *Dumbarton Oaks Papers* 11: 263–77.

Wallace-Hadrill, J. M. 1962, 'The Bloodfeud of the Franks'. In *idem, The Long-Haired Kings* (London), 121–47.

Waterman, L. 1930, *Royal Correspondence of the Assyrian Empire*, pts I and II, trans. and translit. (Ann Arbor).

Weitenberg, J. J. S. 1982, 'Armenian Dialects and the Latin-Armenian Glossary of Autun'. In Samuelian and Stone (eds), 1982, 13–28.

Whitby, M. 1988, *The Emperor Maurice and his Historian. Theophylact Simocatta on Persian and Balkan Warfare* (Oxford).

Whitby, M. and Whitby, M. 1986, trans., *The History of Theophylact Simocatta* (Oxford).

Whitting, P. (ed.) 1981, *Byzantium: An Introduction* (Oxford, revised edn).

Widengren, G. 1956, 'Recherches sur le féodalisme iranien', *Orientalia Suecana 5* (Uppsala), 79–182.

—— 1959, 'The Sacral Kingship of Iran'. In *The Sacral Kingship/La Regalità Sacra* (Leiden), 242–57.

Wilkinson, R. D. 1972, 'Armenia in Hellenistic and Roman Times' (M.A. Diss., Cambridge Univ.).

—— 1982, 'A Fresh Look at the Ionic Building at Garni', *REArm* ns 16: 221–44.

Winkler, G. 1978, 'The History of the Syriac Prebaptismal Anointing in the Light of the Earliest Armenian Sources', *Orientalia Christiana Analecta* 205: 317–24.

—— 1980, 'Our Present Knowledge of the History of Agatᶜangełos and its Oriental Versions', *REArm* ns 14: 125–41.

—— 1982, *Das Armenische Initiationsrituale. Entwicklungs-geschichtliche und liturgievergleichende. Untersuchung der Quellen des 3 bis 10 Jahrhunderts* (*Orientalia Christiana Analecta*, 217) (Rome, Pontifical Institute of Oriental Studies).

—— 1985, 'An Obscure Chapter in Armenian Church History (428–439)', *REArm* ns 19: 85–180.

—— 1994, *Koriwns Biographie des Mesrop Maštocᶜ Übersetzung und kommentar* (*Orientalia Christiana Analecta*, 245) (Rome, Pontifical Institute of Oriental Studies).

Wormald, P. 1978, 'Bede, "Beowulf" and the Conversion of the Anglo-Saxon Aristocracy'. In R. T. Farrell (ed.), *Bede and Anglo-Saxon England* (British Archaeological Reports, 46) (Oxford), 32–95.

Yarnley, C. J. 1976, 'The Armenian Philhellenes, A Study in the Spread of Byzantine Religious and Cultural Ideas among the Armenians in the Tenth and Eleventh Centuries A.D.', *Eastern Churches Review* 8: 45–53.

Yuzbashian, K. N. 1973–1974, 'L'administration byzantine en Arménie aux Xᵉ – XIᵉ siècles', *REArm* ns 10, 139–83.

Zimansky, P. E. 1985, *Ecology and Empire: The Structure of the Urartian State* (Chicago).

Index

bronze, bronze-working, 17, 27, 31,
  36, 38, 39–40
Brown, E. A. R., 240
Browning, R., 248
Bugha, 173, 174, 177, 179, 182, 183,
  186, 221
Bulank, plain, 34
Bulgaria, 228, 231, 241, 242, 248;
  Bulgars, 170, 173, 237, 239, 242,
  246, 248, 250
Bulgarophygon, battle of (896), 204
burial *see* funerals
Byzantium: empire, 6, 22, 159, 166,
  168–70, 172, 173, 174, 175, 177,
  197, 200, 202, 204–5, 210, 211,
  216, 220, 222, 223–7, 228, 229,
  230, 236, 246, 251, 255;
  annexations, 197, 216, 222, 224,
  226–7, 255; and Arabs, 166,
  168–70, 173, 224, 225; Arab
  treaty (689), 169; church building,
  243; coinage, 169–70; Council
  (692), 128; influence of, 214; and
  Khazars, 169; provincial
  organization, 173, 204, 227, 228;
  society, 212, 230, 236–7, 240,
  247, 249; themes, 173, 204, 227,
  228, 236, 240; and Turks, 228,
  229, 263
Bzhnuni family, 54

Caenepolis, 'New City' (Arm.
  Vaḷarshapat, Ējmiatsin, q.v.), 93,
  96, 103
Caesar, Julius, 76
Caesarea in Cappadocia, 95, 96,
  113, 120, 135, 136, 204, 228,
  229
Cambysene, 69
Capetrus, battle of, 228
capital city, capital cities, 25, 29, 30,
  56, 63, 69, 71, 72, 93, 115, 141,
  144, 149, 154, 157, 158, 174,
  209, 220, 224, 225, 227, 243,
  257, 258, 262, 264
Cappadocia, 69, 74, 91, 93, 94, 95, 96,
  111, 112, 113, 144, 204, 227,

229, 237, 239; kingdom, 21, 62,
  65, 67, 68, 69, 71, 76, 78, 81
Caracalla, Roman emperor (AD
  211–17), 93–4, 102
Carcathiocerta (Eğil Arm. Angḷ, q.v.),
  63, 72, 83, 84, 85
Carduchi, 11, 57, 59, 60, 69
Carenitis (Arm. Karin, q.v.), 138, 144,
  153
Carrhae, battle of, 76
Caspian Sea, 10, 85, 137, 156
Caspiane (Arm. Kazbkᶜ), 71, 79, 101,
  135, 137
Cassius Dio (c.164–after 229), 75, 82,
  106
castles *see* forts
Catharism, 241
Catherine the Great of Russia
  (1762–96), 266
Caucasus, 22, 195, 196, 273; mts, 11,
  32, 169; tribes, 181
cavalry, 33, 37, 40, 43, 56, 57, 87, 99,
  106, 115, 129, 137, 149, 168,
  172, 178, 182, 183, 186, 187; *see*
  azats; horses
Çavuştepe, 34, 39, 45, 54, 277
Chalcedon, Council of (451), 151–2,
  174, 239, 249, 250; attitudes to,
  152, 158, 161, 168, 174, 185,
  190, 220, 223–4, 235, 239, 249,
  250–4, 256; *see also* church union
Chalcis, 89
Chaldaeans, 57, 58, 86; mercenaries,
  58
Chaldaei, 50, 51
Chaldia, 173, 225
Chalybes, 2, 17, 32, 51, 57, 59, 60, 63,
  67
charity, 122, 132, 136, 218, 275
Charlemagne, Carolingians, 242, 243
Charles VI, king of France, 1
charters *see* donations
China, 38, 263, 264
Chlomaron (Tigranocerta, q.v.), 138,
  156
Cholarzene (Arm. Klařjkᶜ, q.v.), 63,
  67, 73, 79, 101, 137, 146, 158